# Logistics Management and Strategy

# Logistics Management and Strategy

## Competing through the supply chain

Fourth Edition

## Alan Harrison

## Remko van Hoek

**Financial Times**
**Prentice Hall**
is an imprint of

Harlow, England • London • New York • Boston • San Francisco • Toronto
Sydney • Tokyo • Singapore • Hong Kong • Seoul • Taipei • New Delhi
Cape Town • Madrid • Mexico City • Amsterdam • Munich • Paris • Milan

**Pearson Education Limited**
Edinburgh Gate
Harlow
Essex CM20 2JE
England

and Associated Companies throughout the world

*Visit us on the World Wide Web at:*
www.pearsoned.co.uk

First published 2002
Second edition published 2005
Third edition published 2008
**Fourth edition published 2011**

© Pearson Education Limited 2002, 2005
© Alan Harrison and Remko van Hoek 2008, 2011

ISBN: 978-0-273-73022-4

**British Library Cataloguing-in-Publication Data**
A catalogue record for this book is available from the British Library

**Library of Congress Cataloging-in-Publication Data**

Harrison, Alan, 1944–
   Logistics management and strategy : competing through the supply chain
/ Alan Harrison, Remko van Hoek. -- 4th ed.
        p. cm.
   Includes bibliographical references and index.
   ISBN 978-0-273-73022-4 (pearson : alk. paper)   1. Business logistics.
2. Industrial management.   I. Hoek, Remko I. van.   II. Title.
   HD38.5.H367 2010
   658.5--dc22
                                                    2010041143

10 9 8 7 6 5 4 3
14 13 12 11

Typeset in 9.5pt Stone Serif by 73
Printed by Ashford Colour Press Ltd., Gosport

*The publisher's policy is to use paper manufactured from sustainable forests.*

To Cathi, Nick, Katie, Maryl and Ticho, with love.

# Contents

Foreword                                              xiii
Preface                                               xv
Authors' acknowledgements                             xvii
Publisher's acknowledgements                          xix
How to use this book                                  xxi
Plan of the book                                      xxiii

## Part One  COMPETING THROUGH LOGISTICS

1  Logistics and the supply chain                         3
   Introduction                                           3
   1.1  Logistics and the supply chain                    4
        1.1.1  Definitions and concepts                   6
        1.1.2  Supply chain: structure and tiering        8
   1.2  Material flow and information flow                12
        1.2.1  Material flow                              12
        1.2.2  Information flow                           15
   1.3  Competing through logistics                       16
        1.3.1  Hard objectives                            17
        1.3.2  Supportive capabilities                    19
        1.3.3  Soft objectives                            25
        1.3.4  Order winners and qualifiers               26
   1.4  Logistics strategy                                27
        1.4.1  Defining 'strategy'                        28
        1.4.2  Aligning strategies                        29
        1.4.3  Differentiating strategies                 30
        1.4.4  Trade-offs in logistics                    31
   Summary                                                32
   Discussion questions                                   33
   References                                             33
   Suggested further reading                              34

2  Putting the end-customer first                         35
   Introduction                                           35
   2.1  The marketing perspective                         36
        2.1.1  Rising customer expectations               37
        2.1.2  The information revolution                 37
   2.2  Segmentation                                      38
   2.3  Demand profiling                                  46
   2.4  Quality of service                                50
        2.4.1  Customer loyalty                           51
        2.4.2  Value disciplines                          53

|  | 2.4.3 | Relationship marketing and customer relationship management (CRM) | 53 |
|  | 2.4.4 | Measuring service quality | 56 |
| 2.5 | Setting priorities for logistics strategy | | 56 |
|  | 2.5.1 | Step 1: Diagnose current approach to market segmentation | 58 |
|  | 2.5.2 | Step 2a: Understand buying behaviour | 59 |
|  | 2.5.3 | Step 2b: Customer value analysis | 60 |
|  | 2.5.4 | Step 3: Measure logistics strategy drivers | 60 |
|  | 2.5.5 | Step 4: Specify future approach to market segmentation | 63 |
| Summary | | | 68 |
| Discussion questions | | | 69 |
| References | | | 70 |
| Suggested further reading | | | 71 |

**3  Value and logistics costs**   73

| Introduction | | | 73 |
| 3.1 | Where does value come from? | | 74 |
|  | 3.1.1 | Return on investment (ROI) | 75 |
|  | 3.1.2 | Financial ratios and ROI drivers | 77 |
| 3.2 | How can logistics costs be represented? | | 79 |
|  | 3.2.1 | Fixed/variable | 81 |
|  | 3.2.2 | Direct/indirect | 85 |
|  | 3.2.3 | Engineered/discretionary | 87 |
| 3.3 | Activity-based costing (ABC) | | 89 |
|  | 3.3.1 | ABC example | 91 |
|  | 3.3.2 | Cost–time profile (CTP) | 92 |
|  | 3.3.3 | Cost-to-serve (CTS) | 94 |
| 3.4 | A balanced measurement portfolio | | 95 |
|  | 3.4.1 | Balanced measures | 96 |
|  | 3.4.2 | Supply chain management and the balanced scorecard | 97 |
|  | 3.4.3 | Supply chain financial model | 99 |
| 3.5 | Supply chain operations reference model (SCOR) | | 101 |
| Summary | | | 105 |
| Discussion questions | | | 105 |
| References | | | 106 |
| Suggested further reading | | | 106 |

## Part Two   LEVERAGING LOGISTICS OPERATIONS

**4  Managing logistics internationally**   109

| Introduction | | | 109 |
| 4.1 | Drivers and logistics implications of internationalisation | | 111 |
|  | 4.1.1 | Logistical implications of internationalisation | 114 |
|  | 4.1.2 | Time-to-market | 115 |
|  | 4.1.3 | Global consolidation | 116 |
|  | 4.1.4 | Risk in international logistics | 119 |
| 4.2 | The tendency towards internationalisation | | 120 |
|  | 4.2.1 | Focused factories: from geographical to product segmentation | 120 |
|  | 4.2.2 | Centralised inventories | 121 |

| | | |
|---|---|---|
| 4.3 | The challenges of international logistics and location | 124 |
| | 4.3.1 Extended lead time of supply | 125 |
| | 4.3.2 Extended and unreliable transit times | 125 |
| | 4.3.3 Multiple consolidation and break points | 125 |
| | 4.3.4 Multiple freight modes and cost options | 126 |
| | 4.3.5 Price and currency fluctuations | 126 |
| | 4.3.6 Location analysis | 128 |
| 4.4 | Organising for international logistics | 130 |
| | 4.4.1 Layering and tiering | 130 |
| | 4.4.2 The evolving role of individual plants | 131 |
| | 4.4.3 Reconfiguration processes | 132 |
| 4.5 | Reverse logistics | 141 |
| 4.6 | Managing for risk readiness | 143 |
| | 4.6.1 Immediate risk readiness | 143 |
| | 4.6.2 Structural risk readiness | 144 |
| 4.7 | Corporate social responsibility in the supply chain | 145 |
| | Summary | 150 |
| | Discussion questions | 150 |
| | References | 151 |
| | Suggested further reading | 151 |

**5  Managing the lead-time frontier** | | **153**
| | Introduction | 153 |
| 5.1 | The role of time in competitive advantage | 154 |
| | 5.1.1 Time-based competition: definition and concepts | 154 |
| | 5.1.2 Variety and complexity | 155 |
| | 5.1.3 Time-based initiatives | 156 |
| | 5.1.4 Time-based opportunities to add value | 157 |
| | 5.1.5 Time-based opportunities to reduce cost | 159 |
| | 5.1.6 Limitations to time-based approaches | 161 |
| 5.2 | P:D ratios and differences | 162 |
| | 5.2.1 Using time as a performance measure | 162 |
| | 5.2.2 Using time to measure supply pipeline performance | 163 |
| | 5.2.3 Consequences when P-time is greater than D-time | 165 |
| 5.3 | Time-based process mapping | 168 |
| | 5.3.1 Stage 1: Create a task force | 169 |
| | 5.3.2 Stage 2: Select the process to map | 169 |
| | 5.3.3 Stage 3: Collect data | 170 |
| | 5.3.4 Stage 4: Flow chart the process | 170 |
| | 5.3.5 Stage 5: Distinguish between value-adding and non-value-adding time | 170 |
| | 5.3.6 Stage 6: Construct the time-based process map | 171 |
| | 5.3.7 Stage 7: Solution generation | 171 |
| 5.4 | Managing timeliness in the logistics pipeline | 176 |
| | 5.4.1 Strategies to cope when P-time is greater than D-time | 177 |
| | 5.4.2 Practices to cope when P-time is greater than D-time | 178 |
| 5.5 | A method for implementing time-based practices | 179 |
| | 5.5.1 Step 1: Understand your need to change | 179 |
| | 5.5.2 Step 2: Understand your processes | 180 |
| | 5.5.3 Step 3: Identify unnecessary process steps and large amounts of wasted time | 181 |

5.5.4    Step 4: Understand the causes of waste              181
5.5.5    Step 5: Change the process                          181
5.5.6    Step 6: Review changes                              181
5.5.7    Results                                             182
5.6    When, where and how?                                  183
Summary                                                      183
Discussion questions                                         184
References                                                   184
Suggested further reading                                    184

6    Supply chain planning and control                       185
Introduction                                                 185
6.1    The supply chain 'game plan'                          187
6.1.1    Planning and control within manufacturing           187
6.1.2    Managing inventory in the supply chain              193
6.1.3    Planning and control in retailing                   198
6.1.4    Inter-firm planning and control                     201
6.2    Overcoming poor coordination in retail supply chains  203
6.2.1    Efficient consumer response (ECR)                   204
6.2.2    Collaborative planning, forecasting
and replenishment (CPFR)                                     210
6.2.3    Vendor-managed inventory (VMI)                      214
6.2.4    Quick response (QR)                                 217
Summary                                                      218
Discussion questions                                         219
References                                                   219
Suggested further reading                                    220

7    Just-in-time and the agile supply chain                 221
Introduction                                                 221
7.1    Just-in-time and lean thinking                        223
7.1.1    The just-in-time system                             224
7.1.2    The seven wastes                                    228
7.1.3    JIT and material requirements planning              229
7.1.4    Lean thinking                                       232
7.1.5    Application of lean thinking to business processes  234
7.1.6    Role of lean practices                              235
7.2    The concept of agility                                236
7.2.1    Classifying operating environments                  241
7.2.2    Preconditions for successful agile practice         242
7.2.3    Developing measures that put the end-customer first
to improve market sensitivity                                246
7.2.4    Shared goals to improve virtual integration         247
7.2.5    Boundary spanning S&OP process to improve
process integration                                          248
Summary                                                      249
Discussion questions                                         250
References                                                   251
Suggested further reading                                    252

## Part Three  WORKING TOGETHER

**8  Integrating the supply chain**  255

Introduction  255
8.1  Integration in the supply chain  257
   8.1.1  Internal integration: function to function  258
   8.1.2  Inter-company integration: a manual approach  259
   8.1.3  Electronic integration  260
8.2  Choosing the right supply relationships  264
8.3  Partnerships in the supply chain  270
   8.3.1  Economic justification for partnerships  271
   8.3.2  Advantages of partnerships  271
   8.3.3  Disadvantages of partnerships  271
8.4  Supply base rationalisation  272
   8.4.1  Supplier management  272
   8.4.2  Lead suppliers  272
8.5  Supplier networks  273
   8.5.1  Supplier associations  273
   8.5.2  Japanese *keiretsu*  276
   8.5.3  Italian districts  278
   8.5.4  Chinese industrial areas  280
8.6  Supplier development  284
   8.6.1  Integrated processes  284
   8.6.2  Synchronous production  285
8.7  Implementing strategic partnerships  285
8.8  Managing supply chain relationships  290
   8.8.1  Creating closer relationships  290
   8.8.2  Factors in forming supply chain relationships  291
Summary  292
Discussion questions  294
References  295
Suggested further reading  297

**9  Sourcing and supply management**  299

Introduction  299
9.1  What does procurement do?  301
   9.1.1  Drivers of procurement value  302
9.2  Rationalising the supply base  314
9.3  Segmenting the supply base  316
   9.3.1  Preferred suppliers  319
   9.3.2  Strategic relationships  320
   9.3.3  Establishing policies per supplier segment  320
   9.3.4  Vendor rating  321
   9.3.5  Executive ownership of supply relationships  322
   9.3.6  Migrating towards *customer of choice* status  324
9.4  Procurement technology  326
9.5  Markers of boardroom value  326
9.6  What does top procurement talent look like?  327

Summary                                                                     328
Discussion questions                                                        329
References                                                                  329
Suggested further reading                                                   330

## Part Four  CHANGING THE FUTURE

### 10 Logistics future challenges and opportunities                         333
Introduction                                                                333
10.1  Changing economics?                                                   334
10.2  Internal alignment                                                    336
10.3  Selecting collaborative opportunities upstream and downstream         340
10.4  Managing with cost-to-serve to support growth and profitability       343
10.5  The supply chain manager of the future                                345
10.6  Changing chains                                                       347
Summary                                                                     349
Discussion questions                                                        350
References                                                                  350
Suggested further reading                                                   350

Index                                                                       351

### Supporting resources

Visit **www.pearsoned.co.uk/harrison** to find valuable online resources

For instructors
- Complete, downloadable Instructor's Manual, containing teaching notes, notes on case studies and teaching tips, objectives and discussion points for each chapter
- Downloadable PowerPoint slides of all figures from the book

For more information please contact your local Pearson Education sales representative or visit **www.pearsoned.co.uk/harrison**

# Foreword

I am delighted to introduce *Logistics Management and Strategy*, now in its fourth edition – a further aid in our ability to drive our understanding of such a critical part of the business environment. In Bausch and Lomb logistics remains a key area of management attention, given its central role in customer service and the opportunities it provides for cost control, two fundamental essentials for any global business today.

Bausch and Lomb is built on a tradition of developing state of the art Optical products – from contact lenses to cataract surgery and the fast-growing optical pharmaceutical markets. These complex supply chains cover five continents and serve varying types of customers including hospitals, opticians and multiple retailers. They involve stock-keeping units (skus) requiring temperature control, serial traceability and sterility, and make for a diverse and challenging set of logistics demands.

When you then add these challenges to a range of over 100,000 skus – with some products being offered in over 7,000 different refractive powers/pack sizes – then you can understand why utilising the very latest approaches to logistics management and strategy is absolutely crucial.

In recent years we have invested heavily in automated warehouses, such as at our site in Amsterdam, recently recognised as one of the 'top ten' logistics facilities in the Netherlands. We have also developed our utilisation of agile logistics. This has been addressed by reducing the number of base products produced in our 17 factories, whilst increasing our customer responsiveness through postponement of labelling, bundling, promotional artwork and language compliance. In this regard, being a member of the Agile Supply Chain Research Club at Cranfield and working with Alan has been a rewarding and beneficial experience. I note that some of our experience has been invested in Chapter 7.

In the last two years Bausch and Lomb has greatly reduced inventory holdings through a number of logistics initiatives – improving working capital whilst maintaining, and even improving, customer service levels.

But the fight goes on, and it is with texts such as *Logistics Management and Strategy* in your armoury that you can continue to drive further improvements in your supply chain. The great aspect of this text is its readability – it does not seek to lecture the reader, but imparts its wisdom in a straightforward and practical manner. Fundamentally, I believe that is the essence of the science of logistics. Every element of our complex logistical environment is captured in this book with new sections covering sustainability, planning and control, and particularly the strategic role of procurement – all adding to the rich content.

In introducing this collaboration between Alan and Remko my parentage springs to mind. This was another Anglo-Dutch partnership – albeit with different outcomes!

I have spent the last twenty-five years in logistics, working in both British and Dutch environments. The last ten of these years have been in a global role. The output of Alan's and Remko's partnership rings true in so many areas – and offer methods and approaches which will continue to drive our improvements in the coming years.

Paul Mayhew MSc, MCILT
Vice President, Global Logistics
Bausch and Lomb.

# Preface

Logistics has been emerging from Peter Drucker's shadowy description as 'the economy's dark continent' for some years. From its largely military origins, logistics has accelerated into becoming one of the key business issues of the day, presenting formidable challenges for managers and occupying some of the best minds. Its relatively slow route to this exalted position can be attributed to two causes. First, logistics is a cross-functional subject. In the past, it has rightly drawn on contributions from marketing, finance, operations and corporate strategy. Within the organisation, a more appropriate description would be a *business process*, cutting across functional boundaries yet with a contribution from each. Second, logistics extends beyond the boundaries of the organisation into the supply chain. Here, it engages with the complexities of synchronising the movement of materials and information between many business processes. The *systems nature* of logistics has proved a particularly difficult lesson to learn, and individual organisations still often think that they can optimise profit conditions for themselves by exploiting their partners in the supply chain. Often they can – in the short term. But winners in one area are matched by losers in another, and the losers are unable to invest or develop the capabilities needed to keep the chain healthy in the long term. The emergence of logistics has therefore been dependent on the development of a cross-functional model of the organisation, and on an understanding of the need to integrate business processes across the supply network.

While its maturity as a discipline in its own right is still far from complete, we believe that it is time to take a current and fresh look at logistics management and strategy. Tools and concepts to enable integration of the supply chain are starting to work well. Competitive advantage in tomorrow's world will come from responding to end-customers better than competition. Logistics plays a vital role in this response, and it is this role that we seek to describe in this book.

The globalisation of logistics assumes that quality can be duplicated anywhere, that risks are relatively small, and that sustainability does not really matter. Case study 4.2 quotes an environmental activist as saying 'we are producing food in one corner of the world, packing it in another and then shipping it somewhere else. It's mad.' The reality is that 21st-century supply chains are developing very different profiles from those developed by the mindsets of ten or 20 years ago. Risk will become more important. Plans will need to be in place to prevent or mitigate the impact of financial, operational and political uncertainty. It is both environmentally and economically right to focus on sustainability. Logistics stands at the heart of this debate.

This text has a clear European foundation (its currency is the euro) and an international appeal. In line with the globalisation of logistics, we have included cases from other parts of the world than Europe – diverse though European logistics solutions are – including South Africa, the United States, Japan, China and Australia.

Accordingly, we start in Part One with the strategic role of logistics in the supply chain. We continue by developing the marketing perspective by explaining our view of 'putting the end-customer first'. Part One finishes by exploring the concept of value and logistics costs. In Part Two, we review leveraging logistics operations in terms of their global dimensions, and of the lead-time frontier. Part Two continues by examining the challenges of coordinating manufacturing and retail processes, and the impact on logistics of just-in-time and the agile supply chain. Part Three reviews working together, first in terms of integrating the supply chain and second in terms of sourcing and supply management. Our book ends with Part Four, in which we outline the logistics future challenge.

This text is intended for MSc students on logistics courses, and as an accompanying text for open learning courses such as global MSc degrees and virtual universities. It will also be attractive as a management textbook and as recommended reading on MBA options in logistics and supply chain management.

In the second edition, we listened carefully to students and to reviewers alike and set out to build on the foundation of our initial offering. We updated much of the material while keeping the clear structure and presentation of the first edition. There were lots of new cases and we updated others. We attempted to touch on many of the exciting developments in this rapidly expanding body of knowledge, such as governance councils, the prospects for a radio frequency identification device (RFID) and the future of exchanges. The third edition retains the clarity and up-to-date content which have become hallmarks of the previous editions. This edition continues to provide further new and updated cases to illustrate developments in the subject. This time, Chapters 6, 7 and 10 have been largely reconstructed, but you will also find many improvements to other chapters resulting from our research and work with industrial partners.

The fourth edition continues to build on the foundations we have developed so far, while continuing to update the content and keep it abreast of the rapidly developing logistics body of knowledge. Many of the cases have been updated too and new ones introduced. Chapters 6 and 7 have again been largely reconstructed, and we have refocused Chapter 9 around sourcing and supply management. We have continued to develop the theme of sustainable logistics, which we classify as a competitive priority right from the start. We are grateful to Paul Mayhew of Bausch and Lomb, who has written the Foreword to this edition following the retirement of Alain Le Goff.

We hope that our book will offer support to further professional development in logistics and supply chain management, which is needed today more than ever before. In particular, we hope that it encourages you to challenge existing thinking, and to break old mindsets by creating a new and more innovative future. Transformation of supply chains is a focus for everyone in the 21st century. Since we launched this textbook in 2001, it has become a European best seller – and is popular in Australia, Singapore and South Africa. It is also developing an important following in the United States. Our book has also been launched in local language formats in Japan, Brazil, Russia, China, Poland, Mongolia and the Ukraine.

# Authors' acknowledgements

We should like to acknowledge our many friends and colleagues who have contributed to our thinking and to our book. Cranfield colleagues deserve a special mention: Dr Janet Godsell, Dr Carlos Mena, Simon Templar, Dr Heather Skipworth, Dr Paul Chapman (now at Saïd Business School), Dr Paul Baines and Professor Richard Wilding have all made important contributions. Sri Srikanthan helped us with the financial concepts used in section 3.2. Members of the Agile Supply Chain Research Club at Cranfield also deserve special mention, notably Chris Poole of Procter & Gamble (now of B&Q), Paul Mayhew of Bausch & Lomb (who provides the foreword for the new edition), Ian Shellard and David Evans of Rolls-Royce, Mark Brown of Pentland Brands (who updated the apparel cases 4.4 and 8.1) and Joe Thomas of Tesco (who updated Case study 1.1). We have picked the brains of several who have recently retired from the industry, including David Aldridge (formerly of Cussons UK), Philip Matthews (formerly of Boots the Chemist) and Graham Sweet (formerly of Xerox, Europe). A number of professors from other universities have contributed ideas and cases, including Marie Koulikoff-Souviron (SKEMA Business School, Nice), Jacques Colin (CretLog, Aix-en-Provence), Konstantinos Zographos (Athens University of Economics and Business), Huo Yanfang (University of Tianjin), Thomas Choi (Arizona State University), David Bennett (Newcastle Business School) and Corrado Ceruti (University of Roma Tor Vergata). Many of our MSc graduates, such as Steve Walker and Alexander Oliveira, also made important contributions. Professor Yemisi Bolumole (University of North Florida) helped us to re-draft earlier versions of the first edition. Dr Jim Aitken (University of Surrey) contributed to our supply chain segmentation thinking in Chapter 2, and we have used his work on supplier associations in Chapter 8. We also acknowledge the encouragement of Matthew Walker and Sophie Playle at Pearson Education in the preparation of this text and their encouragement to meet deadlines! Also, we thank the reviewers who made many valuable comments on earlier editions of this book. We are very grateful to all of these, and to the many others who made smaller contributions to making this book possible. Cathi Maryon helped to research several of the cases and to project manage the manuscript. Finally, we thank Lynne Hudston for helping wherever she could – in addition to helping to run our Supply Chain Research Centre at Cranfield!

# Publisher's acknowledgements

*We are grateful to the following for permission to reproduce copyright material:*

**Figures**

Figure 1.2 from *Operations Management*, 2nd ed., FT/Prentice Hall (Slack, N, Chambers, S., Harland, C., Harrison, A. and Johnston, R. 1997); Figure 1.5 from Initial conceptual framework for creation and operation of supply networks, *Proceedings of 14th AMP Conference, Turku, 3–5 September* Vol. 3, pp. 591–613 (Zheng, J., Harland, C., Johnsen, T. and Lamming, R. 1998); Figure 1.6 from JIT in a distribution environment, *International Journal of Logistics and Distribution Management*, Vol. 9, No. 1, pp. 32–4 (Eggleton, D.J. 1990), © Emerald Group Publishing Limited all rights reserved; Figure 1.7 from www.supply-chain.org; Figure 2.4 from Understanding customer expectations of service, *Sloan Management Review*, Spring, pp. 39–48 (Parasuraman, A., Berry, L. and Zeithaml, V. 1991); Figure 2.5 from The impact of technology on the quality-value-loyalty chain: a research agenda, *Journal of the Academy of Marketing Science*, Vol. 28, No. 1, pp. 168–74 (Parasuraman, A. and Grewal, D. 2000), With kind permission from Springer Science and Business Media; Figure 2.6 from *Relationship Marketing for Competitive Advantage*, Butterworth Heinemann (Payne, A., Christopher, M., Clark, M. and Peck, H. 1995); Figure 2.8 from *Developing Supply Chain Strategy: A management guide*, Cranfield University (Harrison, A., Godsell, J., Julien, D., Skipworth, H., Achimugu, N. and Wong, C. 2007); Figures 2.10, 2.10, 2.13 from *Developing Supply Chain Strategy: A management guide*, Cranfield University (Harrison et al 2007); Figure 2.14 from Logistics – the missing link in branding: Bacalhau da Noruega vs. Bacalhau Superior, *ISL – Logistics Conference Proceedings, Lisbon* (Jahre, M. and Refsland-Fougner, A-K 2005); Figures 3.1, 3.3, 3.7, 3.8 from Sri Srikanthan; Figures 3.9, 3.10 from Understanding the relationships between time and cost to improve supply chain performance, *International Journal of Production Economics* (Whicker, L., Bernon, M., Templar, S. and Mena, C. 2006), with permission from Elsevier; Figure 3.11 from Using the balanced scorecard to measure supply chain performance, *Journal of Business Logistics*, Vol. 21, No. 1, pp. 75–93 (Brewer, P.C. and Speh, T.W. 2000), Reproduced with permission of Council of Supply Chain Management Professionals in the format textbook via Copyright Clearance Center; Figure 3.12 from *The Influence of Supply Chains on a Company's Financial Performance*, Cranfield University (Johnson, M and Templar, S.); Figure 3.13 from http://www.tesco-careers.com/home/about-us/visions-and-values; Figures 4.11, 4.12, 4.13 from Reconfiguring the supply chain to implement postponed manufacturing, *International Journal of Logistics Management*, Vol. 9, No. 1, pp. 95–110 (van Hoek, R.I. 1998); Figure 6.1 from *Manufacturing Planning and Control for Supply Chain Management*, 5th Ed., McGraw Hill (Vollman, T.E., Berry, W.L., Whybark, D.C. and Jacobs, F.R. 2005), Reproduced with permission of the McGraw-Hill Companies; Figure 6.8 from 'Relationships in the supply chain' in J. Fernie and L. Sparks (eds) *Logistics and Retail Management: Insights into current practice and trends from leading experts*, Kogan Page (After Fernie, J 1998); Figure 6.9 from *Shrinkage in Europe 2004: a survey of stock loss in the FMCG sector*, ECR-Europe, Brussels (Beck, A 2004); Figure 8.6 from The impact of modular production on the dynamics of supply chains, *International Journal of Logistics Management*, Vol. 9, 25–50 (van Hoek, R. and Weken, H.A.M. 1998), © Emerald Group Publishing Limited all rights reserved; Figure 8.9 from www.santonishoes.com, reprinted by permission of Santoni Shoes; Figure 8.12 from An empirical investigation into supply chain management, *International Journal of Physical Distribution and Logistics Management*, Vol. 28, No. 8, pp. 630–650 (Speckman, R.E., Kamauff, J.W. and Myhr, N. 1998), © Emerald Group Publishing Limited all rights reserved.; Figure 8.14 from The pervasive human resource picture in interdependent supply relationships, *International Journal of Operations and Production Management*, Vol. 27, No. 1, pp. 8–27 (Koulikoff-Souviron, M. and Harrison, A. 2007); Figure 9.6 from McKinsey Quarterly 2007/1, Excerpt from McKinsey Quarterly 2007/1. www.mckinseyquarterly.com Copyright © 2010 McKinsey & Company. All rights reserved. Reprinted by permission.; Figure 9.10 from An integrative framework for supplier relationship management, *Industrial Management and Data Systems*, Vol. 110, No. 4, pp. 595–515 (Park, J., Shin, K., Chang, T-W., and Park, J. 2010), © Emerald Group Publishing Limited all rights reserved; Figure 9.15 from Vendor rating for an entrepreneur development programme: a case study using the analytic hierarchy process method, *Journal of the Operational Research Society*, Vol. 50, pp. 916–30 (Yayha, S. and Kingsman, B. 1999)

**Tables**

Table 2.5 from *Strategy formulation in an FMCG supply chain*, Proceedings of the EurOMA Conference, Copenhagen (Godsell, J. and Harrison, A, 2002); Table 2.6 from Logistics service measurement: a reference framework, *Journal of Manufacturing Technology Management*, Vol. 15, No. 3, pp. 280–90 (Rafele, C. 2004), © Emerald Group Publishing Limited all rights reserved.; Table 3.1 from *Management Accounting, Official Terminology*, CIMA (1989); Table 3.2 from Sri Srikanthan; Table 3.6 from www.supply-chain.org; Table 4.7 from www.rlec.org, reprinted by permission of Reverse Logistics Executive Council; Table 4.8 from CSR Guideline for Suppliers, revision 2, October 2006, www.nec.co.jp/purchase/pdf/sc_csr_guideline_e.pdf, reprinted by permission of NEC Corporation

**Text**

Case Study 1.2 from JIT in a distribution environment, *International Journal of Logistics and Distribution Management*, Vol. 9, No. 1, pp. 32–4 (Eggleton, D.J. 1990); Case Study 1.5 from Backing the future, *Marketing* (00253650), pp. 16–17 (Barry, M. and Calver, L. 2009), Reproduced from Marketing magazine with the permission of the copyright owner, Haymarket Business Publications Limited.; Case Study 2.4 from Based on an article by John Arlidge, *Sunday Times*, 26/10/2003; Case Study 2.6 from Logistics – The Missing Link in Branding: Bacalhau da Noruega vs. Bacalhau Superior, *ISL – Logistics Conference Proceedings, Lisbon* (Jahre, M. and Refsland-Fougner, A-K. 2005); Case Study 4.2 from *Sunday Times*, 20/05/2007 (Jon Ungoed-Thomas); Case Study 4.2 from www.cranfield.ac.uk/cww/perspex, Reprinted by permission of Cranfield University; Case Study 6.1 from Dr. Heather Skipworth, after an original by Dr Paul Chapman; Case Study 8.3 from *Integration of the Supply Chain: The effect of Inter-Organisational Interactions between Purchasing-Sales-Logistics*, PhD thesis, Cranfield School of Management (Aitken, J. 1998); Case Study 8.5 from Professor Huo Yanfang, Tianjin University School of Management; Case Study 8.7 from The pervasive human resource picture in interdependent supply relationships, *International Journal of Operations and Production Management*, Vol. 27, No. 1, pp. 8–27 (Koulikoff-Souviron, N. and Harrison, A. 2007)

In some instances we have been unable to trace the owners of copyright material, and we would appreciate any information that would enable us to do so.

# How to use this book

This book is divided into four parts, centred around a model for logistics. The model for logistics is introduced in the first chapter of Part One, which places logistics in terms of its contribution to competitiveness, customer service and the creation of value. Part Two of the book focuses on leveraging logistics operations within the context of quality of service and cost performance objectives. Part Three focuses on working together, and Part Four pulls together four elements of leading-edge thinking in logistics, homing in on future challenges for the subject.

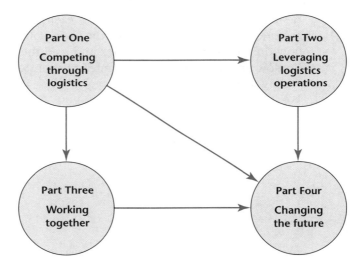

The book has been arranged to take you through the subject in logical stages. The limitation of a text presentation is that the subjects are then arranged in sequence, and links between stages have to be made by the reader. We have set out to facilitate cross-linkages by including:

- *activities* at the end of many of the sections, which are aimed at helping you to think about the issues raised and how they could be applied;
- *discussion questions* at the end of each chapter to help you assess your understanding of the issues raised, and give you practice in using them;
- *case studies*, which draw together a number of issues and help you to think about how those issues are linked together in a practical setting. Use the study questions at the end of each case to guide your thinking.

We have sought continually to break up the text with figures, tables, activities and case studies, so you will rarely find two successive pages of continuous text. You should therefore regard the activities and case studies as an integral part of the method used in this book to help you to learn.

Where possible, discuss the activities and case study questions in groups after you have prepared them individually. Discussion helps to broaden the agenda and create confidence in handling the issues. While you are studying this book, think about the logistics issues it raises – in your own firm or ones that you know well, and in articles in newspapers such as the *Financial Times* and magazines such as *Business Week*. Follow up the website addresses we have included in the text and again link them with the issues raised in the book.

A few words on terminology are appropriate here. We have taken the view that logistics and supply chain management (SCM) are sufficiently different for separate definitions to be needed. We have included these definitions in Chapter 1: logistics is a subset of SCM. 'Supply chain' and 'supply network' are used interchangeably, although we favour 'chain' for a few organisations linked in series and 'network' to describe the more complex inter-linkages found in most situations. Again, our position is explained in Chapter 1.

A summary is provided at the end of each chapter to help you to check that you have understood and absorbed the main points in that chapter. If you do not follow the summary points, go back and read the relevant section again. If need be, follow up on references or suggested further reading. Summaries are also there to help you with revision.

We have designed this book to help you to start out on the logistics journey and feel confident with its issues. We hope that it will help you to improve supply chains of the future.

# Plan of the book

| Part One COMPETING THROUGH LOGISTICS | |
| --- | --- |
| **Chapter 1**<br>Logistics and the supply chain | **Chapter 2**<br>Putting the end-customer first |
| **Chapter 3**<br>Value and logistics costs | |

| Part Two LEVERAGING LOGISTICS OPERATIONS | |
| --- | --- |
| **Chapter 4**<br>Managing logistics internationally | **Chapter 5**<br>Managing the lead-time frontier |
| **Chapter 6**<br>Supply chain planning and control | **Chapter 7**<br>Just-in-time and the agile supply chain |

| Part Three WORKING TOGETHER | |
| --- | --- |
| **Chapter 8**<br>Integrating the supply chain | **Chapter 9**<br>Sourcing and supply management |

| Part Four CHANGING THE FUTURE |
| --- |
| **Chapter 10**<br>Logistics future challenges and opportunities |

# Part One

# COMPETING THROUGH LOGISTICS

Our model of logistics structures the supply network around three main factors: the flow of materials, the flow of information and the time taken to respond to demand from source of supply. The scope of the network extends from the 'focal firm' at the centre across supplier and customer interfaces, and therefore typically stretches across functions, organisations and borders. The network is best seen as a system of interdependent processes, where actions in one part affect those of all others. The key 'initiator' of the network is end-customer demand on the right: only the end-customers are free to make up their mind when to place an order. After that, the system takes over.

Chapter 1 explains how networks are structured, the different ways in which they may choose to compete, and how their capabilities have to be aligned with the needs of the end-customer. Chapter 2 places the end-customer first in logistics thinking, and develops the theme of aligning logistics strategy with marketing strategy. Chapter 3 considers how value is created in a supply network, how logistics costs can be managed, and how a balanced measurement portfolio can be designed.

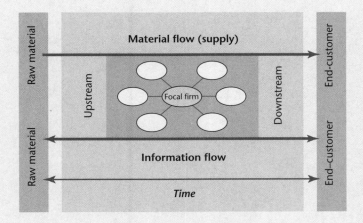

# CHAPTER 1

# Logistics and the supply chain

**Objectives**

*The intended objectives of this chapter are to:*

- identify and explain logistics definitions and concepts that are relevant to managing the supply chain;
- identify how supply chains compete in terms of time, cost, quality and sustainability. Also, how there are supportive capabilities and soft objectives;
- show how different supply chains may adopt different and distinctive strategies for competing in the marketplace.

*By the end of this chapter you should be able to understand:*

- how supply chains are structured;
- different ways in which supply chains may choose to compete in the marketplace;
- the need to align supply chain capabilities with competitive priorities.

## Introduction

It only takes only 17 hours or so to assemble a car, and a couple more days are needed to ship it to the customer via the dealers. So why does it take more than a month for a manufacturer to make and deliver the car I want? And why are the products I want to buy so often unavailable on the shelf at the local supermarket? These are questions that go to the heart of logistics management and strategy. Supply chains today are slow and costly in relation to what they will be like in the future. But let us start at the beginning, by thinking about logistics and the supply chain in terms of what they are trying to do. It is easy to get bogged down in the complexities of how a supply chain actually works (and very few people actually know how a whole supply chain works). We shall address many of those details later in this book. First, let us focus on how a supply chain competes, and on what the implications are for logistics management and strategy.

The overall aim of this chapter is to provide an introduction to logistics and set the scene for the book as a whole. The need is to look outside the individual organisation and to consider how it aligns with other organisations in a given supply chain. This is both a strategic and a managerial task: strategic, because it requires long-term decisions about how logistics will be structured and the systems it will use; managerial, because it encompasses decisions about sourcing, making and delivering products and services within an overall 'game plan'.

**Key issues**    This chapter addresses four key issues:

1 **Logistics and the supply chain:** definitions, structure, tiering.

2 **Material flow and information flow:** the supply chain and the demand chain.

3 **Competing through logistics:** competitive criteria in the marketplace.

4 **Logistics strategies:** aligning capabilities across the supply chain.

## 1.1  Logistics and the supply chain

*Key issues:* What is the supply chain, and how is it structured? What is the purpose of a supply chain?

Logistics is a big word for a big challenge. Let us begin by giving an example of that challenge in practice, because that is where logistics starts and ends.

**CASE STUDY 1.1**

### Tesco

Tesco is the UK's largest food retailer, with a Group sales turnover of more than €67 billion. It has over 2,100 stores in the US, central Europe, Ireland and the Far East, and over 2,300 in the UK alone. This number has increased rapidly as Tesco entered the convenience store market with its Tesco Express store format. The product range held by the stores has grown rapidly in recent years – a larger store can hold up to 20,000 products – as Tesco broadens its presence in the 'non-food' market for electrical goods, stationery, clothing and the like. This massive range is supported by thousands of suppliers, who are expected to meet agreed service levels (correct time and quantities) by delivering to Tesco within specific time 'windows'. Volumes are impressive. In a year, some 2.1 billion cases of product are shipped from suppliers to the stores.

Mindful of its responsibilities, Tesco is the UK's market leader in the use of bio fuels and works hard to reduce its $CO_2$ emissions per case delivered, through initiatives including rail, barge and alternative fuels. The company also buys considerable numbers of double-deck trailers to move more cases per trip.

Tesco states that its core purpose is 'to create value for customers to earn their lifetime loyalty'. A wide product range and high on-shelf availability across that range are key enablers of that core purpose. So how do you maintain high availability of so many product lines in so many stores? This question goes to the heart of logistics management for such a vast organisation. Logistics is about material flow, and about information flow. Let us look at how Tesco deals with each of these in turn.

An early reform for supermarket operation was to have suppliers deliver to a depot rather than to every store. During the 1980s, distribution to retail stores was handled by

26 depots. These operated on a single-temperature basis, and were small and relatively inefficient. Delivery volumes to each store were also relatively low, and it was not economic to deliver to all stores each day. Goods that required temperature-controlled environments had to be carried on separate vehicles. Each product group had different ordering systems. The network of depots simply could not handle the growth in volumes and the increasingly high standards of temperature control. A new distribution strategy was needed.

Many small depots with limited temperature control facilities were replaced by Fresh Food depots which can handle many products at several temperature ranges. The opportunity is to provide a cost-effective daily delivery service to all stores. Typically, a Fresh Food depot can handle over 80 million cases per year on a 40-acre site. The warehouse building comprises 36,000 square metres divided into three temperature zones: $-25°C$ (frozen), $1°C$ (chilled) and $12°C$ (semi-ambient). Each depot serves a group of between 48 and 335 retail stores. Delivery vehicles for Fresh Food depots use insulated trailers divided into chambers by means of movable bulkheads so they can operate at different temperatures. Deliveries are made at agreed, scheduled times. Grocery and Non-Food goods such as cans and clothing are delivered separately.

So much for the method of transporting goods from supplier through to the stores, but how much should be sent to each store? With such a huge product range today, it is impossible for the individual store to reorder across the whole range (store-based ordering). Instead, sales of each product line are tracked continuously through the till by means of electronic point of sale (EPOS) systems. As a customer's purchases are scanned through the bar code reader at the till, the sale is automatically recorded for each stock-keeping unit (sku). Cumulative sales are updated every four hours on Tesco Information Exchange (TIE). This is a system based on internet technology that allows Tesco and its suppliers to communicate trading information. The aim of improved communication is to reduce response times from manufacturer to stores and to ensure product availability on the shelf. Among other things, TIE aims to improve processes for introducing new products and promotions, and to monitor service levels.

Based on cumulative sales, Tesco places orders with its suppliers by means of electronic data interchange (EDI). As volumes and product ranges increased during the 1990s, food retailers such as Tesco aimed to de-stock their depots by ordering only what was needed to meet tomorrow's forecast sales. For fast-moving products such as types of cheese and washing powders, the aim is *day 1 for day 2*: that is, to order today what is needed for tomorrow. For fast-moving products, the aim is to *pick to zero* in the depot: no stock is left after store orders have been fulfilled. This means that the same space in the depot can be used several times over. Deliveries to stores are made in two *waves,* at specific times and within defined windows. This helps to improve product availability at stores throughout the day, and thus support changes in demand.

Updated by Joe Thomas (Tesco) 2010

## Questions

1  Describe the key logistics processes at Tesco.

2  What do you think are the main logistics challenges in running the Tesco operation?

So why is Tesco growing in an intensely competitive market? It describes its core purpose as being 'to create value for customers to earn their lifetime loyalty'. *Loyalty* is an important term that we return to in the next chapter. In order to achieve loyalty, Tesco has to understand customer needs and how they can be served. Its products must be recognised by its customers as representing outstanding value for money. To support such goals, it must ensure that the products that its customers want are available on the shelf at each of its stores at all times, day and night. Logistics is the task of planning and controlling the purchase and distribution of Tesco's massive product range from suppliers to stores. Logistics is concerned with managing two key flows:

- *material flow* of the physical goods from suppliers through the distribution centres to stores;
- *information flow* of demand data from the end-customer back to purchasing and to suppliers, and supply data from suppliers to the retailer, so that material flow can be accurately planned and controlled.

The logistics task of managing material flow and information flow is a key part of the overall task of *supply chain management*. Supply chain management is concerned with managing the entire chain of processes, including raw material supply, manufacture, packaging and distribution to the end-customer. The Tesco UK supply chain structure comprises three main functions:

- *distribution*: the operations and support task of managing Tesco's distribution centres (DCs), and the distribution of products from the DCs to the associated stores;
- *network and capacity planning*: the task of planning and implementing sufficient capacity in the supply chain to ensure that the right products can be procured in the right quantities now and in the future;
- *supply chain development*: the task of improving Tesco's supply chain so that its processes are stable and in control, that it is efficient, and that it is correctly structured to meet the logistics needs of material flow and information flow.

Thus logistics can be seen as part of the overall supply chain challenge. While the terms 'logistics' and 'supply chain management' are often used interchangeably, logistics is actually a subset of supply chain management. It is time for some definitions.

## 1.1.1 Definitions and concepts

A supply chain as a whole ranges from basic commodities (what is in the ground, sea or air) to selling the final product to the end-customer, to recycling the used product. Material flows from raw materials (such as a bauxite mine as a source of aluminium ore) to the finished product (such as a can of cola). The can is recycled after use. The analogy to the flow of water in a river is often used to describe organisations near the source as *upstream*, and those near the end-customer as *downstream*. We refer to firms that are involved in supply chains as partners, because that is what they are. There is a collective as well as an individual role to play in the conversion of basic commodity into finished product. At each stage of the conversion, there may be *returns* which could be reject material from the preceding firm, or waste such as the finished can that needs to be recycled. Sometimes, the whole product is wasted because the consumer throws it away.

> **A supply chain is a network of partners who collectively convert a basic commodity (upstream) into a finished product (downstream) that is valued by end-customers, and who manage returns at each stage.**

Each partner in a supply chain is responsible directly for a process that *adds value* to a product. A process:

> **Transforms *inputs* in the form of materials and information into *outputs* in the form of goods and services.**

In the case of the cola can, partners carry out processes such as mining, transportation, refining and hot rolling. The cola can has *greater value* than the bauxite (per kilogram of aluminium).

Supply chain management (SCM) involves *planning and controlling* all of the processes from raw material production to purchase by the end-user to recycling of the used cans. Planning refers to making a plan that defines how much of each product should be bought, made, distributed and sold each day, week or month. Controlling means keeping to plan – in spite of the many problems that may get in the way. The aim is to coordinate planning and control of each process so that the needs of the end-customer are met correctly. The definition of SCM used in this book is adapted from the Council of SCM Professionals (CSCMP, 2010):

> **SCM encompasses the planning and controlling of all processes involved in procurement, conversion, transportation and distribution across a supply chain. SCM includes coordination and collaboration between partners, which can be suppliers, intermediaries, third party service providers, and customers. In essence, SCM integrates supply and demand management within and between companies in order to serve the needs of the end-customer.**

'Serve the needs of the end-customer' has different implications in different contexts. In not-for-profit environments, such as public health and local government, serving implies 'continuously improving', 'better than other regions/countries', 'best value' and the like. In the commercial sector, serving implies 'better than competition', 'better value for money' and so on. In either situation, the focus of managing the supply chain as a whole is on *integrating* the processes of supply chain partners, of which the end-customer is the key one. In effect, the end-customer starts the whole process by buying finished products. It is the buying behaviour of the end-customer that causes materials to flow through the supply chain.

The degree to which the end-customer is satisfied with the finished product depends crucially on the management of material flow and information flow along the supply chain. If delivery is late, or the product has bits missing, the whole supply chain is at risk from competitors who can perform the logistics task better. Logistics is a vital enabler for supply chain management. We use the following definition of logistics in this book:

> **The task of coordinating material flow and information flow across the supply chain to meet end-customer needs.**

Logistics has both *strategic* (long-term planning) and *managerial* (short- and medium-term planning and control) aspects. Tesco has a clear view about the opportunities here. A breakdown of costs in Tesco's part of the UK supply chain is as follows:

- Supplier delivery to Tesco distribution centre (DC)    18%
- Tesco DC operations and deliver to store    28%
- Store replenishment    46%
- Supplier replenishment systems    8%

Nearly half of supply chain costs are incurred in-store. In order to reduce these in-store costs, Tesco realises that the solution is 'to spend more upstream and downstream to secure viable trade-offs for in-store replenishment'. If a product is not available on the shelf, the sale is potentially lost. By integrating external manufacturing and distribution processes with its own, Tesco seeks to serve the needs of its customers better than its competitors.

## 1.1.2 Supply chain: structure and tiering

The concept of a supply chain suggests a series of processes linked together to form a chain. A typical Tesco supply chain is formed from five such links.

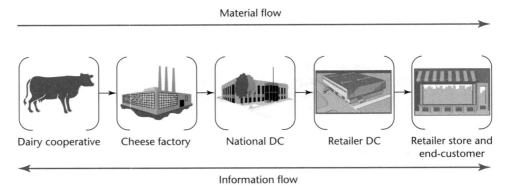

Figure 1.1 **From cow to customer**

In Figure 1.1 milk is produced by a dairy cooperative and shipped to a cheese factory. Once made, the cheese is shipped to the manufacturer's national distribution centre (NDC), where it is stored and matured for nine months. It can then be shipped in response to an order from the retailer, and is transported first to the retailer's regional distribution centre (RDC). From there, it is shipped to the store. Looking at the arrows in Figure 1.1, material flows from left to right. Information is shared across the chain: it is demand from the end-customer that makes the whole chain work.

If we look more closely at what happens in practice, the term 'supply chain' is somewhat misleading in that the 'chain' represents a simple series of links between a basic commodity (milk in this case) and a final product (cheese). Thus the cheese manufacturer will need packaging materials such as film, labels and cases. Cheese requires materials additional to milk in the manufacturing process. So the manufacturer deals with suppliers other than the milk cooperative alone. Once made, the cheese is dispatched for maturation to the supplier's NDC, and then dispatched to many customers in addition to Tesco. Once at a Tesco RDC, the 'chain' spreads again because up to 100 stores are served by a given RDC. The additional complexity prompts many authors to refer to *supply networks* rather than supply chains, a point we return to shortly. Logistics today is also concerned with what happens *after* a product has been sold. Two major concerns are:

- *Reverse logistics*: the return of unwanted goods and packaging in the opposite direction (from right to left) to the normal flow shown in Figure 1.1.
- *Waste*: the discarding of product at any stage in the supply chain due to quality problems – for example, the disposal of out-of-date or damaged stock by a retailer or by an end-customer. We consider waste more generally in Chapter 6.

A more realistic representation of the supply chain is shown in Figure 1.2, where each link can connect with several others. A *focal firm* is shown at the centre of many possible connections with other supplier and customer companies.

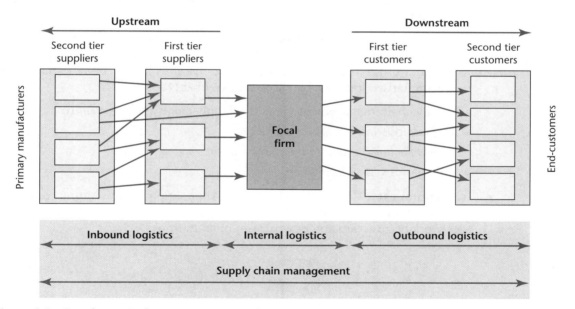

**Figure 1.2  Supply network**
(Source: After Slack *et al.*, 1997)

The supply chain can be seen in this diagram as a number of processes that extend across organisational boundaries. The focal firm is embedded within the chain, and its internal processes must coordinate with others that are part of the same chain. Materials flow from left (upstream) to right (downstream). If everything is as orderly as it seems, then only the end-customer (to the extreme right of the chain) is free to place orders when he or she likes: after that, the system takes over.

The supply chain is *tiered,* in that supply side and demand side can be organised into groups of partners with which we deal. Thus if we place an assembler such as the Ford plant at Valencia as the focal firm, *inbound logistics* comprises tier 1 suppliers of major parts and subassemblies that deliver directly to Ford, while tier 2 suppliers deliver to the tier 1s and so on. *Outbound logistics* covers the supply by the Ford Valencia plant to national sales companies as tier 1 customers, which in turn supply to main dealers at tier 2 and so on. *Internal logistics* covers the planning and control of parts movements within the Ford Valencia plant. The ultimate aim of supply chain management is to *integrate* inbound, outbound and internal logistics into a seamless whole, focused on meeting end-customer needs with no waste.

Other terms that are used to describe aspects of managing the supply chain are:

- *Purchasing and supply* deals with a focal firm's immediate suppliers (upstream).
- *Physical distribution* deals with the task of distributing products to tier 1 customers (downstream).
- *Logistics* refers to management of materials and information. *Inbound logistics* deals with links between the focal firm and its upstream suppliers, while *outbound logistics* refers to the links between the focal firm and its downstream customers. *Internal logistics* deals with planning and control of material flow within the boundaries of the focal firm.

Supply chain management thus appears as the 'end to end' (or 'cow to customer' as we have expressed it in Figure 1.1) management of the network as a whole, and of the relationships between the various links. The essential points were summarised long ago by Oliver and Webber (1982):

- Supply chain management views the supply chain as a *single entity.*
- It demands *strategic decision making.*
- It views *balancing inventories* as a last resort.
- It demands *system integration.*

A natural extension of this thinking is that supply chains should rather be viewed as *networks.* Figure 1.3 shows how a focal firm can be seen at the centre of a network of upstream and downstream organisations.

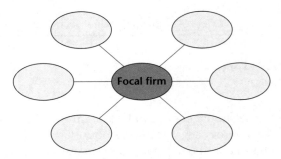

Figure 1.3   **A network of organisations**

The terms 'supply chain' and 'supply network' both attempt to describe the way in which buyers and suppliers are linked together to serve the end-customer.

'Network' describes a more complex structure, where organisations can be cross-linked and there are two-way exchanges between them; 'chain' describes a simpler, sequential set of links (Harland *et al.*, 2001). We have used the terms interchangeably in this book, preferring 'chain' to describe simpler sequences of a few organisations and 'network' where there are many organisations linked in a more complex way.

Figure 1.3 takes a basic view of the network, with a focal firm linked to three upstream suppliers and three downstream customers. If we then add material flow and information flow to this basic model, and place a boundary around the network, Figure 1.4 shows the network in context. Here we have added arrows showing the logistics contribution of material and information flows, together with the time dimension. Material flows from primary manufacture (for example, farming, mining or forestry) through various stages of the network to the end-customer. Material flow represents the *supply* of product through the network in response to demand from the next (succeeding) organisation. Information flow broadcasts *demand* from the end-customer to preceding organisations in the network. The time dimension addresses the question 'How long does it take to get from primary source to the end-customer?' That is, how long does it take to get the product through the various stages from one end of the supply chain to the other? Time is important because it measures how quickly a given network can respond to demand from the end-customer. In fact, the concept of flow is based on time:

**Flow measures the quantity of material (measured in input terms such as numbers of components, tonnes and litres) that passes through a given network per unit of time.**

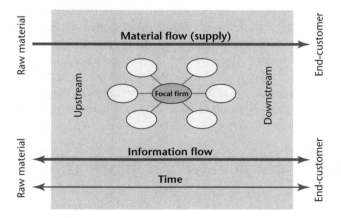

**Figure 1.4    The network in context**

**Activity 1.1**

Figure 1.5 shows an example network map of a chocolate bar. Draw a network map showing how your organisation, or one that you know well, links with other organisations. Explain the upstream, downstream and internal processes as far as you can. We expect you to address at least the first tiers of demand and supply. You will derive further benefit from researching additional tiers, and by developing the linkage of relationships that is involved. Explain how these work in practice, and how materials flow between the different tiers.

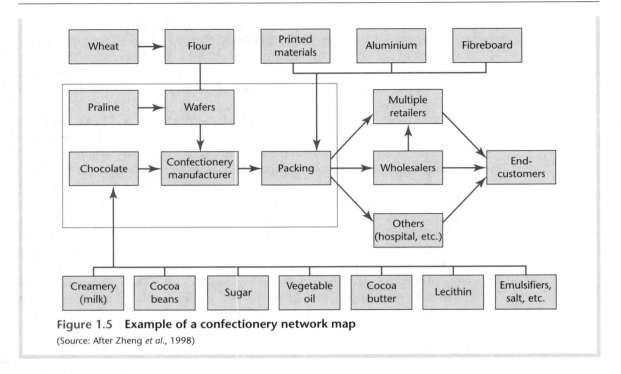

**Figure 1.5** **Example of a confectionery network map**
(Source: After Zheng *et al.*, 1998)

An important point here is that the supply network should be viewed as a *system*. All processes within the network need to be understood in terms of how they interact with other processes. No organisation is an island: its inputs and outputs are affected by the behaviour of other players in the network. One powerful, disruptive player can make life very difficult for everyone else. For example, several auto assemblers optimise their own processes, but disrupt those of upstream suppliers and downstream distributors. The effect is to increase total system costs *and* reduce responsiveness to end-customer demand.

## 1.2 Material flow and information flow

*Key issue:* **What is the relationship between material flow and information flow?**

As we have already seen, logistics is about managing material flow and information flow. In this section, we examine material flow and information flow in more detail.

### 1.2.1 Material flow

The aim within a supply chain is to keep materials flowing from source to end-customer. The time dimension in Figure 1.4 suggests that parts are moved through the supply chain as quickly as possible. In order to prevent local build-ups of inventory, flow must be orchestrated so that parts movement is co-ordinated. The term often used is *synchronous*. Caterpillar Inc. makes complex earth-moving equipment, and there are literally thousands of component parts and subassemblies that must come together in the final assembly processes. The vision is that parts and subassemblies should flow continuously through the supply chain, all orchestrated like a ballet (Knill, 1992: 54):

> The goal is continuous, synchronous flow. *Continuous* means no interruptions, no dropping the ball, no unnecessary accumulations of inventory. And *synchronous* means that it all runs like a ballet. Parts and components are delivered on time, in the proper sequence, exactly to the point they're needed.

Often it is difficult to see the 'end to end' nature of flow in a given supply chain. The negative effects of such difficulty include build-ups of inventory and sluggish response to end-customer demand. And sheer greed by the most powerful members of a supply chain often means that it is weaker partners (notably small to medium-sized enterprises – SMEs) who end up holding the inventories. So management strategies for the supply chain require a more holistic look at the links, and an understanding that organisational boundaries easily create barriers to flow.

Case study 1.2 describes how one company – Xerox in this case – re-engineered material flow in its distribution system.

<table>
<tr><td>CASE STUDY<br>1.2</td><td>

## Xerox

</td></tr>
</table>

Once the problems of introducing 'just-in-time' production systems (internal logistics) had been solved at the Xerox plant making photocopiers at Venray in Holland, attention shifted towards the finished product inventory (outbound logistics). Historically, stocks of finished products had been 'managed' by trying to turn the sales 'tap' on or off as stocks developed. This was characterised by the familiar 'feast or famine' situations. The objective of the next move for Xerox became clear: making only what you need when you need it, then shipping direct to the customer. But the key question had to be answered: just-in-time for what? The answer is – the end-customer. And customer surveys showed that three types of delivery were needed:

- Commodity products should be delivered 'off the shelf'.
- Middle-range products were required in five days.
- Larger products that had to be integrated into existing customer processes and systems had to be planned months ahead, but the quoted delivery date had to be met 100 per cent.

It was envisaged that this would lead to a radically different inventory 'profile' in the supply chain. Figure 1.6 shows a traditional inventory profile on the left. Most of the stock was held in local depots waiting for customer orders. If the mix had been incorrectly forecast, too many of the wrong products were in plentiful supply, while needed products were unavailable. Further, a batch of replacement products would take a long time to fight their way through the pipeline. A new 'just-in-time' strategy was conceived to make the supply chain much more responsive. This strategy had a profound effect on the inventory profile, pushing much of the inventory upstream. The closer that inventory is located towards the end-customer, the higher the value added – and the more that it is committed to a given finished product specification. Instead, inventory was mostly held further upstream. This was a more flexible solution, where product could be finally assembled to known orders, and where it had lower value. Of course, it has since been possible to remove several stages of the distribution process, thereby eliminating some of the sources of inventory altogether.

For commodity products, Xerox coined the term *deliver JIT*: that is, the product had to be delivered out of stock. Where sales forecasts are traditionally poor, the challenge was one of flexibility, simplicity and speed of manufacture. For mid-range products, it was unrealistic to hold 'just-in-case' inventories of products that are too complex to be assembled quickly. Instead, *finish JIT* was the term coined to describe the new policy of building semi-finished products with the minimum of added value, consistent with being able to complete and deliver the product in the five-day target. Finally, *build JIT* was the term used to describe the new philosophy of building larger products quickly within a defined lead time.

The impact of the new build philosophies on the downstream supply chain processes can be judged from Figure 1.6. While the traditional inventory profile shows a maximum number of days of stock (shown in the shaded area) at finished product level, this is risky. It always seems that demand is greatest for the very items that are not available! *Postponing* the decision on exact specification until as late as possible in the process, when we are more likely to know precisely what the end-customer wants, helps to create the much flattened inventory profile to the right of the diagram. These are issues to which we return in Chapter 6. (A development of this case, tracking 'what happened next', is Case study 7.4.)

(Source: After Eggleton, 1990)

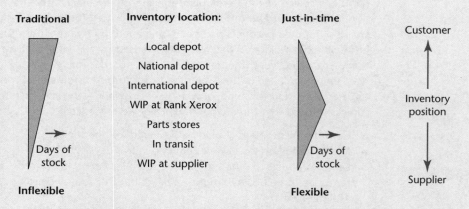

*Notes*: WIP = work in progress, i.e. products being worked on, but not yet ready for sale.
Shaded areas indicate days of stock: the wider the area, the more days of stock in that position.

Figure 1.6　**Xerox: the impact on inventories**

### Question

**1** How did inventory reduction in the supply chain lead to improved competitiveness at Xerox?

### 1.2.2   Information flow

As asked in the Xerox case study, just-in-time *for what*? It is all well and good to get materials flowing and movements synchronised, but the 'supply orchestra' needs to respond in unison to a specific 'conductor'. The 'conductor' in this analogy is actually the end-customer, and it is the end-customer's demand signals that trigger the supply chain to respond. By sharing the end-customer demand information across the supply chain, we create a *demand chain*, directed at providing enhanced customer value. Information technology enables the rapid sharing of demand and supply data at increasing levels of detail and sophistication. The aim is to integrate such demand and supply data so that an increasingly accurate picture is obtained about the nature of business processes, markets and end-customers. Such integration provides increasing competitive advantage, as we explore further in Chapter 8.

The greatest opportunities for meeting demand in the marketplace with a maximum of dependability and a minimum of inventory come from implementing such integration across the supply chain. A focal firm cannot become 'world class' by itself!

Figure 1.7 gives a conceptual model of how supply chain processes (source, make, deliver) are integrated together in order to meet end-customer demand (based on SCOR, 2010). Demand planning information ('plan') is shared across the chain rather than being interpreted and then changed by the 'sell' process next to the market. Demand fulfilment is also envisaged as an integrated process, as materials are moved from one process to the next in a seamless flow. Information is the 'glue' that binds supply chain processes together, and which coordinates planning and fulfilment. (We explain the SCOR model in more detail in section 3.5.)

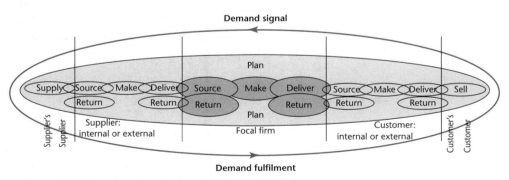

**Figure 1.7   Integrating demand and supply chains**

Activity 1.2

Write a brief (200 words) appraisal of material and information flow in the supply network affecting one of the major products in the response you gave in Activity 1.1. Perhaps the current situation is different from the above ideals?

## 1.3  Competing through logistics

*Key issues:* **How do products win orders in the marketplace? How does logistics contribute to competitive advantage?**

There are many potentially conflicting demands on an organisation today. All those unreasonable customers seem to want it yesterday, at lower prices and to be compensated if it goes wrong! Within a given supply chain, it is important that each organisation understands how each group of products competes in the marketplace, and that it aligns its capabilities with those of its partners.

A 'product' is actually a combination of the *physical product* (for example, a 200g pack of Camembert cheese) and its accompanying *service* (for example, how it is merchandised in the store – easy to find, always available, attractive presentation, lighting, temperature). While the physical product is determined by marketing and research and development (R&D), service is heavily influenced by logistics.

It is impossible to be outstanding at everything, and supply chain partners need to give priority to capabilities that give each product group its competitive edge. These are the advantages where supply chain partners 'dig in deep' by giving priority to investment and training, and by focusing product development and marketing efforts. They need only to match industry average performance on other criteria. Let us now look at the competitive priorities that can be delivered by logistics in the supply chain.

There are various ways in which products compete in the marketplace. Perhaps a given product is something that no one else can match in terms of price. Or maybe you offer a product that is technically superior, such as Gillette razors. While new product development has logistics implications, the key advantage provided by logistics – as suggested in Case study 1.1 about Tesco – is *availability of conforming product in the marketplace at low cost.* Logistics supports competitiveness of the supply chain as a whole by:

**meeting end-customer demand through supplying what is needed in the form it is needed, when it is needed, at a competitive cost.**

Logistics advantage thus shows up in the form of such competitive factors as better product availability in the marketplace and low product obsolescence. Defining logistics advantage means that we need to set goals that are clear, measurable and quantifiable. We distinguish three 'hard objectives' for creating logistics advantage: *quality, time* and *cost*. There are three further important ways of creating logistics advantage: *controlling variability* in logistics processes, *dealing with uncertainty* and *sustainability*. We have called these 'supportive capabilities', and they can be just as important as hard objectives. Finally, there are 'soft objectives', which relate to service aspects such as the confidence customers develop in the way the logistics operation is performed. Let us look at each of these ways of creating advantage in turn.

### 1.3.1  Hard objectives

Traditional ways of competing are to offer the end-customer advantages related to product quality, the speed with which it is delivered, and/or the price at which it is offered. We refer to quality, time and cost as 'hard objectives' because they are easy to measure and relatively obvious to the end-customer.

#### The quality advantage

The most fundamental objective – in that it is a foundation for the others – is to carry out all processes across the supply chain so that the end product does what it is supposed to do. Quality is the most visible aspect of supply chain perform-ance. Defects, incorrect quantities and wrong items delivered are symptoms of quality problems in supply chain processes that are all too apparent to the end-cus-tomer. Such problems negatively influence customer loyalty. Robust processes are at the heart of supply chain performance. Internally, robust processes help to re-duce costs by eliminating errors, and help to increase dependability by making processes more certain. When quality was positioned second to sales growth and cost, even the iconic Toyota Motor Company's brand suffered – as a string of re-calls and safety concerns in recent years has shown (see, for example, Cole, 2010).

While conformance quality in the factory may be controlled to defect levels that are below 25 parts per million (ppm), a product may end up on the retailer's shelf with between 2 and 5 per cent defects, which is 10,000 to 20,000 ppm. This huge escalation takes place as the result of cumulative problems in successive supply chain processes. Cases may be crushed when shrink-wrapped at the manufacturer's NDC. In the back of the retail store, cases may be cut open with a sharp knife – despite instructions to the contrary. The end-customer sees the product on the retail shelf at its *worst* state of quality performance, and that is where the buying decision is made that drives the supply chain as a whole.

In many logistics situations, 'quality of service' is concerned with selecting the right quantity of the right product in the right sequence in response to customer orders. For example, store orders must be picked from a range of thousands of skus (stock keeping units) at a Tesco RDC. This must be carried out accurately (correct sku, correct quantity) against tight delivery schedules day in and day out. *Pick accuracy* (for example, 99.5 per cent correct sku and correct quantity) is widely used to measure the quality of this operation. And increasing require-ments for in-store efficiencies mean that categories of product (for example, shampoos and toothpastes) need to be picked in a set sequence to facilitate direct-to-shelf delivery at the store. Logistics service providers who can imple-ment and maintain the highest standards of service quality place themselves at an advantage over those who cannot.

#### The time advantage

Time measures how long a customer has to wait in order to receive a given prod-uct or service. Volkswagen calls this time the *customer to customer* lead time: that is, the time it takes from the moment a customer places an order to the moment that customer receives the car he or she specified. Such lead times can vary from zero (the product is immediately available, such as goods on a supermarket shelf) to months or years (such as the construction of a new building). Competing on time is about survival of the fastest!

Time can be used to win orders by companies who have learned that some customers do not want to wait – and are prepared to pay a premium to get what they want quickly. An example is Vision Express, which offers prescription spectacles 'in about one hour'. Technicians machine lenses from blanks on the premises. Staff are given incentives to maintain a 95 per cent service level against the one-hour target. Vision Express has been successful in the marketplace by re-engineering the supply chain so that parts and information can flow rapidly from one process to the next. Compare this with other opticians in the high street, who must send customer orders to a central factory. Under the 'remote factory' system, orders typically take about ten days to process. An individual customer order is first dispatched to the factory. It then has to join a queue with orders from all the other high street branches around the country. Once the order has been processed, it must return to the branch that raised the order. While this may be cheaper to do (a central, highly productive factory serves all of the branches), it takes much longer to process an order.

The time advantage is variously described as *speed* or *responsiveness* in practice. Speeding up supply chain processes may help to improve freshness of the end product, or to reduce the risk of obsolete or over-aged stock in the system. Time is an *absolute* measure, that is, it is not open to interpretation as quality and cost are. By following a product through a supply chain, we can discover which processes add value and which add time and cost but no value. We explore this further in Chapter 5, which is about managing time for advantage in the supply chain.

### The cost advantage

Cost is important for all supply chain processes – that goes without saying. Low costs translate into advantages in the marketplace in terms of low prices or high margins, or a bit of each. Many products compete specifically on the basis of low price. This is supported from a supply chain point of view by low cost manufacture, distribution, servicing and the like. Examples of products that compete on low price are 'own brand' supermarket goods that reduce the high margins and heavy advertising spend of major brands. They also perhaps cut some of the corners in terms of product specification in the hope that the customer will consider low price to be more important than minor differences in product quality.

The pressure to reduce prices at automotive component suppliers, and hence costs to the assemblers, is intense. The assemblers have been setting annual price reduction targets for their inbound supply chains for some years. Toyota announced demands for a 30 per cent reduction in prices on many components by the time that new models are launched in 2013. But unless a supplier can match reduced prices at which products are being sold by means of reduced costs, that supplier will gradually go out of business. As a result, many suppliers are cynical about the 'price down' policies of the assemblers. Reduced prices are the reward of cost cutting, and that is most often a collaborative effort by several partners in the supply chain. So suppliers are unlikely to meet Toyota's demands on their own: 'Toyota is going to have to do a lot of work itself, by switching more quickly to global platforms and using more common parts' (Soble, 2009). As indicated in section 1.1, Tesco can make only limited inroads into its in-store costs without the help of its supply chain partners.

## 1.3.2  Supportive capabilities

While the hard objectives listed above are always important to competitive advantage, supportive capabilities can also be key to creating logistics advantage in the marketplace. When there is little to choose in terms of quality, time or cost, supportive capabilities can make all the difference to the end-customer. Variability refers to real and identifiable differences within a population, such as the differences in time each patient at an optician has to wait for his or her eyes to be tested. Uncertainty refers to our lack of knowledge (Thompson, 2002): in logistics terms, uncertainty results in us having to deal with events that are not known in advance. Sustainability addresses the improvement of environmental, social and economic values in the design of logistics systems.

### Controlling variability: the dependability advantage

Time is not just about speed. Quality is not just about meeting defect targets. Behind both 'hard' objectives is the need to *control variability* in logistics processes. Variability undermines the *dependability* with which a product or service meets target. While Vision Express offers a one-hour service for prescription glasses, the 95 per cent service level is a measure of the dependability of that service against the one-hour target. Firms who do not offer instantaneous availability need to tell the customer – in other words to 'promise' – *when* the product or service will be delivered. Delivery dependability measures how successful the firm has been in meeting those promises. For example, the UK's Royal Mail quality of service target for letters posted with a 'first class' stamp is that 93.0 per cent will arrive the next working day (Royal Mail, 2009). It is important to measure dependability in the same 'end to end' way that speed is measured. Dependability measures are widely used in industries such as train and air travel services to monitor how well published timetables are met. And in manufacturing firms, dependability is used to monitor a supplier's performance in such terms as:

- *on time* (percentage of orders delivered on time and the variability against target);
- *in full* (percentage of orders delivered complete and the variability against target);
- *on quality* (percentage of defects and the variability against target).

So logistics is concerned not just with the *average* percentage of orders delivered on time but also with the *variability*. For example, a manufacturer has to cope with the day-to-day variability of orders placed. In practice, this is more important than the average orders placed because of the resource implications of demand variability. Case study 1.3 explores the impact of variability on a supplier's processes.

Measuring schedule variability

A problem that is all too familiar to suppliers in the automotive industry is that of schedule variability. A vehicle manufacturer issues delivery schedules to specify how many parts of each type are required each day for the following month. And each day a 'call-off' quantity is issued, which specifies how many the vehicle manufacturer actually wants. The two sets of figures are not necessarily the same, although they usually add up to the same cumulative numbers for the month as a whole. In other words, the total scheduled quantities and the total call-off quantities are the same. So what is the problem?

The problem is that the supplier has to cope with the variability of call-off quantities that create huge problems for the supplier's process. Let scheduled demand = S, and call-off quantity = A. Then the difference D between schedule and actual is given by D = S − A. If the supplier produces to schedule, then S > A, the supplier will over-produce the part and end up with excess stock. Where S < A, the effects could either be a reduction in stock held by the supplier, or a shortfall of (S − A) of parts from the supplier. The two conditions (S > A and S < A) therefore have different logistics implications.

Figure 1.8 shows that actual demand, totalled across four different parts at PressCo (a supplier of pressed metal components), may be up to 1,600 units above schedule, or 2,200 below schedule in the case of vehicle assembler WestCo. This range has been divided up into intervals of 100 units. The mode (0 − 99) indicates that S = A for a frequency of 18 per cent of the observations.

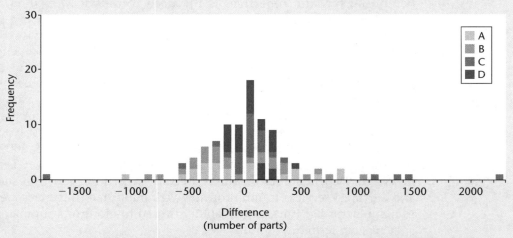

**Figure 1.8 Distribution of differences between scheduled and actual demand for WestCo**

Assuming that the distribution is roughly normal, the standard deviation (SD) is 573, which is characteristic of the flat, wide spread of data. Figure 1.9 shows the distribution of S − A for four similar parts from the same supplier but to a different vehicle assembler; EastCo. This time, the SD for the distribution is 95, representing a much narrower spread of differences than for WestCo.

(Source: Harrison, 1996)

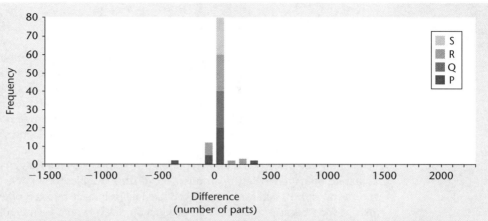

**Figure 1.9  Distribution of differences between scheduled and actual demand for EastCo**

*Questions*

1  What are the logistics implications to PressCo for delivery reliability to customers WestCo and EastCo?

2  What steps will the supplier need to take in order to satisfy call-off orders from WestCo?

3  If separate parts of the PressCo factory were dedicated to production for WestCo and for EastCo, which would be the more efficient in terms of labour costs and inventory holding?

Quality is not just about meeting target pick accuracy or target defect levels. It is also about controlling variability. The same argument can be made about costs. The implication of dependability for logistics is that supply chain processes need to be robust and predictable. In Chapter 6 we develop the case for dependability in supply chains under the themes of planning and control and lean thinking.

### Dealing with uncertainty: the agility advantage

Dealing with uncertainty means responding rapidly to unknown problems that affect logistics processes. Sometimes, problems can be foreseen – even if their timing cannot. Toyota UK manages inbound deliveries of parts from suppliers in southern Europe by a process called *chain logistics*. Trailers of parts are moved in four-hour cycles, after which they are exchanged for the returning empty trailer on its way back from the UK. One hitch in this highly orchestrated process means that incoming parts do not arrive just-in-time at the assembly plant. Toyota demands that its suppliers and logistics partner plan *countermeasures*. This means that alternative routes for suppliers to deliver to its Burnaston assembly plant in the UK have been planned in advance to deal, for example, with a French channel ferry strike at Calais. The weather is also a cause of uncertainty in logistics – for example, it may mean that Tesco has to switch between salads and soups as the result of a cold snap. Other forms of uncertainty concern events where neither the problem nor its timing can be foreseen. Case study 1.4 provides an example of such an event and how two organisations responded differently to it.

CASE STUDY
1.4

## Nokia deals with uncertainty

In March, 2000, a thunderstorm struck the Philips semiconductor plant at Albuquerque in New Mexico, which made silicon chips for products such as mobile phones. Damage at first seemed minor, and firefighters soon left the premises. At first, Philips told major customers such as Nokia and Ericsson that the delay to production would only be one week. But damage to some of the clean areas in the plant – created by smoke and water – was actually going to take months to remedy. Clean rooms in semiconductor plants must be spotless, and particles of more than $0.5\mu$ are filtered out.

The one-week delay was quickly reported by Tapio Markki, Nokia's chief component-purchasing manager, to Pertti Korhonen, Nokia's top troubleshooter. 'We encourage bad news to travel fast', said Mr Korhonen. While Philips initially rejected offers of help from Nokia, it soon became apparent that production delays would be much more than one week. Korhonen put together a team to find solutions to supplying the five chips that were affected by the Philips fire. Three were quickly re-sourced from Japanese and American suppliers, but the other two were only supplied by Philips. This time Philips cooperated at the highest level. Nokia's chairman and chief executive, Mr Ollila, met with the Philips CEO Mr Boostra and the head of the Philips semiconductor division, Mr van der Poel. Factories at Eindhoven and Shanghai were rescheduled to supply the missing chips, and engineers from both Nokia and Philips worked to accelerate the return of the Albuquerque plant to full production. As a result of these intensive efforts, there were relatively minor delays to Nokia's mobile phone shipments.

Executives at Ericsson in Sweden only learned of the problem several weeks after the fire. Company culture was less proactive than at its Finnish rival. The bad news was withheld from senior management long after it became clear that delays were becoming serious. By the time that Ericsson realised the magnitude of the problem, it was too late to find alternative sources. Nokia had seized remaining world capacity, and it took nine months for the situation to be rectified. The disruption led to a 3 per cent loss of market share by Ericsson, and contributed in turn to its exit from the phone handset market (it formed a joint venture with Sony in 2001).

(Sources: Sheffi, 2005; Latour, 2001)

### Question

1 What are the key lessons from this case for dealing effectively with disruptions to the supply chain?

The implication of uncertainty for supply chain processes is that they need to be *flexible*. Flexibility is defined as the 'ability to react or transform [supply chain processes] with minimum penalties in time, cost and performance' (Upton, 1995). Flexibility comes in two basic forms (Sawhney, 2006):

- *Proactive*: to create the capability in advance to handle uncertainty – for example, Toyota's counter-measures.
- *Reactive*: to cope with uncertainty in a focal firm's internal or external environment – for example, Nokia's response to the fire at Philips.

Uncertainties, wherever they originate, may affect other supply chain partners. In Chapter 6, we develop the case for responding to uncertainty in supply chains under the theme of *agility*.

### Acting responsibly: the sustainability advantage

The Bruntland report (UNWCED, 1987) defines sustainability as 'development that meets the needs of the present without compromising the ability of future generations to meet their needs'. Logistics has increasingly been turned to in recent years because it offers enormous potential to mitigate damage to the environment in which we live. Many logistics decisions impact the environment – for example, sourcing from suppliers who use renewable raw materials and who practise ethical labour standards, and transportation modes that minimise carbon dioxide ($CO_2$) emissions. Sustainability emerges as a way of considering the environmental and social values of business decisions alongside their economic value. This thinking gave rise to the term 'triple bottom line' (TBL, Elkington, 1997, 2004). Taking these three 'values' in turn:

- *Environmental*: a focal firm such as Tesco is concerned with reducing consumption of non-renewable energy and materials. It is also concerned with measuring and reducing the environmental impact of processes across the SC – from cow to customer (Figure 1.1). And collection and disposal by the end-user is also factored in – what can be done to reduce the impact of car journeys and the disposal of waste such as packaging? TBL thinking states that environmental polluters should not be given a free ride any more – they should be made to pay. For example, the Australian government introduced carbon trading (Humphreys, 2007, compares tax v trading): under the carbon pollution reduction scheme, the government requires a 5 per cent reduction in $CO_2$ levels by 2020. Accreditation to the ISO 14001 series on environmental management systems is becoming increasingly influential. And the Environmental Protection Agency (EPA, 2010) seeks to 'make sustainability the next level of environmental protection by drawing on advances in science and technology, applying government regulations and policies to protect public health and welfare, and promoting green business practices'.

- *Social*: large focal firms such as Nike and Wal-Mart have been forced to consider the social contexts of the suppliers with whom they deal. Often, suppliers are based on the other side of the world, but consumer pressure has forced such firms to recognise their responsibility in ensuring that goods are manufactured in socially responsible conditions – such as no child labour (see Case study 4.7). Organisations such as the Fairtrade Foundation (2010) aim to help farmers in developing countries:

  > By facilitating trading partnerships based on equity and transparency, Fairtrade contributes to sustainable development for marginalised producers, workers and their communities. Through demonstration of alternatives to conventional trade and other forms of advocacy, the Fairtrade movement empowers citizens to campaign for an international trade system based on justice and fairness.

  Social issues have been developed more broadly under the theme *Corporate Social Responsibility* (CSR), which we examine in more detail in section 4.7.

- *Economic*: this is the net value that a firm generates after social and environmental values have been taken into account. This implies making the connection between TBL values and financial performance. The organisational changes involved in recognising economic value can be wrenching and can take years to implement. Nike – along with other premium brand companies – came under enormous pressure from labour activists in the 1990s to adopt more sustainable codes of conduct in their global supply chains. For example, purchasing teams had to be constrained from going for lowest prices from suppliers, which threatened short-term profitability. So Nike had to 'offset any first-mover disadvantage by getting both its competitors and suppliers involved . . . it is essential to work with others to move toward the adoption of a common approach to labour compliance codes, monitoring and reporting to help ensure broader accountability across the industry as a whole' (Zadek, 2004).

Supplier Codes of Conduct (such as Cisco Systems, 2009) are used to 'give preference to suppliers who are socially and environmentally progressive'. In other words, sustainability has become a competitive advantage in its own right. Case study 1.5 outlines the operation of the Marks and Spencer 'Plan A'.

<table>
<tr><td>CASE STUDY<br>1.5</td><td>

## Plan A at Marks and Spencer

</td></tr>
</table>

In January 2007 Marks and Spencer (M&S) launched 'Plan A', its five-year strategy to improve the retailer's social and environmental impact. Plan A currently sets out 100 commitments – goals to be achieved by 2012 – covering climate change, raw materials, waste, health and fair partnership. €300 million has been set aside to fund the plan over the five years, and 14 staff applied to its delivery. Noted in particular for its comprehensive approach and willingness to use the company's influence with customers, suppliers, investors and politicians, the plan has been praised as an example of best practice as well as a means by which other agents may join M&S to change the way companies do business along more socially, environmentally and ethically beneficial lines. Plan A has so far won 27 independent awards.

In June 2009 M&S reported on Plan A's progress to date and revealed that 39 commitments had been achieved, 24 of which have been extended. Another 50 are on or ahead of target. Ten are behind, and only one commitment has been put on hold; to make a 50 per cent switch to bio-diesel in its lorries, due to emerging concerns about deforestation. Thus M&S can claim that, at the two-fifths mark, it is on track to deliver its commitments, and furthermore stated that Plan A was cost positive by 2009.

It is not all plain sailing: carbon footprint reduction, as one example, has presented several challenges to M&S. Its reported 18 per cent net reduction in greenhouse gas emissions is largely based on the company's switch to buying electricity under 'green' tariffs – reductions that have already been counted by energy suppliers. M&S now report gross emissions excluding this saving – which show a 2 per cent growth. A factor in the rise is a 10 per cent increase in store size, also, M&S international air travel has increased. Mike Barry, head of sustainable business at M&S, points out that the company has 'decoupled' emissions growth from commercial growth, and is firm on its commitment to reduce emissions; nevertheless this marker alone shows the conflict between business growth and a target of reduced environmental impact.

M&S maintains that Plan A is not just another CSR ploy. Jonathon Porritt, adviser to M&S, agrees and points to its integration through the whole company, its detailed measurement of non-financial data and its focus on outcomes. Porritt asserts that Plan A 'really works' for shareholders as well as other stakeholders.

So how has M&S made sure Plan A 'really works'? Feedback tells the company that customers discern and value the Plan A difference between M&S and other retailers, and this translates into increased foot traffic and a wider customer base. And there are savings: increased energy efficiency; reduced fuel use; cutting food waste by discounting short shelf-life products; recycling internally, including coat hangers; innovation in recycling/re-use and purchasing, e.g. using PET plastic for home product filling as well as clothes; reducing water consumption; and being a good employer, thus reducing staff turnover and maximising payback on investment in training and good working conditions. All this, plus a name for encouraging customers and suppliers to change their behaviour, being a fair partner with suppliers, raising money for charity and promoting healthy lifestyles, makes customers want to buy more from M&S. Richard Gillies, Director of Plan A and Sustainable Business at the company, sums it up with 'As well as saving costs, Plan A differentiates our business and brings more customers into our stores.'

(Source: Barry, M. and Calver, L. (2009), 'Backing the future', *Marketing* (00253650), pp. 16–17.

### Question

1 How has M&S made the social and environmental impacts of Plan A acceptable to its shareholders?

## 1.3.3  Soft objectives

There are other ways in which logistics advantage may be gained, but these are not so readily measurable as those listed above. They are referred to as 'soft' objectives as distinct from the more easily measurable 'hard' objectives. Examples of soft objectives are:

- *confidence*: queries answered promptly, courteously and efficiently;
- *security*: customer's information and property treated in a confidential and secure manner.

Soft objectives need to be measured in different ways to hard objectives, such as customer attitude surveys.

Logistics is not the only way in which product competitiveness in the marketplace can be enhanced. The performance objectives listed above can be added to (and in some cases eclipsed by) other ways in which products may win orders, such as design and marketing features. No matter how good the logistics system might have been, lack of an early 'clam shell' design led to the reduction of Nokia's market share for mobile telephone handsets in Europe. Superior product or service design – often supported by brand image – may become the dominant ways of achieving advantage in the marketplace. Here, the logistics task is to support the superior design. BMW's supply chain is one of the most efficient there is, mainly because its products are sold (at least in Europe) as soon as they have been made. Finished cars do not accumulate in disused airfields across Europe, like those of the mass producers. Finished product storage adds cost, with no value added from an end-customer perspective.

### 1.3.4 Order winners and qualifiers

The relative importance of the above logistics performance objectives is usually different for a given market segment. A helpful distinction is that between order winners and order qualifiers (Hill, 2000):

- *Order winners* are factors that directly and significantly help products to win orders in the marketplace. Customers regard such factors as key reasons for buying that product or service. If a firm raises its performance on those factors, it will increase its chances of getting more business. Thus a product that competes mainly on price would benefit in the marketplace if productivity improvements enabled further price reductions.
- *Order qualifiers* are factors that are regarded by the market as an 'entry ticket'. Unless the product or service meets basic performance standards, it will not be taken seriously. An example is quality accreditation: a possible supplier to major utilities such as PowerGen in Britain and EDF in France would not be considered seriously without ISO 9000 certification. And delivery reliability is a must for newspapers – yesterday's news is worthless. Note that, in both examples, order qualifiers are *order-losing sensitive*: loss of ISO 9000 accreditation would make it impossible to supply to major utilities, and late delivery of newspapers would miss the market.

Order winners and qualifiers are *specific to individual segments,* a point we develop in the next chapter. Table 1.1 provides an example of how two different products made by the same manufacturer and passing through the same distribution channel have different performance objectives. The first product group comprises standard shirts that are sold in a limited range of 'classic' colours and sizes. The second product group comprises fashion blouses that are designed specially for each season in many colours and a choice of styles with associated designer labels.

Analysis of the order winners and qualifiers shows that the two product ranges have very different performance criteria in the marketplace. Of the two, the range of fashion blouses presents more logistics challenges because demand for individual skus are much more difficult to forecast. It is not until the season is under way that a picture begins to emerge about which colours are selling most in which region of the market. The logistics challenge is therefore concerned with speed of response and flexibility to changing demand. The logistics challenges between the two ranges are quite distinctive.

Not only can order winners and qualifiers be different for different products and services. They can also *change over time*. Thus, in the early phase of a new product lifecycle, such as the launch of a new integrated circuit, the order winners are availability and design performance. Price would often be a qualifier: provided the price is not so exorbitant that no one can afford it, there is a market for innovators who want the best-performing chip that is available. But by the maturity phase of the lifecycle, competitors have emerged, the next generation is

Table 1.1   **Different product ranges have different logistics performance objectives**

|  | Classic shirts | Fashion blouses |
|---|---|---|
| *Product range* | Narrow: few colours, standard sizes | Wide: many colours, choice of styles, designer labels |
| *Design changes* | Occasional | Frequent (at least every season) |
| *Price* | Everyday low price | Premium prices |
| *Quality* | Consistency, conformance to (basic) spec | High grades of material, high standards of workmanship |
| *Sales volumes* | Consistent sales over time | Sales peak for given fashion season |
| *Order winners* | Price | Time-to-market<br>Brand/label<br>Quality |
| *Order qualifiers* | Quality<br>Availability | Price<br>Availability |
| *Logistics priorities* | Cost<br>Dependability<br>Quality | Speed<br>Flexibility<br>Quality |

already on the stocks, and the order winners have changed to price and product reliability. The former order winners (availability and design performance) have changed to become order qualifiers. The logistics challenge is to understand the market dynamics and to adjust capabilities accordingly.

The *actions of competitors* are therefore a further influence on logistics performance objectives. For example, low-price competitors are a feature of most markets, and attempt to differentiate themselves from the perhaps higher-grade but pricier incumbents. Thus competitors such as Matalan have sparked fundamental changes in logistics strategy at M&S (see Case study 1.5). In response to loss of sales to cheaper new entrants, M&S ditched long-standing agreements with local UK suppliers and sourced garments from new, lower-priced suppliers in the Far East.

While the above helps to show some of the thinking in setting logistics strategy, there are limitations to the use of order winners and qualifiers. They are subjective, and so provide *perceived* relative priorities. While this creates useful debate between marketing and logistics, it lays the foundation for more informed strategy setting in the context of the values of other variables in Table 1.1 such as volumes. We develop this point in section 2.4. It is also important to share understanding of these priorities with partners, a point which we develop next.

## 1.4  Logistics strategy

*Key issues:* **What is 'strategy'? How can competitive criteria be aligned within a supply chain? How can logistics strategies be tuned to different product needs?**

## 1.4.1 Defining 'strategy'

Strategy is about planning as distinct from doing. It is about formulating a long-term plan for the supply chain, as distinct from solving the day-to-day issues and problems that inevitably occur. Extending the concept of 'strategy' from Hayes and Wheelwright (1984):

> **Logistics strategy is the set of guiding principles, driving forces and ingrained attitudes that help to coordinate goals, plans and policies, and which are reinforced through conscious and subconscious behaviour within and between partners across a network.**

All too often, logistics 'strategy' is set using few such characteristics: decisions are made piecemeal by accident, muddle or inertia. We need, however, to recognise that strategic decisions may indeed be made by such means.

Whittington (2000) proposes four approaches to setting strategy. He starts by suggesting different motivations for setting strategy:

- *How deliberate are the processes of strategy setting?* These can range from clearly and carefully planned to a series of ad hoc decisions taken on a day-to-day basis.

- *What are the goals of strategy setting?* These can range from a focus on maximising profit to allowing other business priorities such as sales growth to be included.

If we make these two considerations the axes of a matrix, Figure 1.10 suggests four options for crafting strategy.

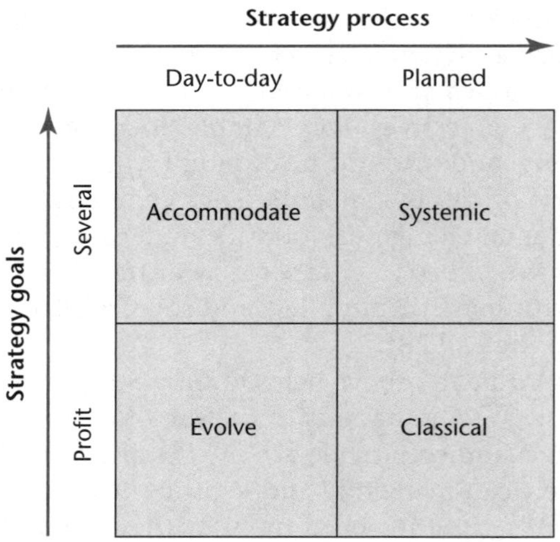

**Figure 1.10  Four options for crafting strategy**

What are the implications for the way in which supply chain strategy is approached in different organisations? Following is a brief description of the four options:

- *Evolve.* 'Strategy' is not something that is formally undertaken at all. 'Our strategy is not to have a strategy' is a typical viewpoint. Operating decisions are taken in relation to the needs of the moment, with financial goals as the main guiding principle.

- *Classical.* While financial goals are again the main guiding principle, these are achieved through a formal planning process. This is called 'classical' because it is the oldest and most influential option.

- *Accommodate.* Here, decisions are back to the day-to-day mode, but financial objectives are no longer the primary concern. Strategy is accommodated instead to the realities of the focal firm and the markets in which it operates.

- *Systemic.* This option for strategy setting sees no conflict between the ends and means of realising business goals. While goal setting takes place across all major aspects of the business (including human resources, marketing and manufacturing policies), these are linked to the means by which they will be achieved in practice.

Logistics strategy usually demands systemic strategy setting between network partners, who may have to coordinate order winners and qualifiers across different market segments.

## 1.4.2 Aligning strategies

In section 1.1 we showed the supply chain as a network of operating processes. In section 1.2 we emphasised the need to 'integrate' these processes to maximise flow and focus on the end-customer. And in section 1.3 we saw how supply chains can choose to compete on a range of different competitive priorities. Now it is time to put these ideas together and show how strategies need to be *aligned* across the supply chain.

If different links in the supply chain are directed towards different competitive priorities, then the chain will not be able to serve the end-customer as well as a supply chain in which the links are directed towards the same priorities. That is the basic argument for alignment in the supply chain (Cousins, 2005). Where the links are directed by a common and consistent set of competitive criteria, then that supply chain will compete better in the marketplace than one in which the links have different, conflicting priorities. This is the concept of 'focus'.

Focus is based on the view that you cannot be good at everything. For example, it is difficult to handle high volume, low cost products in the same channel to market as low volume, high variety products, for which flexibility is the name of the game. While the assembly line is the method of choice for manufacturing cars in volume, development of prototypes for new models is kept well away from the factory in special facilities until close to launch. This is because the development process demands quite different technical skills and equipment that are better physically separated from the more routine, efficient and repetitive assembly line. In the example of the standard shirts and fashion blouses in section 1.3, the associated operations processes would be kept separate ('focused') for similar reasons. And the separation could be thousands of kilometres. 'Classic' shirts could be sourced from China, where prices are low, and long delivery lead times are not so important. 'Fashion' shirts may be sourced nearer to home, because response time is key and cost is less important (see Case study 8.1).

What happens when the processes are not aligned within a supply chain? Let us address that question with Case study 1.6 to show the problems that can arise.

CASE STUDY
1.6

## Talleres Auto

Talleres Auto (TA) is an SME based in Barcelona. TA attends to broken-down vehicles, providing a roadside repair and recovery service. Two of the parts that TA frequently uses are starters and alternators, which were obtained from a local distributor. In turn, the local distributor ordered parts from a prime distributor. Starters and alternators were obtained from a remanufacturer, who replaced the windings and tested the products using parts bought from a component supplier. A diagram of this part of the supply chain is shown in Figure 1.11.

Component supplier → Remanufacturer → Prime distributor → Local distributor → TA: installer

- Talleres Auto is the installer
- TA buys starters and alternators from a local distributor
- The local distributor buys from a prime distributor
- The prime distributor buys from the remanufacturer
- The remanufacturer buys components from a component supplier

**Figure 1.11    The Talleres Auto supply chain**

Most of TA's customers made 'distress purchases' – their car had broken down and they wanted it to be fixed quickly. So TA needed a fast replacement service from the local distributor. While the distributors both recognised the need for fast replacements, the performance of the purchasing department at the remanufacturer was measured on cost savings. Thus the component supplier thought that the name of the game was low cost.

(Source: Harland, 1997)

### Questions

1  What were the order winners and order qualifiers at TA?

2  What were the order winners and order qualifiers at the component supplier?

3  What impact on customer service was this lack of alignment likely to cause?

## 1.4.3  Differentiating strategies

A supply chain, then, may choose to compete on different criteria. Such criteria need in turn to be recognised and form part of the business strategies of all the members of a given network. The choices so made have major implications for the operation of each member. Failure to recognise competitive criteria and their implications for a given product or service *by any member* means that the supply chain will compete less effectively. It is like playing football when the goalkeeper makes an error and lets in a goal that should not have happened – he or she lets the whole side down.

What makes a successful strategy? Five principles of strategic positioning, related to logistics strategy, are as follows (after Porter, 1984):

- *A unique value proposition*: determining what makes the product/service different from its competitors.
- *A tailored supply chain*: governed by consistent order winning and qualifying criteria.
- *Identify the trade-offs*: by choosing not just the priorities but also what not to do. A responsive supply chain is not compatible with an efficient supply chain (Fisher, 1997).
- *Align logistics processes*: so that processes are mutually reinforcing.
- *Continuity*: logistics processes are continually and consistently improved over time.

### 1.4.4 Trade-offs in logistics

To reinforce the issue of differentiating strategies, let us look at two commonly used strategies that have very different logistics implications. Consider products with different logistics priorities, such as those in Table 1.1:

- *Cost*: a high volume product for which demand is relatively stable throughout the year. While subject to occasional enhancements, these are usually small scale: the lifecycle is comparatively long. Forecast error is relatively low.
- *Time*: a high variety product, which is designed for a given season and which is completely redesigned for the next season. Often, it is impossible to predict which colour or style will sell best. The product lifecycle is short, and forecast error is relatively high.

Cost and time have quite different logistics implications. The very actions that help to reduce costs, such as Far East sourcing, are completely the wrong strategy when speed and responsiveness are top of the agenda. Similarly, investing in high volume, low variety equipment in the factory may create efficiency and low cost, but limit a firm's ability to offer variety and fast response times. Developing the capability to support more of one priority (cost) hobbles the capability to support another (time). This is the principle of *trade-off* in logistics: more of one thing means less of another. Ideally, we want two separate supply chains, one focused on cost, the other on time. This may not be fully practical because of the need to maintain a single European distribution centre. But logistics operations within the DC may well be kept separate to avoid product lines where the priority is low cost from interfering with time sensitive product lines. The same thinking may also apply *within* a given product range, when everyday ('base') demand may need to be kept separate from promotional demand. These are two examples of the various ways in which trade-offs may apply in practice. We return to these concepts in the next chapter.

*Activity 1.3*

1 Using the concepts from this section, analyse the supply chain support for both of the products you analysed in Activity 1.2. What should the supply chain be *(functional-efficient or innovative-responsive)*? What is the reality, and why are the two different?
2 To what extent is there alignment of strategy in the supply chains for these two products?

## Summary

*How does logistics work within the supply chain?*

- Supply chain management is defined as 'SCM encompasses the planning and controlling of all processes involved in procurement, conversion, transportation and distribution across a supply chain. SCM includes coordination and collaboration between partners, which can be suppliers, intermediaries, third party service providers and customers. In essence, SCM integrates supply and demand management within and between companies in order to serve the needs of the end-customer.'

- Logistics is defined as 'the task of coordinating material flow and information flow across the supply chain to meet end-customer needs'.

- In a supply chain, materials flow from upstream to downstream. Demand information from the end-customer flows in the opposite direction. A focal firm is positioned within a supply 'network', with tier 1 suppliers and tier 1 customers its immediate neighbours. Material flow measures the quantity of material that passes through a given network per unit of time.

- A supply network is a system in which each organisation is linked to its immediate neighbours. Therefore the overall performance of the network results from the combined performance of the individual partners.

- Logistics supports competitiveness of the supply chain as a whole by meeting end-customer demand through supplying what is needed when it is needed at low cost.

*What are the performance objectives of the supply chain, and how does logistics support those objectives?*

- 'Hard objectives' are quality, speed and cost because they are easy to measure and relatively obvious to the end-customer. Briefly, quality is about doing things right, speed is about doing things fast, and cost is about doing things cheaply. Supporting capabilities are concerned with controlling variability (the dependability advantage), dealing with uncertainty (the rapid response advantage) and acting responsibly (the sustainability advantage). Uncertainty can be addressed by flexibility in logistics processes – either proactively or reactively. Sustainability is concerned with addressing the 'triple bottom line' – social, environmental and economic values. 'Soft objectives' are service-oriented, such as security and confidence. They are less easily measurable than hard objectives.

- Such performance objectives can, and often are, augmented by other objectives that are outside logistics. These include product superiority, innovation and brand. Here the logistics task is to support such performance objectives in the marketplace.

- The relative importance of logistics performance objectives varies from one situation to another. It can also vary over time. The concept of order winners and qualifiers helps to prioritise the logistics task. Key influences on relative importance are individual product needs in the marketplace, position in the product lifecycle and competitor activity.

● Logistics strategy is the set of guiding principles, driving forces and ingrained attitudes that help to communicate goals, plans and policies, and which are reinforced through conscious and subconscious behaviour within and between partners across a network.

## Discussion questions

1 Bill Gates of Microsoft describes the 2000s as 'business @ the speed of thought'. Discuss the importance of speed in the supply chain. How can speed be increased within the supply chain?

2 Suggest logistics performance priorities for the following, explaining why you have come to your conclusions:
   a a low fare airline such as Ryanair;
   b a fast food chain such as McDonald's;
   c an overnight parcels service such as DHL.

3 What is meant by the term *alignment* in relation to supply chain processes? Why is alignment important in setting a strategy for a given supply chain?

4 What does *flow* mean in a supply chain context? Explain how material flow relates to information flow in a supply network.

## References

Cisco Systems (2009) 'Cisco supplier code of conduct', 9 November; at http://docs.google.com/viewer?a=v&q=cache:JOImGD-wmoMJ:www.ciscosystems.lt/legal/Cisco_Supplier_Code_of_Conduct.pdf+supplier+codes+of+conduct&hl=en&sig=AHIEtbTlHMdx7kwTQXLY6lVn4mnmiAF-tw

Cole, E. (2010) 'No big quality problems at Toyota?', *Harvard Business Review* blog, at http://blogs.hbr.org/cs/2010/03/no_big_quality_problems_at_toy.html

Cousins, P. (2005) 'The alignment of appropriate firm and supply strategies for competitive advantage', *International Journal of Production and Operations Management,* Vol. 25, No. 5, pp. 403–28.

CSMP (2010) http://csmp.org/aboutcsmp/definitions.asp

Eggleton, D.J. (1990) 'JIT in a distribution environment', *International Journal of Logistics and Distribution Management,* Vol. 9, No. 1, pp. 32–4.

Elkington, J. (1997) *Cannibals with Forks: the triple bottom line of 21st century business.* Oxford: Capstone.

Elkingon, J. (2004) in Henrriques, A. and Richardson, J. (eds) *The Triple Bottom Line – does it all add up?* London: Earthscan.

Environmental Protection Agency (2010) http://www.epa.gov/sustainability/basicinfo.htm

Fairtrade Foundation (2010): http://www.fairtrade.org.uk/what_is_fairtrade/ fairtrade_foundation.aspx

Fisher, M. (1997) 'What is the right supply chain for your product?', *Harvard Business Review,* March/April, pp. 105–16.

Harland, C. (1997) 'Talleres Auto', in Johnston, R., Chambers, S., Harland, C., Harrison, A. and Chambers, S. (eds) (1997) *Cases in Operations Management,* 2nd edn, pp. 420–8. London: Pitman.

Harland, C., Lamming, R., Zheng, J. and Johnsen, T. (2001) 'A taxonomy of supply networks', *Journal of Supply Management*, Fall, pp. 21–7.

Harrison, A. (1996) 'An investigation of the impact of schedule stability on supplier responsiveness', *International Journal of Logistics Management*, Vol. 7, No. 1, pp. 83–91.

Hayes, R.H. and Wheelwright, S.C. (1984) *Restoring Our Competitive Edge*. New York: John Wiley.

Hill, T. (2000) *Manufacturing Strategy*, 2nd edn. London: Macmillan.

Humphreys, J. (2007) *Exploring a Carbon Tax for Australia*, Centre for Industrial Studies, at http://www.cis.org.au/policy_monographs/pm80.pdf

Knill, B. (1992) 'Continuous flow manufacturing', *Material Handling Engineering*, May, pp. 54–7.

Latour, A. (2001) 'Trial by fire: a blaze in Albuquerque sets off major crisis for cell phone giants', *Wall Street Journal*, 29 January, p. A1.

Oliver, R.K. and Webber, M.D. (1982) 'Supply chain management: logistics catches up with strategy', *Outlook*, 6, pp. 42–7.

Porter, M. (1984) *Competitive Advantage*. New York: Free Press.

Royal Mail (2009) 'Scheduled services and standardised measures: summary of actions for 2009/10', at ftp://ftp.royalmail.com/Downloads/public/ctf/rmg/SummaryStatement OfActionsToAchieve2009-10QualityOfServiceTargets.pdf

Sawhney, R. (2006) 'Interplay between uncertainty and flexibility across the value chain: towards a transformational model of manufacturing flexibility', *Journal of Operations Management*, Vol. 24, pp. 476–93.

SCOR (2010) http://supply-chain.org/f/SCOR%2090%20Overview%20Booklet.pdf

Sheffi, Y. (2005) *Resilient Enterprise: overcoming vulnerability for competitive advantage*. Cambridge, MA: MIT Press.

Slack, N., Chambers, S., Harland, C., Harrison, A. and Johnston, R. (1997) *Operations Management*, 2nd edn. Harlow: FT/Prentice Hall.

Soble, D. (2009) 'Toyota ratchets up pressure for price cuts on component suppliers', *Financial Times,* 23 December, p. 1.

Thompson, K.M. (2002) 'Variability and uncertainty meet risk management and risk communication', *Risk Analysis*, Vol. 22, No. 3, pp. 647–54.

UNWCED (1987) *Our Common Future* (The Bruntland Report). Oxford: Oxford University Press.

Upton, D.M. (1995) 'What makes factories flexible?,' *Harvard Business Review*, July/Aug., pp. 74–84.

Whittington, R. (2000) *What is Strategy and Does it Matter?* London: International Thomson Business Press.

Zadek, S. (2004) 'The path to corporate responsibility', *Harvard Business Review*, December, pp. 125–32.

Zheng, J., Harland, C., Johnsen, T. and Lamming, R. (1998) 'Initial conceptual framework for creation and operation of supply networks', *Proceedings of 14th AMP Conference*, Turku, 3–5 September, Vol. 3, pp. 591–613.

## Suggested further reading

Chopra, S. and Meindl, P.S. (2010) *Supply Chain Management,* 4th edn. (global). Upper Saddle River, NJ: Pearson.

Stock, J.R. and Lambert, M. (2001) *Strategic Logistics Management*, 4th edn. Boston, MA: McGraw-Hill/Irwin.

Willard, R. (2002) *The Sustainability Advantage*. Gabriola Island, BC: New Society Publishers.

# CHAPTER 2

# Putting the end-customer first

**Objectives**

*The intended objectives of this chapter are to:*

- develop the marketing perspective on logistics and the need for close coordination between the two functions;
- explain how customer segmentation works, and to emphasise its importance to logistics;
- outline the role of demand forecasting and the links with marketing;
- explain the connection between quality of service and customer loyalty;
- show how current segmentation practice can be re-engineered to set logistics priorities.

*By the end of this chapter you should be able to understand:*

- how supply chains should compete by aligning logistics strategy with marketing strategy;
- how to use logistics strategy drivers to help redefine segments to achieve this alignment.

## Introduction

In Chapter 1 we looked at the logistics task from the perspective of material flow and information flow. We also saw how logistics contributes to competitive strategy and the performance objectives by which we can measure this contribution. But what is it that drives the need for flow in the first place? The key point to recognise here is that it is the behaviour of the end-customer that should dictate what happens. The end-customer starts the logistics response by buying finished products. It is this behaviour that causes materials to flow through the supply chain. Only end-customers should be free to make up their minds about when they want to place an order on the network – after that, the system takes over.

Quality of service addresses the process of handing over products and services to end-customers. It is after this process has been completed that a product/service reaches its full value. And the handover process offers many opportunities for adding value. Instead of picking up a product from a distributor who is remote from the focal firm, there are opportunities during the sales transaction (for example, help and advice in using the focal firm's products), as well after the sales transaction (for example, after sales service and warranty).

This chapter explores the link between marketing strategy and logistics strategy. It introduces this link, and shows how it is possible to identify logistics priorities – and hence the tasks at which logistics needs to excel.

This chapter addresses four key issues:

1 **The marketing perspective:** the impact of rising customer expectations and the information revolution.

2 **Segmentation and demand forecasting:** and their implications for logistics strategy.

3 **Quality of service:** the link between customer satisfaction and customer loyalty.

4 **Setting priorities for logistics strategy:** creating advantage by redefining segments in logistics terms.

## 2.1 The marketing perspective

*Key issue:* What are the marketing implications for logistics strategy?

'Marketing' has traditionally been associated with anticipating, identifying and satisfying customer requirements profitably. In our terms, such a definition emphasises the focal firm and outbound logistics. But a more current definition emphasises value in the context of the broader supply chain – and that includes partners rather than just customers:

> Marketing is the activity, set of institutions, and processes for creating, communicating, delivering, and exchanging offerings that have value for customers, partners, and society at large.

> (American Marketing Association, 2007)

Marketing in practice comprises the plans and decisions that determine how these processes will be carried out.

Ultimately, satisfied end-customers are seen as the only source of profit, growth and security. Sir Terry Leahy, Chief executive of Tesco plc, talks of harnessing customer power (2005):

> The basic assumption that customers choose – that they know best what they want – means that they have become the centre of the retailer's universe. In the best businesses, their decisions drive everything. These choices are also judgements. They pick the winners and losers in retail and in manufacturing. This is not theoretical: they regularly pass verdicts, moving from product to product and store to store. These judgements send strong feedback – shocks might be a better word – forcing change.

Louis Gerstner (2002: 47) explained that the amazing turnaround of IBM in the 1990s was about 'a customer was now running IBM'.

In Chapter 1, we referred to 'tier 1 customers' with whom a focal firm deals directly, and to 'end-customers' who are the individuals or businesses that buy the finished 'product' at the downstream end of the supply network. It is therefore usual to refer to two types of customer:

● *business customers*: who represent the focal firm's immediate trading environment (see Figure 1.2);

● *end-customers*: who represent the ultimate customer for the network as a whole (see Figure 1.4).

We refer to these types of relationships as 'business to business' (B2B) and 'business to customer' (B2C) accordingly. In section 1.2.2 of Chapter 1, we referred to the need to integrate supply chain processes so that they are aligned towards end-customer needs. In this sense, B2B integration should be aligned towards the ultimate B2C process.

We also need to distinguish here between customers and consumers. Webster (2000) defines them thus:

- *consumers* are people who use or consume the product;
- *customers* are individuals or businesses who buy the product, meaning that they acquire it and pay for it.

It is usual in business today to refer to 'customers' as the next process downstream in a supply chain. This includes 'all types of marketing intermediaries or channel members who buy for resale to their customers' (Webster, 2000).

But 'satisfied customers' are increasingly hard to find. This has been caused by widespread changes that are affecting the world we live in. Two of the major changes are rising customer expectations and the information revolution (Doyle, 2000). We expand on these below.

## 2.1.1  Rising customer expectations

Expectations have risen among customers in line with a general increase in the wealth of developed countries over the last half century. This increase in expectations has many causes, including:

- better levels of general education;
- better ability to discern between alternative products;
- exposure to more lifestyle issues in the media.

These expectations have led to customers not only aspiring to more desirable products, they are also demanding much better levels of service to be associated with those products.

Businesses are also expecting more from their suppliers. Suppliers need to pay increasing attention to the service aspects of their dealings with industrial customers. This is especially true when the customer has implemented more customer-centric management systems such as just-in-time (Chapter 6).

## 2.1.2  The information revolution

The explosion in applications of internet technology continues to have sweeping effects on the way that business is transacted today. Applications that have sprung from the world wide web have impacted both B2C and business to business B2B relationships.

- *Business to consumer (B2C):* online retailing has developed rapidly in recent years, and organisations such as Amazon.com continue to extend the range of products they offer, Many retail firms based on the traditional 'bricks and mortar' model have fought back by launching their own websites and online catalogues. The world wide web has become another channel to market for the retail industry, as home shopping accelerates in industry sectors as diverse as books, music and furniture.

- *Business to business (B2B):* here, the impact has been even greater than in B2C, but perhaps less visible. Businesses increasingly use web portals, online marketplaces and other collaborative online applications to exchange information, undertake transactions (such as buying and selling) and organise delivery and payment. These forms of inter-firm collaboration are leading to closer integration of processes between businesses and helping to break down some of the traditional barriers in buyer–supplier relationships.

- *Supply chain implications:* developments in B2B and B2C exchanges also have an impact on how the supply chain operates. The ability to exchange information more effectively and accurately should enable more reliability in supply chain operations, as well as lowering the costs of ordering. The availability of shared information also facilitates improved management of inventory, forecasts and use of assets. Web-enabled data exchange facilitates replacement of inventory with information, resulting in lower working capital.

Faced with rising customer expectations and the information revolution, supply chain partners are increasingly looking at how they can be more demand-led, and respond more rapidly to market requirements. The starting point is to put the end-customer first by analysing their needs and wants. The marketing perspective has a well-known way to help in this analysis – segmentation.

## 2.2 Segmentation

*Key issue:* What is segmentation, and what are its implications to logistics strategy?

Segmentation describes how a given market might be broken up into different groups of customers with similar needs. It means 'describing the market as simply as possible while doing our best to emphasise its variety' (Millier and Palmer, 2000). We start by considering market segmentation from a *customer* perspective in what are usually described as 'fast-moving consumer goods (FMCG)' markets. For example, segmentation of the market for suntan creams and lotions would begin with an understanding of:

- the benefits wanted (e.g. water resistance, oil/non-oil, sun factor);
- the price consumers are prepared to pay;
- the media to which they are exposed (television programmes, magazines, Google ads, etc.);
- the amount and timing of their purchases.

Profiles of the segments and evaluation of their relative attractiveness to a focal firm can then be developed.

There are many possible ways in which markets can be segmented, including:

- *demographic:* such as age, sex and education;
- *geographic:* such as urban v country, type of house and region;

- *technical*: the use that customers are going to make of a product;
- *behavioural*: such as spending pattern and frequency of purchase.

Of the various ways to segment markets, we have found that behavioural segmentation, which 'divides buyers into groups based on their knowledge of, attitude towards, and use of or response to a product' (Kotler and Keller, 2009) is a powerful way to bridge marketing and logistics. For example, Finne and Sivonen (2009) describe a study of behavioural segments in convenience stores in Europe. Six segments were identified – main, top-up, impulse, distress, grab-and-go and habitual shoppers. 'Top-up' shoppers may only value bread, milk and convenience foods, while an 'impulse' shopper is attracted by special offers and displays.

It is vital that the definition of segments is not a marketing-only task, but that logistics is involved. The key point is that defining segments that cannot be served because logistics capability does not exist is unlikely to work. For example, if most of the spending pattern is around Christmas, then logistics must be capable of supporting the huge surge in demand at that time. Case study 2.1 explains how a retailer views its behavioural segments.

| CASE STUDY 2.1 | Managing events and promotions in the retail sector |
|---|---|

If end-customers only purchased their requirements in line with their use, then it would be relatively easy to reorganise the end-to-end supply chain from shelf to national warehouse using lean principles (see Chapter 6). A simple demand–pull system replenishing tomorrow that which has been sold today, direct to shelf, would streamline store operations and reduce inventories significantly. Retailers such as Wal-Mart in the US and Tesco in Britain have pursued an everyday low price policy in an attempt to maximise this 'steady state' replenishment policy. However, in Europe, most retailers have found that customers enjoy promotions and that promotions boost sales. In any case, events such as Christmas and back to school create huge surges in demand.

Events may be divided in two: seasonal events and promotional events, as shown in Table 2.1.

Table 2.1   **Example seasonal events and promotions**

| Seasonal events | Promotions |
|---|---|
| ● Valentine' Day <br> ● Mother's Day <br> ● Summer holidays <br> ● Back to school <br> ● Christmas | ● Three for two <br> ● Buy one get one free <br> ● 10% off for a week <br> ● Happy hour −20% <br> ● Triple loyalty card points <br> ● Gift with purchase |

Retailers have no control over the timing of seasonal events and it is usually very difficult to forecast likely demand with normal levels of accuracy. In contrast, promotional events are planned by retailers and their suppliers. Consequently, while demand may be unpredictable, the timing of such events is known in advance. It is surprising, therefore, how often consumers will find that items on promotion are not on the shelf and that display aids and promotional material will be missing. The event that has the greatest effect is

▶

Christmas – where sales usually start growing in October, ramp up in November and peak in December. This is the *only* profitable quarter for many retailers. The product is frequently sourced from the Far East and once the order has been delivered there will be no further shipments. Retailers need to plan for this activity months in advance and cross their fingers that they will not miss sales through under-ordering or buy too much with the consequent write-downs in the January sale. The position is further complicated in a national chain where demand patterns will be different store by store and region by region.

Many retailers allocate their Christmas merchandise to individual stores on the basis of previous year's sales for the particular product category and hope for the best. A lean design supply chain is unable to cope with such spiky demand, which will be affected further by marketing efforts and the latest fad. Retailers therefore need to be particularly agile in their approach in order to satisfy unknown demand.

Boots the Chemist (BTC) – the leading UK health and beauty retailer – has approached this problem by outsourcing specific Christmas merchandise deliveries. These deliveries are scheduled at different times of the day from 'normal' deliveries. In this way, while not dealing with the issues created by unpredictable demand, store operations can apply appropriate resources to unload vehicles and put away directly to shelf or indirectly to stockroom. Historically, promotional events in BTC were a fairly hit and miss affair with hundreds of products being promoted within a four-week window. There was a high reliance on good luck for all the elements to come together prior to the start of the promotional period. Inevitably some products, display aids and show material arrived late. Store operations at the end of the supply chain then had to try and mount the promotions with what had been delivered. Consumers were dissatisfied with the result and sales were lost.

The solution was to create a dedicated promotions team within the categories. The team masterminded the overall promotional plan and were made responsible for the delivery of products, display aids and show materials into the national distribution centres (NDCs). A successful trial was then conducted whereby most of the work required to mount the promotion was done by logistics staff in the regional distribution centres (RDCs) for each of the individual stores.

The trial comprised sending allocations of all the promotional requirements to the RDCs from the NDCs. Staff in the RDCs then picked products for a week's anticipated sales (based on historical data for that line by individual store) into totes for direct-to-shelf delivery together with appropriate display aids and show material. The totes were then placed on dollies, rolled on and off vehicles, and wheeled into the shop to the correct gondola end (end of free-standing 'island' shelf in a store). After three days, EPOS data were reviewed, and an accurate prediction of future sales to the end of the promotion was made. This was then used to calculate future replenishment requirements. Finally the merchandising teams were invited to devise clever ways to make shelves look full at the end of the promotion without using a lot of stock. This resulted in fewer 'remainders' from a promotion that had to be written down. BTC is currently implementing its design for a transformed end-to-end supply chain and the work described above is being gradually rolled out.

(Source: Philip Matthews, formerly Supply Chain Director, BTC)

## Question

1  List the logistics challenges of mounting promotions and coping with events at a retailer such as BTC.

**Activity 2.1**

Figure 2.1 shows a Pareto analysis of the annual sales to 886 customers in the portfolio of a book stockist. What actions could the stockist take to segment its market? How could each segment best be served? What are the operational implications for the stockist? (Check out Chris Anderson, 'The Long Tail' at http://www.thelongtail.com/about.html).

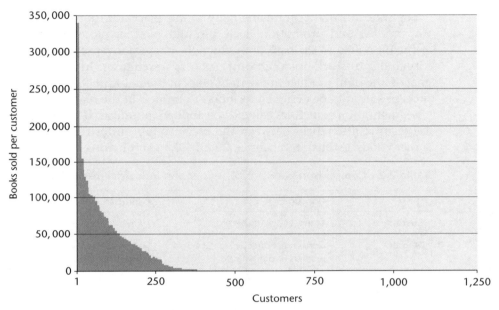

Figure 2.1    **Annual sales per customer for a book distributor, shown as a Pareto diagram**

The important characteristics of segments (McGoldrick, 2002) are that they must be:

- *measurable*: variables that can be easily identified and measured;
- *economically viable*: capable of producing the contribution that justifies the effort and cost of marketing;
- *accessible*: geographically or in terms of media communications;
- *actionable*: can be attracted and served effectively.

The next step is to select target segments and identify how a focal firm is going to win orders in each. In other words, to define *differential advantage* that distinguishes our offerings from those of our competitors. In logistics terms, the important issues here are the order winning criteria (OWC), and qualifying criteria (QC) for the target segments. These help in turn to define the *marketing mix*.

The marketing mix is the set of marketing decisions that is made to implement positioning strategy (target market segments and differential advantage) and to achieve the associated marketing and financial goals. The marketing mix has been popularly termed the '4 Ps' (McCarthy, 1964):

- *product*: range, sizes, presentation and packaging, design and performance;
- *price*: list price, discounts, geographical pricing, payment terms;
- *promotion*: sales force, advertising, consumer promotion, trade promotion, direct marketing;
- *place*: channel selection, market coverage, distribution systems, dealer support.

Logistics contributes fundamentally to the 'place' decisions, as well as supporting 'product' and 'promotion' decisions. All too often, 'place' activities are viewed as the bit bolted to the back of production that gets inventory away from the factory and into stock-holding points such as warehouses. In order to achieve the goal of 'the right product in the right place at the right time', logistics systems and processes need to be designed to support products in the marketplace.

Segmentation principles can also be applied to industrial marketing. But 'there are distinct differences between the marketing of industrial products and consumer goods' (Millier and Palmer, 2000: 60), as summarised in Table 2.2.

Table 2.2　**Comparison between consumer and industrial marketing**

|  | Consumer | Industrial |
|---|---|---|
| **Customers** | Many, widely dispersed | Few, concentrated |
| **Market** | Consumers directly served by retailers and distributors | Derived demand<br>Industrial chain, long and complex |
| **Buying behaviour** | Individual and family decision | Group decision<br>Formal procedures<br>High buyer power |
| **Relationships** | Low individual buying power | Formal procedures<br>High buyer power |
| **Product** | Standard<br>Positioned on emotional and perceptual factors | Technical complexity<br>Specification important<br>Bespoke and customised |
| **Price** | Low unit price<br>Take it or leave it<br>No negotiation | High unit price<br>Tender and negotiation<br>Standard items from price list |
| **Promotion** | Mass media advertising<br>Role of the brand | Emphasis on personal selling<br>Reputation important |
| **Place** | Established retail chain<br>Stock availability, Seasonality | Direct made to order<br>Standard items in stock |

Let us turn to an industrial marketing example to illustrate how new segments can impact on logistics capability.

**CASE STUDY 2.2**

## Powerdrive Motors

Tom Cross took over as Managing Director at Powerdrive Motors in South Africa three years ago. At the time, the company was an established manufacturer of small electric motors with a strong reputation for product reliability and technical leadership. On the downside, it was also regarded in the trade as having high prices and variable delivery. Tom's first task was to tackle the huge product variety on offer. He saw this as the major problem in addressing the negative views in the marketplace, and also saw opportunities in streamlining design and production. The product range was replaced with a new generation of designs based on a few hundred 'modules', which could be assembled in many different combinations to give variety at low cost. This meant the loss of some customers who had gone to Powerdrive because they could rely on the company's technical leadership to produce designs that suited their particular needs. This was not considered important because the combined sales volume of such customers was under 5 per cent.

Using the new designs, Tom was now able to reorganise the factory into cells that produced major subassemblies such as rotors and stators. The work flow was transformed, and manufacturing throughput time was reduced from six weeks to just four days. Cost improvements meant that average price reductions of between 10 and 15 per cent could be offered.

Powerdrive's customer service policy was redrafted to offer quotations within a maximum of one hour of any enquiry, and for deliveries of finished product to be made within one week 'anywhere in northern Europe'. This new policy was explained to internal sales staff, and to sales representatives and agents employed by the organisation. If 'old' customers wanted special designs that were no longer in the range, the sales staff were instructed to explain Powerdrive's new policy and politely decline the order.

At first, business soared. Impressed by the lower prices and short delivery times, customers flocked to Powerdrive and sales jumped by 50 per cent. But then things began to go sour. First, the factory could no longer cope with the demands being placed on it. The addition of a large order for lawnmower motors blocked out a lot of production capacity from January to June. Order lead times during this period in particular slid back to former levels. Second, a Brazilian supplier spotted the opportunity to enter the market with prices that undercut Powerdrive by 20 per cent. While only half of the product range was covered by this new entrant, it was the high volume products that were especially threatened. Further, the new competitor offered three-day lead times from stock that had been established in the country. Third, some of the former customers who could no longer obtain their bespoke designs from Powerdrive were complaining within the industry that Powerdrive's technical leadership had been sacrificed. Although small in number, such customers were influential at trade fairs and conferences.

### Questions

1 Evaluate the changes that took place in the segmentation of Powerdrive's market.

2 Characterise the changes using the concept of order winners and qualifiers.

Segmentation is often undertaken by adopting the easy way to group customers – by account size. While this is easily measurable, it fails on the fourth of McGoldrick's criteria listed above: it is not actionable in logistics terms. An example from our research in the fast-moving consumer goods (FMCG) sector illustrates the problems of poor alignment between marketing and logistics.

## Segmentation at CleanCo

CleanCo is a Polish manufacturer of cleaning products that serves the European grocery retailing market. CleanCo currently segments its customers on the value of customer accounts. The primary division is between *national accounts*, for which ten accounts constitute 70 per cent of sales by value, and *field sales*, which comprise a long 'tail' of more than 200 accounts that together make up only 30 per cent of sales. Due to the size of the field sales structure, a secondary classification groups accounts by channel type: neighbourhood retail, discount and pharmacy. CleanCo recognises the need to reduce the long customer 'tail' and is introducing distributors for orders below a minimum quantity. CleanCo's current approach to segmentation is summarised in Table 2.3.

Table 2.3   **CleanCo – current approach to market segmentation**

| National accounts | Field sales | | |
|---|---|---|---|
| 70% sales | 30% sales, 200+ accounts | | |
| 10 accounts | Neighbourhood retail | Discount sector | Pharmacy |

While CleanCo currently segments its retail customers by account size, its sales organisation has identified two significant types of buying behaviour displayed by the customer base, shown in Table 2.4:

- *volume-driven* buying behaviour;
- *margin-driven* buying behaviour.

Volume-driven customers are keen to capitalise on both product and supply chain cost savings in order to pass them on to their customers to drive volume sales. There are two variants of the volume-driven behaviour:

- everyday low price (EDLP);
- discount.

Retailers pursuing an EDLP strategy strive for continuous price reduction from suppliers such as CleanCo to drive a fairly consistent, high volume of sales. This should result in a relatively stable pattern of demand in the washing and bathing sector. Discounters, on the other hand, are looking for bargains so they can 'stack 'em high and sell 'em cheap', a strategy more likely to result in a volatile demand pattern. Margin-driven customers are keen to add value for their customers by offering a wide selection of products and value-adding services. This strategy also results in a relatively stable demand pattern in this sector.

Table 2.4   **CleanCo – potential for behavioural segmentation**

| Volume-driven | Margin-driven |
|---|---|
| Everyday lowprice (EDLP) | |
| Discount | |

A complicating factor when trying to deconstruct the buying behaviour of CleanCo's customers is that several secondary factors are used to support products in the marketplace.

Such factors include product types (e.g. premium, mid, utilitarian), product range (e.g. current products, end of lines, 'b' grade), merchandising requirements (e.g. category captains) and promotions strategy (e.g. roll-back, 12-week, 4-week, Hi-Lo). Promotions are by far the most disruptive of these factors. Although the promotions are generally planned well in advance with the retailers, they cause significant disruption to the supply chain operations due to the peaks and troughs in demand that they create. Furthermore, the deeper the promotional activity the greater the volatility created and the greater the disruption to the supply chain. This has the effect of masking what is fundamentally a fairly stable demand pattern with somewhat artificial volatile demand.

Strategic alignment can only be achieved if the supply chain is aligned behind the segmentation strategy that CleanCo has adopted. This is not currently the case with the CleanCo supply chain. Each operation within the supply chain makes decisions or segments its customers based on the functional criteria that affect its part of the supply chain. We have called this lack of alignment 'matrix twist', because the matrix of business processes at each stage of the supply chain has been apparently twisted so that the processes fail to fit with each other. As illustrated in Table 2.5, the decision criteria for CleanCo and its suppliers and customers change at each stage. This not only complicates material flows, but becomes a minefield if one considers it in terms of behavioural segments.

**Table 2.5   Supply chain segmentation criteria**

| Management process | Supply chain decision | Determined by |
|---|---|---|
| Source | Which suppliers? | Raw material commodity type |
| Make | Which manufacturing site? | Product family type |
| Deliver | Which manufacturer order size? | Historically a function of warehouse?<br><br>In process of being divided by export paperwork requirements and customer account (arbitrary split) |
|  | Which customer RDC? | Product type and location of store to serve |
|  | Which products to which store? | Demographics of the store's catchment area, which drives layout and range decisions |

(Source: Godsell and Harrison, 2002)

We develop the management processes 'source', 'make' and 'deliver' in the next chapter.

## Questions

1  What has caused the 'matrix twist' between CleanCo and its retail customers?

2  What actions are needed to straighten out the 'matrix twist'?

## 2.3  Demand profiling

Marketing people want to forecast demand in order to plan broad goals such as allocating the salesforce, setting sales goals, promotions planning and advertising campaigns. But logistics people need to know how many to deliver, where and when to do so, for each sku in the product range and for each channel – not just for the range as a whole. This leads to a common perception of the two functions – marketing dealing in the abstract and logistics dealing in the day-to-day realities. The two business functions must be careful not to talk past each other, for both have important insights into what the end-customer wants. For many firms, of course, this is not an issue, and the two functions collaborate extensively. The aim is to combine forces and produce the most accurate profile of future demand.

It is impossible to predict the future with certainty, so it is necessary to *forecast* what will happen. Accurate forecasts of demand are one of the key starting points for achieving competitive supply chains, reflected in such measures as high on-shelf availability (the percentage of a trading day for which a given sku is available 'on the shelf' to be purchased by an end-customer) and low inventories. The key approaches to forecasting demand are explained at length in such texts as Wild (2002) and Waters (2003). Here, we will stick to some of the broad principles that apply to forecasting: first when there are limited or no historical data available, and second when such data are available.

First, consider the demand profiles in Figure 2.2 when forecasting demand for a new product during the early stages of its lifecycle (introduction and growth).

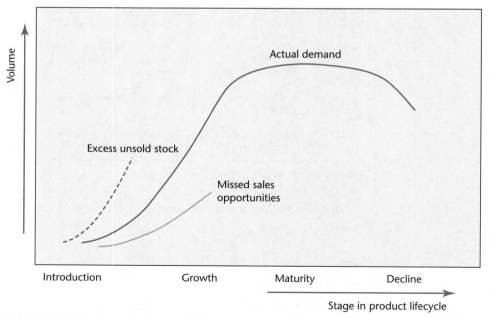

Figure 2.2  **The impact of uncertainty**

A forecast which over-estimates the way that demand takes off results in too much inventory too early in the product lifecycle. If this situation is allowed to continue, it will result in the need to get rid of the surplus unsold stock by mark-downs or by disposal. On the other hand, a forecast which under-estimates actual demand results in insufficient stock to meet what the end-customer wants. If allowed to continue, this results in lost sales opportunities and hence loss of market share to competitors who can better meet demand. Both scenarios are familiar challenges for grocery (such as managing promotions) and planning fashion goods for a new season when there is no directly usable history of demand, and forecasting relies on *judgemental* methods such as historical analogy, perhaps augmented by market research. New drugs (called 'new pharmaceutical entities', NCEs) are especially problematic because of the uncertainties of approval from the Food and Drug Administration (FDA) – which takes five years on average – and the take-up by physicians after launch. Lifecycle curves and growth functions can be used to model demand by incorporating 'market based evidence, uncertainty and judgements about what might happen during the drug's lifetime' (Latta, 2007).

When historical demand data such as point of sale (POS) are available, various modeling techniques can be used to produce *projective forecasts*. Consider the demand profile in Figure 2.3a, which shows actual demand for years 1–3, and forecast demand for years 1–4. It is based on the profile of sales of a product called 'barbecue sauce', which is produced in many flavours and is sold mainly in the summer.

Differences between actual A and forecast demand F (Case study 1.3 uses scheduled demand, S) for each period *n* of years 1–3 are termed the *error*, E:

$$E_n = A_n - F_n$$

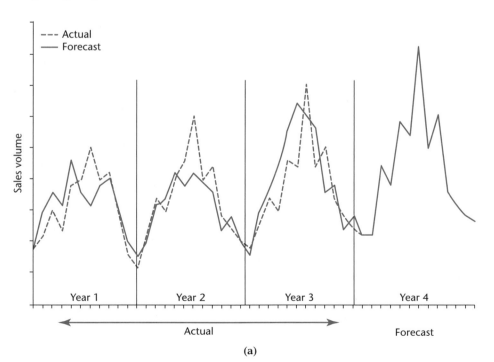

Figure 2.3a **Modelling trend and seasonality**

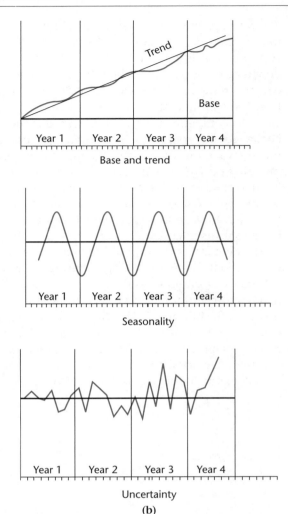

Figure 2.3b  **Modelling trend and seasonality  - continued**

If data are collected over a number of periods *n* (here, *n* = 36), then the *mean absolute deviation* (MAD) is a widely used measure of forecast error:

$$\text{MAD} = 1/n^* \sum_{n-1}^{n} |A_n - F_n|$$

In practice, the MAD may be exponentially weighted to give higher weightings to the most recent demand data (Wild, 2002: 176).

Figure 2.3b shows how the total (aggregate) demand for this product can be broken down into four components:

- *Base*: the level demand that needs to be adjusted for trend and seasonality.
- *Trend*: the long-term trend, which shows a healthy increase year-on-year from base.
- *Seasonality*: the periodic increase and reduction in demand as a result of consumer behaviour – in this case between summer and winter. This can be measured by

means of a *seasonal index* – which is the seasonal value divided by the trend, calculated for each period.

- *Uncertainty:* sometimes called 'randomness', this is the balance of demand due to effects we cannot explain. These effects may include short-term weather variations, which mean that the consumer is put off barbecuing because it is too cold, wet or windy. Other demand 'spikes' may be due to special causes like the promotion of a particular flavour of sauce by a chef in a popular television programme.

Base and trend demands can be found by linear regression analysis, and a seasonality index can be found by dividing the original data by the trend for each period. Uncertainty is usually allowed for by *increasing* the forecast to provide a safety margin to make it unlikely that there are missed sales opportunities (see Figure 2.2). Forecast demand for a future period $n$ is then calculated from;

$$F_n = (base + trend_n) \times seasonality\ index_n + uncertainty_n$$

So forecast demand for year 4 was based on projecting historical data for these four components into the future.

So far, the forecast has been carried out at the aggregate level, 'barbecue sauce'. And this is what forecasting professionals often encourage you to do – forecast accuracy is best at aggregate level and worst at sku level. But there are many flavours in the range – such as sweet hickory, Cajun and peri-peri. And there are different pack sizes and territories that are supplied. So the aggregate plan has to be *disaggregated* into individual skus. This is often achieved by calculating the percentage of the total demand for each sku from historical data, and then applying a seasonality index to refine the forecast for each period (see, for example, Ogrodowczyk, 2008). We return to the issue of disaggregation in section 6.1.1.

Forecasting is a major factor in logistics today, and we have only touched on some of the key issues in this section. We address further issues in other sections of this book as follows:

- Because of uncertainty, it is better to rely less on forecasting by shrinking lead times and engaging more closely with actual demand (section 5.1.4).
- Several management approaches can be used to improve forecast accuracy (section 7.1.3).
- Forecasting should be recognised as a key business process (section 7.2.5).
- Poor internal coordination compounds forecasting problems (section 6.1.4).
- External coordination with partners in a supply chain can be used to develop better forecasts through collaborative planning, forecasting and replenishment (CPFR, section 6.2.2).

### Activity 2.2

Explain how marketing and logistics functions should work together to develop segmentation plans that can more easily be made to work in practice, and to create more accurate forecasts of demand.

## 2.4  Quality of service

*Key issues:* How do customer expectations affect logistics service? How does satisfaction stack up with customer loyalty?

Most supply chains that involve physical products end with *service* processes such as retailing (grocery or apparel), healthcare (pharmaceutical and other medical goods) and distribution (motor cars). Service processes mean that the customer is present in some way, although distribution through web-based shopping, telephone and mail order mean that customers do not have to be physically present. Performance of service processes often differs between employees, between customers and from one hour to the next. If you want good service from the local supermarket, do not go on Saturdays or near to Christmas when the service is under severe capacity pressure: on-shelf availability is at its lowest, and queues at the checkout are at their longest. The key point is that 'service is the combination of outcomes and experiences delivered to and received by the customer' (Johnston and Clark, 2008).

Quality of service takes place during service delivery, which is the interaction between the customer (B2B or B2C) and the service process. 'Gaps' can emerge between what the service is supposed to be, what the customer expects it to be, and how the customer perceives it when it is delivered (Zeithaml *et al.*, 1988; Parasuraman *et al.*, 1991). We can illustrate these gaps as a simplified gap model (Figure 2.4):

- *Gap 1* refers to differences between customer expectations and how these have been developed into a service specification by the supplier.
- *Gap 2* refers to differences between how the specification was drawn up and how it was delivered.
- *Gap 3* refers to differences between what the customer expected and what he or she perceived was delivered.
- *Gap 4* refers to differences between how supplier and customer perceived the service delivery.

Gaps in quality of service can arise, as seen in Case study 2.4 on IKEA.

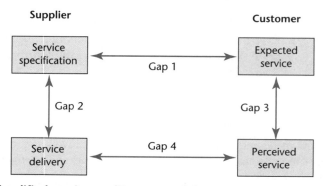

**Figure 2.4    Simplified service quality gap model**
(Source: After Parasuraman *et al.*, 1991)

## Tears at teatime at IKEA

Next week, Jane Fillimore will move into a new flat. You can tell something about the 28-year-old music-industry publicist from Kilburn, north-west London, from the list of furniture she is buying. There is the Pax Brivic wardrobe, the Norden dining table and the Bonde media storage combination. Fillimore wants style – but on a budget. She is part of Generation IKEA.

Not that she wants to be. She hates the Swedish retailer, and only last Sunday had her worst shopping day ever at the firm's superstore in a drab retail park near the new Wembley stadium in London.

She wanted to pick up the Pax Brivic wardrobe she had ordered the week before. Easy, you might think, but just getting served was an ordeal. When she entered the store, an assistant told her to 'walk the mile of hell' past wannabe-stylish urban living rooms to the giant storage zone.

The store did not have her wardrobe and a salesman sent her back through road works to IKEA's nearby distribution centre. The distribution centre had the wardrobe, but could not give it to her without a receipt. To get one, she had to go back to the main store. But the main store had lost her order, so she had to go to customer service. This department is not called customer service at IKEA, it's called customer returns, and it took her half an hour to find.

By 4.30 pm, Fillimore was right back where she started. Exasperated, she put her head in her hands and burst into tears. 'I don't even like the wardrobe', she sobbed. 'I bought it because it's cheap. That's the only reason I come here.' By 5.00 pm, the store is closing, and she can only dream of getting her wardrobe by Friday. She could walk back through the little sets that represent the nation's living rooms to try one last time to find her wardrobe, but she can't face it. As she walks out, I ask her if she knows that Argos and Sainsbury's (two other UK retailers) are selling furniture. For the first time all day, she breaks into a smile.

'Really?' she grins. 'I'll go there tomorrow. I never want to come back to this place again.'

(Source: Based on an article by John Arlidge, *Sunday Times*, 26 October 2003)

### Question

1 When IKEA was founded 60 years ago by Ingmar Kamprad, he realised that customers did not mind queuing, collecting their purchases and assembling the furniture themselves as long as the price was right. Suggest why gaps in quality of service have opened up.

## 2.4.1 Customer loyalty

While plugging gaps in service quality helps to improve customer satisfaction, this is a 'qualifier' for long-term customer loyalty. The two concepts are not the same. Piercy (2009) distinguishes them as follows:

- *Customer satisfaction* is what people think of us – quality of service, value for money. It is an *attitude* (how does a customer feel about our product/service?).

- *Customer loyalty* is how long we keep a customer (or what share of his or her business we take). It is a *behaviour* (does he or she buy from us more than once?).

Nevertheless, the attitude of customer satisfaction is key to the behaviour of customer loyalty. Parasuraman and Grewal (2000) link the two concepts by proposing the 'key drivers of customer loyalty', shown in Figure 2.5. Also, note the connection to Tesco's core purpose on page 6. There is a purpose to this beyond the words: Tesco seeks actively to extend its relationships with customers by offering a broad range of services such as optician, pharmacy, non-food, and bank and insurance products. All purchases in these diverse categories and its core grocery business are rewarded by the firm's *loyalty programme*, which provides Tesco with further detailed insights into the behaviour of its customers. This data can be used for sophisticated segmentation that allows all customers to be 'scored' in one or more segments to allow accurate measurement and targeting (Finne and Sivonen, 2009).

The benefits of customer loyalty are potentially huge. The loyal customer should be viewed in terms of lifetime spending potential. Thus, a customer of VW Audi Group could be viewed as worth €300k rather than the €30k of today's sales transaction. As Johnston and Clark (2005) put it, loyal customers:

- generate long-term revenue streams (high lifetime values);
- tend to buy more than new customers;
- tend to increase spending over time;
- may be willing to pay premium prices;
- provide cost savings compared with attracting new customers.

The logistics challenge is to support the development of customer loyalty by designing and delivering quality of service. Of the three drivers of customer loyalty shown in Figure 2.5, quality of service is 'essential for excellent market performance on an enduring basis' (Berry, 1999: 8–9). The rationale for this is that 'service quality is much more difficult for competitors to copy than are product quality and price'. Supporting product availability through such means as channel selection, market coverage, distribution systems and dealer support all help to nourish customer loyalty. So does logistics support of product characteristics (such as variety or product range) and of marketing initiatives (such as promotions).

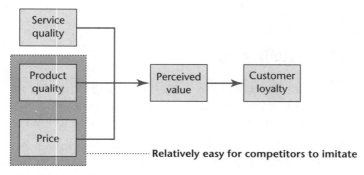

**Figure 2.5   Key drivers of customer loyalty**

(Source: After Parasuraman and Grewal, 2000)

## 2.4.2  Value disciplines

Figure 2.5 refers to 'perceived value'. A development of the service quality–product quality–price model is that of *value disciplines*. Instead of competing on all of these fronts equally, Treacy and Wiersema (1997) argue that companies taking leadership positions do so by narrowing their competitive focus, not by broadening it. They propose three strategies, or 'generic value disciplines' that can be followed:

- *Operational excellence.* Here, the strategy centres on superb operations and execution, often by providing a reasonable quality at low price. The focus is on efficiency, streamlining operations, supply chain management and everyday low price. Most large international corporations use this discipline.
- *Product leadership.* Here, the leaders are very strong in innovation and brand marketing and operate in dynamic markets. The focus is on development, innovation, design, time-to-market and high margins in a short timeframe. 'It was the ability of Apple to innovate in many spaces – getting the music companies to agree to 99 cent pricing, creating wonderful iTunes software, making a terrific physical product, the iPod, that just works in your hand – that gave Steve Jobs his success. It was building an ecosystem of innovation, not just the iPod, that did it' (http://www.businessweek.com/innovate/NussbaumOnDesign/).
- *Customer intimacy.* Here, leaders excel in customer attention and customer service. They tailor their products and services towards individual or almost individual customers. The focus is on customer relationship management (next section): they deliver products and services on time and above customer expectations. They also look to lifetime value concepts, reliability and being close to the customer.

While most organisations are under pressure to reduce prices, speed up delivery and improve customer service, the best will have a clear focus (page 29) as a key part of their competitive strategy. This focus needs to be improved and adapted over time.

### Activity 2.3

Evaluate Treacy and Wiersema's value disciplines based on Porter's views on differentiating strategies (section 1.4.3).

## 2.4.3  Relationship marketing and customer relationship management (CRM)

A development of customer intimacy is relationship marketing. Here, the aim is to develop long-term, loyal customers through 'bonding' with them. This development can take place at three levels (de Chernatony and McDonald, 2003):

- *Financial incentives*: such as frequent flyer schemes and reward cards.
- *Social and financial bonds*: from a dentist making personal notes about clients that can be used on subsequent visits to accountants taking their clients to rugby matches.
- *Structural bonds*: such as IT systems that bind client and customer together, sometimes called 'electronic handcuffs'.

This development process becomes a strategic task. The principle behind customer relationship management (CRM) is that marketing strategies are continuously extended in order to strengthen customer loyalty. Eventually, customer and supplier are so closely intertwined that it would be difficult to sever the relationship. In other words, the exit barriers become higher and higher. CRM 'provides enhanced opportunities to use data and information to both understand customers and co-create value with them. This requires a cross-functional integration of processes, people, logistics and marketing capabilities that is enabled through information, technology and applications' (Payne and Frow, 2005). Figure 2.6 compares CRM thinking with traditional relationships that are limited to buying and selling functions of the organisations concerned (Payne *et al.*, 1995). We explore the issue of partnerships in the supply chain further in Chapter 9. Case study 2.5, Batman, illustrates the evolution of diamond-type relationships in an industrial setting.

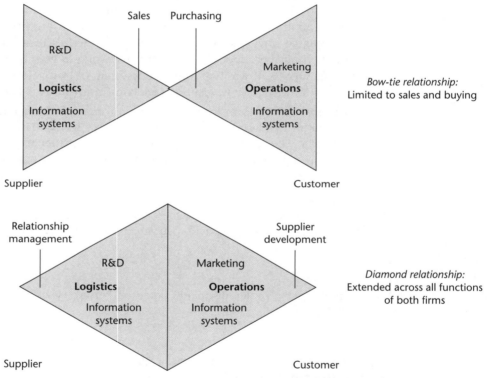

**Figure 2.6    Customer relationship management: bow tie and diamond**
(Source: After Payne *et al.*, 1995)

| CASE STUDY 2.5 | Batman – adding value through quality of service |

Everglo Battery, the premier battery manufacturer and service provider in South Africa, looked back on the development of its marketing strategy in four stages. Each had been signalled by advancing the concepts of what is meant by 'quality of service'. Stage 1 had been the basic product: a sealed lead-acid battery for use in mining applications. Batteries were regarded by customers as a mature product and as a 'grudge buy'.

Each year, the basic product was under heavy downward price pressure. Stage 2 had been the industry reaction to customer service: the addition of warranty replacement of defective products, of quality assurance (QA) audits of a supplier's design and manufacturing processes, and of parts and service provision.

Stage 3 had recognised the need to go much further in terms of customer service. A whole raft of additional services had been conceived with a view to adding value. Breakdowns were fixed at short notice by means of field service engineers. Everglo products could now be delivered and installed at customer premises. Price lists were simplified by including peripheral equipment, such as contactors, that had to be added to a battery rack in order to make it work. Advice and tips were added to help customers warm to Everglo products. In a proactive move, Everglo introduced charts and advice about the application of battery products in general, and the resulting tables became an industry standard. Parts and service in the field were upgraded to a '24-hour, no-nonsense back-up service'. And customer training built on Everglo's position as an industry leader. Rather than sales seminars, Everglo's were customer training seminars, where the company spoke on behalf of the industry rather than as a supplier.

In spite of having reached a pre-eminent position in mining power supply, Everglo recognised that the centre of Figure 2.7 was in effect a 'black hole'. Each year,

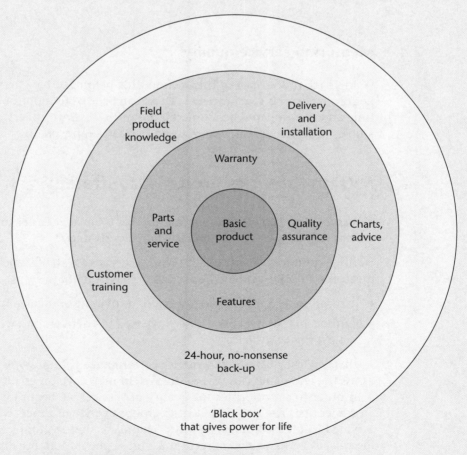

Figure 2.7   Adding value by quality of service

competitors added more services to their basic products too. In effect, the second and to some extent the third circles were being absorbed into the 'commodity' category, and customer expectations increased all the time. A new stage 4 strategy was conceived to take Everglo into a position that competitors would find even more difficult to follow. The new strategy was coined 'Batman': battery management for life. The aim was nothing less than a total, customer-oriented product management service that provides 'power for life'. The supplier takes over the task of managing the customer's assets, including problem identification, training and managing cash flow. The objective of 'Batman' is to look at the product the way the customer does, performing best at what the customer values most rather than at what the supplier values most.

### Questions

1  Has Everglo reached the end of the line in terms of its quality of service strategy?

2  As a competitor to Everglo, what would be your options in response to Everglo's latest moves?

### 2.4.4  Measuring service quality

Going back to the start of this section, it is helpful to have in place measures of performance of service processes. These can be used to monitor performance over time and to compare ('benchmark') the processes with others. Table 2.6 lists examples of service level measures used in retail supply chains.

## 2.5  Setting priorities for logistics strategy

*Key issues:* **How can we segment our market to make it easier to supply? How can we use such knowledge to improve logistics strategy?**

Setting priorities to assure quality of service leads to establishment of performance measures. Priorities should be used to help ensure that:

- partners in a supply network focus on providing end-customer value;
- partners in that network can see how well the network as a whole is performing against this yardstick.

In this way they can judge whether performance is improving or declining, and assess the effect that changes to the system may have on quality of service.

In order to set priorities for quality of service, we begin by putting the end-customer first. The aim is to identify groups of end-customers whose needs can be serviced in focused, targeted ways. The needs define groups and give them an identity, as we explained in section 2.2 on segmentation. Because segments therefore have different characteristics, it is usually a mistake to take a 'one size fits all'

**Table 2.6   Selected service level measurements in retail supply chains**

| | |
|---|---|
| **Inventory/availability** | *Physical and accounting correspondence*: number of orders with mistakes divided by the total number of orders in the warehouse in the same period of time |
| | *Stock turnover*: quantity delivered or shipped divided by the average stock in the warehouse in the same period of time |
| | *Stockout*: number of orders out of stock divided by the total number of orders placed in the same period of time. |
| **Flexibility** | *Flexibility*: number of special/urgent/unexpected orders confirmed to the customer divided by the total number of special/urgent/unexpected orders required by the customer multiplied by 100 in the same period of time |
| **Service care** | *Punctuality*: number of orders delivered on time divided by the total number of orders delivered multiplied by 100 in the same period of time |
| | *Regularity*: number of orders delivered with a n*t* of delay/advance divided by the total number of orders delivered multiplied by 100 in the same period of time |
| | *Completeness*: number of full orders delivered divided by the total number of orders delivered multiplied by 100 in the same period of time |
| | *Correctness*: number of orders with mistakes dispatched divided by the total number of orders dispatched multiplied by 100 in the same period of time, or |
| | Number of codes/articles sent back divided by the total number of codes/articles sent multiplied by 100 in the same period of time |
| | *Harmfulness*: number of damaged orders dispatched in a period divided by the total number of orders dispatched in the same period multiplied by 100 |
| | *Delay*: number of days of delay (or number of days of delay divided by the number of days promised) multiplied by 100 |
| **Supply conditions** | *Delivery frequency*: number of orders delivered in a certain period of time |
| | *Shipped quantity*: quantity shipped in a certain period of time or quantity dispatched for each shipment |
| | *Presentation*: method of packaging and of shipment, alignment with customer process |
| **Lead time** | *Total order cycle time*: occurring from the arrival of a customer order to the receipt of goods or cycle time of the single activities (order transmission, order processing, order composition, order transfer to the production plant, article production, warehouse delivery, final delivery to the customer) |
| | *Response time*: to order tracking requests, etc. |
| **Marketing** | Range completeness, information on products and selling assistance |
| **Order management** | Documents management (invoices and orders), client contacts and order advancement state, etc. |
| **After sales** | *Speed of response*: to back orders, claims management, use assistance and payment management, fulfilment of warranty conditions, etc. |
| **e-information** | Web site completeness, ease of making orders by network and data transmission security, etc. |

(Source: After Rafele, 2004)

approach to servicing them. Our research has shown that the starting point for segmentation is often conceived by marketing in isolation, and does not make any sense in logistics terms (Godsell *et al.*, 2006). Logistics is therefore left with an impossible task. Since logistics is actually part of the marketing mix (see 'place' under section 2.2 above), ability to provide quality of service is off to a bad start!

Our framework for creating logistics advantage (Harrison, 2010), shown in Figure 2.8, therefore starts by reviewing and re-engineering the current approach to market segmentation in a focal firm and its immediate supply chain partners. Typically, this re-engineering takes place in collaboration with strategic suppliers two tiers upstream and strategic customers two tiers downstream.

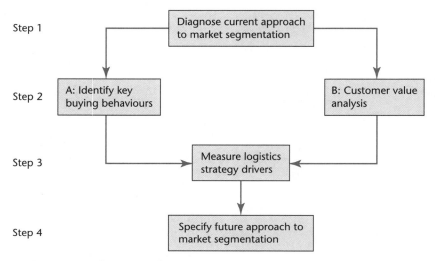

**Figure 2.8   Creating logistics advantage: a four-step process**
Source: (Harrison, 2010)

### 2.5.1  Step 1: Diagnose current approach to market segmentation

Current approaches to segmentation may drive elements of logistics strategy to a limited extent, or they may have no relevance in logistics terms. Segmentation in the CleanCo case (Case study 2.3) was based on national accounts and field sales, that is, by account size. This was in line with the way that sales and marketing functions were organised. There were no effective links between marketing and logistics – in logistics terms, only the distribution function was differentiated according to channel.

Another example from our research is AutoCo, a manufacturer of automotive seat subassemblies which supplies seat manufacturers such as The Lear Corporation, and automotive assemblers such as BMW. AutoCo currently segments its customers first by the country from which customers purchase, and second by customer within that country. Customer facing teams (CFTs) comprise a sales manager, an engineer and a product designer. These teams deal with each of the segments, and place orders on manufacturing units (based in England, Poland, Norway and Sweden). While this made sense in marketing terms, CFTs were not coordinated between customer countries. The supply network was therefore fragmented, and manufacturing units were left to compete with each other for business.

### 2.5.2   Step 2a: Understand buying behaviour

The sales organisation in the CleanCo case (Case study 2.3) had identified two significant types of buying behaviour by its retail customers: volume driven and value driven.

- *volume-driven behaviour* is driven by the retailers who want to offer low prices to end-customers in order to drive high volumes. The EDLP variant of this behaviour places pressure on supply partners such as CleanCo for continuous price reduction. In turn, this generates a relatively stable demand pattern for the supply chain – unlike a retailer who regularly promotes the same product by means of special offers.

- *margin-driven behaviour* is driven by offering a wide selection of products and value adding services. Cost savings were not necessarily passed on to the customer but could be used to invest in additional value adding activities. This strategy also resulted in a relatively stable demand pattern.

Other behaviours by retailers are also possible – such as discounting and promotion. But the key point is that the different behaviours must be characterised and specified in terms of their logistics implications, along the lines of Table 1.1. Using order winners and qualifiers helps to bridge marketing and logistics perspectives. While there are dangers in a 'one size fits all' logistics strategy (low cost but low service) in the same way that there are dangers in over-customisation (high cost and complexity), the compromise solution is to specify three or four substantive segments (Gattorna, 2006).

Discussing the characteristics of customer behaviour within a cross-functional group in a workshop setting helps to spawn ideas on patterns. It is often easier to make sense of the data if they are used to plot graphs and charts. Venn diagrams such as the one shown in Figure 2.9 are helpful to illustrate patterns that may appear among the analysed data.

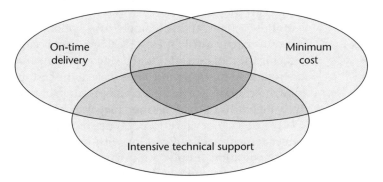

Figure 2.9   **Analysing the influence of demand characteristics**

### 2.5.3  Step 2b: Customer value analysis

Customer value is the customer-perceived benefit gained from a product/service compared with the cost of purchase. In order to measure customer value, we need to understand what *aspects* of a product or service a customer values (Johnson and Scholes, 2008). Here, we are primarily interested in aspects of customer value which impact on logistics strategy. Three aspects in particular relate to buying behaviours:

- *demand profile*: the characteristics of demand in terms of volume and variety, and of demand variability and uncertainty (section 2.3);
- *competitive profile*: how the focal firm chooses to compete in the marketplace (section 1.3);
- *product profile*: the extent to which the product is customised to specific customer requirements.

Customer value is assessed by means of a questionnaire to measure customer views of these aspects in terms of:

- *importance* (on a 0–100 scale);
- *performance* of the focal firm and a key competitor (0–5 Lickert scale);
- *price level* of the focal firm relative to the key competitor (0–5 Lickert scale).

Examples of customer value profiles for two customers of AutoCo (referred to in step 1 above) are shown in Figure 2.10

We return to the concept of 'value' in Chapter 3. Meanwhile, we will continue to use the AutoCo example to illustrate steps 3 and 4.

### 2.5.4  Step 3: Measure logistics strategy drivers

Here, we examine demand profile and competitive profile as drivers of logistics strategy (based on Godsell *et al.,* 2006):

- *Demand profile.* The time that the customer is prepared to wait to have his or her order fulfilled is defined as 'D time', which is further explored in section 5.2. D time may be measured in time-related measures from months to seconds. Essentially, this sets time objectives for the supply chain. Response in seconds means that there is no time to procure materials or to process them. Therefore, inventories of finished product are inevitable. However, as D times reduce in turbulent markets, holding inventories becomes an increasingly risky option, and in turn places increasing pressure onto supply capabilities. A focal firm may decide to respond to such pressure by reducing the range on offer, and by increasing the commonality of parts between different skus. At the other end of the scale, if the customer is prepared to wait for a long enough period to enable design and procurement processes to be completed, a relatively high level of customisation may be possible.

  Forecast accuracy (section 2.3) ties in with the logistics need to align mid- to longer-term capacity decisions with demand. In Chapter 5, we argue that reducing the total supply chain throughput time (P time) reduces the need to rely on forecasts. But clearly there is a limit to how far this ideal can be pushed. Being able to respond immediately to actual demand means that logistics

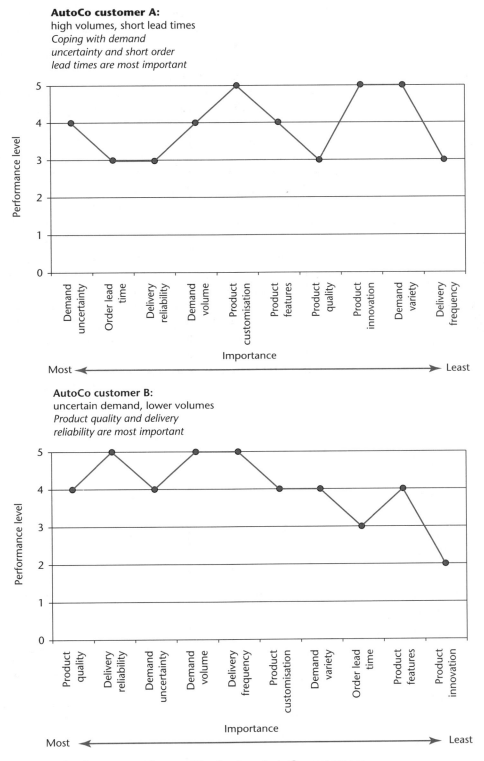

Figure 2.10   **Customer value profiles for two AutoCo customers**

capabilities have been put in place to do so. In particular, it is still necessary to make mid- to longer-term forecasts – for example to allow for advanced orders to suppliers, long cycle time production processes and to expand facilities.

It is also tough in logistics terms to support high levels of *volume variation* of demand across a given time period in a given supply chain. Constraints such as capacity limitations and fixed order quantities and lead times inhibit what may be done. Building *buffer capacity* into the supply chain (in the form of in-ventories or spare production capacity) may be too costly. Instead, it helps to analyse the causes of volume variation. Two main factors are the differences between peaks and troughs of demand, and the frequency with which peaks and troughs occur. A standard seasonal pattern may have just one peak (sum-mer for garden furniture, for example), whereas fashion industries may have six seasons or more. Retail promotions may create peaks every other week, which lead to volume variations of 60 to 70 per cent of 'normal' demand. Figure 2.11 shows how demand characteristics can be analysed.

- *Competitive profile.* This is based on the competitive factors we introduced in section 1.3 – hard objectives (quality, time and cost), supporting capabilities (controlling variability, dealing with uncertainty in logistics processes and sustainability) and soft objectives (such as confidence and security). For exam-ple, Ford chooses to compete on low price and delivery speed (by making to stock), while BMW chooses to compete by making more expensive and highly specified cars to customer order while the customer waits. While they also appear in the demand profile as characteristics, we refer here to variability and uncertainty in terms of a focal firm's capability to cope with them better than competition.

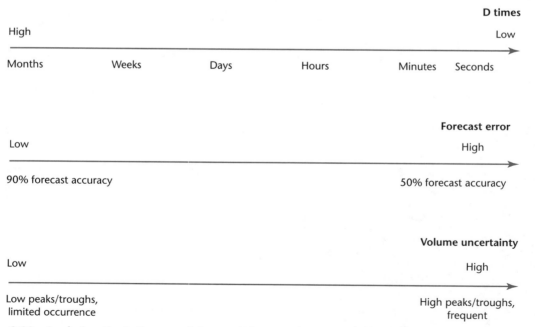

**Figure 2.11    Analysing the influence of demand characteristics on a supply chain**
Source: (Harrison, 2010)

● *Product profile.* Determining the level of customisation requires analysis at two levels. First, the proportion of products and sourced components that are customised is measured for each sku supplied to the final process in the supply chain (e.g. retailer or distributor). This analysis can result in the categorisation of skus on the basis of levels of customisation: high, medium and low. Second, we need to understand which processes or components are customised and where they are positioned in the supply chain. For high levels of customisation, particularly where it occurs early in the supply chain, the complexity that is caused may be reduced in two ways. The relevance to customers may be questioned – is this extra variety giving value to the end-customer? Or, different options could be built in as standard. While some redundancy is created, greater standardisation of supply chain processes and shorter lead times are gained.

All three of these profiles have profound implications for logistics strategy, some of the key implications for which are summarised in Figure 2.12.

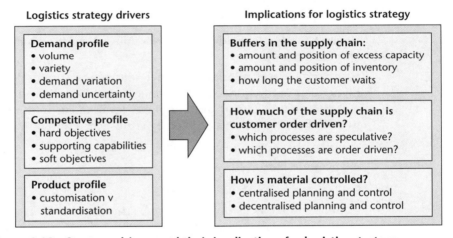

Figure 2.12 **Strategy drivers and their implications for logistics strategy**

For example, the higher the demand variability and uncertainty, the greater the need for buffers. Buffers can be in the form of spare capacity, inventory and order lead times. If we want to shorten the time the customer has to wait, then it is necessary to make speculatively – perhaps finishing off (customising) the product once the final order details are known. Finally, planning and controlling the flow of materials across the supply chain needs to be carried out centrally, when in high demand variability and uncertainty conditions in order to coordinate the response of supply partners. In more stable demand conditions, it is possible to relax controls and allow more local flexibility.

### 2.5.5 Step 4: Specify future approach to market segmentation

Using logistics strategy drivers it is now possible to revisit the customer value profiles in Figure 2.11 and develop a fresh approach to segmentation that makes sense in logistics terms. In Figure 2.13, the two customers (A and B) in Figure 2.10 are analysed in terms of their key demand and competitive profiles. Customers A and B both want 100 per cent on time – in full – on quality delivery. However,

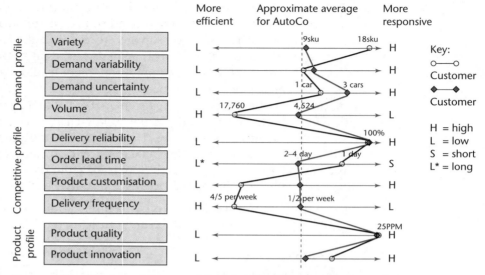

**Figure 2.13   Strategy drivers and their implications for segmentation**
Source: (Harrison, 2010)

customer A places priority on higher volumes on shorter delivery lead times with higher delivery frequencies. Customer B places priority on AutoCo's capability to meet uncertain demand, and on higher levels of customisation. It is now possible to describe the segments typified by customers A and B in terms of:

• buying behaviour relevant to logistics strategy;

• customer-perceived value;

• profile of logistics strategy drivers.

All other major customers at AutoCo then need to be evaluated in similar terms so that an overall segmentation strategy for the focal firm can be developed and refined. As indicated earlier, the aim is to develop a 'compromise' strategy that – like segmentation itself – seeks to describe logistics strategy 'as simply as possible while doing our best to emphasise its variety' (Millier and Palmer, 2000). Case study 2.6 gives you an opportunity to try out these concepts in the setting of a food supply chain.

---

**CASE STUDY 2.6**

## Bacalao – two supply chains for two markets

Bacalao is fish that has been salted and dried, traditionally in the open air on rocks; today it is done in a drier. It has been produced in Norway since about 1640, can be kept refrigerated for several years, and is said to improve over time. It has developed a strong position in the food cultures of many Latin countries – such as Brazil, the Dominican Republic and Portugal – where consumers often follow the Catholic tradition of eating more fish on Fridays and in the run-up to Easter. Marketing over many years has created the association with Norway as 'the land of bacalao', or 'bacalhau da Noruega' as it is called. It is a matter of great pride among consumers to master a variety of recipes for serving bacalao.

The overall supply chain is illustrated in Figure 2.14. It takes at least four weeks to make the end product. The best fish is wild and taken by line, but trawled fish is also

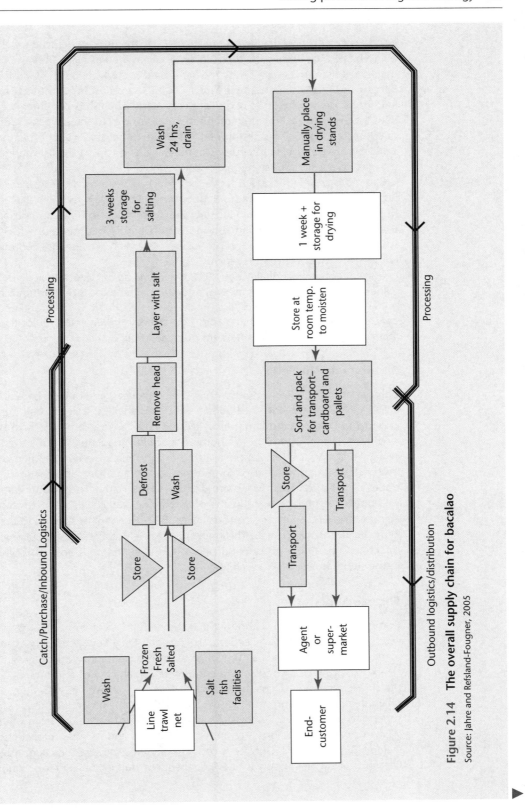

**Figure 2.14   The overall supply chain for bacalao**

Source: Jahre and Refsland-Fougner, 2005

good, while nets give the lowest quality because the fish can be dead for a while before being hauled up. Today, the fish is increasingly farmed as well. The raw material is the major cost item: prices are set by the Råfiskelaget (the Norwegian raw fish association). Prices can vary a lot – for example from NOK 26/kg to NOK 15/kg within a year. Electricity and insurance are the other two major cost items. The fish is slaughtered (and bled on boat for the best quality), then matured in salt for two to three weeks. After salting it is dried, sorted, packed and distributed. There are no reliable ways of measuring salt and water content, so manual methods of touching and feeling the fish during each stage are used to ensure consistent quality and weight.

Bacalao is mainly produced from cod, which is preferred by Portuguese customers. But consumers in the Dominican Republic prefer pollock, which is a darker-fleshed fish that is more abundant in the North Atlantic. Cod is up to three times more expensive than pollock. The Norwegian fish industry is highly fragmented, with many small-scale fish farmers, fishermen and producers. Marketing activities are coordinated by the Norwegian Seafood Export Council.

Consumers are very quality conscious when buying bacalao. Quality is determined by colour, texture and firmness, as well as water content and size. Portuguese consumers prefer smaller cod around 2.5 kilos, while consumers in the Dominican Republic are less concerned with size. Note that quality here refers to *grade* of fish rather than to conformance quality: both grades are fit for purpose in the markets they serve.

### Bacalhau da Noruega

Company Noruega (CN) company has 150 employees, and built its bacalao production facility in 1997 in the port of Ålesund – which has one of the largest harbours in Norway and one of the most modern fishing fleets in Europe. The company focuses on volume in order to benefit from the economies of scale. Production is stabilised through the year by ensuring a stable supply of fish through sourcing a combination of frozen and fresh fish, creating a buffer of some three to four months supply. The company only trades in full truckloads, which are distributed via Hamburg or Rotterdam. Product is sold under the generic brand name of *Bacalao da Noruega* in standard transport packaging. While CN serves most Latin markets, 80 per cent of its sales go to the Dominican Republic as pollock bacalao. This market is relatively stable throughout the year, which matches CN's stable production policy. CN is experimenting with pollock farming further to improve supply reliability.

### Bacalao Superior

Company Superior (CS) is also based in the Ålesund area, and accounts for 15–20 per cent of Norwegian bacalao exports to Portugal. Only cod bacalao is exported to this market, which commands a 10–15 per cent price premium over other Norwegian bacalao. The product is popular with consumers, which creates a strong relationship with the single supermarket chain that sells it. Fish are sold whole, with a CS tag showing guarantee of origin from fresh Norwegian cod, which was an idea that came from the supermarket customer. This ensures that CS bacalao stands out from other offerings. Joint marketing campaigns are funded by both CS and its supermarket customer, and include TV promotions. Only fresh cod is used in *bacalao superior*, caught by the coastal fleet in small boats. Supply is heavily dependent during the winter on quotas that are permitted in the famous Lofoten fishing field in the far north. CS buys from three fresh cod suppliers, and from 15–20 suppliers of salt fish. Processing follows traditional routes, but some technology has been introduced into cutting and drying. Finished product is transported to Portugal in 22-tonne truck loads three times per week. Storage of finished product is in Lisbon at the customer's warehouse.

## Comparing da Noruega and superior

Table 2.7 summarises some of the major differences between these two products.

**Table 2.7  Comparing da Noruega and superior**

| Characteristic | da Noruega (Dominican Rep) | Superior (Portugal) |
|---|---|---|
| Raw material | ● Fresh/frozen pollock<br>● Different sizes<br>● Line/trawl/net/farm<br>● Continuous supply<br>● 3–4 months inbound stocks | ● Fresh cod, some salted<br>● Size specific<br>● Mostly line<br>● Seasonal supply<br>● Small inbound stock |
| Production process | ● High volume<br>● Single facility<br>● All types of fish processed in a single factory: more efficient<br>● Undifferentiated packaging | ● Customised<br>● Many dedicated facilities<br>● Cod only in single, focused factory<br>● Fish individually tagged |
| Marketing | ● Continuous consumption<br>● Generic marketing through Seafood Export Council<br>● Low price<br>● Generic packaging<br>● Little differentiation | ● Special occasions<br>● Joint promotion with supermarket customer<br>● Premium price<br>● Tagged to show origin<br>● Differentiated by market |

CN accepts more variation in its raw material source to enable continuous supply. This applies to type of fish as well as where and how it is caught. Farming and a healthy stock of frozen fish help to reduce further supply variations. On the other hand, CS seeks the best quality with minimum variation. The only inbound stock that is permitted is small quantities of salted cod.

While the raw materials and end-product have many similarities, there are substantial differences in inbound and outbound logistics as well as processing and distribution strategies. These differences are fundamental to the need to support the brand (raising consumer expectations) by means of logistics strategy (meeting consumer expectations). We can conclude as follows:

● *Two fundamentally different inbound strategies*: CN focuses on secure, continuous supply and accepts greater variation in terms of type of fish, where and how caught – so farming is encouraged. They buffer and store extensively. CS goes for consistently high quality by not accepting much by way of variation: size, line catching and location are all important requirements. They do not store fresh fish or use frozen.
● *Internally consistent marketing and logistics*: CN matches the low price, continuous availability marketing mix by means of efficient sourcing and continuous availability, and of 'lean' (see Chapter 6) production and distribution methods. This enables

▶

high and consistent production volumes supported by a flexible product mix. There is less to go wrong in terms of supply, but the generic nature of the product militates against better margins or customer loyalty. CS matches the high price, seasonal availability marketing mix by means of highly selective sourcing and by focused factory production that is seasonal and relatively inefficient. Production is possible only when high-quality, line-caught fresh fish are available. Limited and sporadic availability mean that the product has to reassert itself following supply interruptions, so the marketing pull must be consistent and strong. Traceability through tagging reinforces the superior quality image in consumers' minds, supported by joint marketing with the major retail customer.

The way that the two supply chains have evolved illustrates the *tradeoffs* at stake: more of one thing means less of another. The CS supply chain has become focused on top quality (grade) product, but at relatively high cost and sporadic availability. The CN supply chain has become focused on the opposite: low cost and continuous availability, but at average quality (grade).

Sources: Jahre and Refsland Fougner, 2005; Harrison, 2010

## Question

1 Using Figures 2.12 and 2.13, summarise the key strategy drivers for products from CN and CS as far as you can with the information given in the case.

## Summary

*What is customer service in the context of logistics?*

- Marketing is defined as 'the activity, set of institutions, and processes for creating, communicating, delivering, and exchanging offerings that have value for customers, partners and society at large'. Loyal customers are seen as the source of profit, growth and security. Marketing in practice starts with analysing segments, evaluating those segments and targeting them. Segments need to be measurable, economically viable, accessible and actionable. Marketing in practice continues by market positioning, which requires differential advantage to be defined, and the marketing mix to be formulated.

- The key logistics contribution to the marketing mix is in the 'fourth P', place. This includes decisions about factors such as channel selection, market coverage, distribution systems and dealer support. Logistics also supports product decisions (for example, product range) and promotion activity.

- An important logistics contribution to putting the end-customer first is to forecast demand. This can be undertaken using judgemental forecasting (where no demand history exists) or by causal forecasting (where historical data are available).

- Business to business (B2B) refers to upstream relationships between members of a network. Business to customer (B2C) refers to handover to the end-customer. B2B relationships therefore need to be aligned towards B2C.

- Supply networks end with service processes, where the end-customer is present in some way. 'Gaps' can emerge between what the service is supposed to be, what the customer expects it to be, and how the customer perceives it when it is delivered. The size of these gaps has implications for quality of service, a major driver of customer loyalty.

*How do we win and retain customers through logistics?*

- The principle here is that loyal customers have many advantages over new ones. The logistics challenge is to reinforce loyalty by exceeding customer expectations via superior quality of service.

- Customer relationship management is based on the principle that marketing strategies should be continuously extended to strengthen customer loyalty. Phases of logistics development are needed, each phase placing increasing demands on the development of logistics capabilities.

- Setting logistics priorities should be carried out with market segments in mind. This is a joint task between marketing and logistics functions. Order winners and qualifiers by segment help develop a common language to assist this task.

- Often, the current approach to segmentation is unsatisfactory in logistics terms. We present a four-step model to diagnose the current approach, and to re-engineer that approach using the concept of logistics strategy drivers (demand profile and competitive profile).

## Discussion questions

1  suggest ways in which logistics can play a part in the marketing mix for:
   **a**  a manufacturer of cleaning products like CleanCo (Case study 2.4);
   **b**  a retailer such as Tesco (Case study 1.1);
   **c**  an automotive repair and recovery firm such as Talleres Auto (Case study 1.6);
   **d**  food suppliers such as CN and CS (Case study 2.6).

   In each case, specify the organisation you have in mind and explain the reasons for your suggestions.

2  The 'Batman' case (Case study 2.5) presents what might be described as a 'marketing wish list'. Analyse the likely logistics challenges at each stage of development, and suggest how these might be addressed.

3  While top companies such as IBM and Tesco say that the customer is king, will customer choice continue to be unrestrained in a) 2020 and b) 2050? Explain your thinking in each future state scenario.

4  Explain what is meant by uncertainty in demand forecasting.

   The barbecue sauce focal firm described in section 2.3 has manufacturing facilities in the Netherlands which are described as 'high on quality and reliability, but low on responsiveness'. In order to maximise production efficiency, large batches of each flavour are made so that process cleanouts (each lasting > four hours) are kept to a minimum. After manufacturing, each batch of a given flavour is transported to an off-site finishing operation, where bottles of the different flavours are packed into a display box for attractive presentation to the end-customer at the firm's retail customers. This process takes an average of two weeks because of the need to ensure that all flavours are available. Finally, the display boxes are distributed through warehousing operations which have been situated in six carefully selected locations around the product's major European market in Germany.

Management of the focal firm is under pressure to reduce inventories and stock write-offs (the sauce has a shelf life of three months). Propose what actions could be taken to improve the supply chain to permit improved responsiveness to end-customer demand.

## References

American Marketing Association (AMA) (2007) *Definition of Marketing*, at http://www.marketingpower.com/Community/ARC/Pages/Additional/Definition/default.aspx?sq=definition+of+marketing.

Berry, L.L. (1999) *Discovering the Soul of Service: The nine drivers of sustainable business success.* New York: Free Press.

de Chernatony, L. and McDonald, M. (2003) *Creating Powerful Brands in Consumer Service and Industrial Markets,* 3rd edn. Oxford: Butterworth Heinemann.

Doyle, P. (2000) *Value-based Marketing: Marketing strategies for corporate growth and shareholder value.* Chichester: Wiley.

Finne, S. and Sivonen, H. (2009) *The Retail Value Chain.* London: Kogan Page.

Gattorna, J. (2006) *Living Supply Chains: How to mobilise the enterprise around delivering what your customers want.* Harlow: Financial Times/Prentice Hall.

Gerstner, Jr, L.V. (2002) *Who Says Elephants Can't Dance?* London: HarperCollins.

Godsell, J. and Harrison, A. (2002) 'Strategy formulation in an FMCG supply chain', *Proceedings of the EurOMA Conference,* Copenhagen.

Godsell, J., Harrison, A., Storey, J. and Emberson, C. (2006) 'Customer responsive supply chain strategy – an unnatural act?', *International Journal of Logistics: Research and Applications,* Vol. 9, No. 1, pp. 47–56.

Harrison, A. (2010) *Delivering Agility in Food Supply Chains* in Mena, C. and Stevens, G. *Delivering Performance in Food Supply Chains.* Cambridge: Woodhead Publishing.

Jahre, M. and Refsland-Fougner, A.-K. (2005) 'Logistics – The Missing Link in Branding – Bacalhau da Noruega vs. Bacalhau Superior', *ISL – Logistics Conference Proceedings 2005,* Lisbon.

Johnson, G. and Scholes, K. (2008) *Exploring Corporate Strategy,* 8th edn. London: Financial Times/Prentice Hall.

Johnston, R. and Clark, G. (2008) *Service Operations Management,* 3rd edn. London: Financial Times/Prentice Hall.

Kotler, P. and Keller, K.L. (2009) *Marketing Management,* 13th edn. Harlow: Pearson Education.

Latta, M. (2007) 'How to forecast the demand for a new drug in the pharmaceutical industry', *The Journal of Business Forecasting,* Fall, pp. 21–8.

Leahy, T. (2005) 'Sir Terry Leahy at the Guardian summit', at http://www.guardian.co.uk/print/0,,5120038-113379,00.html.

McCarthy, E.J. (1964) *Basic Marketing: a managerial approach.* Homewood, IL: Irwin.

McGoldrick, P. (2002) *Retail Marketing,* 2nd edn. Maidenhead: McGraw-Hill Education Europe.

Millier P. and Palmer, R. (2000) *Nuts, Bolts and Magnetrons: a practical guide for industrial marketers*. Chichester: Wiley.

Ogrodowczyk, J. (2008) 'Disaggregating forecasts: Fairchild semiconductor's experience', *Journal of Business Forecasting*, Spring, pp. 34–43.

Parasuraman, A., Berry, L. and Zeithaml, V. (1991) 'Understanding customer expectations of service', *Sloan Management Review*, Spring, pp. 39–48.

Parasuraman, A. and Grewal, D. (2000) 'The impact of technology on the quality–value–loyalty chain: a research agenda', *Journal of the Academy of Marketing Science*, Vol. 28, No. 1, pp. 168–74.

Payne, A., Christopher, M., Clark, M. and Peck, H. (1995) *Relationship Marketing for Competitive Advantage*. Oxford: Butterworth Heinemann.

Payne, A. and Frow, P. (2005) 'A strategic framework for customer relationship management', *Journal of Marketing*, Vol. 69 (Oct.), pp. 167–76.

Piercy, N. (2009) *Market-led Strategic Change*, 4th edn. Oxford: Butterworth Heinemann.

Rafele, C. (2004) 'Logistics service measurement: a reference framework', *Journal of Manufacturing Technology Management*, Vol. 15, No. 3, pp. 280–90.

Treacy, M. and Wiersema, F. (1997) *The Discipline of Market Leaders*. Reading, MA: Addison-Wesley Publishing Co.

Waters, D. (2003) *Inventory Planning and Control*. Chichester: Wiley.

Webster, F. (2000) 'Understanding the relationships among brands, consumers and retailers', *Journal of the Academy of Marketing Science*, Vol. 28, pp. 17–23.

Wild, A. (2002) *Best Practice in Inventory Management*, 2nd edn. Oxford: Elsevier.

Zeithaml, V., Berry, L. and Parasuraman, A. (1988) 'Communication and control processes in the delivery of service quality', *Journal of Marketing*, Vol. 52, pp. 35–48.

## Suggested further reading

Christopher, M. and Peck, H. (2003) *Marketing Logistics*, 2nd edn. Oxford: Butterworth-Heinemann.

Doyle, P. and Stern P. (2006) *Marketing Management and Strategy,* 4th edn. Harlow: Pearson Education.

McDonald, M. and Dunbar, I. (2004) *Market Segmentation*. Oxford: Elsevier Butterworth-Heinemann.

# CHAPTER 3

# Value and logistics costs

**Objectives**

*The planned objectives of this chapter are to:*

- explain the concept of value and its implications for managing the supply chain;
- explain how total costs can be divided up in different ways, and how they can be applied to managing the supply chain;
- identify how better cost information can be used to create more value.

*By the end of this chapter you should be able to understand:*

- what is meant by the term 'value creation';
- how logistics costs can be managed for better value creation;
- how activity-based management can be used to identify the cost drivers in your business.

## Introduction

In section 1.3 we reviewed the way in which different products may have different logistics strategies. While the range of classic shirts compete on price and brand, and demand is relatively stable over the year, fashion blouses compete on style, responsiveness to market and brand. For a fashion product, the logistics challenge is to be able to support highly uncertain demand in the marketplace. The logistics task for the two supply chains is essentially different, and some companies refer to a 'supply chain for every product' to emphasise this difference. In Chapter 2, we stated the need for compromise here – between 'one size fits all' on the one hand, and endless customisation of the supply chain on the other.

Here, we develop the information flow aspects of our model in Figure 1.4. We also show how there is another flow in supply chains – *funds flow*. Funds flow in the opposite direction to materials. Funds – in the form of cash – originate from the end-customer, and are used to pay the bills progressively from one supply chain partner to the next upstream.

While funds flow has not yet been formally included in the logistics domain, the integration of finance and logistics is an increasingly important aspect of logistics in the 21st century. The acquisition of Vastera (a third party logistics company) by JP Morgan Chase Bank (a financial institution) to form JP Morgan

Chase Vastera is aimed at 'driving cost savings and global supply chain efficiencies while providing best-in-class compliance with government regulations'.

This chapter probes the financial implications of different logistics strategies. While it may be clear that cost must form a central plank of supply chain strategy for classic shirts, the product team for fashion blouses cannot ignore the cost implications of their actions (see Table 1.1). The common theme is the concept of *value*, and the extent to which both management teams are creating value for the end-customer. Here, we advance the concept of 'value' beyond the mainly end-customer view that we took in Chapter 2, and extend it to other stakeholders in the supply chain.

While value is based on *cost* from the point of view of the company accountant, the concept of value may have different interpretations outside the company. In section 2.5.3, we stated that value from the end-customer's point of view is the *perceived benefit* gained from a product/service compared with the cost of purchase. From the shareholder's point of view, value is determined by the *best alternative use* of a given investment. In other words, value is greatest where the return on investment is highest.

**Key issues**

This chapter addresses five key issues:

1 **Where does value come from?**: different views of value, and how it can be measured using return on investment.

2 **How can logistics costs be represented?**: three different ways to divide up total costs.

3 **Activity-based costing (ABC)**: a process-based alternative to allocating overheads.

4 **A balanced measurement portfolio**: balancing the needs of all stakeholders.

5 **Supply chain operations reference (SCOR) model**: a further process-based approach to measuring supply chain costs and performance.

The chapter assumes a basic knowledge of a profit/loss account and balance sheet. If finance is not your long suit, then a helpful accompanying financial text is *Management Accounting for Non-specialists* (Atrill and McLaney, 2008). We acknowledge the assistance from our colleague at Cranfield, Sri Srikanthan, for his help with sections 3.1 and 3.2. Figures 3.2 and 3.7 and Table 3.2 are from his lectures.

## 3.1 Where does value come from?

*Key issue:* How can shareholder value be defined? What is economic value added, and how does it help in this definition?

Creating shareholder value is widely used today to describe the main objective of a business. In its simplest form, shareholder value is created when the shareholder gets a better return by investing in your business than from a comparable investment. A *comparable investment* is one that has a similar level of risk. You might make the same return on €100,000 from playing roulette as you do from buying a house, but the risk profiles are very different! In order for a business to create superior shareholder value, it must have a competitive advantage. Return on investment is an important measure that is widely used to assess shareholder value.

### 3.1.1  Return on investment (ROI)

One way of looking at the creation of shareholder value is to end the year with a lot more money than at the start. If this extra money results from profitable trading, then management has been successful in *improving the productivity of capital.* Return on investment (ROI) is measured as profit (in €) before interest and tax as a percentage of capital employed (also in €):

**% ROI = 100 × € Profit/€ Capital employed**

The term 'investment' is used because capital employed is equivalent to the money invested in the business. ROI can also be seen as the outcome of profitability and asset utilisation:

$$\% \text{ ROI} = 100 \frac{\textbf{Profit}}{\textbf{Sales}} \times \frac{\textbf{Sales}}{\textbf{Capital employed}}$$

Let us look at the detail behind each of these ratios, and the way they fit in with each other. Figure 3.1 provides a family tree of the way ROI is made up. Let us look at the potential for improving each from a point of view of managing the supply chain better.

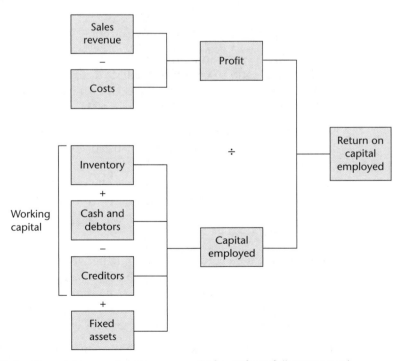

**Figure 3.1  The make-up of return on capital employed (investment)**
(Source: Courtesy of Sri Srikanthan)

### Sales

Superior customer service improves sales, and makes a focal firm more valued by the customer in the long term.

- Improving customer responsiveness is a key goal for managing the supply chain.

### Costs

The supply chain is a potential gold mine for making bottom line improvements to business performance. But directors of many businesses are impatient for cost improvement, and consider that cutting stocks and headcount is the primary task – as in the 'evolution' strategy in Figure 1.10. This may achieve short-term margin improvement, but strategic supply chain management is more importantly concerned with process improvement over the long term.

- Supply chain modelling shows that manufacturing and distribution costs together with inventories can be optimised while customer service is maximised.
- Studies in efficient consumer response (ECR) have shown that cutting out non-value-added products and inefficient promotional activity can reduce overall costs by 6 per cent. (ECR is discussed in Chapter 6.)

### Working capital

Note that the combination of inventory, cash and debtors *less* creditors is called working capital. Each of the elements of working capital is considered in turn.

### Inventory

This is a major asset in many businesses. It is there to buffer uncertainty of supply and demand, and to permit immediate availability when replenishment times are too lengthy. However, inventory is often regarded as a hindrance rather than a help: it ties up cash, it needs resources to be stored and it becomes obsolete.

- A primary goal for supply chain management is to replace inventory with information. Try to minimise the use of forecasts and to increase the use of real demand.
- Question any means for automatically replenishing inventory (such as the re-order level used in stock control, described in section 6.1.2).

### Cash and debtors

The key task here is to make the time between receipt of customer order and receipt of the cash as short as possible. Progress against this ideal not only makes the company more competitive by reducing lead times, but also improves its cash position. This means that business processes from sales order processing to distribution should be integrated and free from waste.

- Debtors (customers who owe us money) can be minimised by basic controls such as regular review and problem resolution. Sending out incomplete or inaccurate invoices is an invitation for delays or even non-payment!

## Creditors

Creditors are people we owe money to. In supply chain terms, this term applies mainly to our suppliers. Many organisations think that lengthy payment terms to suppliers maximise credit and therefore improve the balance sheet. The downside of this thinking is that suppliers factor in the credit terms to their prices, and their own balance sheets become saddled with debt.

- Plan material requirements and distribution requirements to maximise flow of parts through the supply chain as needed.
- Discipline goods inwards to check delivery date, quality and correct prices. There is no point in starting the credit cycle early by accepting goods before they are due.
- If the supplier is a smaller company, it may be that the cost of capital is higher than it is for your company. It may then be worthwhile to consider negotiating with the supplier to pay early, and therefore getting a share of the money that the supplier is paying in interest to the bank.

## Fixed assets

The value-generating assets of a business that form the focus of supply chain management are a heavy drain on capital. They include manufacturing facilities, warehousing and distribution. They contribute to high *fixed costs* for an operation: that is, costs that do not change much with throughput. Such costs are therefore highly volume sensitive, as we shall see.

- Many organisations respond by a 'maximum variable, minimum fixed' policy. This refers to keeping fixed costs to a minimum, and is helped by *outsourcing* all but the core capabilities, which are retained in-house. Outsourced processes can then be cut more easily in the event of a downturn such as the recession of 2009/10. Thus transport and warehousing are today often outsourced to specialist 'third party logistics providers' such as DHL Exel and UPS.

### Activity 3.1

1 Review the categories in Figure 3.1 and compile your own list of the way in which these categories can be influenced (made better or worse) in an organisation.
2 What are the implications for logistics strategy?

## 3.1.2 Financial ratios and ROI drivers

ROI is an important measure for assessing shareholder value and is underpinned by two main drivers:

- increased profitability;
- increased asset utilisation.

As discussed section 3.1.1, these two supporting drivers are the key determinants for increasing ROI and hence shareholder value. An understanding of the financial ratios that affect these two drivers is essential when formulating a focal firm's supply chain strategy. While financial ratios are based on historical information, and therefore have limitations, they have a number of advantages for an organisation. They can be:

- a benchmark for comparing one organisation with another;
- used as a comparator for a particular industrial sector;
- used to track past performance;
- a motivator for setting performance targets;
- an early warning indicator if the organisation's performance starts to decline.

Table 3.1 provides a guide to linking ROI and its drivers with the financial ratios for a manufacturing company (CIMA, 1989).

Table 3.1 **ROI and its key drivers**

| Level 1 | Level 2 | Level 3 | Level 4 |
|---------|---------|---------|---------|
| **Return on investment** | $\dfrac{\text{Net profit}}{\text{Sales}}$ | Production costs as % of sales | Labour costs as % of sales<br>Materials as % of sales |
| | | Selling costs as % of sales | Labour costs as % of sales |
| | | Administration costs as % of sales | Labour costs as % of sales |
| | $\dfrac{\text{Sales}}{\text{Total assests}}$ | Fixed assets as % of sales | Property as % of sales<br>Plant as % of sales<br>Vehicles as % of sales |
| | | Current assets as % of sales | Inventory as % of sales<br>Debtors as % of sales<br>Cash as % of sales |

Section 3.2 of this chapter tackles the issues concerning the visibility of costing information. This form of analysis can be applied to benchmark an existing operation with a competitor, or it can be used to assess the implications on ROI against potential *trade-offs* (see section 1.4.4), such as comparing an in-house operation with a third party outsourcing alternative.

The use of financial ratios in relation to time is key to monitoring working capital and the 'cash to cash' cycle. Key time-related ratios include:

- *average inventory turnover*: the number of times inventory is turned over in relation to the cost of good sold;
- *average settlement period for debtors*: the time taken for customers to pay their invoices;
- *average settlement period for creditors*: the time taken for an organisation to pay its creditors.

Reductions in working capital will have a beneficial effect on an organisation's ROI. For example, inventory reductions increase both profitability (reduced costs) and capital (increased asset utilisation). Supply chain decisions have an impact on costs *and* assets, so they affect both the drivers of ROI. Understanding the trade-offs involved is key to increasing value.

## 3.2  How can logistics costs be represented?

*Key issues:* **What are the various ways of cutting up the total cost 'cake', and what are the relative merits of each?**

We all have a pretty good idea of what the total costs of a business are in practice. The costs of such items as materials used, power and wages all lead to bills that have to be paid. What is not so clear is how these costs should be allocated to supply chain processes – or even to products for that matter. Figure 3.2 shows a breakdown of the costs of producing a bottle of mineral water against

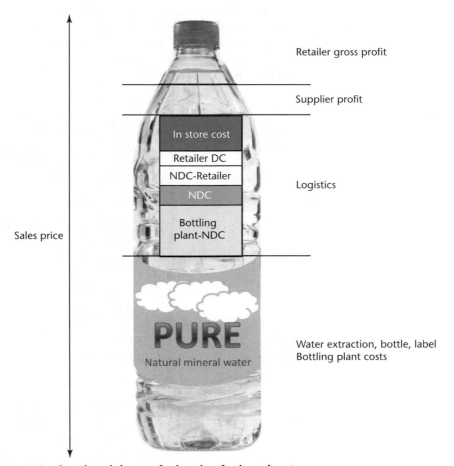

**Figure 3.2   Cost breakdown of a bottle of mineral water**

its total sales price, showing the approximate proportions of each. Starting at the bottom:

- *Manufacturing costs*: of extracting the water from source, testing and purifying. Add on the costs of plastic and labels for the bottles.
- *Transport costs*: from bottling plant to the supplier's national distribution centre (NDC) in a given territory.
- *Processing costs*: in the supplier's NDC.
- *Transport costs*: from supplier's NDC to retailer's regional distribution centre (RDC).
- *Processing costs*: in the retailer's RDC.
- *Processing costs*: in the retailer's store.

The balance of the sales revenue-costs is shared between supplier and retailer as profit (or 'margin'). But how are costs allocated to product lines (for example, plastic bottles, glass bottles, facial spray) and individual skus (for example, 1.5 litre, 500ml)?

This section reviews three commonly used ways of representing costs: fixed and variable, direct and indirect, and engineered and discretionary. If you are already familiar with the concepts of variable and fixed costs and break-even charts, then start at section 3.3. Bear in mind that the *total cost* picture is the same: the three different ways of allocating them to products are simply different ways of 'cutting the cake'. Let us look at total cost as a cube instead of a cake. Then the three different ways of representing costs can be shown as different ways of cutting up the cube (Figure 3.3).

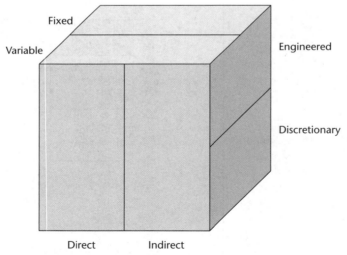

**Figure 3.3  Three ways to cut the 'total cost cube'**
(Source: Courtesy of Sri Srikanthan)

The important point here is that the total cost is constant: it is the ways we *analyse* that cost that are different. Why analyse it in different ways? To gain better information about our cost basis so that we can manage the business better. Let us look in turn at each of these ways to cut the total cost cube.

## 3.2.1  Fixed/variable

One popular way of analysing costs is to consider the effect of *volume of activity* on them. Costs tend to respond differently as the volume changes:

- *fixed costs* tend to stay the same as volume of activity changes, or at least within a given volume range;
- *variable costs* change as the volume of activity changes.

Fixed costs include items such as warehouse rental, which is charged on a time basis (€/month). As volume of activity increases, additional warehouses may be added around Europe, and we get the familiar *stepped fixed costs*, as shown in Figure 3.4. The same relationship would apply if volumes were reduced and a warehouse closed.

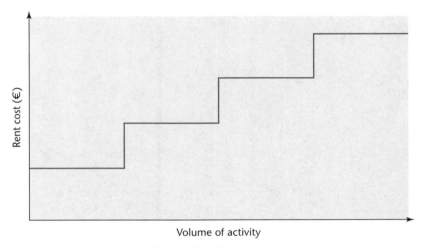

Figure 3.4  **Rent cost against volume of activity**

Variable costs include things such as direct materials, which are ordered in line with demand. If demand increases, we buy more. Starting with zero cost at zero activity, variable costs increase roughly in line with volume, as shown in Figure 3.5.

If we add the variable costs to the fixed costs against a given range of volume (so that the fixed costs remain completely fixed), and add in the sales revenue (which also increases in line with volume), we arrive at the break-even chart shown in Figure 3.6. The sloping line that starts at O is the sales revenue. The total cost line starts at F, and represents the sum of fixed and variable costs. The point at which the sales revenue line crosses the total cost line is the break-even point. Below this point, a loss will be incurred; above it a profit will be made.

A helpful concept in evaluating break-even charts is that of contribution:

**Contribution = Sales less variable costs**

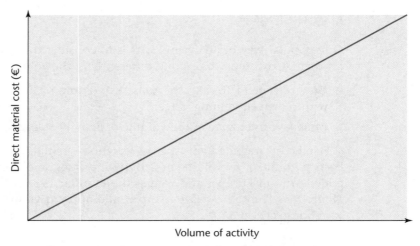

**Figure 3.5    Direct material costs against volume of activity**

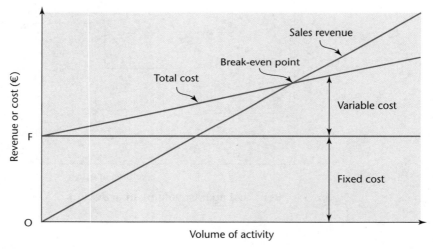

**Figure 3.6    Break-even chart**

Therefore contribution is the fixed costs plus the profit. Contribution is useful in decision making. High contribution per unit indicates a more volatile business: that is, one that is more risky. Therefore we should expect a business with high contribution/unit to provide a higher return on investment in the longer term. Look at the two break-even charts in Figures 3.7 and 3.8. What are the differences between the two situations? What has happened to the break-even point and why?

Chart A (Figure 3.7) shows a situation with high variable costs and low fixed costs. In chart B (Figure 3.8), the situation is reversed. The break-even point has moved well to the right: that is, chart B requires a higher volume to break-even

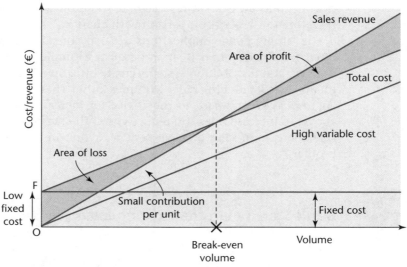

**Figure 3.7  Break-even chart A**
(Source: Courtesy of Sri Srikanthan)

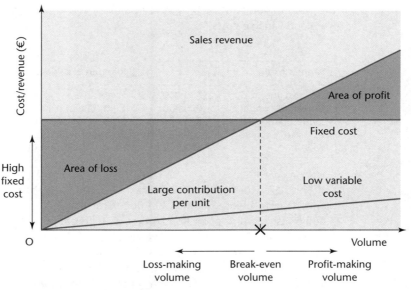

**Figure 3.8  Break-even chart B**
(Source: Courtesy of Sri Srikanthan)

than A. This is because a much higher volume of sales is needed to cover the high level of fixed costs.

Furthermore, additional volume has a small impact on chart A, whereas it has a much higher impact on chart B. So high fixed costs and low variable costs lead to greater volume sensitivity. Accordingly, profitability (the area above the break-even point) is affected much more by volume changes in chart B. In terms of contribution, chart A represents a situation with low contribution/unit, and therefore low risk in comparison with chart B.

The supply chain implications of such considerations are that we are most often faced with chart B situations. For example, core resources such as warehousing and distribution systems create little opportunity to reduce investments in line with reducing sales volumes other than the step changes shown in Figure 3.4. We are back to the advice for increasing ROI given in section 3.1.1 above: to increase sales and reduce costs. The reassuring point is that every 1 per cent increase in sales or 1 per cent reduction in costs has a leveraged effect on profits.

## CASE STUDY 3.1

## Bond SA – a marginal costing example

Bond SA is planning to manufacture a new product with an initial sales forecast of 3,600 units in the first year at a selling price of €800 each. The finance department has calculated that the variable cost for each truck will be €300. The fixed costs for the manufacturing facility for the year are €1,500,000. Using the information provided by the sales forecast and the finance department, it is now possible to calculate the planned profit, the contribution and the break-even point for this venture by leveraging the nature of fixed and variable costs.

| Planned profit | € | Planned break-even point | € |
|---|---|---|---|
| Sales revenue | 2,880,000 | Fixed costs | 1,500,000 |
| Less variable costs | 1,080,000 | Contribution per unit | |
| Contribution | 1,800,000 | Sales value – variable cost | 500 |
| Less fixed costs | 1,500,000 | Break-even point (units) | |
| Profit | 300,000 | Fixed costs/contribution per unit | 3,000 |

If Bond SA achieves its sales forecast of 3,600 units then the company will make a planned profit before tax of €300,000. Crucially the company's break-even point is 3,000 units, at which point Bond SA makes no profit but also no loss, because sales revenue (€2,400,000) equals all the variable costs (€900,000) and all the total fixed costs associated with production process (€1,500,000). Any additional unit sold after this point will provide Bond with profitable sales revenue. The difference between the planned profit and the break-even point is called the margin of safety. In the case of Bond SA, this equates to 600 units.

(Source: Simon Templar, Cranfield)

### Questions

What happens to the break-even point if:

1 Fixed costs increase by 10 per cent?

2 The sales price reduces by 5 per cent?

### 3.2.2  Direct/indirect

Another way to cut up the total cost 'cube' is to analyse costs in terms of whether or not they can be directly allocated to a given product. Two further categories emerge:

- *Direct costs* can be tied to specific products. The most obvious examples are direct labour and direct materials. Thus we can allocate exactly the cost of bought-in parts to the products into which they are built.

- *Indirect costs* are whatever is left over after direct costs have been allocated. Indirect costs are also called 'overheads', and include everything from the managing director's salary to the rent rates paid for the distribution centre – anything that cannot be allocated directly to a given product.

*Directness* of costs is concerned with the extent to which costs can be allocated directly to given products. This is a completely different concept from that of fixed/variable costs. While there is a tendency to associate fixed costs with indirect and variable with direct, there is no necessary relationship at all. Thus direct labour costs tend to be fixed, at least in the short term.

As stated above, the reason for analysing costs differently is *to gain better information about our cost basis so that we can manage the business better*. Direct and indirect costs help us to decide the full cost of a product or service when more than one is offered. If there were just a single product, life would be easy, because all of the costs could be allocated to that one product. Most businesses are much more complex than that, and are faced with the issue of how indirect costs should be apportioned to products. The most popular way to spread indirect costs is on the basis of direct labour. This is not the 'correct way', nor is it the only way.

A closer view of how fixed costs behave by product is achieved by using a method called *direct product profitability* (DPP). This method has been widely used in the retail industry to understand the way in which logistics costs behave for each product. The understanding is achieved by allocating fixed costs by making assumptions about how these are incurred by a product as it moves through the logistics system.

A good DPP system should take account of all the significant differences in the ways products are developed, sourced, produced, sold and distributed. In order to make this analysis practical, products will normally need to be grouped together. Product groups need to recognise shared technologies, processes, fixed assets, raw material inputs and packaging methods. The key objective of product groupings is to remove the need for apportioning costs, and thereby not to apportion profit across the products.

An example DPP is shown for a manufacturing company in Table 3.2. Note that not all of the fixed costs have been assigned. DPP assumes that only those costs that can rationally be allocated may be deducted. Thus DPP may be viewed as a development of direct/indirect costing in that it attempts to convert into direct costs logistics costs that would otherwise have been regarded as fixed. In this way, DPP seeks to provide more accurate information about which products are contributing most to profitability – and which are contributing least.

Table 3.2  **Direct product profitability (DPP)**

| | € | € |
|---|---|---|
| Gross sales for product group<br>● Less product-specific discounts and rebates | | X<br>X |
| Net sales by product<br>● Less direct costs of product | | X<br>X |
| Gross product contribution<br>● Less product-based marketing expenses | X | X |
| Product-specific direct sales support costs<br>● Less product-specific direct transportation costs:<br>   Sourcing costs<br>   Operations support<br>   Fixed-assets financing<br>   Warehousing and distribution<br>   Inventory financing<br>   Order, invoice and collection processing | X<br><br>X<br>X<br>X<br>X<br>X<br>X | <br><br><br><br><br><br><br>X |
| ● Less product-attributable overheads<br>Direct product profitability | | X<br>X |

(Source: Courtesy of Sri Srikanthan)

The principle at stake here is that good accounting and financial analysis force us to ask more questions about what is going on in our business. DPP can have a role to play here: it attempts to allocate logistics costs more specifically to products (and, in this case, orders as well) than is possible by spreading 'fixed' costs on the basis of an assumption such as direct labour. The assumption would otherwise be that direct labour actually 'drives' the overheads, which is highly doubtful.

---

**CASE STUDY 3.2**

## Direct product profitability

Filmco makes two thin film (gauge = 12μm) products for packaging applications in the food industry. Product A is coated so that it can subsequently be printed on; product B is uncoated. There is no changeover time on the production line, because all that needs to happen is that the coating drum is switched on or off. Once produced on the film-making lines, the film is slit to width and length to customer order. Roughly 40 per cent of Filmco's output is A, and 60 per cent B, and film-making takes place 360 days/year on a continuous basis because of the high capital cost of the process.

A DPP study was carried out at Filmco to determine the relative profitability of the two products A and B by major customer. The method was adapted from that shown in Table 3.1 because Filmco is a manufacturing environment. Here is how it was done:

1 Invoice price: this was the total sales value invoiced to the customer.
2 Cost of placing orders: the total cost of the sales office (salaries, etc.) was divided by the number of orders dispatched that month. This cost per order (€150) was allocated to each order placed by each customer.
3 Manufacturing cost: a variable cost for each product was found by collecting raw material, labour, power, packaging and waste costs. Manufacturing overheads

(fixed costs) were allocated on the basis of direct labour. Because of the small difference in manufacturing methods, the manufacturing costs for the two products were similar. They were €2,107 for A and €2,032 for B.

4 Storage costs: the total cost of the warehousing operation is €800k/year. There are 8,300 pallet locations, and the cost/day for a pallet was calculated as €0.30 assuming 360 working days. The storage cost for a given order was calculated as the number of pallets × the number of days × €0.30.

5 Opportunity costs: orders must wait in the warehouse until the last reel has been produced. An order with a value of €3,000 that stays for seven days in the warehouse with an interest rate of 14 per cent is said to have an opportunity cost of €8.20.

6 Transport cost: this was based on a price per tonne delivered to a given customer.

7 Total cost: this was the sum of b to f for a given order.

8 DPP: this was sales price less total cost g.

Table 3.3 gives a sample of the DPPs for four orders for customer P. The average DPP for customer P over all orders shipped over a given month was 19.6 per cent, while that for customer Q was 23.1 per cent and customer R was 33.0 per cent.

**Table 3.3   DPP for customer P for a sample of four orders in a given month**

| Order no. | Film | Weight (t) | a | b | c | d | e | f | g | h(%) |
|---|---|---|---|---|---|---|---|---|---|---|
| 186232 | A | 482 | 1,210 | 150 | 876 | 1.08 | 1.88 | 79 | 1,108 | 8.4 |
| 185525 | A | 2,418 | 5,997 | 150 | 4,344 | 7.83 | 9.33 | 190 | 4,702 | 21.6 |
| 185187 | B | 4,538 | 13,000 | 150 | 8,402 | 20.80 | 30.33 | 343 | 8,946 | 31.2 |
| 185351 | B | 2,615 | 7,576 | 150 | 4,897 | 14.58 | 17.68 | 198 | 5,277 | 30.3 |

*Question*

1 What can we tell from the above analysis in Table 3.3 and the average DPPs per customer? (Consider in particular the differences in DPP between the four orders shown, and between the three customers P, Q and R.)

## 3.2.3  Engineered/discretionary

A third way of analysing costs is to consider *the ease of allocating* them. Some things are easy to cost; others may require considerable thought and analysis because they are difficult to cost under current methods. This line of thinking creates a third way of cutting the total cost cube:

● *Engineered costs* have a clear input–output relationship. In other words, the benefit of a given cost is measurable. For example, if it takes ten hours to produce ten boxes of product A in the factory, then we have a clear output benefit (one box) for the cost of each hour of input.

● *Discretionary costs* do not have a clear input–output relationship. Here, the input cost is clear but the output benefit is unclear. For example, the cost of the contract cleaners who clean the factory is clear, but the benefit they produce is not easily quantifiable.

The challenge is to convert discretionary costs into engineered costs, so that we can better quantify the competitive impact of a given course of action. A classic example of converting discretionary costs into engineered costs has been the conversion of 'quality' as a discretionary concept into engineered 'quality costs' (Dale and Plunkett, 1995). This was achieved by breaking down the concept of quality into three cost drivers:

- *Prevention.* This comprises the costs of measures to prevent defects from taking place, such as training and process capability studies.
- *Appraisal.* This comprises the costs incurred in detecting defects, which would include testing and inspection.
- *Internal and external failure.* Internal costs are scrap, rework and the associated costs of not getting it right the first time. External failure costs are rectification after products have reached the final customer, such as warranty claims, returns and repairs.

In this case, it was argued, greater investment in prevention would result in the overall cost of quality being reduced over time.

The principle is to convert discretionary costs into engineered costs where possible. As indicated in the above examples, it is usually possible to make an estimate of what the engineered costs are, perhaps accompanied by a sensitivity or risk analysis. Without such guidelines, decisions would have to be taken on 'gut feel' – or, as usually happens, not taken at all! In other words, the logistics team may have an excellent project for increased flexibility in the distribution centre, but because they have not quantified the outputs (for example, the cost savings) the application for funding is rejected.

---

**CASE STUDY 3.3**

## Glup SA

Glup SA supplies a range of household soaps to supermarkets in northern Europe. There are 12 stock-keeping units (skus) in the range. The logistics manager has determined that an investment of €0.5 million on improved material handling equipment would convert the main distribution centre into a more flexible facility. A number of benefits in improved product availability has been identified – but current information is largely in the form of discretionary costs. Glup's assessment of the benefits and its plans to convert the justification into engineered costs are outlined below.

### Improved in-store availability

This is the percentage of time for which a product is available on the shelf. If the product is not available on the shelf, then it will lose sales to competitive products that are available, such as supermarket own brands. (Availability is a classic 'order losing sensitive' qualifying criterion as described in section 1.3.) Current available data at Glup are scant, but suggest that average in-store availability is as low as 85 per cent for a given sku. In order to convert this discretionary benefit into an engineered cost, Glup intends to measure the time for which each of the 12 product lines is unavailable each week. One way to do this is to use a market research agency to conduct sample studies of product availability in selected stores at random times across the working week.

This will yield an availability guide, such as the 85 per cent figure referred to. The new system will, it is believed, reduce this unavailable time. Glup then plans to model the new material-handling equipment methods using simulation, and to calculate the new in-store availability. The reduced non-availability time could then be converted into additional contribution for each sku to give an engineered cost saving.

### Reduced transportation costs

The new equipment would also allow lower transportation costs, because trays of different skus could be mixed together on the same pallet. Glup again intends to use simulation modelling to identify the opportunities for savings using this method. It is considered that this will offer the opportunity to reduce overall transport costs by more flexible loading of the trailers used to distribute the products to Glup's customers.

### Promotions and new product launches

It is considered that the new equipment will enable promotions and new product launches to be delivered to selected stores more accurately and more quickly. Demand uncertainty in such situations is very high: for example, a recent 'three for the price of two' promotion created a fivefold increase in sales. In order to launch a new product it is first necessary to drain the pipeline of the old product, or to 'write it off' as obsolete stock. If the more flexible warehouse system can reduce the length of the pipeline from factory to supermarket, it is argued, then a real saving in time or obsolete stock is possible. Glup again intends to measure this by simulation. It will then be necessary to determine by how much sales will increase as a result of the new product advantages. This will be estimated by Glup marketing people, who will use experience of previous promotions and new product launches. The engineered cost will be the additional time for which the new product is available multiplied by the additional estimated sales volume multiplied by the contribution per unit. Alternatively, it will be the reduction in obsolete stocks multiplied by the total cost per product plus any costs of double handling and scrapping.

### Question

1  Comment on Glup's plans to create engineered costs from the perceived benefits of the new material-handling equipment.

## 3.3 Activity-based costing (ABC)

*Key issues:* **What are the shortcomings of traditional cost accounting from a logistics point of view? How can costs be allocated to processes so that better decisions can be made?**

The driving force behind activity-based costing (ABC) is that the traditional way of allocating indirect costs by spreading them to products on the basis of direct labour is becoming difficult to manage. While direct labour used to constitute a substantial portion of product costs, today that rarely applies. Therefore overhead rates of 500 per cent or more on direct labour are not uncommon. Just a small change in direct labour content would lead to a massive change in product cost.

Cooper and Kaplan (1988) explain the problem by referring to two factories, which we here refer to as Simple and Complex. Both factories produce 1 million ballpoint pens each year; they are the same size and have the same capital equipment. But while Simple produces only blue pens, Complex produces hundreds of colour and style variations in volumes that range from 500 (lavender) to 100,000 (blue) units per year. A visitor would notice many differences between the factories. Complex has far more production support staff to handle the numerous production loading and scheduling challenges, changeovers between colours and styles, and so on. Complex would also have more design change issues, supplier scheduling problems, and outbound warehousing, picking and distribution challenges. There would be much higher levels of idle time, overtime, inventory, rework and scrap because of the difficulty of balancing production and demand across a much wider product range. Because overheads are allocated on the basis of direct labour, blue pens are clobbered with 10 per cent of the much higher Complex overheads. The market price of blue pens is determined by focused factories such as Simple, so the blue pens from Complex appear to be unprofitable. As a result, the management of Complex considers that specialist products such as lavender – which sell at a premium – are the future of the business, and that blue pens are low priority. This strategy further increases overheads and costs, and perpetuates the myth that the unit cost of each pen is the same. Traditional cost systems often understate profits on high-volume products and overstate profits on low-volume, high-variety products. ABC principles would help the management of Complex to make more informed product decisions. The management of Simple has no need for another costing system; the current one works well for them.

ABC recognises that overhead costs do not just happen, but are caused by activities, such as holding products in store. ABC therefore seeks to break the business down into major processes – such as manufacture, storage and distribution – and then break each process into activities. For example, the distribution process would include such activities as picking, loading, transport and delivery. For each of these activities, there must be one cost driver: what is it that drives cost for that activity? For example, the cost driver for the storage activity may be the volume of a case, whereas the transport activity may be driven by weight. Once we know the cost driver, we need to know how many units of that cost driver are incurred for that activity, and the cost per unit for the cost driver. For example, the cost driver for the transportation activity may be the number of kilometres driven, and therefore cost per kilometre would be the cost per unit of the cost driver. This yields the cost of the activity and, when summed across all of the activities in a process, the total cost of that process.

ABC is difficult to implement because we need first to understand what the discrete processes are in a business where the existing links between functions are not well understood. There is then the issue of identifying the cost driver, which requires a fresh way of looking at each activity. For example, the cost driver for a warehouse fork-lift operator would be the number of pallets moved. The cost driver for stocking shelves would be the number of pieces that must be stacked in a given time period. A further problem occurs if there is more than one cost driver for a given activity. You are then faced with the same problem as with overhead allocation: on what basis should the cost drivers be weighted? Usually, this problem shows that activities have not been broken down into sufficient detail, and that more analysis is needed. ABC can therefore become resource-intensive to implement.

In spite of the implementation challenges, logistics and ABC go hand in hand (van Damme and van der Zon, 1999). It is a very rational way to analyse costs, and logistics practitioners recognise that providing a service is about managing a sequence of processes. Logistics or supply chain managers are particularly well placed to understand, analyse and apply ABC. They understand business processes and the activities that go with them. Theirs is a cross-functional task. The value chain stares them in the face.

The procedure of determining cost drivers is often considered to be more valuable than the ABC system itself. Activity-based management enables the cost structure of a business to be examined in a new light, allowing anomalies to be resolved and sources of waste highlighted. It may also help in better targeting investment decisions.

## 3.3.1 ABC example

Komplex GmBH has four production lines, which each operates for 8,000 hours a year. Each line makes a number of products, which are based on size and colour. Many changeovers are therefore required, each incurring set-up and maintenance costs. Traditionally the maintenance costs have been allocated on the basis of machine hours, so each production line is charged equally. This year, the maintenance budget of €1 million has been divided into four, so each line is charged with €250,000.

Sales and marketing are concerned that certain products are losing market share, and this is due to prices relative to the competition. All departments have been instructed to investigate costs and suggest improvements. How can activity-based costing improve this situation? By identifying the cost driver for maintenance, in this case the number of changeovers, costs can be allocated to each production line on this basis. Costs are then matched to the activity that generates them, so avoiding cross-subsidies.

The results are illustrated in Table 3.4. Maintenance costs have now been transferred to the production lines that incur the activity. For example, costs on

Table 3.4   **Different ways of allocating maintenance costs**

| Production lines | A | B | C | D | Total |
|---|---|---|---|---|---|
| Machine hours | 8,000 | 8,000 | 108,000 | 258,000 | 1,032,000 |
| No. of changeovers | 50 | 30 | 15 | 5 | 100 |
| Equal allocation | 250,000 | 250,000 | 250,000 | 250,000 | 1,000,000 |
| Allocation by activity | 500,000 | 300,000 | 150,000 | 50,000 | 1,000,000 |
| Difference | 250,000 | 50,000 | −100,000 | −200,000 | 1,000,000 |

line A have doubled to €500,000, while costs on line D have reduced to €50,000. ABC in this example has not taken cost out of the process, but has reallocated the costs to give a better understanding of the cost base. Complex is now in a better position to make decisions that affect the cost competitiveness of the product range.

### 3.3.2 Cost–time profile (CTP)

A key benefit of being able to cost logistics processes is that cost information can be used in conjunction with time information. The synergies of the two can then provide opportunities for identifying activities which create either value or waste.

The cost–time profile (CTP) (Bicheno, 2005) is a graph, which plots cumulative time against cumulative cost for a set of discrete activities that together form a process or a supply chain. The CTP utilises outputs from two sources:

- *activity times*: from the time-based process mapping (TBPM) process time recording system (see Chapter 5);
- *activity costs*: from a process costing system that is underpinned by activity-based costing.

As discussed earlier, ABC strives to achieve an equitable distribution of over-head costs to activities. Table 3.5 illustrates cumulative time and cost for a process comprising six activities.

Table 3.5   **Cumulative time and cost data by activity**

| Activity | A | B | C | D | E | F |
|---|---|---|---|---|---|---|
| Cumulative time (%) | 14 | 64 | 65 | 67 | 97 | 100 |
| Cumulative cost (%) | 25 | 45 | 83 | 85 | 95 | 100 |

Such data can be used to construct a *cost–time profile*. Bernon *et al.* (2003) record the process in terms of time and cost for a poultry product from receipt of live bird to delivery of finished product to the retailer. Overall, the process takes an average of 175 hours to complete. The profile shows areas that consume time and cost within the supply chain, highlighting those for future investigation that could yield savings. For example, distribution accounts for 35 per cent of process time, but only 3 per cent of total cost. Slicing and packaging are more in line, since they account for 25 per cent of total cost and are responsible for 28 per cent of the total process time. Figure 3.9 shows the time–cost profile for this process.

The profile shows that time and cost are *not related linearly*. Bicheno and Holweg (2008) stress the importance of interpreting both the horizontal and vertical lines of the CTP:

- *Long, horizontal lines* tend to occur when there is a relatively small increase in total cost as a result of an activity that runs over a relatively long period of time. An example is storage of finished product after slicing and packing.

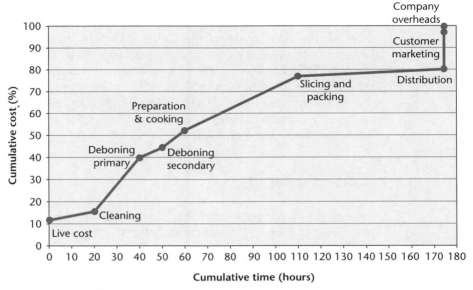

**Figure 3.9   Cost–time profile for poultry product**
(Source: After Bernon *et al.*, 2003, reprinted by permission of EIASM)

- *Steep, vertical lines* tend to occur when costs are consumed over a relatively short period of processing time. An example is deboning, where the cumulative cost rises sharply.

A focus on the long, horizontal sections of the CTP graph may help reduce cumulative time (see Chapter 5). A focus on steep, vertical lines may help reduce cumulative cost. The CTP can be used to prioritise improvement processes, as shown in Figure 3.10:

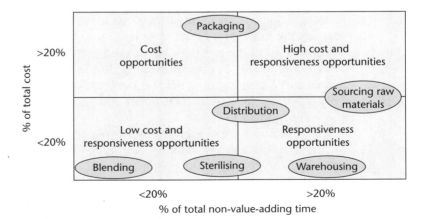

**Figure 3.10   Cost–time grid**
(Source: Whicker *et al.*, 2009)

Processes in the top right-hand box are prime candidates for savings in both time *and* cost. Processes in the bottom left-hand box are low on the list of priorities.

A further conclusion of the Cranfield study shown in Figure 3.8 was that decisions to optimise cost in one area could have a detrimental effect downstream (Whicker *et al.*, 2009). Large batch sizes reduced the need for machine changeovers in manufacturing. But this meant that the NDC was often running over capacity, and that overspill inventories had to be extracted and sent to third-party warehouses. Savings in manufacturing efficiency were causing extra costs and lead times in distribution.

### 3.3.3 Cost-to-serve (CTS)

So far, we have focused on manufacturing costs, but what about the cost of distributing products to customers? 'Putting the end-customer first' (Chapter 2) includes the need to serve customers in different ways. *Cost to serve* (CTS) is defined (Guerreiro *et al.*, 2008) as:

> **the cost of the administrative, commercial and logistics activities related to customer service delivery, as measured through ABC methodology.**

Identical manufactured products may be distributed in many different ways, each of which affects CTS. Examples of factors that may influence CTS are:

- Distribution channel used (for example, wholesalers, supermarkets, hypermarkets – see Case study 2.3).
- Delivery frequency (for routinely planned replenishment deliveries – daily, weekly, etc.).
- Customised deliveries (requiring special planning).
- Promotional activity (see Case study 2.1).
- Contractual terms used (for example, pricing by full truck loads, full pallet loads, pallet layers).

Recognising and allocating these costs to specific products and customers means *re-balancing* total costs better to reflect the actual CTS (Braithwaite and Samakh, 1998). Results of the re-balancing on customer profitability – made on the basis of margin after CTS – can be astonishing. In place of the traditional Pareto curve, a 'whale curve' may result, where 80 per cent of the margin after CTS comes from only 6 per cent of customers (Cooper and Kaplan, 1988; Guerreiro *et al.*, 2008) as shown in Figure 3.11.

This reveals a large proportion of loss-making customers for this Brazilian food business. Axing the loss-making customers needs to be undertaken with great care, because 'a significant proportion of service activity costs are fixed costs' (Guerreiro *et al.*, 2008). Such action would remove the contribution that these customers provide, thus reducing the margins of the remaining customers. Rather, knowledge of the causes of higher and lower margins and of relatively high CTS costs for certain customers can lead to better decisions regarding prices, commercial terms and investment.

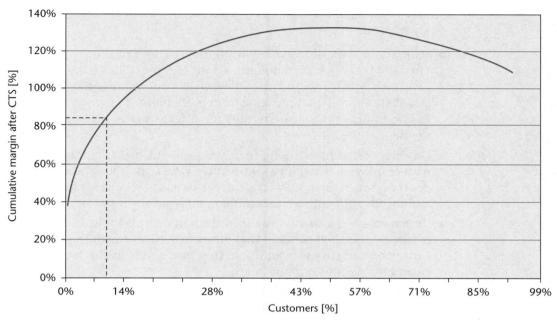

**Figure 3.11    Customer profitability curve**
(Source: After Guerreiro *et al.*, 2008)

## 3.4  A balanced measurement portfolio

*Key issues:* Who are the key stakeholders in a business, and what needs to be achieved in order to satisfy them? How can a balanced set of measures of performance be developed in order to address stakeholder satisfaction and stakeholder contribution?

Many organisations have suffered from undue emphasis on particular measures of performance within the firm. For example, a preoccupation with labour productivity may lead to excessive stocks of inbound parts ('do not run out of raw materials otherwise bonuses will suffer'). Such a preoccupation may also lead to excessive stocks of outbound products, because the most important priority is to keep workers busy, whether the product can be sold or not. While this priority may be good for productivity, it may well disrupt flow in the supply network: inbound parts are ordered too early, and outbound products are made too early. What is good for one measure (productivity in this case) is bad for others (inventories and material flow).

In reality, management today is faced with the challenge of performing across a whole range of objectives. Different groups of stakeholders in a firm include shareholders, employees, customers, suppliers, the local community and government. This is not a comprehensive list, and industries such as pharmaceuticals have other important stakeholders, including regulators such as the Drug Enforcement Agency. The challenge for the directors of a firm is to *balance* the diverse interests of these groups of stakeholders. We review the interests of each group in turn:

- *Shareholders* typically have a passing interest in a firm in which they invest. They will keep their shareholding as long as it provides a return that is competitive with other investments. Shareholders are impressed by high dividends and share appreciation resulting from profitability and growth of the business. Failure to deliver adequate returns often turns shareholders against the management of the day.

- *Employees* often have a long-term commitment to a firm, and are concerned with employment stability, competitive wages and job satisfaction. Failure to deliver on such goals may create negative reactions such as loss of motivation and loyalty, difficulty in recruitment, and various forms of industrial action.

- *Customers* are, in theory, the most important stakeholders in a free market economy. It is their demand that draws material through the supply network. Customers can choose from whom they buy, and failure to keep them satisfied creates the risk of loss of business.

- *Suppliers* are interested in such benefits as long-term business, involvement in new product development and, of course, payment on time. Failure to meet such benefits leads to sanctions such as disruption of supply and higher prices.

- *Local community*. Here, the interests are in the firm as a local employer, with a reputation for civic responsibility and long-term commitment to the region as an employer and as a ratepayer. Failure to deliver against such interests may lead to environmental disputes and difficulty in obtaining planning permission.

- *Government* is interested in the firm as a contributor to employment and value creation in the economy, and as a source of revenues. Failure to meet government laws, on the other hand, may lead to prosecution or even closure of the business.

Thus the directors of a business are faced with the need to manage the potentially conflicting interests of the stakeholders, keeping each within what Doyle (1994) refers to as a *tolerance zone*. Each stakeholder has a limit beyond which the risk of disruption to the business increases rapidly. An upper limit exists as well. For example, a preoccupation with profits may please shareholders for the time being, but may result in negatives from labour exploitation and low levels of investment. While bumper profits appear in year 1, these are rapidly eroded as the negatives cut in during later years. In the end, the whole business suffers. And customers can disrupt the business too: a preoccupation with customers at the expense of everything else can lead to shrinking margins and loss of focus. The challenge for the directors is to keep all stakeholders just satisfied, keeping each within the tolerance zone.

### 3.4.1  Balanced measures

While balance between stakeholders is one issue, another is the balance between financial and operational measures of performance, and between history and the future. Kaplan and Norton (1996) point to the shortcomings of traditional cost accounting systems. Traditional systems are geared to the needs of the stock market, and are essentially historical and financial in emphasis. Modern systems, they argue, need to be balanced between financial and operations, and between history and the future. A way of showing the relative emphasis between traditional measures and balanced measures is to show relative priorities by means of circles, where larger circles imply a greater priority and number of measures in use, as shown in Figure 3.12.

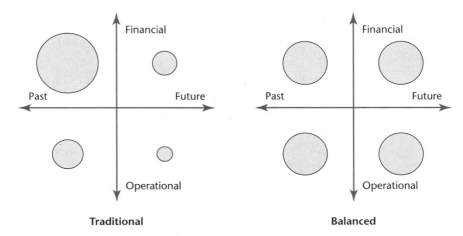

Figure 3.12  **Traditional and balanced priorities**

In developing a modern performance measurement system it is necessary to take all of these factors into account, and to create a balanced performance measurement system. That is the objective of the 'balanced scorecard'.

In practice, Kaplan and Norton propose that the balanced scorecard should balance the financial perspective (goals for future performance and measures of past performance) with similar goals and measures for the underlying drivers of long-term profitability. These drivers are identified as the business process perspective, the innovation and learning perspective, and the customer perspective.

## 3.4.2  Supply chain management and the balanced scorecard

Extending the balanced scorecard into the context of the supply chain, Brewer and Speh (2000) consider that performance measurement systems must be aligned to supply chain practices:

> **If firms talk about the importance of supply chain concepts, but continue to evaluate employees using performance measures that are . . . unaffected by supply chain improvements, then they will fail in their supply chain endeavours.**

Traditional performance measurements within a focal firm have a number of significant deficiencies. They often track individual activities within functions: this can promote the optimisation of the function rather than of the supply network as a whole.

As a general rule, effective cross-supply chain measures should have the following characteristics (Derocher and Kilpatrick, 2000):

- simple to understand;
- no more than ten in total number;
- representative of a significant causal relationship;
- have an associated target;
- capable of being shared across the supply chain.

The following are eight such measures, which can be adapted to focus on specific sectors:

- *on time in full, outbound*: a measure of customer orders fulfilled, complete and on time, conforming to specification;
- *on time in full, inbound*: a measure of supplier deliveries received, complete and on time, conforming to specification;
- *internal defect rates*: a measure of process conformance and control (rather than inspection);
- *new product introduction rate*: a measure of supply chain responsiveness to new product introduction;
- *cost reduction*: a measure of sustainable product and process improvement;
- *stock turns*: a measure of supply chain goods flow. This measure is useful when applied to supply chains focused on segments: as a 'blanket' measure, it can be misleading;
- *order to delivery lead time*: a measure of supply chain process responsiveness;
- *financial flexibility*: a measure of how easy it is to structure the supply chain for financial advantage (with international supply chains, channelling operations through low-tax locations for purposes of gaining supply chain cost benefits should be considered).

The main benefits of these measures are that they can be applied to all partners in a supply chain, and can thereby help to improve visibility and control *between* partners. Consistent with our view that different supply strategies are needed to support different product needs in the marketplace, the aim should be to identify consistent groups of measures that support specific supply strategies.

Just as important is the need to coordinate measures to improve visibility and control *within* a focal firm. The challenge is especially tough when there are many operating units in a large, decentralised organisation. Tesco provides an example of the communication needed by means of its 'corporate store steering wheel' (shown in Figure 3.13). Case study 1.1 describes the sheer scale of the Tesco operation – manned by some 400,000 employees in many countries. How do you keep so many people in such a large organisation 'facing the same direction' – that is, pursuing corporate strategy consistently? Tesco's answer has been to focus on 20 measures within five key areas – customer, finance, people, operations and community (Tesco, 2010).

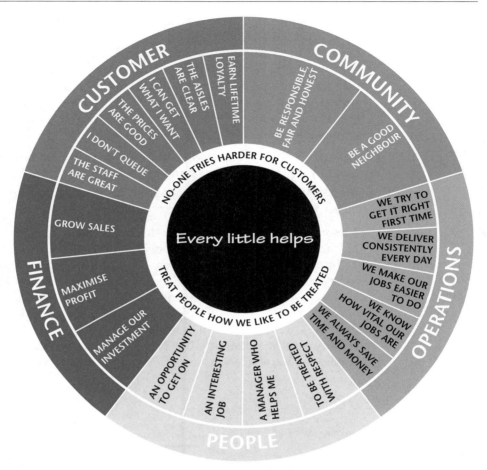

**Figure 3.13    Tesco's corporate store steering wheel**
(Source: Tesco, 2010)

> Throughout all our businesses across the world we measure our performance through the Steering Wheel, whether we work in distribution, head office or in stores. This helps maintain focus and balance in what counts to run each of our businesses successfully, be it wage costs or whether customers can get everything they want.

For example, each store receives a monthly update of its performance against each of the measures. 'Shopping lists' are selected extracts from Steering Wheel measures which direct individual groups of employees in their everyday jobs.

### 3.4.3    Supply chain financial model

Similar arguments can be made about linking supply chain practices to financial performance. Authors such as D'Avanzo *et al.* (2003) conclude that there is a strong link between supply chain performance and financial performance: 'supply chain leaders are showing market capitalization growth rates significantly higher than the industry growth rate'.

We have been working on a model which links decisions about the supply chain (such as inventory holding, outsourcing and supplier reduction) with a focal firm's financial performance (Johnson and Templar, 2007, 2010). The model is shown in Figure 3.14, and starts off with two ratios for a given financial period. These are adaptations of the ROI model we considered in 3.1.1 above (see, for example, Ellram and Liu, 2002):

- *cash generation* is the net cash inflow (operating profit before deducting depreciation) adjusted for changes in working capital divided by sales;
- *asset efficiency* is the sales divided by the value of the firm's total assets less current liabilities.

The product of these two ratios is the *supply chain ratio*.

Any tactical decision in the supply chain (five are shown) influences these ratios either positively or negatively. As a result, we can predict the impact of tactical supply chain decisions on financial performance. Equally, we can use the model to predict the impact of top-down decisions (for example, 'cut working capital', or 'increase sales through promotions') on supply chain positives and negatives. The link between positives and negatives – for example, reducing inventory improves liquidity but places adverse pressure on relationships with customers and suppliers – is a further example *of trade-offs* (section 1.4.4) at work.

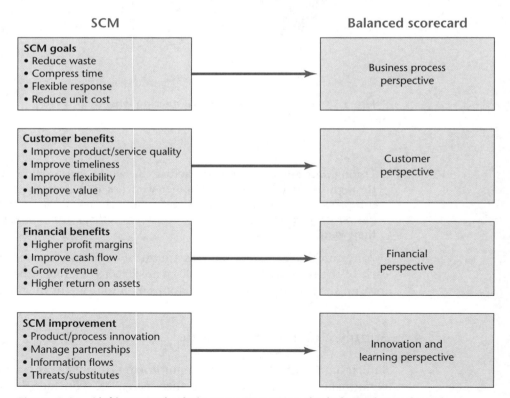

**Figure 3.14   Linking supply chain management to the balanced scoreboard**
(Source: After Brewer and Speh, 2000)

## 3.5  Supply chain operations reference model (SCOR)

*Key issues:*  How can *process* thinking be applied to measures across the supply chain? What is the supply chain operations reference model, and how is it constructed?

The previous two sections looked at process-based performance measures within an organisation. This section reviews a model that places a focal firm in the context of the supply chain. In order to help companies to understand their supply

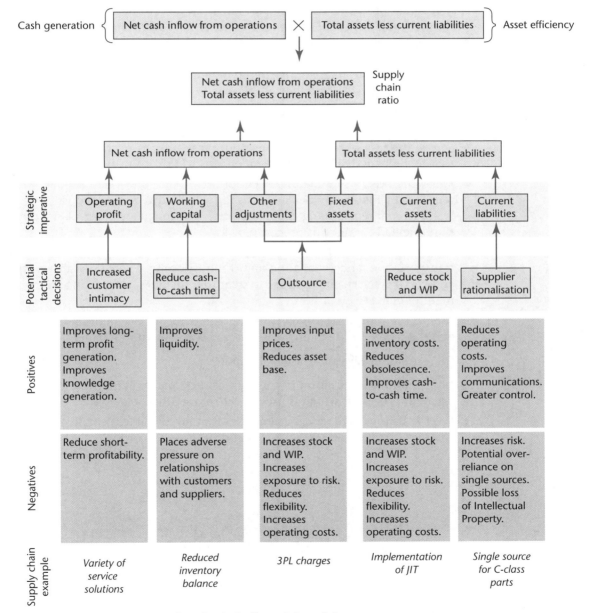

**Figure 3.15  Supply chain financial model**
(Source: © Cranfield and PA Consulting Group)

chain performance and opportunities for improvement, a cross-industry frame-work has been developed by the Supply Chain Council. You can visit the Council website at http://www.supply-chain.org.

This section gives an introduction to SCOR based on publicly available material; in order to obtain detailed benchmarking data from the model, your organisation would need to become a member. In common with ABC, the SCOR model uses a process-based approach to the supply chain.

The supply chain operations reference model (SCOR) is founded on five distinct management processes. The supply chain is viewed in terms of overlapping management processes – source, make, deliver and return – within an integrated planning framework that encompasses all of the organisations in the chain, as shown in Figure 3.16. It is a process-based version of Figure 1.1 in Chapter 1. The management processes of the 'focal firm' are seen as linked with corresponding processes within supplier and customer organisations. The five distinct management processes can be described as follows:

- *Plan*: the tasks of planning demand and supply set within an overall planning system that covers activities such as long-term capacity and resource planning.
- *Source*: the task of material acquisition, set within an overall sourcing system that includes activities such as vendor certification and vendor contracting.
- *Make*: the task of production execution, set within an overall production system that includes activities such as shop scheduling. Any added value activity (e.g. material repackaging at a distribution centre; quality control at a production line) falls under this process type as well.
- *Deliver*: the day-to-day tasks of managing demand, orders, warehouse and transportation, and installation and commissioning. These tasks are set within an overall delivery management system that includes order rules and management of delivery quantities.
- *Return*: the return of non-conforming goods for replacement or rectification, and the recycling of materials no longer needed by the customer.

There are three levels to the SCOR model:

- *Level 1*: a broad definition of the plan, source, make, deliver and return management processes, which is used to set competitive objectives.
- *Level 2*: defines core process categories that are possible scenarios of a supply chain (e.g. make to stock; make to order; engineer to order).

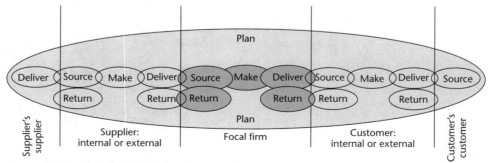

**Figure 3.16 Five distinct management processes**
(Source: After Supply Chain Council www.supply-chain.org)

- *Level 3*: provides the process breakdown needed to describe each element that comprises the level 2 categories. Detailed performance metrics are set at this level.

Table 3.6 shows 13 metrics at level 1 in the SCOR model, and is taken from the SCOR website (http://www.supply-chain.org). As with processes, the model's hierarchical structure is repeated also for the metrics. This means that the SCOR model provides a breakdown of level 2 and level 3 subcomponents of the level 1 performance metrics. The intention is that an individual company should not attempt to be 'best in class' in all areas. Rather, a given company should target its strength in four to six selected areas to create differentiation in the marketplace. The company will also need to ensure that it stays competitive in the other areas. Note that the customer-facing measures are what we referred to in section 3.2 as 'discretionary costs', while the internal-facing measures are 'engineered costs'. By drilling down into levels 2 and 3 of the SCOR model, the aim is to identify the cost drivers and so convert discretionary costs into engineered costs: that is, to convert supply chain performance directly into revenue, cost and margin. Also note that the internal-facing metrics encourage improvement of ROI (section 3.1) by reducing costs and maximising asset turns. Participating companies in the Supply Chain Council may obtain benchmarking information on how their organisation's performance compares with others: see the website given above.

In order to illustrate how such concepts could be applied in practice, Table 3.7 shows actual performance against the SCOR level 1 metrics for a given company. It also shows how those metrics compared with the SCOR database in terms of what was needed to achieve parity with the 'competitive population', what was needed to gain advantage and what was needed to show superior performance. Where is this supply chain positioned in terms of its competitive performance?

Table 3.6   **Supply chain performance is tied to measurements that can be benchmarked**

| | Customer-facing | | Internal-facing | |
|---|---|---|---|---|
| *SCOR Level 1 supply chain management* | *Supply chain reliability* | *Flexibility and responsiveness* | *Cost* | *Assets* |
| Delivery performance | ◀ | | | |
| Order fulfillment performance | ◀ | | | |
|   Fill rate | | | | |
|   Order fulfillment lead time | | | | |
| Perfect order fulfillment | ◀ | | | |
| Supply chain response time | | ◀ | | |
| Production flexibility | | ◀ | | |
| Total logistics management cost | | | ◀ | |
| Value-added productivity | | | ◀ | |
| Warranty cost or returns processing cost | | | ◀ | |
| Cash-to-cash cycle time | | | | ◀ |
| Inventory days of supply | | | | ◀ |
| Asset turns | | | | ◀ |

(Source: http://www.supply-chain.org)

Table 3.7  **Supply chain performance evaluated within the context of the competitive environment**

| | | Supply chain scorecard v 3.0 | | Performance v competitive population | | |
|---|---|---|---|---|---|---|
| | Overview metrics | SCOR level 1 metrics | Actual | Parity | Advantage | Superior |
| | | Delivery performance to commit date | 50% | 85% | 90% | 95% |
| EXTERNAL | Supply chain reliability | Fill rates | 63% | 94% | 96% | 98% |
| | | Perfect order fulfillment (on time in full) | 0% | 80% | 85% | 90% |
| | | Order fulfillment lead times (customer to customer) | 7 days | 7 days | 5 days | 3 days |
| | Flexibility and responsiveness | Production flexibility (days master schedule fixed) | 45 days | 30 days | 25 days | 20 days |
| INTERNAL | Cost | Total logistics management costs as % of revenues | 19% | 13% | 8% | 3% |
| | | Warranty cost, returns and allowances | NA | NA | NA | NA |
| | | Value-added per-employee productivity | $122K | $156K | $306K | $460K |
| | Assets | Inventory days of supply | 119 days | 55 days | 38 days | 22 days |
| | | Cash-to-cash cycle time | 196 days | 80 days | 46 days | 19 turns |
| | | Net asset turns (working capital) | 2.2 turns | 8 turns | 12 turns | 28 days |

Not very well, it seems! *All* of the level 1 metrics are below parity with the exception of order fulfillment lead times. External metrics such as delivery performance and perfect order fulfillment are seriously adrift. Production flexibility is way behind the competitive population, suggesting that the master schedule is 'fixed' for too long a period – and there will no doubt be underlying causes of that. Internal measures are not in good shape either, with a poor cost performance and a seriously uncompetitive asset utilisation record. The model associates level 2 and 3 process elements to the various metrics, so that, once the worst performing metrics have been identified, the user has an indication of what are the processes to look after in order to reduce the gap.

## Summary

### What is 'value' in the context of the supply chain?

- Return on investment (ROI) is a widely used method for measuring shareholder value. ROI encourages logistics management to control costs, working capital and fixed assets.

- Logistics is increasingly concerned with funds flow as well as material flow and information flow (Chapter 1). It is a cross-functional discipline that addresses management processes of plan, source, make, deliver and return. These processes are repeated across the supply chain.

- Traditional cost accounting is unhelpful in making logistics-related decisions because it is insensitive to processes and cost drivers. Traditional cost accounting tends to understate profits on high-volume products and overstate profits on low-volume/high-variety products.

### How can logistics costs be better represented?

- Logistics costs can be better described by using a variety of methods of allocating costs to products. The purpose of such a variety of allocations is to gain better information about the cost base of logistics operations, and hence to take better decisions. For example, direct product profitability (DPP) attempts to allocate logistics costs more specifically to products by considering how they use fixed resources. Another principle is to convert discretionary costs such as product availability into engineering costs such as profit contribution from increased sales.

- Activity-based costing (ABC) seeks to understand what factors drive costs, and how costs are incurred by logistics processes that span the organisation – and the supply chain in general. It is essentially a process-based view of costing, and again seeks to enhance the quality of logistics decision making. Cost-to-serve (CTS) is an extension of ABC thinking that seeks to identify how distribution and service costs vary between customers.

- Financial measures that are rooted in the past are insufficient for taking logistics decisions in today's fast-moving environment. A balanced measurement portfolio is called for, one that takes into account the needs of different stakeholders in a business. A balanced measurement portfolio is extended into the supply chain by means of the supply chain operations reference model (SCOR).

## Discussion questions

1 Explain what is meant by the term *value* in a supply chain. How can value best be measured in a supply chain context?

2 Why are processes important in terms of managing logistics? Suggest how the processes of plan, source, make, deliver and return might differ in the case of the two factories Simple and Complex described in section 3.3.

3 What are the advantages of cutting the 'total cost cube' in different ways? Summarise the different perspectives on logistics costs provided by fixed/variable, direct/indirect and engineered/discretionary costs, and by activity-based costing.

4 Suggest balanced measurement portfolios for the two factories Simple and Complex described in section 3.3. In particular, suggest key performance measures in the areas of strategy, process and capability.

## References

Atrill, P. and McLaney, E. (2008) *Managing Accounting for Non-Specialists*, 6th edn. Harlow: Financial Times/Prentice Hall.

Bernon, M., Mena, C., Templar, S. and Whicker, L. (2003) 'Costing waste in supply chain processes: a European food drink industry case study', *Proceedings of the 10th International EurOMA Conference, Copenhagen, June 2003*, Vol. 1, pp. 345–54.

Bicheno, J. (2005) *The 'New' Lean Toolbox*, Buckingham: Picsie Books.

Bicheno, J. and Holweg, M. (2008) *The Lean Toolbox – the essential guide to lean transformation*, 4th edn. Buckingham: Picsie Books.

Braithwaite, A. and Samakh, E. (1998) 'The cost-to-serve method', *International Journal of Logistics Management*, Vol. 9, No. 1, pp. 69–84.

Brewer, P.C. and Speh, T.W. (2000) 'Using the balanced scorecard to measure supply chain performance', *Journal of Business Logistics*, Vol. 21, No. 1, pp. 75–93.

CIMA (1989) *Management Accounting, Official Terminology*. London: CIMA.

Cooper, R. and Kaplan, R.S. (1988) 'Measure costs right: make the right decisions', *Harvard Business Review*, September/October, pp. 96–105.

Dale, B.G. and Plunkett, J.J. (1995) *Quality Costing*, 2nd edn. London: Chapman & Hall.

D'Avanzo, R., van Lewinski, H. and van Wassenhove, L. (2003) 'The link between supply and performance', *Harvard Business Review*, Nov./Dec., pp. 40–7.

Derocher, R. and Kilpatrick, J. (2000) 'Six supply chain lessons for the new millennium', *Supply Chain Management Review*, Vol. 3, No. 4, pp. 34–40.

Doyle, P. (1994) *Marketing Management and Strategy*. New York: Prentice Hall.

Ellram, L.M. and Liu, B. (2002) 'The financial impact of supply management', *Supply Chain Management Review*, Vol. 6, pp. 30–37.

Guerreiro, R., Rodrigues Bio, S. and Vasquez Villamor Merschmann, E. (2008) 'Cost-to-serve measurement and customer profitability analysis', *The International Journal of Logistics Management*, Vol. 19, No. 3, pp. 389–407.

Johnson, M. and Templar, S. (2007) 'The influence of supply chains on a company's financial performance', London: PA Consulting Group.

Johnson, M. and Templar, S. (2010) 'The relationships between supply chain and firm performance: the development and testing of a unified proxy', *International Journal of Production, Distribution and Logistics Management* (forthcoming).

Kaplan, R. and Norton, D. (1996) *The Balanced Scorecard*. Boston, MA: Harvard Business School Press.

Tesco (2010) 'Tesco Careers', at http://www.tesco-careers.com/home/about-us/visions-and-values

van Damme, D.A. and van der Zon, F.L. (1999) 'Activity based costing and decision support', *International Journal of Logistics Management*, Vol. 10, No. 1, pp. 71–82.

Whicker, L., Bernon, M., Templar, S. and Mena, C. (2009) 'Understanding the relationships between time and cost to improve supply chain performance', *International Journal of Production Economics*, Vol. 121, No. 2, pp. 641–50.

### Suggested further reading

Camerinelli, E. (2009) *Measuring the Value of the Supply Chain*. Farnham: Gower.

Ellram, L. (2002) 'Strategic cost management in the supply chain: a purchasing and supply management perspective', Center for Advanced Purchasing Studies, Arizona State University.

# Part Two

# LEVERAGING LOGISTICS OPERATIONS

Part Two uses the foundation of logistics management and strategy developed in Part One to concentrate on key tasks for logistics operations. This covers the centre panel of our logistics model: the flow of materials, lead times and the network of operations in a global context.

Despite its role in corporate success, the logistics task ultimately boils down to orchestrating the flow of materials and information in the supply chain. The aim is to support products and services in the marketplace better than competitors. You could say that the logistics task is about making strategic objectives a reality by executing against demand and making value propositions to customers a reality. Logistics delivers value. Increasingly, this means improving sustainability, reducing operational risks in the international pipeline and considering a focal firm's social responsibilities in an international context.

Chapters 4 and 5 look at the basic dimensions of logistics operations: their international reach and their contribution to a timely response to demand. Chapters 6 and 7 then take that thinking a level higher by introducing key managerial concepts that support logistics operations. Chapter 6 addresses the immense amount of detail that is needed to plan and control material flow – both in the focal firm and more broadly in the supply chain. Chapter 7 reviews the role of just-in-time and lean thinking in reducing waste in the supply chain, and in improving coordination of material movements. We also review the role of agility in elevating the speed of response to uncertain end-customer demand.

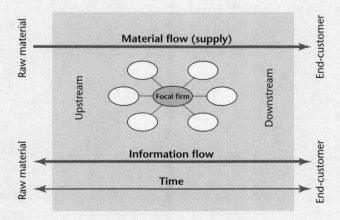

# CHAPTER 4

# Managing logistics internationally

**Objectives**

*The intended objectives of this chapter are to:*

- identify challenges that internationalisation presents to logistics management;
- analyse the structure and management of a global logistics network.

*By the end of this chapter you should be able to:*

- understand the forces which are shaping international logistics;
- understand challenges of international logistics networks;
- understand how to begin to balance these in organising for international logistics – bearing in mind risks and sustainability considerations

## Introduction

The early roots of logistics are in international transport, which was a central element of many fundamental models in economic theory. In traditional location theory, for example, transport costs were optimised in relation to distance to market and production locations. The origins of internationalisation can be traced back to the expanding trade routes of early civilisations. Discoveries made in excavations from Europe, Asia, Africa and the Americas reveal artefacts made hundreds or even thousands of miles away from the site, at the edges of their respective known worlds. Developments in transport, navigation and communication have progressively expanded our horizons. Measured in transport time and costs, the world has shrunk to the dimensions of a 'global village'. Many take for granted the availability of products from around the world and safe, fast intercontinental travel on container carriers and aircraft. It is in this context that a clear link exists between logistics and economic development. The connectivity of all regions of the world is essential for international trade. As a result, many projects aimed at supporting regional economic development focus on the infrastructure needed to support integration into the global economy.

The logistics dimension of internationalisation conjures up a vision of parts flowing seamlessly from suppliers to customers located anywhere in the world, and a supply network that truly spans the entire globe. Often basic products such as deep-freeze pizzas combine a multitude of locations from which ingredients are sourced, and an international transport network that links production locations to warehouses and multiple stores. The enormous geographical span of this logistics system cannot be recognised in the price of the product. This can be explained by transport having become just a commodity in the global village. At the micro level of the individual company, however, the reality is that there are few examples of truly global supply chains. There are many barriers to such a vision. For example, local autonomy, local standards and local operating procedures make the integration of information flow and material flow a challenging task. Local languages and brand names increase product complexity. Global supply chains are made more complicated by uncertainty and difficulty of control. Uncertainty arises from longer lead times and lack of knowledge over risks and local market conditions. Coordination becomes more complex because of additional language and currency transactions, more stages in the distribution process, and local government intervention through customs and trade barriers. But there are many instances where a truly globalised logistics system is not necessary, and where 'internationalisation' is a more accurate description. Internationalisation is an increasing feature of the majority of supply chains. International sourcing of component parts and international markets for finished goods are extending as world trade increases. The move of supply and production to 'off-shore' locations has been steady and stable. However, this does not mean that internationalisation is without risks. Challenges in migrating supply to remote locations, breakdowns in product flow, environmental considerations resulting from greater shipping distances and corporate social responsibility considerations are added challenges and considerations.

The factoring in of risks, environmental and social considerations into the design of international logistics operations has made longstanding logistics formulas more problematic to apply. And it has helped the mindset of logistics managers to move beyond 'available everywhere at low cost' towards a more qualified approach of 'available at a certain price and within a defined risk/reliability'.

Within the context of this changing global landscape for logistics, the overall aim of this chapter is to analyse the internationalisation of logistics, and to explore how to begin to organise international supply chains. Figure 4.1 shows the framework for this chapter: drivers and enablers need to be countered by risk

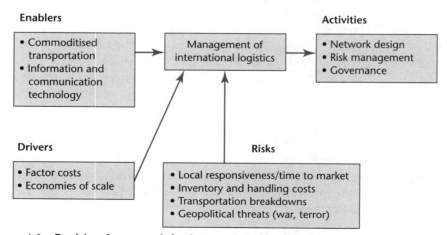

**Figure 4.1  Decision framework for international logistics**

factors in organising logistics internationally. Essentially, this means developing and designing an international logistics network, managing risks and developing international governance structures, while keeping social responsibility and environmental concerns in mind.

Key issues This chapter addresses seven key issues:

1  **Drivers and logistics implications of internationalisation:** the trade-off facing internationally operating businesses.

2  **The tendency towards internationalisation:** three strategies for improving the transition to global supply chains.

3  The challenges of international logistics and location: barriers to international logistics.

4  **Organising for international logistics:** proposes principles by which international logistics networks can be organised, including offshoring considerations.

5  **Reverse logistics:** developing the 'returns' process.

6  **Managing for risk readiness:** two levels of risk readiness and several specific steps to take.

7  **Corporate social responsibility in the supply chain:** the need to include social responsibility in supply chain design.

## 4.1  Drivers and logistics implications of internationalisation

*Key issue:* What are the trade-offs between responsiveness to local markets and economies of scale?

The business approach towards internationalisation is not taking place according to any common pattern. In assessing the nature of cross-border logistics, three questions can be asked:

- Does internationalisation imply a universal global approach to supply chain management?

- Does internationalisation require a 'global' presence in every market?

- Does internationalisation distinguish between the companies that globally transfer knowledge and those that do not?

The arguments presented in this section suggest that the answer to each of these questions is 'no'.

The 'single business' concept of structuring the supply chain in the form of uniform approaches in each country is losing ground. 'McColonisation' was effectively abolished when McDonald's announced localisation of its business in such areas as marketing and local relations. In response to local crises in quality, and suffering from local competition, the corporate headquarters were downsized to help empower the local organisation. (This also means localising the focal firm's human resource practices, a point we return to in Chapter 8.) The same applied to the Coca-Cola Company, which abandoned 'CocaColonisation' – based on a universal product, marketing, and production and distribution model – for the same reasons. In favour of local brands and product varieties, Procter & Gamble is doing the same. In supply chains we find regional variations in the application of international principles.

This does not mean to say that localisation is the new mainstay. Unilever, a traditionally localised competitor of Procter & Gamble, has announced a decrease in the number of brands, and has rationalised operations away from strict localisation over the past decade, and probably will continue to do so for a while. Somewhere between local and global extremes, Procter & Gamble and Unilever will meet each other in a new competitive area.

Looking at the different drivers of internationalisation, three basic global shifts in international investment and trade have been identified, with a possible fourth coming to the forefront in modern markets, as listed in Table 4.1. Such shifts of course have an impact on international trade and the flow of goods. In particular, destinations change as well as logistics requirements. The 'fourth generation' recognises the logistics trade-off between responsiveness to local markets, environmental and risk concerns with the benefits of internationalisation.

**Table 4.1    The fourth-generation global shift in Europe**

| Generation | First | Second | Third | Fourth |
|---|---|---|---|---|
| Period | 1950s–1960s | From 1960 | From 1980 | Emerging now |
| Primary drivers | Labour shortage | Labour costs and flexibility | Market entrance | Responsiveness to customer orders, risk reduction, and social and environmental responsibility |
| Shift of labour and investment towards | European countries without labour shortage | Newly industrialised countries, low labour cost countries | Eastern Europe, China, Latin America | Market region for responsiveness and lower risk. To low-cost region for social responsiveness initiatives |
| Transport routes | Still significantly continental | Increasingly intercontinental | Adding additional destination regions | Beginning to refocus on continental |
| Nature of international flow of goods | Physical distribution of finished products from new production locations | Shipping parts to production locations and exporting finished products | Physical distribution towards new market regions | Shipping (semi-) finished products to markets, reduction of eco footprint and risk exposure where possible |

At a company level, generic drivers of internationalisation include:

- a search for low factor and supply costs (land, labour, materials);
- the need to follow customers internationally in order to be able to supply locally and fast;
- a search for new geographical market areas;

- a search for new learning opportunities and exposure to knowledge (such as by locating in Silicon Valley – a 'hot spot' in development of international electronics, software and internet industries).

The importance of these drivers varies by company and with time. Considering the sequence of global shifts, proximity to production factors such as labour and low material costs can be considered more basic than market- or even knowledge-related drivers. Furthermore, the importance of the respective drivers is dependent upon the internationalisation strategy of the company involved. Table 4.2 provides examples of strategic contexts, and – in the bottom row – the logistics implications of those strategies. The multi-domestic and global strategies represent two extremes, while the integrated network strategy represents a balance between them. The consequences of this 'balancing act' for logistics are analysed below. Case study 4.1 about Airbus offers illustrations of how complex and comprehensive supply chain management in an international context can be and how hard it can be to manage against risks for service and value.

**Table 4.2   Dimensions of different internationalism strategies**

| Dimension | Setting in a pure multi-domestic strategy | Setting in a pure global strategy | Setting in an integrated network strategy |
|---|---|---|---|
| Competitive moves | Stand-alone by country | Integrated across countries | Moves based on local autonomy and contribution of lead subsidiaries, globally coordinated |
| Product offering | Fully customised in each country | Fully standardised worldwide | Partly customised, partly standardised |
| Location of value-adding activities | All activities in each country | Concentration: one activity in each (different) country | Dispersal, specialisation, and interdependence |
| Market participation | No particular pattern; each country on its own | Uniform worldwide | Local responsiveness and worldwide sharing of experience |
| Marketing approach | Local | Integrated across countries | Variation in coordination levels per function and activity |
| Logistical network | Mainly national; sourcing, storage and shipping on a national level and duplicated by country | Limited number of production locations that ship to markets around the globe through a highly internationalised network with limited localised warehouse and resources | Balanced local sourcing and shipping (e.g. for customised products and local specialities) and global sourcing and shipping (for example for commodities) |

(Source: Based on Yip, 1989, and Bartlett and Ghoshal, 1989)

---

**CASE STUDY 4.1**

## Launching a new aeroplane at Airbus

When Airbus introduced its Airbus A380 double decker superplane in January 2005 to the press and the world it was an impressive show that brought out government leaders and made headlines all over the world. A little while later, however, delays to the

▶

actual delivery of the first planes were announced. The causes for this were largely found in the international supply chain and its design.

In October 2006, the then Airbus president and CEO Christian Streiff said: 'This is a very long and complex value chain. While everyone on board was on top of their job, the production process . . . not the aeroplane . . . but the production process has one, big flaw – one weak link in the chain: that of the design of the electrical harnesses installation in the forward and aft fuselage. To be clear: this is the weak link in the manufacturing chain, this is the reason why ramping up the production is hampered. But the electrical harnesses are not the root causes why we at Airbus are in a crisis. The issue of the electrical harnesses is extremely complex, with 530 km of cables, 100,000 wires, and 40,300 connectors.'

This quote clearly points to the supply chain and design as the cause for delays. In addition to the wiring issues there were some further supplier-related challenges as well. A lot of different locations are an inherent aspect of the supply chain, not least because customers and sponsoring countries require a share of the production process to be located in their countries. So many locations, and design and make tasks are involved. This created a lot of challenges that needed detailed coordination. For example, one small component was supposed to be built in a plant in Italy for which a location was selected, but no permit had been granted by local authorities. It turned out that there were some very old olive trees on this site that had protected status. This is just one example of how local considerations can be specific and detailed, hard to predict yet potentially having a big impact on the supply chain. Additionally a Japanese supplier of seats was said to have caused further delivery delays. A complex project such as developing and building a new plane across multiple countries and locations can be very challenging in terms of scale and scope.

When Airbus launched the A380, the early signs of supply chain shortfalls already existed, but they were well hidden. Under the paint, screws were missing. Behind the panels, lots of parts were missing. The launch was a great spectacle, but you cannot hide a supply chain that is not working behind some paint for long . . . .

(Source: quote from: http://blog.seattlepi.com/aerospace/archives/107302.asp)

### Question

1 Brainstorm in groups how locating parts of the supply chain around the world might be more difficult than locating it on a single site and location.

## 4.1.1 Logistical implications of internationalisation

Internationalising logistics networks holds consequences for inventory, handling and transport policies.

### Inventory

Centralising inventories across multiple countries can hold advantages in terms of inventory-holding costs and inventory levels that are especially relevant for high-value products. On the other hand, internationalisation may lead to product proliferation due to the need for localisation of products and the need to respond to specific local product/market opportunities.

### Handling

Logistics service practices may differ across countries as well as regulation on storage and transport. Adjusting handling practices accordingly is a prerequisite for internationalisation. Furthermore, the opportunity to implement best practice across various facilities may also be possible. Both of these practices assist the process of internationalisation.

### Transport

Owing to internationalisation, logistics pipelines are extended and have to cope with differences in infrastructure across countries, while needing to realise delivery within the time-to-market. This may drive localisation. On the other hand, the opportunity for global consolidation may drive international centralisation.

Within this final, central, consideration in the globalise–localise dimension of logistics, global businesses face a challenge that can be summarised in terms of a simple trade-off between the benefits of being able to consolidate operations globally on the one hand, and the need to compete in a timely manner on the other.

## 4.1.2 Time-to-market

Time-to-market has particular significance for the management of the global logistics pipeline. The subject of time is considered in depth in Chapter 5, although we shall touch on the following issues here:

- product obsolescence;
- inventory-holding costs.

### Product obsolescence

The extended lead time inherent in international logistics pipelines means that products run the risk of becoming obsolete during their time in transit. This is especially true for products in industries with rapid technological development, such as personal computing and consumer electronics, and for fashion goods such as clothing and footwear.

### Inventory-holding costs

Lead time spent in the logistics pipeline increases the holding cost of inventory. In addition to the time spent in physical transit, goods travelling internationally will incur other delays. These occur at consolidation points in the process, such as in warehouses where goods are stored until they can be consolidated into a full load, such as a container. Delay frequently occurs at the point of entry into a country while customs and excise procedures are followed. We review these issues in more depth in Chapter 7.

### 4.1.3  Global consolidation

Global consolidation occurs as managers seek to make best use of their assets and to secure lowest-cost resources. This approach leads to assets such as facilities and capital equipment being used to full capacity, so that economies of scale are maximised. Resources are sourced on a global scale to minimise cost by maximising purchasing leverage and to pursue economies of scale. The types of resource acquired in this way include all inputs to the end-product, such as raw materials and components, and also labour and knowledge. Familiar features of global consolidation include:

- sourcing of commodity items from low-wage economies;
- concentration at specific sites;
- bulk transportation.

*Sourcing commodity items from low-wage economies*

Two sourcing issues are used by internationally operating organisations:

- consolidation of purchasing of all company divisions and companies;
- sourcing in low-wage economies.

Internationally operating organisations seek to consolidate the purchasing made by all their separate divisions and operating companies. This allows them to place large orders for the whole group, which enables them to minimise costs by using their bargaining power and by seeking economies of scale. At its extreme, a company may source all of its requirements from its range of a given commodity, such as a raw material or a component, from a single source.

Internationally operating companies are on a constant quest to find new, cheaper sources of labour and materials. This trend led to the move of manufacturing from developed industrial regions to lower-cost economies. Examples of this are:

- Western Europe to Eastern Europe;
- USA to Mexico;
- Japan to China, India and Vietnam.

These developing economies have seen impressive growth over recent years. This has led to increased prosperity for their people and rising standards of living. However, these advances in social standards raise the cost of labour and other resources. Therefore, the relentless search for the lowest production cost has led to some companies re-sourcing commodity items to lower-wage countries in Asia, North Africa and South America.

In some cases this movement of facilities around the globe has come full circle, with Asian companies setting up plants in the UK not only to gain access to the EU market but also to take advantage of lower overall costs.

## Logistics in the news

*The subject of air miles appears regularly in media headlines today. Here are two contrasting views of what is happening.*

Supermarkets and food producers are taking their products on huge journeys, despite pledging to cut their carbon emissions. Home-grown products are being transported thousands of miles for processing before being put on sale back in Britain. Jason Torrance, campaigns director of Transport 2000, the environmental transport group, said 'we are producing food in one corner of the world, packing it in another and then shipping it somewhere else. It's mad.'

Dawnfresh, a Scottish seafood company that supplies supermarkets and other large retailers, cut 70 jobs last year after deciding to ship its scampi more than 8,000km to China to be shelled by hand, then shipped back to Scotland and breaded for sale in Britain. The company said it was forced to make the move by commercial pressures. 'This seems a bizarre thing to do but the reality is that the numbers don't stack up any other way', says Andrew Stapley, a director. 'We are not the first in the industry that has had to do this. Sadly, it's cheaper to process overseas than in the UK, and companies like us are having to do this to remain competitive.'
(Source: Jon Ungoed-Thomas, *Sunday Times*, 20 May 2007)

Commissioned by World Flowers, a study was carried out by Adrian Williams of Cranfield University's Natural Resources Department to establish the actions needed to reduce Sainsbury's [a retailer] carbon footprint regarding Kenyan roses. Results have provided a fresh challenge to much current thinking on local sourcing and the impact of air freight. The high environmental cost of heating and lighting for growing roses in the Netherlands outweighed emissions caused by flying them in from Kenya, with its naturally warm all-year temperatures. It also indicated that carbon dioxide ($CO_2$) emissions from Kenyan roses were just 17 per cent of Dutch roses, including the larger impact of $CO_2$ emissions to high altitude by air freighting. The study found that 6kg of $CO_2$ was produced per dozen Kenyan roses, as opposed to 35kg for production in the Netherlands. Whereas 99 per cent of the Dutch emissions were caused by producing the roses, only 7 per cent of the emissions from the Kenyan flowers were accounted for by growing them there. In contrast, nearly 99 per cent of the $CO_2$ emissions from the Kenyan roses were accounted for by the 6,000km clocked up by air freighting them to the UK.
(Source: http://www.cranfield.ac.uk/cww/perspex)

### Question

1  What are the pros and cons of sourcing commodity items in low wage economies?

## Concentration at specific sites

Consolidation of purchasing applies not only to commodity goods but also to high-value or scarce resources. Research and development skills are both high value and scarce. Therefore there is an incentive to locate at certain sites to tap into specific pools of such skills. Examples of this are 'Silicon Valley' in California and 'Silicon Fen' near Cambridge as centres of excellence in IT. Companies originally located in these areas to benefit from research undertaken in the nearby universities.

Companies become more influential in directing such research and benefiting from it if they have a significant presence in these locations. This is helped if global research is consolidated onto a single site. While this may mean missing out on other sources of talent, consolidated R&D gives a company a presence that helps to attract the bright young minds that will make their mark in these industries in the future, and it allows synergies to develop between research teams.

## Activity 4.1

An international logistics pipeline is represented in Figure 4.2 as a set of logistics processes that are connected together like sections of a pipe. However, the sections may be in different countries – requiring planning and coordination of the processes on a global scale. The international pipeline therefore has a number of special characteristics, some of which are suggested in Case study 4.2 on the previous page. Use Table 4.3 to make a list of the characteristics that you believe make a global logistics pipeline different from one that operates only nationally.

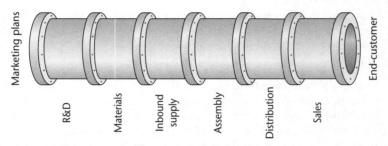

**Figure 4.2   The international logistics pipeline**

Table 4.3   **Characteristics of the international pipeline**

| Elements of the pipeline | Special characteristics of the international pipeline |
|---|---|
| Research and development | |
| Material/component sourcing | |
| Inbound supply | |
| Assembly | |
| Distribution | |
| Selling/retailing | |

## Bulk transportation

One of the more obvious advantages of operating a company in a global manner is the cost advantage of consolidated transportation. Taking Procter & Gamble as an example, 350 ship containers, 9,000 rail car and 97,000 truck loads are transported every day. The opportunity for cost saving by coordinating these movements and maximising utilisation is significant.

### 4.1.4  Risk in international logistics

In addition to time-to-market and inventory risks, events of recent years have forced companies to adapt to the new supply chain reality of expecting the unexpected. Companies are not only responding to current volatility and geopolitical risks, they are also developing new risk management approaches based upon the realisation that decades of globalising supply chains has come at a price: a heightened and different risk profile.

#### Geopolitical threats

The 2003 SARS crisis and the second Gulf War were major events in and of themselves; they were also consecutive and had huge impacts on supply chain continuity and execution feasibility. Major trade routes had to be altered and global travel was limited. In addition, structurally heightened government security measures and screening are indicators of risks involved in international logistics. Logistics making the global economy a reality can never be a given that deserves no second thought.

#### Transportation breakdowns

Transportation may be a commodity, but that does not mean that nothing can go wrong. A several-week strike in the US west coast ports in 2002 lasted long enough to almost cripple the US economy. With hundreds of cargo ships floating outside the ports, shipments were not arriving at US destinations. This meant that factories were shut down and stores were emptying. It also had a ripple effect on global trade overall. For example, return shipments were delayed because no ships were leaving the ports either. In addition, with so many ships and containers tied up, other routes could not be served. And in fact a resulting global shortage of containers caused a slowdown of shipments in many other port regions. So shipments on other routes, in different harbours and even shipments using different modalities were affected.

Risk and security concerns are not a one-time issue but require continuous risk management. Helferich and Cook (2002) found that this is necessary because, for example:

- only about 61 per cent of US firms had disaster recovery plans;
- those that do typically cover data centres, only about 12 per cent cover total organisational recovery;
- few plans included steps to keep a supply chain operational;
- only about 28 per cent of companies have formed crisis management teams, and even fewer have supply chain security teams;
- an estimated 43 per cent of businesses that suffer a major fire or other major damage never reopen for business after the event.

According to Helferich and Cook (2002) this can partially be explained by the fact that there are competing business issues, managers might not recognise their vulnerability and might assume that the government will bail them out. Peck (2003) has published a self-assessment for supply chain risk and an operational-level tool kit.

## 4.2 The tendency towards internationalisation

*Key issue:* How can we picture the trade-offs between costs, inventories and lead times in international logistics?

In order to remain competitive in the international business environment, companies seek to lower their costs while enhancing the service they provide to customers. Two commonly used approaches to improve the efficiency and effectiveness of supply chains are focused factories and centralised inventories.

### 4.2.1 Focused factories: from geographical to product segmentation

Many international companies, particularly in Europe, would have originally organised their production nationally. In this situation, factories in each country would have produced the full product range for supply to that country. Over time, factories in each country might have been consolidated at a single site, which was able to make all the products for the whole country. This situation, in which there is a focus on a limited segment of the geographical market, is shown in Figure 4.3a.

The focused factory strategy involves a company's consolidating production of products in specific factories. Each 'focused factory' supplies its products internationally to a wide market and focuses on a limited segment of the product assortment. This situation is shown in Figure 4.3b.

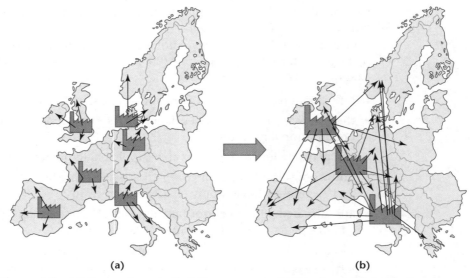

(a)                                             (b)

Figure 4.3   (a) Focused markets: full-range manufacture for local markets

(b) Focused factories: limited range manufacturing for all markets

Traditional thinking is that this organisational strategy will deliver cost advantages to a global company. While this is true for production costs, the same is not necessarily true for inventory-holding costs and transport costs.

Focused factories have an impact on the important trade-off between cost and delivery lead time. Make a list of the advantages and disadvantages of focused factories. One example of each has been entered in the table below to start you off.

|  | Cost | Lead time |
|---|---|---|
| **Advantages** | Lower production costs through economies of scale | Specialised equipment may be able to manufacture quicker |
| **Disadvantages** | Higher transport cost | Longer distance from market will increase lead time |

## 4.2.2  Centralised inventories

In the same way that the consolidation of production can deliver cost benefits, so can the consolidation of inventory. Rather than have a large number of local distribution centres, bringing these together at a small number of locations can save cost. Savings can be achieved in this way by coordinating inventory management across the supply pipeline. This allows duplication to be eliminated and safety stocks to be minimised, thereby lowering logistics costs and overall distribution cycle times. Both may sound contrary to the fact that the transport pipeline will extend, owing to the longer distribution legs to customers from the central warehouse in comparison with a local warehouse. Nevertheless, through centralising inventory, major savings can be achieved by lowering overall speculative inventories, very often coupled with the ability to balance peaks in demand across regional markets from one central inventory. Figure 4.4 characterises the different operating environments where centralised inventory may be a more relevant or a less relevant consideration, based upon logistics characteristics.

In product environments where inventory costs are more important than the distribution costs, centralised inventories are a relevant concern. This is typically the case for products of high value (measured in costs per volume unit). Microchips are an extreme example: these products are of such high cost per volume unit that distributing from the moon could still be profitable! Distribution costs have a marginal impact on logistics costs per product, assuming of course that transport costs are mainly a function of volume and weight. Products that require special transport, such as antiques, art, confidential documents or dangerous chemicals, may represent a different operating environment.

A second dimension that needs to be taken into consideration is that of distribution lead times. Here, we focus on physical distribution from warehouse to customer, and not on the inbound pipeline. Centralising inventory may lead to lower factory-to-warehouse distribution costs because shipments can be

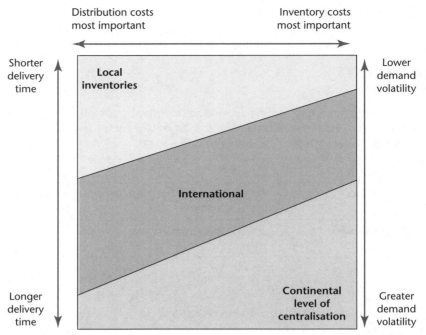

**Figure 4.4   Inventory centralisation against logistics costs and service dimensions**

consolidated into full container loads. Where service windows to customers are very compressed there may not be sufficient time to ship products from a central warehouse and allow for the required transit time within the service window. This is why, for example, hospitals and pharmacies retain in-house stocks of products, almost irrespective of their inventory costs. Critical medicines and surgical appliances need to be available instantly and locally, regardless of inventory costs.

In general, transport costs have continued to decline over time as a relative cost item because of innovations in transport technology, the commoditisation of transport (such as container ships), and the oversupply of transport capacity for basic transport. These factors in themselves contribute to the increasing internationalisation of logistics: physical distance becomes less important, even for bulky products. However, the lead-time dimension loses some of its relevance, from a transport point of view. Customer demand can be very volatile and unpredictable. *Accuracy* of delivery (the right quantity) can therefore be a more demanding challenge than *speed* (the right time). Speed is available through different transport modes (container ship, air cargo, express, courier, for example) at reasonable prices. In very volatile markets, control over international inventories by means of centralised inventories can be crucial. Overall delivery reliability ('on time in full') tends to increase significantly, to the benefit of an organisation's performance in terms of service requirements. The ability to balance peaks across market regions from a central inventory is among the additional advantages. Different levels of inventory centralisation can be applied according to different dimensions. Taking the European market as an example, the range is from local inventories (by country or even by location) through international (a selection of countries) to the complete continent. Many companies now include the Middle East and Africa as a trading bloc (Europe, Middle East and Africa–EMEA).

Centralised inventory management and focused factories enable different delivery strategies to be combined. Figure 4.5 depicts a simple distribution network that enables three different delivery strategies (listed in Table 4.4) to be applied as appropriate. For example, an opportunity to think globally arises where the key product relies more on the designer label and its promotion and marketing and less on its manufacturing origins. The key to success in clothing is often about fashionable design and labelling. Low labour costs (rather than material costs) of production can then be achieved by outsourcing to low-wage economies, often in the Far East.

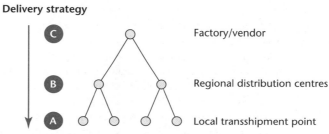

**Figure 4.5    Delivery strategies in a global network**

Table 4.4    **Three different delivery strategies**

| Delivery strategy | Description | Pros | Cons |
|---|---|---|---|
| A | Direct shipment of fast-moving, predictable lines. Held locally, probably pre-configured | Short lead time to customer | Multiple inventory points leading to duplication of stocks |
| B | Inventory of medium velocity, less predictable demand lines held at generic level awaiting final configuration | Lower overall levels of inventory, consolidated shipments to distribution centres and concentrated handling | Longer lead time to customers |
| C | Slowest-moving lines, least predictable. Perhaps one shared global inventory or make to order | Low overall inventory levels | Long lead time to customers |

<br>

**CASE STUDY 4.3**    **Centralised distribution at Nike**

'centralised and specialised, but not standardised'

Nike has a central customer service centre (distribution centre) located at Laakdal in Belgium. The centre is 200,000 square metres in size and serves 45,000 customers in EMEA with footwear, apparel and equipment. The centre receives products from supplier

▶

factories around the world for distribution to retail clients both before the start of all four seasons each year, as well as during a given season. Prior to the start of a season, when work is at a peak, the workforce stands at some 2,300 operational staff. Off peak, that drops to 1,350 staff. Deliveries are very time critical, given the seasonal nature of the business. Retailers demand in-store availability on day one of a new season. The centre is a clear example of a company deciding to centralise receiving, storage and shipment to customers at one location in Europe. The benefits including consolidation of inbound shipments, lower inventory levels and better delivery service (in comparison to fragmented warehouses scattered around Europe). This does not mean, however, that the logistics operations are standardised for all flows of goods and all customers.

Not every shipment is handled in a standard way through a single distribution pipeline:

- About a quarter of the volume of shipments is shipped to customers directly. These are larger shipments such as full pallets for larger customers – for which there is no need to consolidate with other shipments. As a result it is cheaper and quicker to make these shipments directly.
- New growth areas that are served from the centre are Russia, Turkey and South Africa. For Russia, the first satellite centre with small inventories was recently opened to enable faster local replenishment of selected products.
- Selected shipments to selected retailers are dealt with by a materials handling operation at the centre. This mainly involves labelling and re-packing operations.
- Some retailers share weekly point of sale data with Nike, enabling it to replenish inventories based upon actual sales.

### Questions

1 What are the reasons for a company, such as Nike, with a centralised distribution centre to ship some products directly to customers, not through the distribution centre?

2 What are the reasons to start satellite centres when a company such as Nike has a centralised distribution centre?

3 What are the pros and cons of locating materials handling operations such as labelling and packing in a distribution centre, as opposed to in the factory?

4 What are the pros and cons for a company such as Nike to take on these materials handling services as opposed to leaving them to retail customers?

## 4.3 The challenges of international logistics and location

*Key issues:* **What are the risks in international logistics in terms of time and inventories, and how can they be addressed?**

International logistics is complex, and different from localised logistics pipelines. The main differences that need to be taken into consideration are:

- extended lead time of supply;
- extended and unreliable transit times;

- multiple consolidation and break points;
- multiple freight modes and cost options;
- price and currency fluctuations.

Information technologies can help to circumvent these challenges in general, and the proper location of international operations in particular can help to resolve some of these challenges. Another key point is that the benefits of sourcing from low-cost locations could be lost by the operating costs and challenges of international logistics. Hence it is key to consider these prior to making decisions about global sourcing and offshoring.

### 4.3.1 Extended lead time of supply

In an internationally organised business most products produced in a particular factory will be sold in a number of different countries. In order to manage the interface between the production and sales teams in each territory, long lead times may be quoted. This buffers the factory, allowing it to respond to the local variations required in the different markets.

### 4.3.2 Extended and unreliable transit times

Owing to the length and increased uncertainty of international logistics pipelines, both planned and unplanned inventories may be higher than optimal. A comparison of the length of domestic and international product pipelines and their associated inventories is shown in Figure 4.6, which uses a similar 'pipeline' illustration to activity 4.1. Variation in the time taken for international transport will inevitably lead to increased holding of inventory with the aim of providing safety cover.

### 4.3.3 Multiple consolidation and break points

Consolidation is one of the key ways in which costs in pipelines can be lowered. Economies of scale are achieved when goods produced in a number of different facilities are batched together for transport to a common market.

The location of consolidation points depends on many factors that are not really appropriate to consider in a simple assignment such as this. That said, the following is one solution. Products manufactured in India should be consolidated at the site on the east coast (near Madras) for shipping to Singapore. Here they are combined with the output from the Thai and Singapore factories and shipped to Hong Kong. Products are consolidated at a Chinese port, possibly Shanghai, and transported by rail or sea to Hong Kong. All the other manufacturing sites deliver direct to Hong Kong, where products from all the various facilities are consolidated and shipped to Los Angeles.

It is worth noting that, after arrival in LA, this process runs in reverse. The consignment will be broken down at various 'break points' throughout North America and the goods distributed to market via hubs.

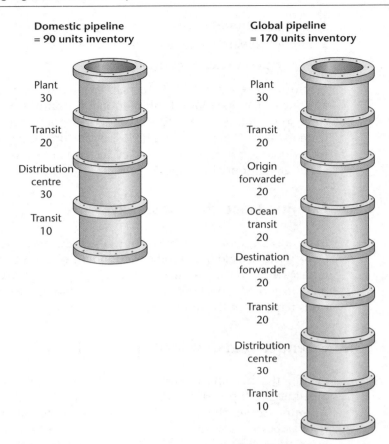

**Domestic pipeline
= 90 units inventory**

Plant
30

Transit
20

Distribution
centre
30

Transit
10

**Global pipeline
= 170 units inventory**

Plant
30

Transit
20

Origin
forwarder
20

Ocean
transit
20

Destination
forwarder
20

Transit
20

Distribution
centre
30

Transit
10

**Figure 4.6    Comparison of domestic and international logistics pipelines**
(Source: After van Hoek, 1998)

### 4.3.4 Multiple freight modes and cost options

Each leg of a journey between manufacture and the market will have a number of freight mode options. These can be broken down in simplistic terms into air, sea, rail and road. Within each of these categories lies a further range of alternative options. Each of them can be assessed for their advantages and disadvantages in terms of cost, availability and speed. When the journey along the supply chain involves multiple modes, the interface between them provides further complication.

### 4.3.5 Price and currency fluctuations

When operating around the globe, fluctuations in currencies along the supply chain can have an impact on how the supply chain is configured. While it can take years to develop a global supply chain structure and operational footprint, currencies fluctuate daily – and sometimes wildly. Such fluctuations do not favour operations in countries with an unstable currency, and explain why some countries and industries do most of their business in a single currency, even if not their own. For example, price fluctuations of fuel have impacted the feasibility of international shipping against the benefits of lower, centralised inventories. Figure 4.7 shows that inventory holdings become less cost justifiable as the costs of shipping increase. Essentially, global transport is not free.

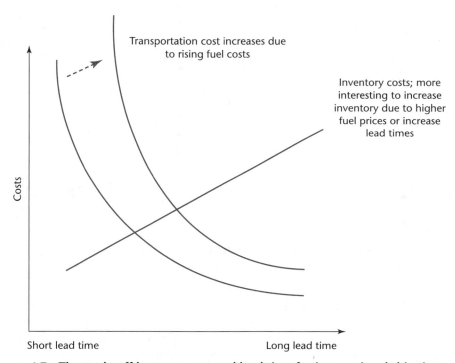

**Figure 4.7   The trade-off between cost and lead time for international shipping**

A footwear company has a number of manufacturing facilities around Asia, as shown in Figure 4.8. There are five manufacturing sites in China, three in India, and one each in Thailand, Singapore and Taiwan. Singapore and Hong Kong also have the facility to act as regional consolidation sites.

Draw arrows on the map showing where the flow of exports to the North American market could be consolidated. Write a brief description that explains your reasons for choosing these consolidation points and the flows between them.

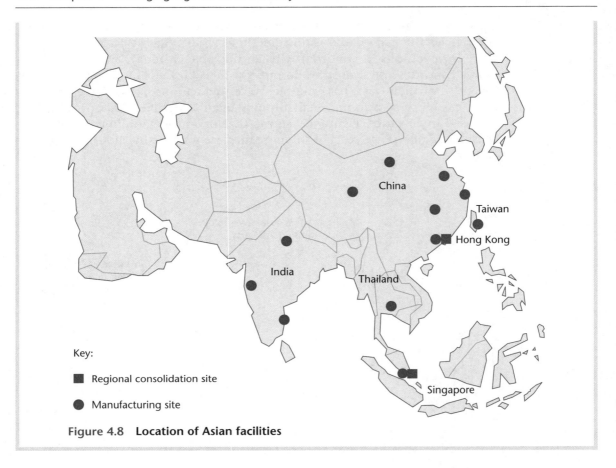

Key:

■  Regional consolidation site

●  Manufacturing site

Figure 4.8  **Location of Asian facilities**

### 4.3.6  Location analysis

A structural component of international logistics pipeline design is the location design, or, in other words, deciding where operations are going to be performed. As Figure 4.9 shows, there is a sequence to the decision-making process involved that incorporates the business (left-hand side) and geographical decision making (right-hand side). Business decision making evolves from a strategic commitment through a decision support analysis project to implementation of the resulting plan at a selected location. In parallel, the location analysis starts at the level of relevant continent, through consideration of relevant countries and regions, to the selection of a location.

**Activity 4.4**

Consider each of the four freight modes in terms of their cost, speed and availability, and write in the respective box in the table 'high', 'medium' or 'low'. Explain your answers in the 'Rationale' box on the right.

| Freight mode | Cost | Speed | Availability | Rationale |
|---|---|---|---|---|
| Air | | | | |
| Sea | | | | |
| Rail | | | | |
| Road | | | | |

Note that these comparisons are fairly subjective, and your answers will reflect your experience of the different freight modes in your industry, product type and geographic location.

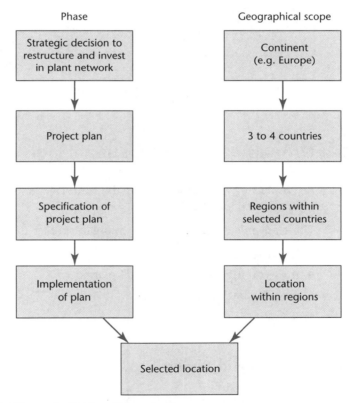

**Figure 4.9   Phases in the location selection process**

The typical four-phase decision-making process can be structured using the following steps:

1 Deciding upon the appropriate level of centralisation–decentralisation using, for example, Figures 4.4 and 4.9.

2 Selecting relevant location criteria.

3  Selecting criteria weightings.

4  An economic trade-off analysis of structures and relevant locations.

Table 4.5 displays a representative trade-off table for two locations by relevant weighted criteria.

Table 4.5    **Trade-offs between two locations**

| Location criteria | Weight | Score region A | Score region B |
|---|---|---|---|
| Railways | 1 | 4 | 1 |
| Water connections | 1 | 4 | 1 |
| Road connections | 2 | 2 | 4 |
| Site availability | 2 | 2 | 3 |
| Central location | 3 | 1 | 2 |
| A . . . | . . . | | |
| Total | | 19 | 22 |

Key: Score on a five-point scale ranging from poor to excellent.

## 4.4  Organising for international logistics

*Key issue:* **How can supply chains be better organised to meet the challenges of international logistics?**

There are at least three elements in organising for international logistics. These are:

- layering and tiering;
- the evolving role of individual plants;
- reconfiguration processes.

These will be outlined in the following subsections.

### 4.4.1  Layering and tiering

Internationalisation is often looked at from the point of view of asset centralisation and localisation. However, the wider organisational setting needs to be taken into account as well.

A commonly used maxim is *global coordination and local operation*, which relates to laying out the flow of information and coordination differently from the map of the physical operations. For example, Hewlett-Packard (HP) operates a globally consistent and coordinated structure of product finalisation and distribution in contrast to its continental operations. The company runs a final manufacturing and central distribution operation in Europe, the US and Asia for each continent.

The operations are structured and run exactly the same, with the only difference being the way that products are configured to suit end-customers in the specific regions. This final configuration process (which in the case of HP may include fitting power leads and local instructions) is referred to as *postponement*, which we review in more detail in Chapter 6. Regional facilities are often owned and operated on a dedicated basis by a contract manufacturer and *third party logistics providers* (3PL, reviewed in Chapter 7). HP brings only limited management expertise to these regional operations to assure global coordination. Thus, although HP operates in a globalised way, its products are tuned to local markets by means of local logistics operations. Therefore developments in ICT do not eliminate the need for such local operations.

Another example can be found in the automotive industry. In this industry, major original equipment manufactuers (OEMs) structure their plant networks globally, while making suppliers build their plants in the immediate vicinity of the OEM plant. The distance or broadcasting horizon between the two plants is defined by the time between the electronic ordering of a specifically finalised single module on the online system and the expected time of delivery in sequence along the assembly line. Time horizons for order preparation, finalisation, shipment and delivery tend to be in the area of an hour and a half or less. This causes localisation of the supplier or co-location, while the OEM plant services a continental or even global market.

## 4.4.2  The evolving role of individual plants

Ferdows (1989) projects the theories by Bartlett and Ghoshal (1989) onto the role of individual plants/factories in achieving the targeted international capabilities of global efficiency, local responsiveness and worldwide learning, or a combination of the three. Using the same type of approach, with location considerations on the horizontal axis and performed activities on the vertical axis, van Hoek (1998) adjusted the model for distribution centres. The model indicates the way in which the growth of performed activities changes the demands placed on the capabilities of the plant and changes the location requirements. Location is concerned with the response of governments to globalisation: adjusting local taxes, incentives and infrastructure to favour selection of their territory.

In Figure 4.10 a traditional warehouse is projected to possibly develop into a semi-manufacturing operation with product finalisation among its responsibilities and added value. This also contributes to the creation of a flexible facility for responding to local markets. The model also indicates a possible downgrading of the plant, with its two-way arrows showing development paths. These developments could be driven by poor location conditions, an inability to reach supply chain objectives, or the ability to reach the supply chain objectives more easily at other plants in the company's network. This suggests that the role of individual plants could be seen as an internal competitive issue for plant management. Most relevant, the evolutionary roles and functions of individual plants within the evolving supply chain are specific issues of concern for the realisation of global objectives.

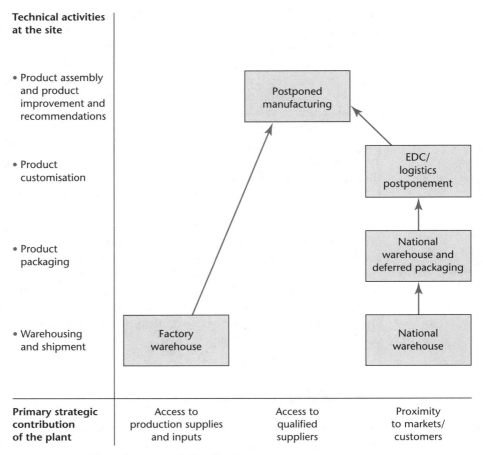

Figure 4.10   **Changing role of distribution centres**

## 4.4.3  Reconfiguration processes

Related to this last point, the achievement of the required changes in international logistics pipelines is a central issue. In the research presented in Figure 4.6 (van Hoek, 1998), it was found that, across companies, large differences can be found in reconfiguration paths. This was found even in cases where the same supply chain structure (a traditional factory warehouse, as displayed in Figure 4.10) was targeted. Differences included:

● *Supply chain scope/activities involved.* Was only final manufacturing relocated, or did sourcing undergo the same treatment?

● *Focus.* Were activities moved into the market, e.g. localised or centralised within the market? Did the move have a single or multiple focus?

● *Tendency.* Were activities moved out of the (European) market or vice versa, with single or multiple tendencies?

- *Timetable.* Was it a single-step process or did it involve various steps spanning out the process over a longer period of time?
- *Pace.* Was it an overnight change or the result of a gradually changing process?
- *Authority.* Was it directed from a global base (top down) or built up region by region (bottom up)?

The differences can be explained through differences in the supply chain characteristics of companies, among which are:

- *Starting point:* Is the base structure localised or globalised?
- *Tradition:* Does the company have a long preceding history with the baseline in the market, or can it be built up from scratch, in supply chain terms (brownfield or greenfield)?

Table 4.6 summarises the differences found in companies implementing postponed manufacturing as an example of a reconfiguration process. The same argument could be applied to the difference between a central European warehouse and a country-based, localised distribution network.

Table 4.6    **Differences in reconfiguration processes for companies depending upon starting point (global or local)**

| Starting point | Global structure | Localised structure |
|---|---|---|
| Heritage in market | Little, greenfield approach | Extensive, brownfield approach |
| Supply chain scope | Narrow, involving inventory and final manufacturing | Broad, involving inventory, manufacturing, and sourcing |
| Focus | Decentralising final manufacturing and inventory into market | Centralising inventory and final manufacturing at continental level and globalising manufacturing and sourcing |
| Tendency | Single, placing activities into market | Multiple, relocating within market and moving outside market |
| Timetable | Short (1–10 months) | Long (number of years) |
| Authority | Global, top-down directions | Local, bottom-up iterative process |

Figures 4.11 and 4.12 represent the reconfiguration process from local distribution through logistics centralisation to postponed manufacturing (final manufacturing in the warehouse). The differences in the implementation path are based upon the different starting points. The path with a localised starting point goes through centralisation within Europe starting from autonomous, duplicated local structures. The path with a global starting point builds a small European presence and then migrates through the increase of European presence centrally (representing a further location into Europe, rather than a further centralisation from within Europe).

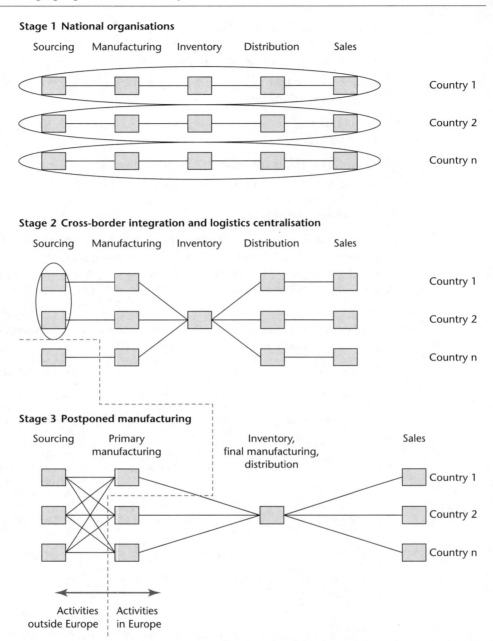

**Figure 4.11 Stages in the implementation of postponed manufacturing: local starting point**

(Source: van Hoek, 1998)

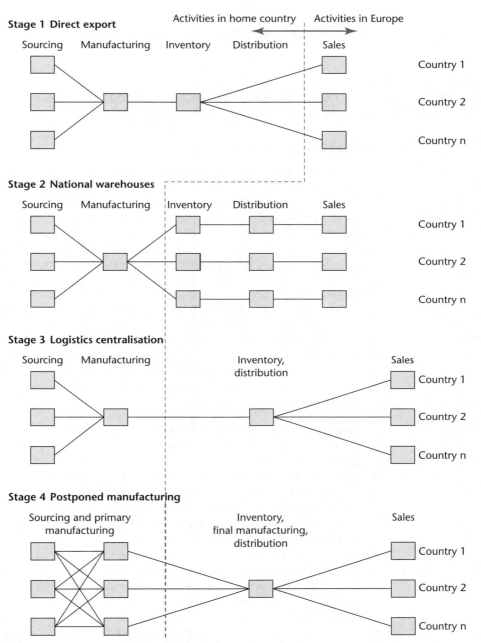

Figure 4.12    **Stages in the implementation of postponed manufacturing: global
starting point**

(Source: van Hoek, 1998)

Case study 4.4 explores issues and trade-offs found in developing competitive solutions when organising for international logistics.

# The trade-off between time and cost in global supply chains: lessons from the apparel industry

### Vertical integration v outsourcing

The enormous success of vertical retailers such as H&M, Zara, Gap and Next in the apparel industry in the last ten years has forced manufacturers of brand labels such as Esprit and Levi, and department stores such as El Corte Ingles and Marks & Spencer, to speed up their supply chains. Partly, this has been achieved by integrating their processes and systems upstream (towards their suppliers) and for wholesale brands downstream (towards their wholesale customers) in the supply chain.

The competitive environment in the apparel industry is increasingly tough. Retail prices are under pressure; there is increasing polarisation of pricing, with growth in the premium luxury brands at one end and low cost segments at the other, resulting in a constriction in the middle ground, driven by vertical retailers such as Primark and Matalan; competition is extending from products that were traditionally limited to upper, middle or lower segments of the market – and increasingly with 'fashion' product from the sports industry; gross margins are shrinking; retail store costs and personnel costs are going up. Those who do not manage their assortment planning and inventories well are continuously under pressure to mark down their merchandise. *Vertical retailers* have found an answer to this hostile environment by:

- increasing the probability of designing a bestseller product by dramatically shortening its time-to-market, designing and delivering product closer to the on-market trend (see Chapter 5);
- piloting products in the stores and then replenishing the best sellers within two to three weeks by utilising new types of make-to-order processes;
- driving the inventory sales productivity (as measured by stock turn, sales per square metre and mark down percentage) by keen assortment planning, sales performance feedback and delivery planning;
- integrating the IT systems from point of sale back into garment production factories and from there towards fabric suppliers, using product lifecycle management systems that incorporate data and workflow along the supply chain;
- identifying a product category mix that, where possible, can take advantage of longer lead time, higher margin products;
- focusing on quality of workmanship through fitting and process quality.

Brand label manufacturers traditionally do not own their retail stores, and department stores do not have own their factories. This easily leads to competitive disadvantage in comparison with the vertical retailers, who have their own retail stores and have tight control over their manufacturers. To survive in today's marketplace against the vertical retailers, brand labels and department stores need to integrate their processes and systems from point-of-sale back into the factory. How can this be done?

## Core competencies and time-to-market

Companies such as Esprit have initiated strategies to become vertical retailers themselves. They have also set up their own e-commerce website, a direct distribution channel to their consumers. This strategy not only generates additional revenue but also supports direct and immediate product performance feedback. Elements of this strategy are to focus on core competencies and to offload all non-core activities to specialists who can such activities better and at a lower price. Another element of the strategy is to increase the number of collections from four to between six and twelve per year. This enables them to be closer to market and thus to forecast and fulfil product demand more accurately. Of course, closeness to market increases the pressure on faster, timely product development and product delivery. The product lifecycles of the individual collections are shorter, which leads to enhanced requirements for responsiveness on all supply chain partners. There can be no buffers, and deliveries have to be on time and in full. As a result of this each partner in the chain has increased needs for information, flexibility and transparency. Therefore, vertical retailers must have an excellent supply chain that is fast, flexible, reliable and which provides full transparency at low cost. That's in addition to having good products and closeness to market!

## Developing a global SCM network

Re-engineering supply chain processes as part of the verticalisation strategy forces apparel and sports companies to focus on outsourcing all non-core activities and development of a global supply network. Outsourcing of non-core activities, such as managing warehousing and distribution centres, frees up management time which can be utilised for managing the supply chain end-to-end. The development of a global supply network consists basically of four components:

- enforcing end-to-end supply chain thinking within the focal firm, its suppliers and its logistics service providers;
- setting up a physical infrastructure with selected lead logistics providers (LLPs) who manage the logistics hubs at sourcing origin and market destination (see Figure 4.13);
- using central databases on the internet (SCM portal and Supplier portal) where all logistics partners, suppliers and buyers can view order status and workflow, product specifications and development in real time;
- empowering LLPs to manage selected service level agreements on behalf of the focal firm in terms of cost and time

Besides development of the above components of the supply chain, it is important to consider *trade-offs*. These are decisions that have to be made for each step in the supply chain. Figure 4.14 provides an overview of the steps and trade-offs in the supply chain from sourcing areas in Asia, Eastern Europe and South America towards a European market destination.

## The trade-off between time and cost

Which trade-offs are to be made? For example, when sourcing in Asia whilst selling in Europe, what process set ups are possible? When focusing on *cost* the focal firm needs to make sure that shipments are in full container loads, shipped by sea, packed as cross-

▶

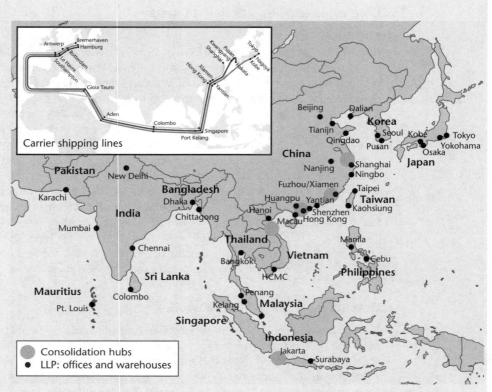

**Figure 4.13 Example of physical infrastructure set-up with LLP origin in Asia**
(Source: Leeman, 2007)

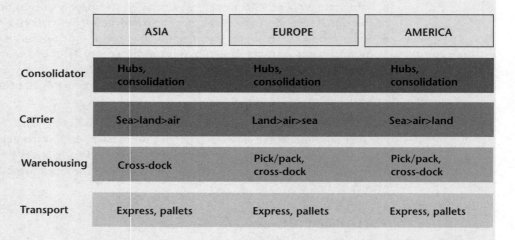

**Figure 4.14 SCM tools and trade-offs in the supply chain**

dock shipments which are then transported to retail stores via a cross-dock warehouse as consolidated shipments once a week. However, this slows down the process time substantially to approximately 20 days. Also, different countries of manufacture have considerably different levels of duty tariff when landing product in Europe and this needs to be considered in the total acquisition cost. When focusing on *time*, the focal firm needs to ensure that shipments are packed by retailer store at the factory, shipped by air and transported directly to stores upon arrival without going through a cross-dock warehouse. Of course, this process is fast (two–five days) but it is also very costly, and can only be justified with exclusive branded products with high gross margins. Also, Asian manufacturing is in developing countries and therefore local infrastructure and the time required to move product to the hub needs consideration. The product category mix, levels of assortment and replenishment product volumes also require that logistics managers plan for timely availability of capacity at suppliers. It is also becoming important to global brands to plan for how quickly they can manufacture and replenish for growing *local* Asian markets from the same supply base. Therefore, companies such as Esprit and Nike have a *range* of supply chain solutions. Some of these set delivery windows which focus on time, while others organise supply chain processes to focus on minimising cost.

(Source: Based on Leeman 2007; updated by Mark Baker, 2010)

### Questions

1 What are the strategic drivers that are forcing focal firms in the apparel industry to change their supply strategy?

2 Why is time-to-market so important in the apparel industry? How does it impact supply chain processes?

3 Which trade-offs must be made when setting up a global SCM network for the apparel industry? Also discuss the trade-offs regarding sourcing countries versus quality.

Case study 4.5 offers an example of an approach to outsourcing that provides an insight into the hidden difficulties that may be faced when moving from 'local' to 'low cost' supply.

CASE STUDY
4.5

## Moving offshore – not so easy or straightforward: the experience of Smiths Aerospace

Smiths Aerospace is a largely UK-based supplier to both military and civilian aircraft and engine manufacturers, and is owned by General Electric of the US. Several years ago, Smiths launched an initiative to outsource production of parts from UK suppliers to Chinese suppliers in a drive to benefit from lower costs. Among the beneficiaries of

▶

the new initiative was the Mechanical Systems division, which intended to source high volume, low cost products from lean, low cost suppliers in China. The remaining volume was to be sourced from domestic suppliers which could operate more flexibly (section 1.3.2). The scope of the restructuring included machined civilian aircraft parts from four UK sites under the Mechanical Systems Division: based in four locations in the UK: Wolverhampton, Cheltenham, Hamble and Dowty Propellers (Gloucester).

Global supply chain teams based in the UK and the US, in conjunction with each of the Smiths Aerospace divisions, were given responsibility for the deployment of the outsourcing programme. The reconfigured supply chain will result in the transition of approximately 5,000 to 15,000 parts from traditional suppliers to low cost economy suppliers over a five-year period. Plans state that, on average, 40 per cent of the spend will remain within the UK because of high switching costs. As the long-term contracts expire, the parts will either be manufactured internally or outsourced depending on intellectual property rights and technology protection. However, several years into the initiative, only parts of the original plans have been accomplished. Much of the delay was attributable to the change process, which was not so simple as originally envisioned. There were also challenges with how that change was being managed. For example, in the words of one company executive:

> 'Failure to manage exit from the existing supplier, and failure to coordinate the transition, led to catastrophic failure of supply'.

In this restructuring initiative, several keys to a successful supply chain initiative have been met:

- The initiative directly relates to corporate strategic priorities and there is top executive recognition of its importance.
- There are clear considerations for switching production to China.
- There is a clear business (four units two of which serve as pilots) and operating scope defined (those that require less flexibility).
- There is a launch point for 'quick wins' (high volume, labour intensive parts)
- Teams around the world have been allocated to the initiative.

However, as is also clear from the above quote from the executive, there are real risks involved. As much as there have been many companies moving supply chain operations to China, there are also clear negative impacts on supply chain performance that need to be considered and incorporated into the change plan.

### Questions

1  Which are risks in relocating parts of the supply chain and how can they be incorporated into the plan for change?

2  Despite the recognised need to coordinate the transition process, the sites lacked a documented method to specify *how* this would take place. There were also challenges with the change process itself. Propose what steps might have been included to address these shortcomings.

## 4.5  Reverse logistics

*Key issue:* factoring in the return flow of goods when designing international networks.

Reverse logistics deals with the flow of goods that go back up the supply chain for a number of reasons, including: product returns, repairs, maintenance and end-of-life returns for recycling or dismantling. Reverse logistics has both a service (repair, recalls, etc.) and an environmental component. Corporate social responsibility considerations will be covered in more detail in section 4.7. Meanwhile, Table 4.7 – from the Reverse Logistics Executive Council – compares reverse logistics with forward logistics.

Table 4.7  **Comparing forward and reverse logistics**

| Forward logistics | Reverse logistics |
| --- | --- |
| Forecasting relatively straightforward | Forecasting more difficult |
| One to many distribution points | Many to one distribution points |
| Product quality uniform | Product quality not uniform |
| Product packaging uniform | Product packaging often damaged |
| Destination/routing clear | Destination/routing unclear |
| Pricing relatively uniform | Pricing dependent on many factors |
| Importance of speed recognised | Speed often not considered a priority |
| Forward distribution costs easily visible | Reverse costs less directly visible |
| Inventory management consistent | Inventory management not consistent |
| Product lifecycle manageable | Product lifecycle issues more complex |
| Negotiation between parties straightforward | Negotiations complicated by several factors |
| Marketing methods well known | Marketing complicated by several factors |
| Visibility of process more transparent | Visibility of process less transparent |

(Source: Reverse Logistics Executive Council, http://www.rlec.org)

Reasons why reverse logistics is often only partially incorporated into international network design include:

- no infrastructure: companies often try to use the same outbound distribution system to handle returns without considering whether it is fit for purpose;
- reverse logistics is often a 'corner-of-the-desk concern', and does not receive sufficient resources;
- much attention on the subject is driven by legislation, not yet by recognised business value;
- focal firms see reverse logistics as a cost of doing business;
- the subject is intuitively not popular: it means something has gone wrong, so people are tempted to ignore it or hide it;
- it is hard to forecast the reverse flow and composition – what is going to come back.

Opinions indicate that there are operational shortcomings such as using the same infrastructure for the return flow, and the difficulty of forecasting reverse flow. These might be explained by a lack of management attention, and by lack of appreciation of the full costs of reverse logistics. On the other hand, potential downsides of a reactive approach include image risks, service shortfalls and being a nuisance to customers. Suggested ways forward include considering the full impact of reverse logistics and approaching it as a business:

- consider reverse logistics for its full cost and negative potential market impact;
- seek green as a business ('green is green');
- design for disassembly and recycling;
- outsource reversed operations to a specialist 3PL;
- create dedicated (parts of) operations.

Cisco Systems offers a good case example of the migration from reversed logistics as a burden to it as a business opportunity.

---

**CASE STUDY 4.6**

## Cisco Systems value recovery programme

In 2005, Cisco Systems dealt with US$500 million of returned products and parts through a cost centre whose annual operating cost was just US$8 million. All returns were treated as defective product and service returns with the rationale being that all returns were without value. Furthermore, 95 per cent of all returns were scrapped. The 5 per cent of returns that were re-used were therefore more accidental than by design. The US$500 million in scrap products and parts was equal to a volume of 12 football fields covered knee high with defective products and parts.

Cisco Systems made the transition towards a profit-making value recovery operation by setting criteria for value recovery and screening all returns for embedded value. The criteria include:

- Can a cosmetic 'touch up' or software upgrade be performed?
- Can they be broken down into spares or parts or go into the secondary market or even be donated to philanthropy?

The lessons learned from this programme for Cisco Systems included:

1 Do not treat all returns the same. There are products and parts that are beyond saving but more often than not things can be used in different ways to generate value.
2 Uncovering this value requires getting into the details of the product to identify possible ways to recover value and assess the opportunity to do this with a specific product.
3 Most returns are not defective but are returned for other reasons.
4 Take a broad view of the opportunity. Think of reverse logistics as a business and approach it like a general manager, not looking only for pennies or operational issues, but instead looking for what value can be brought to other parts of the organisation such as the corporate social responsibility (CSR) department and social efforts.
5 Learn from other functions. It may require you to take pages from the service manual, learn from finance on quantifying value (returns can provide a tax write-off when they are donated to philanthropic causes) and learn from the sales department in running a value recovery programme effectively (focus on solution selling, segment the business for opportunities, establish return quotas and value recovery targets).

As a result of the programme, 44 per cent of returns are now re-used and returns have moved from a cost centre to a net contribution of US$85 million. This is on top of the non-financial environmental and social benefits.

*Note: A further description of this programme is available from the CSCMP website,* http://cscmp.org *It contains a further write-up of this supply chain innovation award winning case.*

### Question

1  Do you consider Cisco's value recovery criteria can be applied to any supply chain? Consider a supply chain for fashion goods (illustrated in Case study 4.4) as an example.

## 4.6  Managing for risk readiness

*Key issue:* developing appropriate responses to risk in both the short and long term.

Supply chain disruptions such as transportation breakdowns and geopolitical risks can have many impacts: empty distribution channels, stores and goods stuck upstream leading to lost sales, revenue and customers. And they can be the result of plant shutdowns due to supplier discontinuity or collapse, bottlenecks in the transportation system or many other events in the supply chain. There are at least two levels at which companies are responding to risk in international logistics; preparing for immediate response to risks and structurally preparing for risk in international supply chains.

### 4.6.1  Immediate risk readiness

Recent events have shown that immediate responses to risks can include four things:

- raised inventory levels to assure a cushion for supply disruptions of key parts and supplies;
- redrawing transportation scenarios in the light of the possible logistics meltdown of global trade routes;
- supplier hedges are put into place; and
- global sourcing and supplier rationalisation efforts are being reconsidered actively.

#### Inventory policies to reflect volatility levels

Shortly before the second Gulf War, GM and Toyota asked their just-in-time suppliers to raise inventory levels in order to avoid early and extensive plant shutdowns. It added short-term costs but as a hedge against supply disruptions it can be a real money saver down the line while assuring service to the customer that competitors might not be able to offer. LaCrosse Footwear raised its safety stock sixfold for certain products in order to ensure the ability to ship to customers on short notice.

### Re-do transportation network redesign

Based upon possible risks or a real situation, scenarios for transportation routes at risk can be developed together with contingency plans on a route-by-route and plant-to-plant basis. Airlines altered services to the Middle East before the Gulf War, for example. Here are three other examples:

- Hewlett Packard maintains the ability to shift production between assembly facilities in Europe, North America, South America and Asia as part of a formal continuity plan to be implemented in a crisis.
- Chrysler quickly shifted component shipment from air to express truck service in response to transportation bottlenecks after 9/11.
- Continental Tyres' crisis team put together a list of all customers' orders, parts and suppliers outstanding, identified critical shipments by the afternoon of 9/11, and expedited those critical parts by land transport and through contingency relationships with transport firms.

### Reconsider sole and global sourcing arrangements

Despite the benefits of supplier rationalisation and focused factories, risk management does imply there is real rationale for lining up alternative suppliers in different locations, and for manufacturers to develop a thorough understanding of their suppliers' capabilities and vulnerabilities. Companies are responding in two ways: considering alternative and back-up sources; and proactively auditing the supply base for financial and operational sustainability in these tough times. Hewlett Packard, for example, has secondary suppliers for all critical components as part of its continuity plan.

## 4.6.2  Structural risk readiness

Because risk needs to be an ongoing focus, companies are increasingly devoting dedicated teams to risk management in the supply chain. These teams can do several things:

- develop contingency plans and risk protocols;
- audit preparedness;
- train plant management and staff;
- report to senior management on risk profiles and preparedness.

Most important, however, is not to leave risk management in the supply chain solely the responsibility of a team, but to use the team to create an ongoing organisation-wide focus and effort. Most often teams *help* plant management and various functions in the organisation, instead of telling them what to do. Henkel, the German consumer goods company, for example, has appointed risk teams to work with various departments in assessing risk. It raises fundamental awareness across the organisation, and is the basis for developing contingency plans proactively.

## 4.7 Corporate social responsibility in the supply chain

*Key issue:* Companies operating international or global supply chains need to incorporate social responsibility into their supply chain design.

In Chapter 1, we included corporate social responsibility (CSR) under the overall concept of sustainability and the 'triple bottom line'. CSR has developed a momentum of its own, and now largely overlaps sustainability. Here, we explore the concept of CSR as it is being developed by various focal firms, especially in the context of international logistics. Broadly defined, CSR in the supply chain deals with the social and environmental consequences of supply chain operations. Making a global supply chain environmentally sustainable and socially considerate is harder than just doing so for a focal firm. This is due to global reach and the fact that multiple companies are involved. As a result, it is harder to assess and improve operating policies across the entire supply chain. Yet this is a key opportunity to bring CSR to life.

Two examples illustrate the issues:

- In 2006 the ship *Probo Koala* was redirected from the port of Amsterdam in the Netherlands to Côte d'Ivoire, where it dumped its waste. But a Dutch inquiry found the 'waste' was more than 500 tonnes of a mixture of fuel, caustic soda and hydrogen sulphide. The waste was dumped in 12 sites around the capital of Côte d'Ivoire, Abidjan. The gas released by these chemicals was blamed by the United Nations and the government of Côte d'Ivoire for the deaths of 17 and the injury (ranging from mild headaches to severe burns of skin and lungs) of over 30,000 Ivorians. A November 2006 Ivorian government report into the incident said that Trafigura was to blame for the dumping of waste, and was aided by Ivorians. A government committee concluded that Trafigura knew that the nation had no facilities to store such waste and knowingly transported it from Europe to Abidjan. In late 2008 a criminal prosecution was begun in the Netherlands by the Dutch Public Prosecutors office: Trafigura (the ship's owner), the captain of *Probo Koala* and the port of Amsterdam authorities were charged with 'illegally transporting toxic waste into and out of Amsterdam harbour' and falsification of the chemical composition of the ship's cargo (Leigh and Hirsch, 2009).

### Activity 4.5

Review the evidence for this disaster which is detailed at:
http://en.wikipedia.org/wiki/ 2006_C%C3%B4te_d'Ivoire_toxic_waste_dump
Who was to blame for the *Probo Koala* disaster in Côte d'Ivoire in 2006? What are the CSR implications of what happened?

- Nike came under heavy scrutiny from customers in the 1990s for its use of low cost labour, predominantly in Asia. There were suspicions of use of child labour (Case study 4.7), and other unethical labour practices among Nike suppliers. Nike launched a comprehensive CSR effort – including the appointment of a vice-president for CSR – and now is considered to be a leader for improving supplier practices and for responsible behaviour along the supply chain.

CSR has caught both public and political attention, and companies are developing approaches that span the spectrum displayed in Figure 4.15. Worst practice in CSR is for companies to publish a CSR report and to engage in PR efforts to make the company look responsible, yet hide behind the approach:

> I can't see everything in my supply chain that happens on the other side of the globe in another company, so I can't manage that.

So not much changes in day-to-day operations – other than telling suppliers that they 'need to be responsible for their actions'.

Telling suppliers to 'shape up' cannot be expected to have much of an impact. One example of a weak response to CSR is that of a focal firm which said, 'we ask our suppliers to adhere to the rules, and if we have a continued suspicion of improper conduct we send them a letter'. Not only does that not help suppliers to develop, it also does not take active ownership of the challenge. Even worse – while this was happening – the firm continued to award business based on supplier price levels, with no consideration for the impact of these price levels on labour practices. But progress can be made in comparatively difficult circumstances, as Case study 4.7 illustrates.

---

**CASE STUDY 4.7**

## Eliminating child labour from the Sialkot soccer ball industry

Nearly 75 per cent of soccer balls were produced in Pakistan, mostly in the Sialkot district, Pakistan's 'export capital' close to the border with India. However, an International Labour Organisation (ILO) study in 2002 showed that more than 7,000 children aged between seven and 14 were stitching footballs on a full-time basis, working between ten and 11 hours/day and earning between PKR 20 and 22 per ball (€1 = PKR 81). Production ranged from three to five balls/day per person. An article in *Life* magazine appeared in June 1996, featuring Tariq, a 12-year-old, stitching balls in Sialkot. This resulted in pressure on international brands such as Adidas, Reebok and Nike to ensure that their products were not produced with child labour. The ILO brokered the *Atlanta Agreement* (2001) to eliminate child labour from the soccer ball industry through improved monitoring.

However, monitoring was difficult to implement. Local 'manufacturers' outsourced work to middlemen, who in turn dealt with home-based stitchers. These could be whole families, including children. Payment was on a 'fixed price' basis, so there was no cost advantage whether the worker was adult or child. The anonymous nature of the network meant that manufacturers had no idea what age of worker was involved.

An independent monitoring committee was set up, and manufacturers were invited to register. Once registered, manufacturers had to declare details of their entire network – including the number of stitchers, daily production, location of stitching centres and names of the middlemen. This was to be done gradually over a period of 18 months. And, once declared, stitching centres were to be subject to random visits. If child labour was discovered, the manufacturer was instructed to fix the situation. Repeated violations resulted in the manufacturer being withdrawn from the register and reported to international buyers and retailers. Within a few years, practically all of the manufacturers had registered.

Saga Sports, the largest manufacturer, decided to go a step further. It would stop the use of child labour completely by eliminating outsourcing and concentrating production in custom-built stitching facilities which Saga would manage. While Pakistani law allowed children to start work at the age of 14, Saga decreed that it would only employ workers aged 18 or over. Age would be verified against national identity cards and birth certificates. Once confirmed, employees benefited from a pay structure 'equivalent to university teachers in Pakistan'. Employee benefits, such as free health checks and medical help, meals and transport, were introduced. Saga saw these benefits as compensation to families who had lost income as a result of the elimination of child labour.

While Saga's actions have helped to purge child labour from the football stitching industry in an exemplary way, there are other sectors in which children can earn money. Sialkot is also famous for leather goods and surgical goods, where international pressures are more difficult to focus. Easy availability of work, lack of meaningful education opportunities and a 'poverty of thought' prevalent in the community could mean that the problem may only be transferred elsewhere.

(Source: Adapted from Hussain-Khaliq, 2004)

### Question

1 What further changes are needed for there to be a sustainable change in the incidence of child labour in developing countries such as Pakistan?

More progressive firms are now beginning to use CSR as a market lever – not only to make them look good in the eyes of the consumer, but to expand the firm with new products at premium prices. An example is 'fair trade' products. Such firms are taking active ownership over the challenge – for example, NEC goes into considerable detail to specify CSR actions for suppliers in a lengthy handbook it has published. Nike has appointed a CSR vice-president, as noted above. Finally, companies such as NEC, Nike and HP invest time and resources in helping suppliers develop into more CSR-adept firms. They visit suppliers, conduct

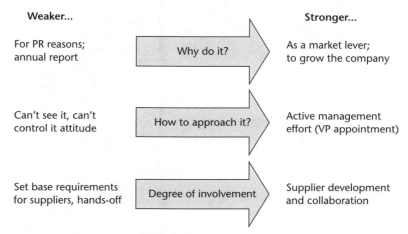

Figure 4.15  **CSR practices in the supply chain**

audits to identify improvement opportunities and proactively carve out opportunities to collaborate on achieving improvements.

Examples of CSR efforts include:

● incorporating CSR standards and suggested efforts in purchasing policies (see the NEC example above and Table 4.8);

Table 4.8   NEC CSR supplier requests

| Risk management priority | Action item |
| --- | --- |
| CSR general requirement | Promote positive CSR activities<br>Contribute to the society and community |
| Product quality and safety | Ensure product safety<br>Establish and apply a quality management system |
| The environment | Control hazardous chemicals in products<br>Control hazardous chemicals in manufacturing<br>Establish and apply an environmental management system<br>Minimise environmental pollution (water, soil, air)<br>Obtain environmental permits<br>Promote resource and energy saving by reusing, reducing and recycling<br>Promote greenhouse gas reduction<br>Promote waste reduction<br>Disclose environmental preservation activities |
| Information security | Secure computer networks against threats<br>Prevent the leakage of personal information<br>Prevent the leakage of confidential information of the customer and third party |
| Fair trading | Prohibit corruption and bribery<br>Prohibit abuse of a superior position<br>Prohibit the offering and receiving of inappropriate profit and advantage<br>Prohibit impediment to free competition<br>Provide correct information on products and services<br>Respect intellectual property<br>Use appropriate company information<br>Detect injustice promptly |
| Occupational health and safety | Apply safety measures for equipment and instruments<br>Promote safe activities in the workplace<br>Promote hygiene in the workplace<br>Apply appropriate measures for occupational injuries and illnesses<br>Properly manage disasters and accidents<br>Be careful about physically demanding work<br>Promote safety and hygiene in all company facilities<br>Promote health maintenance programmes for employees |
| Human rights | Prohibit forced labour<br>Prohibit inhumane treatment and infringements of human rights<br>Prohibit child labour<br>Prohibit discrimination<br>Pay appropriate wages<br>Control working hours<br>Respect the right to freedom of association |

(Source: NEC Group CSR Guideline for Suppliers, http://www.nec.co.jp/purchase/pdf/sc_csr_guideline_e.pdf)

- conducting supplier audits to identify improvement opportunities, and following up on issues that are found (do not say you can't see it when you can go and look);
- taking ownership of CSR initiatives by running supplier development sessions, and by collaborating on improvement projects.

## CASE STUDY 4.8

### Embedding CSR at Akzo

Akzo, the Dutch-based chemicals and coatings company, owner of ICI and many other brands, has appointed a CSR officer to drive and coordinate CSR efforts across the company. To drive ownership, consideration and focus broadly across the company and in all the decisions it makes, two simple things are done:

1 Every proposal that the Board is asked to decide upon must be accompanied by a CSR and sustainability evaluation otherwise it will not be considered by the Board.
2 Personal targets for senior management across the company include as a KPI the company's position in the Dow Jones sustainability index.

As (a) the largest company in the world by revenue taking sustainability seriously, (b) doing so in a cost effective manner and (c) on an international scale, Wal-Mart is setting some challenging targets with its supply chain partners, as described in Case study 4.9.

## CASE STUDY 4.9

### Wal-Mart's sustainability programme

Wal-Mart has set three ambitious goals for sustainability:

1 To be supplied by 100 per cent renewable energy.
2 To create zero waste.
3 To sell products that sustain the environment.

In moving towards these goals several key projects have been rolled out, including changing store design to use more natural light as opposed to electrical light, and catching rain from store roofs and AC units for watering the landscape.

On its fleet the company has introduced auxiliary power units so that when waiting idle for more than three minutes the main engine turns off. It is estimated that this alone will lead to US$23 million in fuel savings per year.

Furthermore, the company worked with its supplier of private label toys to remove excess packaging from 277 children's construction toy skus and to reduce the size of the package. This alone will lead to 727 fewer shipping containers and a US$3.5 million saving in transportation costs. Additionally the company recognises a marketing advantage as customers frequently ask for sustainability improvements.

## Activity 4.6

List possible CSR concerns in the supply chain, and the possible impact on the focal firm making and selling the end product (a) if they go wrong and (b) if they go right.

## Summary

*Why international logistics?*

- A major driver of the internationalisation of business has been labour shortages and costs in established markets, and the availability of low cost production in newly industrialised regions. A further driver has been the need to follow customers into new local markets, and to create new learning opportunities.

- This has created phases in internationalisation of operations, and hence of the logistics pipelines that are associated with them. Logistics pipelines differ from market to market and from company to company over time.

- Global sourcing can create economies of scale for transportation through multiple consolidation as organisations orchestrate their global networks, and focus key areas such as manufacturing and R&D.

*What are the logistics implications of internationalisation?*

- Despite the obvious benefits of global sourcing, firms should not ignore the logistical complexities and operational costs associated with sourcing globally (including longer shipment times and higher shipping costs) when deciding their internationalisation strategies. Increased complexities and costs are often ignored or only partially recognised in the rush to obtain lower piece part prices.

*How do we organise for international logistics?*

- New solutions for layering and tiering the supply network are being tried out, such as co-location of suppliers with OEM plants in the auto industry. Meanwhile, the role of individual plants may be modified to allow more flexible response to local markets, for example by carrying out final assembly in local distribution centres.

- The key to success of internationalisation strategies is the rationalisation of sourcing, production and distribution. At the same time, the organisation needs to be sensitive to local markets and preferences. Crucial also is to ensure risk preparedness in international supply chains and to factor in corporate social responsibility policies proactively.

## Discussion questions

1  What are the benefits and limitations of international logistics? Illustrate your response by referring to sourcing of standard shirts and fashion blouses (shown in Table 1.1 in Chapter 1) from manufacturers in the Far East. Also, refer to the time v cost trade-off illustrated in Case study 4.4.

2  Tiering of the supply network is referred to in section 4.4.1, and in Chapter 1, section 1.1. Describe the advantages of tiering in terms of globalisation, touching on areas such as outsourcing and the focused factory.

**3** Identify six potential sources and causes of risk in global supply chains. Use the reference to Peck (2003) below to propose counter measures.

**4** What is meant by the term 'corporate social responsibility' as it applies to international logistics? Illustrate your answer by referring to the *Probo Koala* disaster and the issue of child labour in the Sialkot soccer ball industry described in section 4.7.

# References

Bartlett, C.A. and Ghoshal, S. (1989) *Managing Across Borders*. Boston, MA: Harvard Business School Press.

Ferdows, K. (1989) 'Mapping international factory networks', in Ferdows, K. (ed.), *Managing International Manufacturing*, pp. 3–22. Amsterdam: Elsevier Science.

Helferich, O.K. and Cook, R.L. (2002) *Securing the Supply Chain*. Oak Brook, IL: Council of Logistics Management.

Hussain-Khaliq, S. (2004) 'Eliminating child labour from the Sialkot soccer ball industry', *The Journal of Corporate Citizenship*, Spring, pp. 101–7.

Leeman, J. (2007) *Supply Chain Management: Integrale ketenaansturing*. The Hague: Pearson Benelux.

Leigh, D. and Hirsch, A. (2009) Papers prove Trafigura ship dumped toxic waste in Ivory Coast. *The Guardian*, Thursday 14 May.

Peck, H. (2003) *Creating Resilient Supply Chains: A practical guide*, and *Understanding Supply Chain Risk: a self-assessment work book*. Available for free download, courtesy of the UK Department for Transport, at http://www.som.cranfield.ac.uk/som/scr

van Hoek, R.I. (1998) 'Reconfiguring the supply chain to implement postponed manufacturing', *International Journal of Logistics Management*, Vol. 9, No. 1, pp. 95–110.

Yip, G.S. (1989) 'Global strategy . . . in a world of nations?', *Sloan Management Review*, Fall, pp. 29–41.

## Suggested further reading

Dicken, P. (2003) *Global Shift: Reshaping the global economic map in the 21st century*. London: Sage Publications.

Dyckhoff, H., Reese, J. and Lackes, R. (2004) *Supply Chain Management and Reverse Logistics*. New York: Springer.

Gourdin, K.N. (2006) *Global Logistics Management: A competitive advantage for the 21st century*, 2nd edn. Oxford: Blackwell Publishing.

Grayson, D. and Hodges, A. (2004) *Corporate Social Opportunity!: Seven steps to make corporate social responsibility work for your business*. Sheffield: Greenleaf Publishing.

Rubman, J. and del Corral, D. (2009) *Creating Competitive Advantage through Integrated PLM and Sourcing Systems*. New York: Kurt Salmon Associates.

# CHAPTER 5

# Managing the lead-time frontier

**Objectives**

*The intended objectives of this chapter are to:*

- introduce time-based competition definitions and concepts;
- show how the lead time needs to be managed to serve customer expectations;
- explain how organisations compete through responsiveness.

*By the end of this chapter you should be able to understand:*

- how organisations compete through managing lead time;
- how time can be used as a performance measure;
- P-times and D-times and the consequences when they do not match;
- different solutions to reduce P-times;
- how to apply a methodology for implementing these solutions.

## Introduction

This chapter takes a strategic and a managerial view of time, and of the impact of time on logistics performance. It provides an introduction to the nature of time-based competition and how time can provide competitive advantage in logistics. As we saw in section 1.3, logistics supports the competitiveness of the supply chain as a whole by meeting end-customer demand through supplying what is needed, when it is needed and at low cost. Because logistics supports time and place commitments in the supply chain, it can be argued that the lead-time frontier accounts for at least half of logistics success.

Competing on time is the principle of taking timely completion of supply chain tasks to a higher level: that of compressing cycle times for supply chain operations for internal and external benefits. External benefits include:

- lowering overall cycle time and providing services faster;
- outrunning competition.

These benefits are especially important in the context of improving responsiveness to customers and volatile markets. Chapter 7 will return to these points.

Internal benefits include:

- shorter cash-to-cash cycles, thereby releasing working capital and reducing asset intensity of the supply chain;
- lowering inventories in the pipeline and storage by speeding up turnover times for work in progress and inventory.

These benefits are especially important within lean or waste elimination approaches, as will be developed in Chapter 6. This chapter focuses on how time-based solutions link with competitive strategy.

**Key issues**   This chapter addresses five key issues as follows:

1 **The role of time in competitive advantage:** using time in logistics management and strategy.
2 **P:D ratios and differences:** the gap between the time it takes to get the product to the customer (P-time) and the time the customer is prepared to wait (D-time).
3 **Time-based process mapping:** how to create visibility of time across the network.
4 **Managing timeliness in the logistics pipeline:** strategies and practices for coping when P-time is greater than D-time.
5 **A method for implementing time-based practices:** implementing time-based practices across the network.
6 **When, where and how?** Tactical considerations in planning a time-based strategy.

## 5.1 The role of time in competitive advantage

*Key issues:* **What is time-based competition, how does it link to other initiatives, and what is the purpose of it?**

### 5.1.1 Time-based competition: definition and concepts

Many attempts at business improvement focus on cost reduction and quality improvement. While a great deal of benefit has been achieved by many organisations through these efforts, most of the obvious opportunities for improvement have now been taken. This has led to time emerging as a fresh battleground in the search for competitive advantage. A working definition of competing on time is:

**The timely response to customer needs.**

The emphasis in this definition is on 'timely'. This means responding to customers' needs on time – neither early nor late. The implication of this definition is that the organisation must focus its capabilities on being responsive to the customer.

Traditionally, people often have the opinion that you cannot have low cost *and* high quality, or low cost *and* fast delivery, or fast delivery *and* high quality. The belief is that some kind of trade-off is necessary, meaning that more of one advantage means less of another. For example, better quality means putting in more inspectors, which increases costs. Such thinking was shown to be flawed when the quality movement of the 1980s demonstrated that good quality actually *reduces* costs (Crosby, 1979). The trade-off between cost and quality can be altered by *preventing* defects from happening in the first place through such measures as:

- designing the process so that defects cannot occur (error proofing);
- designing products so that they are easy to make and distribute;
- training personnel so that they understand the process and its limitations.

This leads to savings in *detecting* defects, by removing the need for inspection, and in avoiding the *failures* that lead to scrap and the cost of resolving customer complaints. The result is that overall quality costs (prevention + detection + failure) can be reduced by spending more on prevention.

Understanding trade-off relationships lies at the heart of a focal firm's ability to achieve competitive advantage. Relationships that need to be understood and harnessed include recognising that:

- costs do not have to increase in order to improve quality, they can reduce;
- costs do not have to increase when lead times are reduced. It may be possible to reduce both in some processes (see Figure 3.10);
- costs do not have to go up as product variety increases and times reduce, they can also reduce.

Each of these trade-offs has important links with strategy. A focus on responsiveness to the customer means that a focal firm needs to change the way it goes about its business. This involves redesigning systems and processes to give priority to time. In these circumstances, cost plays a supporting role – since time and cost have distinctive strategy implications (section 1.4.4) and are not linearly related (section 3.3.2).

## 5.1.2 Variety and complexity

One of the first challenges we have in describing logistics systems is to understand the terms variety and complexity. *Complexity* is often used casually to refer to things that we do not understand: as we understand more about a system, the boundary of 'complexity' recedes. Thus Galbraith (1977) defines complexity as the difference between the information needed to perform a task and the information actually possessed. A more helpful definition for logistics purposes, taken from the science of evolution (Edmunds, 1999) is:

> **A system is complex when it is difficult to formulate its overall behavior, even when given almost complete information about its components and their relationships**

In logistics terms, we start to lose control as a system becomes more complex. And the less complete the information, the more rapidly that control is lost. Eventually, the system may descend into *chaos*, the potential supply chain impacts of which we explore in section 6.1.4. Mercedes offers $3.3 \times 10^{24}$ possible variations on its E class model, which is 'far more than the company could ever sell in its entire existence' (Pil and Holweg, 2004). Only 17,000 of these variations are said to matter to the end-customer, a situation which appears to be making the logistics challenge unnecessarily complex. Here, the complexity of the E class is being driven by *variety*, and it is useful to distinguish two types of variety:

- *External variety*: is the choice offered to the end-customer, or potential finished product skus. Choice soon builds up – an automotive example would be:
  - 2 body styles × 15 power train combinations × 19 painted body colours × 15 trim colours × 70 factory fitted options ≈600,000 variations
- *Internal variety*: converts external variety into the internal requirements placed onto the supply chain. Holweg and Pil (2004) measured internal variety at three levels in the product structure (for an example of a product structure, see Case study 6.1): the basic product (models and body styles), intermediate (such as power trains, wiring harnesses and body colours), and peripheral (number and variety of components used).

These authors have used variety as a measure of complexity. Complexity makes it progressively more challenging to plan and control the supply chain. Cooper and Griffiths (1994) state that 'issues of variety and complexity are strongly linked', and list three rules for managing complexity:

- Increased variety tends to add to the complexity of logistics operations, and so increases both direct and indirect costs (section 3.2.2).
- Variety should only be increased when it contributes to added value. Heineken, the Dutch beer manufacturer, has 10 skus today compared with 2,500 across Europe a few years ago. The 'right' level of product variety starts with consumer research (Mahler and Bahulkar, 2009) rather than 'tail cutting' (Activity 2.1).
- System redesign can enhance added value through reducing the cost impact of an increase in variety. The antidote to complexity is *simplicity*, so auto manufacturers have implemented several ways to offer external variety without making internal operations too complex (see Case study 8.2).

Let us now return to the main theme of this chapter – time. Speed and dependability can both be improved by simplifying logistics processes.

## 5.1.3  Time-based initiatives

When a company attacks time directly, the first benefits to show up are usually shorter cycle times and faster inventory turns. Lower overhead costs usually follow, as the costs of dealing with breakdowns and delays begin to disappear from the system. So by seeking time reduction, *both* time reduction and cost reduction are often the rewards.

Attacking the sources and causes of delays helps reduce quality defects in product and service. Thus, by focusing on time, customers' needs are met more quickly and a quality benefit will often accompany the time benefit.

### 5.1.4 Time-based opportunities to add value

There are several ways in which a company can use time to help meet customer needs better and therefore add more value. The most common examples of this are:

- increased responsiveness to customer needs;
- managing increased variety;
- increased product innovation;
- improved return on new products;
- reducing risk by relying less on forecasts.

We deal with each of these opportunities in turn.

#### *Increased responsiveness to customer needs*

Increased responsiveness to customer needs is the most common reason for organisations to invest in time-based approaches to performance enhancement. Many elements of customer service are dependent upon time. These include how long it takes to deliver a product or service, achieving on-time delivery and how long it takes to deal with customer queries, estimates and complaints.

High levels of responsiveness to customers tend to correlate to greater loyalty from them and therefore more business over time. Such responsiveness is also addictive to the customer, creating customer lock-in. Once they get used to short lead times they often reorganise their own products and services to customers to make use of responsiveness from their suppliers, such as by holding less inventory and promising their own customers shorter lead times. Once they start to do this they find it hard to accept longer times again.

Customers of time-based organisations do not have to carry as much raw material or component stock and therefore benefit from a cost saving. In order to profit from the service they provide, a time-based organisation needs to demonstrate to customers that the total cost of doing business is lower, and then recover some of this value. This can be achieved by winning more business and/or by charging more.

#### *Managing increased variety*

We discussed the impact of variety on complexity of logistics operations in section 5.1.2. Shortened lead times in product development, the supply chain and manufacturing help factories deliver a variety of products without the traditional cost penalty. The same is also true of service organisations that can design and supply a range of new offerings in line with changes in market needs. By reducing overall lead time, product complexity and process set-up times, the production of a particular product can be scheduled more frequently with smaller production batches. This improves the variety of products available to a customer over a given time.

#### *Increased product innovation*

Time-based organisations are more likely to meet customer needs accurately by using short product development times to produce new products that meet customer needs. The shortening of product development lead time means that innovations can be capitalised on to maximum effect. If a company innovates through product design faster than its competitors it will become increasingly competitive. Conversely, if your competitors are innovative then reducing the time to develop imitations will underpin a 'fast follower' strategy to keep up.

### Improved return on new products

Reducing product development lead time means that a product can get to market earlier. This has a number of important advantages:

- the sales life of the product is extended;
- a higher price can be charged;
- new customers can be won;
- a high market share can be won through building upon the initial lead.

Each of these benefits can add to the other. Therefore, being first to the market allows a higher initial price to be charged, helping to recoup development costs quicker. This revenue will support investment into further developments necessary to retain these initial customers. Meanwhile, the initial product can continue to be sold, generating cash through its high market share. Being first in the market maximises the product life until the time when it becomes obsolete.

An impressive approach to the issue of obsolescence is attributed to Akio Morita, the co-founder of Sony and inventor of the Walkman. He believed that it was his job to make his own products obsolete before competitors did so. In effect, not only was his aim to make innovative products, he also sought to build on this success in the knowledge that if he did not then someone else soon would.

The related argument here is that of *break-even time* rather than the break-even volumes discussed in Chapter 3. Traditional break-even analysis focuses on the volume of product needed to be moved before the investment pays off. Given shortening times-to-market and compressed product lifecycles (e.g. from six months to 45 days of shelf-life for Nike footwear) the analysis shifts towards the question 'how long before break-even is reached?' Figure 5.1 illustrates the point.

As product lifecycles shrink, so the time window of opportunity for making profits also shrinks. This consideration means that a new product must achieve its break-even time more quickly.

### Reducing risk by relying less on forecasts

There is a saying in industry that there are only two types of forecast: wrong ones and lucky ones, and there are precious few of the latter! It is certainly true that the further ahead a company tries to forecast, the less likely the forecast is to be correct.

One of the aims of a time-based initiative is often to minimise how much forecasting is needed. By reducing the production lead time, the period when demand is uncertain becomes shorter. Forecasting over a shorter time period results in a more reliable forecast and therefore less risk of stockouts or obsolete stock. It also reduces the amount of finished goods stock needed, which frees up working capital.

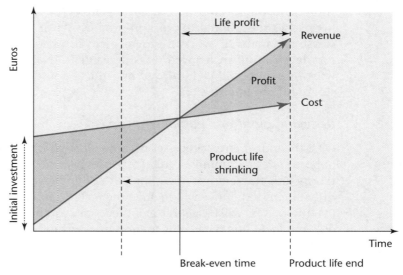

Figure 5.1    **Break-even time**

In product development, risk is also reduced by shortening lead times. This is achieved when the specification for the new product can be fixed with more certainty, thus improving the chances of market success.

The ultimate goal is to reduce production time so it lies within the lead time it has been given by the customer to deliver. In this situation, no forecasting is needed and all production is done in line with actual customer orders. The implications of reducing production time in relation to the demand time of customers are very significant and we have devoted the whole of section 5.2 to addressing them.

### 5.1.5   Time-based opportunities to reduce cost

The second key element of time-based competition is to reduce cost and therefore improve productivity through the elimination of non-value-added time in processes. This means that wasted lead time and unnecessary tasks that are not actually adding any value in the customers' eyes should be identified and eliminated. Stopping unnecessary tasks and removing wasted time from those that remain lowers cost by:

- reducing the need for working capital;
- reducing the need for plant and equipment capital;
- reducing development costs;
- reducing quality costs.

We address each of these in turn.

### *Reducing working capital*

Increasing the speed of flow through processes by eliminating unnecessary steps and wasted time reduces the amount of money tied up in the system. In the short term the focus will be upon inventory. Here, manufacturing lead time is inversely proportional to work-in-progress levels. By focusing on time we decrease raw material, work-in-progress and finished good stocks. Lowered inventory levels result in reduced working capital. As already mentioned, returns on working capital will be improved by reducing obsolescence caused by making to stock and not to order.

### Reducing plant and equipment capital

Over the longer term, processes become more visible, inventory levels reduce and opportunities to minimise capital expenses become more visible. These opportunities include the removal of equipment not employed in activities that add value. Initial items to remove will include the racking and pallets formerly used to store inventory. Next will be a purge of unnecessary equipment in offices, stores and production, including the jigging for unnecessary operations of obsolete parts.

In terms of what to do with superfluous items, some may be sold and capital recovered. The remaining items should just be skipped. While it may seem stupid to simply throw away equipment given how much some items have cost, these are sunk costs. If the equipment can no longer be used to generate revenue, all it does is incur further costs, such as maintenance, and the floor space it occupies will have many better uses.

As a company embraces time-based competition then success in the marketplace will increase demand for products and services that the customer really values. To make way for these means that space will be at a premium in the company. This is just the driver needed to replace the old with the new.

### Reducing development costs

Shortened lead times in product development are achieved in part by more effective use of development resources through elimination of rework and reduction of distracting superfluous projects. This leads to cost reductions as the time spent on a given project is less.

### Reducing quality costs

One of the main elements in improving quality is to reduce the time between an error being made and the problem being detected. The sooner the error is detected the smaller the amount of the product affected by it. Reducing lead times has a positive effect on the speed of feedback and hence quality costs are reduced.

In keeping with the total quality movement, time-sensitive organisations will only become consistently responsive if they strive to maintain quality processes. This means that as defects and errors arise they are detected quickly, root causes identified and effective solutions installed to ensure they cannot recur.

**Activity 5.1**

List six applications of responsiveness in an organisation; for example, 'external phone calls answered within five rings'. How many organisations can you think of that compete overtly on time, such as the Vision Express example given in Chapter 1?

### 5.1.6  Limitations to time-based approaches

Despite the clear benefits of time-based approaches to logistics management described above, there are often barriers to its application, as well as limitations to its relevance.

Two basic limitations to the need for time-based logistics management are the need for speed and the degree of speed required. Not all operating environments require speed. Product demand that is very predictable such as high-volume, low-value commodity products can be planned well in advance and processed without a particular speed. Not all customers value speed as they may be able to order well in advance of delivery. Delivery before the parts are needed creates unnecessary inventories. In particular, when there are costs involved in creating speedy delivery, customers may trade that off against ordering in advance. Only selected parcels need to be shipped with express carriers, for example.

A particular issue with the costs involved in speeding up logistics processes in the supply chain is the distribution of those costs between companies in the supply chain. It is well known that JIT deliveries, for example, may generate significant costs for suppliers whereas the customer may experience most of its benefits (such as low process inventories and rapid delivery). Toyota is capable of manufacturing a car in five days but has decided not to do so because of the pressure it would place on its suppliers and its distribution processes, creating costs that are not expected to be outweighed by revenue opportunities in current market circumstances.

An additional issue is that time-based approaches might lead to superior performance only being achieved on a limited number of occasions. An illustration of this situation is shown in Figure 5.2. In this example a supplier demonstrates that it is able to deliver in only one day. However, it is clear that this was achieved for only a minor portion of shipments, which does not mean that customers can depend on shipments being consistently completed within a day. Rather customers will order seven days in advance, where the required 99 per cent service level for deliveries is achieved. Time-based approaches are not about managing exceptions but managing for speed reliably.

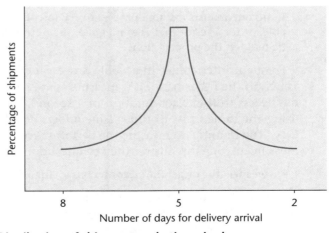

Figure 5.2  **Distribution of shipment cycle times in days**

## 5.2 P:D ratios and differences

*Key issues:* **What are P- and D-times, and why are they important to logistics strategy?**

P-time and D-time are measures of performance of the supply pipeline. They are explained in section 5.2.2, but let us first look at the importance of time as a performance measure.

### 5.2.1 Using time as a performance measure

One of the major advantages of a time-based approach to managing processes over one based on cost or quality is the ease with which time is understood as a measure. While cost and quality are open to differences in interpretation, time is an absolute measure. Stalk and Hout (1990) refer to the 'time elasticity of price', where the price that customers are prepared to pay is often related to the delivery speed. For example, Talleres Auto in Case study 1.4 was able to charge premium prices for spare parts in breakdown situations because these were 'distress purchases'.

Cost is a more subjective measure that is open to interpretation, three examples of which we saw in section 3.2. Many people have a poor grasp of how costs work in practice, and do not understand how the actions they take affect others. An all too frequent example is saving costs in one part of the supply network only to cause extra costs elsewhere. While quality is an important area for organisations to improve, there is a number of different ways to interpret 'quality'. Garvin (1988) lists eight *dimensions of quality*, which depend on the perspective taken, such as product quality (design), conformance quality (manufacturing) and fitness for use (customer). In order for quality measures to be useful they often require a statistical approach that can easily be misunderstood by those who have not been explicitly trained. Deming's famous Monte Carlo experiments with a funnel and glass marble (Deming, 1986: 327) illustrate the perils of interfering with a stable process:

> If anyone adjusts a stable process to try to compensate for a result that is undesirable, or for a result that is extra good, the output that follows will be worse than if he had left the process alone.

Frequent interference in a stable process increases the variability of its output! Time, on the other hand, is a measure that everyone understands. Every person has access to the exact duration of a second, minute or hour, thanks to clocks using the same units of time. Time allows people across an organisation, with very little training, to measure the performance of a process or activity. Using this measure anyone can answer the key question:

> Do we meet the target the customer has set for us?

By comparing this measure with one taken for the performance of competitors, we can easily answer the next key question:

> How good are we compared with the competition?

If we take a reason for measuring performance as being to understand the effect of making changes to a process, we can more easily answer the question:

**Is our performance getting better or worse?**

By using measures that are simple to understand, people can see the big issues more easily. They can measure and quantify the flow of activities directly, and ask themselves whether each of the steps in a process is adding real value or just adding cost. By following the flow through a process we can see where time is lost (see Chapter 3). This allows us to translate the data into time-reduction and cost-reduction opportunities. Looking at cost analyses alone does not tell anyone where to save time.

## 5.2.2  Using time to measure supply pipeline performance

In the same way that time can be used to measure the performance of a process within a company so it can be used to measure the supply pipeline. Two measures are presented below that are key to understanding supply pipeline performance: P-time and D-time.

### P-time

The first measure of performance for the total supply process is to determine how long it takes for a product or service to pass through it. This measure is used to identify the total logistics lead time, also known as the *P-time* or production time.

Just to be clear, the P-time is a measure of the total time it takes for a product to go through a pipeline. Thus it includes source, make and deliver lead times: it is not just the time it takes to supply from stock.

The measure starts the moment a new order is raised. It includes all the time needed to take a product through all the processes necessary to make and deliver that product. It is important to be clear about when these activities start and end in order for the measure to be consistent should you want to measure performance for a number of processes, including those of competitors. For a first attempt at this measure take the starting time as the point when an order is raised. Consider the total time needed to make and deliver a new product or batch of products. This includes the time needed to procure the longest lead parts and the total manufacturing time. The end of the process is the time when you fulfil an order and send the product to the customer.

When you are competent in measuring this time and creating useful data you should improve the measure you take. Instead of measuring from when you receive the order, measure from when the person in the customer's company realises they have a need. The end point is not when you send the product but when it is received by that person. This measure incorporates the internal process of the customer's company for informing you of the order and the steps they take to receive your delivery and get it to where it is needed. Exploring this process will reveal useful opportunities where you can help the customer to help themselves, thus strengthening your competitive position.

### D-time

The time for which customers are willing to wait to have their demand fulfilled is the *D-time* or demand time. D-time varies considerably. For example, the time a customer is willing to wait for 'fast food' is comparatively short. Assuming you are in a city with plenty of options, once you realise you are hungry you will probably want to be eating within ten minutes. This D-time will include the time it takes to walk to the cafeteria/restaurant, wait in a queue, sit at a table and be served. By contrast, as a customer of an up-market restaurant, you may have travelled for an hour, spent 20 minutes in a reception area over an aperitif and study the menu for 15 minutes, before happily waiting for a further half an hour for the meal to be cooked and served.

In addition to the obvious differences in grade and choice of food, the implication from a supply chain point of view is that the two restaurants must be organised in totally different ways to deliver the food within their customers' D-time. Interestingly, the same customer may visit both restaurants on the same day and accept the two different delivery systems. You do not *expect* to wait at a fast-food counter, but you *do* expect to linger over a meal in a high-quality restaurant.

Similar examples can be found in other industries. Buyers of new premium cars expect to wait a month or two for delivery when they place an order. Some people are not prepared to wait so long, but are prepared to accept a second choice of colour instead of their first, especially if the dealer gives a discount! Manufacturers of vehicles for customers with short D-times face increased supply chain challenges compared with those who have long ones. If it is not possible to make a car to order within the expected D-time, then the manufacturer is forced to carry out some or all of the logistics processes speculatively. The most risky scenario is to make the whole car for stock, hoping that the forecast mix of diesel and petrol, of left- and right-hand drive and so on is correct. But taking such a risk is necessary to cope with the customer who wants to drive away a vehicle the same day he or she enters the dealer's showroom.

It is worth pointing out the parallels in new product development. Some new product development is a race to get new ideas and innovations to market. However, others involve hitting specific customer-defined windows of opportunity for getting products to market. This is particularly true for lower-tier suppliers in supply chains. These two concepts have different objectives, as shown in Table 5.1.

Suppose your customer announces their intention for the launch of their new product. They usually give a number of deadlines to would-be suppliers, including:

- date for tenders;
- date for first-off samples;
- date for volume launch.

These are the D-times for each stage of product development. As a potential supplier, you must be able to meet all of these windows. Indeed, each supplier must be capable of meeting all of these deadlines for the product to meet its launch date successfully.

Table 5.1   **Getting ideas to market**

|  | **Idea to market** | **Meet window of opportunity** |
|---|---|---|
| **Objective** | Reduce lead time for turning idea into cash | Delay commitment of cash<br>Develop fresher, more fashionable product<br>Operate within shorter, less unstable forecast period |
| **Examples** | Electronics – maximise advantage in a new market segment before competitors respond | Summer clothing – delay outlay on raw materials to improve cash flow and delay commitment to particular designs until last possible time |
|  | Pharmaceuticals – get new drug to market to (1) save life and (2) begin to recover development spending | New car launch in four years' time – delay spend on tooling and delay design freeze so latest technologies can be incorporated |

## 5.2.3   Consequences when P-time is greater than D-time

P-time should be measured for each separate product group, because each will have different internal processes. D-time should be measured for each different market segment that is served, because customers may have different needs (e.g. prepared to wait/not prepared to wait).

Armed with this data, P-times and D-times should be contrasted for each product/customer group to see if P-time is more than D-time. A simple way to do this is by drawing them on a graph as time lines, as shown in Figure 5.3. The length of the arrows shown in Figure 5.3 represents *time*. The arrow for the P-time represents the time taken for buy, make and sell processes. The D-time arrow represents the time the customer is prepared to wait for an order to be fulfilled.

Comparing the length of the two arrows, it can be seen that the time it takes to respond to an order is longer than the customer is prepared to wait. Thus the P-time is greater than D-time. The consequence is that this focal firm is not able fully to make to order. On the other hand, it may be possible to complete the final 'make' processes such as assembly and test within the customer-required D-time. Such a strategy is called *assemble to order* (ATO). This is basically how Dell manages to supply the computer you want so quickly.

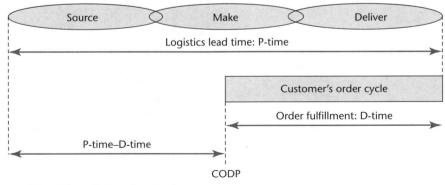

Figure 5.3   **When P-time is > D-time**

## Activity 5.2

Assess the benefits and concerns that may arise as a result of the relative sizes of P-time and D-time. Compile your views in the table below:

|  | P-time greater than D-time | P-time = D-time | P-time less than D-time |
|---|---|---|---|
| Benefits | ● <br> ● <br> ● | ● <br> ● <br> ● | ● <br> ● <br> ● |
| Concerns | ● <br> ● <br> ● | ● <br> ● <br> ● | ● <br> ● <br> ● |

The vertical broken line which separates D-time from P–D time in Figure 5.3 is *the customer order decoupling point* (CODP). This divides the point to which a focal firm carries out processes to known customer orders from the processes it has to carry out speculatively. We return to the importance of the CODP in terms of planning and controlling materials in the next chapter.

## CASE STUDY 5.1

# Wiltshire Distribution Transformers

Sid Beckett, the Managing Director of Wiltshire Distribution Transformers (WDT), had concentrated on a new generation of simplified, modular designs that used proven US technology. He had energetically exploited the market advantages this had given. WDT now has two major product ranges:

- TR 100: 3-phase, oil-cooled transformers with a power rating from 200 to 2000 kVA;
- PS 300: packaged substations that utilise TR 100 transformers with appropriate switchgear and LV control panels.

Judging by the number of enquiries, the market for both product ranges was now increasing.

### The new JIT system

Each product must be individually engineered to order (ETO). Formerly, this process had taken two weeks, because a design engineer had to develop an entirely new design from scratch based on the customer order. Designs have now been modularised as a result of the new system: that is, a new design is produced from a few hundred standard 'modules' that are held on file. This can be done by a sales engineer in a matter of hours. If a tender is accepted by a customer, it had formerly taken another two weeks to convert the tender information into specifications and drawings for manufacture. Today, it is possible simply to send the accepted tender information to the shop floor, and to use the set of standard engineering information already held on file to act as manufacturing instructions. The following is a list of the main features of the new JIT system.

## Enquiry processing

The engineer enters major design details (kVA rating, voltage ratio, product classification and quantity) into a computerised estimating program. From a list of 700 possible options, the selected ones to suit the tender requirements are added. From a library of material, labour and overhead costs, a tender price is calculated.

Should the customer accept this price, then a customer delivery date is agreed and the tender becomes the works order.

## Engineering instructions

WDT's efforts had resulted in the completion of a comprehensive library of standard drawings and instructions that covered all major options. The works order simply calls these up by reference number and description. The one exception is the fabricated cubicle that houses the packaged substations. This has to be individually designed. A simple CAD/CAM system enables the design and associated manufacturing instructions to be completed quickly. Presentations of the panels can be separately worked on and designed. The output is a set of computer numerical control (CNC) tapes for the relevant machines in the fabrication shop, and a set-up schedule indicating sheet size, clamp positions, list of tools, etc.

## Master production scheduling (MPS)

Standard networks are kept on file. Activity durations for each manufacturing process vary according to specific designs, and are picked up from the works order. Only bottleneck operations are scheduled, and can be loaded only up to 100 per cent of their capacity. Given the customer requirement date, the scheduling programme works backwards and loads activities to key resources so that the final assembly date will be met. The MPS acts by pulling demand through the manufacturing system (a process called pull scheduling).

Material requirements for each work centre for each order are calculated by means of a modular bill of material, which has been simplified as a result of the modular designs.

## Shop scheduling

The MPS generates operation release tickets (ORTs) for each scheduled process. The type and quantity of units required by the next process are withdrawn from the previous one as they are needed. When a work square becomes empty, an ORT is passed back to the preceding work centre to trigger a manufacturing operation. This serves as

▶

a signal (*kanban*) to the previous process to produce just enough units to replace those withdrawn.

Work is performed in sequence of ORTs, and is carried out only when an output square is available. Completed operations are marked up on the hard copy of the MPS, which is pinned to the wall of the works manager's office by the supervisors at the end of each shift. The MPS is updated for completed operations and new orders each week.

A combination of four weeks' reduction in the time taken to tender and the time taken to produce a manufacturing design, and a further two weeks' reduction in manufacturing times, has placed WDT in a pre-eminent position in the marketplace. Customers want to place orders for this type of equipment later and later in their own projects, so short lead times are a major benefit to WDT in the marketplace.

### Questions

1 Sketch out the main processes between a customer placing an enquiry and receiving delivery of a WDT transformer. Where has WDT really scored in terms of reducing this time?

2 What are the potential negatives of WDT's new JIT system in terms of limiting customer choice and short-circuiting the design process?

## 5.3 Time-based process mapping

*Key issue:* **How do you go about measuring time in a supply network?**

The purpose of supply chain mapping is to generate visibility of the processes within the supply chain. Once this visibility has been achieved it is possible to benchmark similar processes. The processes we need to map are the actual processes that are taking place, not what is supposed to happen. Quality standards based on ISO 9000 require processes to be documented, but within the organisation the actual process undertaken may often differ considerably. When undertaking a supply chain mapping exercise it is the *actual* process that we need to focus on. The key is to track one order, one product or one person through the process with respect to time. A map is a snapshot taken during a given time period. Workloads may vary during the course of a month, and so may the individual process times. Record the actual times that you observe. Most processes take place in batches, so if you are mapping a trailer being filled with tyres, record the time that the median (middle) tyre waits before being moved. The method of documentation of the process and the symbols to use are illustrated in Table 5.2.

Key operations and the subprocesses that can consume the most time and generate the greatest inefficiencies (e.g. waiting for transport) are revealed, enabling problem solving and improvement of the supply chain.

Table 5.2  **Example of process document**

| Step | Description | Symbol | Time | Notes |
|------|-------------|--------|------|-------|
| 1 | Machine complete | ○ | 1:37 | |
| 2 | Inspect | ❐ | 0:45 | |
| 3 | Wait transport | D | 5:53 | |
| 4 | Transport to heat treat | ⇨ | 0:08 | |
| 5 | Wait heat treat | D | 3:34 | |
| 6 | Heat treat | ○ | 4:15 | |

| Symbol | Description |
|--------|-------------|
| ⇨ | transport |
| ▼ | store |
| ○ | operation |
| ❐ | inspect |
| D | delay |

The following sections give an overview of the key stages involved in the time-based mapping process.

## 5.3.1  Stage 1: Create a task force

Before the mapping process can be undertaken it needs to be recognised that supply chain processes cross all functions of the organisation. It is therefore important to have all key functions represented. The task force must be assured of top management support. A project champion may also need to be appointed.

## 5.3.2  Stage 2: Select the process to map

It may not be feasible to map the total supply chain initially. Take an overview of the core processes within the organisation and the time they take before deciding on the priorities for detailed mapping. To get the organisation to 'buy in' to the project, a subprocess may be identified that has been a particular problem. This can act as a pilot for the task force, enabling them to prove that their methods really work. When selecting the process, ensure that there is a generic customer or group of customers that the process serves. A clear start (or trigger) and finish to the process should also be present.

### 5.3.3 Stage 3: Collect data

The most effective way to collect the data is to follow an item through the process. This is often referred to as *walking the process*. An actual component or order will be followed through all the stages of the process. Identify someone who is actively involved in each part of the process and knows what is really happening within the process: interview these key individuals. Get the interviewee to describe each movement of the item with respect to time. It can be useful to ask the interviewee to describe 'a day in the life of' that product or order. Remember the steps an item goes through are not just those where something is done: for example, items could be waiting or being moved, or may be sitting waiting for a decision to be made. Identify an appropriate level of detail at which to map the process. Initially it might be better to map at a high level to gain an overview of the process; one can always map in more detail if needed later.

### 5.3.4 Stage 4: Flow chart the process

Use the data collected by walking the process and the interviews with operators to sketch a flow chart so linkages and dependencies between steps can be clarified before constructing the time-based process map. This flow chart is used by the task force to ensure they have not missed any steps in the process.

### 5.3.5 Stage 5: Distinguish between value-adding and non-value-adding time

A rough definition of value-adding time is time when something takes place on the item that the end-customer is willing to pay for. The definition of value-adding time requires due consultation, and should be aligned with the overall business strategy. The business strategy should define the markets and segments, and the accompanying order qualifiers and order winners (see Chapters 1 and 2). Once the value-adding criteria at the strategic level have been defined, these can be translated into value-adding criteria at an operational level. The time data collected in stage 3 can then be analysed to identify the value-adding time. Value-adding time is characterised using three criteria:

- whether the process (or elements of the process) physically transforms the material that forms the input to that process;
- whether the change to the item is something that the customer values or cares about and is willing to pay for;
- whether the process is right the first time, and will not have to be repeated in order to produce the desired result that is valued by the customer.

Non-value-adding activity can be split into four categories: delay, transport, storage and inspection, using the categories from Table 5.2.

## 5.3.6   Stage 6: Construct the time-based process map

The purpose of the time-based process map is to represent the data collected clearly and concisely so that the critical aspects of the supply network can be communicated in an easily accessible way. The ultimate goal is to represent the process on a single piece of paper so that the task force and others involved in the project can easily see the issues. A simple Gantt chart technique can be used to show the process, and different categories of non-value-adding time can be represented on this. These categories will be dependent on the nature of each process. Figure 5.4 shows three operations processes (delivery, production and goods in), with the last one magnified to show four types of waste.

From the interviews and data from walking the process, extract the relevant data. It is sometimes useful to sketch a flow diagram so that linkages and dependences between steps can be clarified before constructing the map. This flow diagram can be used to approximate the total time that the business process consumes.

## 5.3.7   Stage 7: Solution generation

Once the time-based process map has been produced, the opportunities for improvement are generally all too obvious. The task force can collect ideas and categorise causes of non-value-adding activity using problem-solving approaches such as cause-and-effect diagrams. (A helpful condensed guide to problem-solving tools and techniques will be found in Bicheno and Holweg, 2008.)

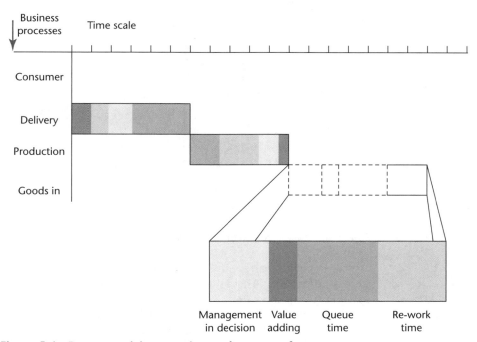

**Figure 5.4   Process activity mapping and sources of waste**

The Electro-Coatings case study (Case study 5.2) describes how the above principles were applied to a focal firm that produces electroplated parts for the automotive industry.

## Electro-Coatings Ltd

Electro-Coatings Ltd electroplates parts for the automotive industry; for example, the marque badges fitted to the front of prestige cars. Customers were becoming increasingly demanding, resulting in Electro-Coatings' undertaking a review of its internal supply chain. The initial analysis by walking the process identified 12 key processes, as shown in Figure 5.5.

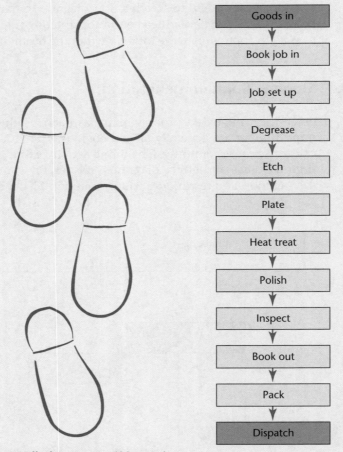

Goods in
↓
Book job in
↓
Job set up
↓
Degrease
↓
Etch
↓
Plate
↓
Heat treat
↓
Polish
↓
Inspect
↓
Book out
↓
Pack
↓
Dispatch

Figure 5.5   **Walk the process (12 steps)**

Once this initial map has been produced, each step was mapped in detail and some 60 steps were identified. These steps have been summarised as a flow diagram in Figure 5.6, showing every process step.

An initial analysis of value-adding and non-value-adding time was undertaken. This is shown in Table 5.3, which summarises the total time, wasted time and value-adding time for each of the 12 steps. These data were then used to produce a map with the value-adding (activity) time and non-value-adding (wasted) time shown as the series of 11 steps (etch and plate were combined) against total elapsed time in hours (Figure 5.7).

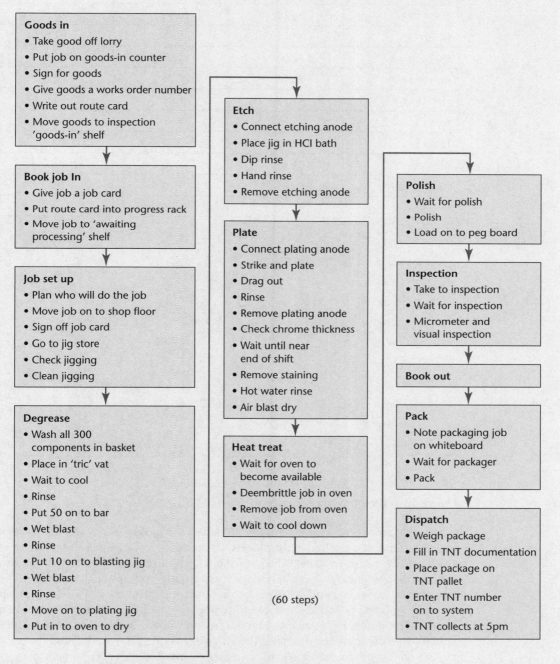

**Figure 5.6   Identify every process step**

**Table 5.3   Time-based analysis data**

|  | Total time/hours | Wasted time/hours | Activity time/hours |
|---|---|---|---|
| Goods in | 0.00 | 3.91 | 0.41 |
| Book job in | 4.32 | 20.00 | 0.41 |
| Job set-up | 24.73 | 5.50 | 1.77 |
| Degrease | 32.00 | 1.00 | 0.60 |
| Etch and plate | 33.60 | 8.75 | 2.20 |
| Heat treat | 44.55 | 0.00 | 4.50 |
| Polish | 49.05 | 1.95 | 1.95 |
| Inspect | 52.95 | 9.50 | 1.00 |
| Book out | 63.45 | 0.00 | 0.40 |
| Pack | 63.85 | 4.00 | 0.85 |
| Dispatch | 68.70 | 0.00 | 0.40 |

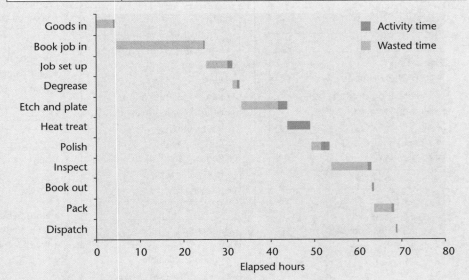

**Figure 5.7   Time-based process map: current**

The total process took approximately 70 hours. The project team held an afternoon meeting with those involved in the process, and the results of this brainstorming session produced the cause-and-effect diagram shown in Figure 5.8. This was then used to identify opportunities for improving the process. For example, the analysis revealed that jobs arriving goods inwards at 9.00am might not be input into the system until 5.00pm because the operator would undertake the computer inputting in one go at the end of the day. This resulted in manufacturing not having visibility of the updated order book until 9.00am the following morning. This was easily addressed by combining the booking-in process with the good inwards process, removing a further lead time. Figure 5.9 depicts the re-engineering process.

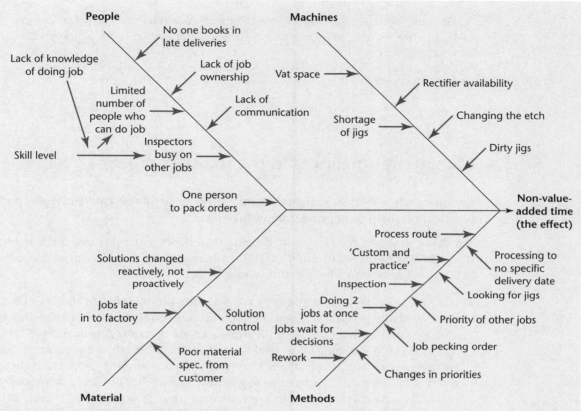

**Figure 5.8    Cause-and-effect diagram**

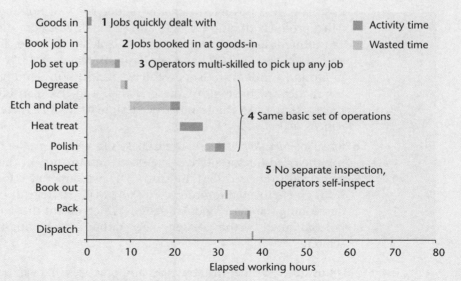

**Figure 5.9    Time-based process map: re-engineered**

The simple actions undertaken by the company resulted in the total process taking 37 hours. This led to a more responsive service being offered to its customers and increased business.

(Source: Based on a study by Dr Paul Chapman and Professor Richard Wilding, Cranfield Centre for Logistics and Supply Chain Management)

## 5.4  Managing timeliness in the logistics pipeline

*Key issue:* When P-time is greater than D-time, what time-based strategies and practices can help to improve competitiveness?

Two basic strategies for managing timeliness in the logistics pipeline are make to stock (MTS) and make to order (MTO). In between, we have assemble to order (ATO). We begin with a brief description of each:

- *Make to stock (MTS).* Here, the key task is to offer products for customers to buy from available inventory. Customer service is determined by this availability, so a key performance measure in supermarkets is *on-shelf availability* (OSA). Achieving 100 per cent OSA would mean holding infinite inventories, so in practice a compromise of say 98.5 per cent OSA across most products at most times is targeted. MTS firms have to plan the availability of their inventory by means of a distribution network which may involve several levels (regional, national and local). In turn, this requires that models are determined for *stock replenishment* – how much, when and where.

- *Assemble to order (ATO).* By shifting the decoupling point (CODP, Figure 5.3) upstream, it is possible to greatly reduce risk – of holding inventories of finished products that do not sell, and of missing out on sales opportunities because the desired product was unavailable at the time. Thus Dell computers and BMW cars use ATO as their basic strategies. A BMW 3-series is available in around a million finished vehicle specifications, and it would be risky and impractical to have all of these available in the distribution pipeline. This means that the vehicle must be designed flexibly in terms of *components, options and modules.*

- *Make to order (MTO).* Here, the CODP is moved to product design, thus reducing the need for speculative processes even further. In the Wiltshire Distribution Transformers case (Case study 5.1), we saw how a focal firm had moved from an engineered to order (ETO) to a MTO strategy. It had achieved this by developing standard modular designs which meant that customer orders could be configured by the sales engineer, rather than having to be designed from scratch.

Let us now consider the strategies and practices that can be used to cope when P-time is greater than D-time.

### 5.4.1  Strategies to cope when P-time is greater than D-time

When faced with a D-time shorter than the corresponding P-time, a company has a number of options. In the short term it can attempt to make to order, or it can forecast demand and supply from stock (MTS). Making to order in these circumstances is likely to dissatisfy customers. If competitors exist that can deliver within the customer's D-time, or there are substitute products available that will, then the customer is likely to select them. If there are no alternatives then it may be possible to continue supplying to order for the short term. In the longer term it is likely that the customer will seek to develop alternative suppliers, or re-engineer its products to remove the need for yours.

The more common solution is to forecast customer demand, make products to stock and supply from there. This stock may be held as finished goods if the D-time is very short, or it could be work-in-progress held in the manufacturing process that can be finished in time. This option incurs a number of penalties. The stocks of goods will need to be financed, as will the space needed to store them. There is also the risk that the customer may not order those goods already made within their shelf-life, causing them to become obsolete.

Both make to order and make to stock have associated costs and risks, so a company should look at ways to reduce these costs and risks in the longer term. Reducing risks can be grouped into three inter-linked areas. These are marketing, product development and process improvement. Each of these areas is analysed below.

#### Marketing

There are various ways in which you could reduce risk, with customer help. For example, ask the customer to cooperate by supplying more detailed demand information at an earlier stage. Speed up the access to demand data, perhaps by locating one of your people in the customer's scheduling process. Perhaps the customer is prepared to wait longer than stated, if you can guarantee delivery on time.

#### Product development

There are only so many improvements to the reduction of production time that can be made when a process is based around existing products. With time-based thinking in mind, next-generation products can be designed for 'time to market'. Such thinking aims for products that can be made and distributed quickly, and which offer product variety without unnecessary complexity.

#### Process improvement

Time-based organisations come into their own by changing the way they go about their business. They engineer their processes to eliminate unnecessary steps, and take wasted time out of those that remain. Engineering your key processes means focusing on those things the customer cares about and getting rid of all the rest. Having done this once, the best organisations go on to do it again and again as they learn more about their customers and grow in confidence in what they can change.

## 5.4.2 Practices to cope when P-time is greater than D-time

There are a number of ways to reduce P-time. These can be summarised as follows:

- *Control* by optimising throughput and improving process capability.
- *Simplify* by untangling process flows and reducing product complexity.
- *Compress* by straightening process flows and reducing batch sizes.
- *Integrate* by improving communications and implementing teams.
- *Coordinate* by adding customer-specific parts as late as possible.
- *Automate* with robots and IT systems.

### Control

In any process, lead time depends on the balance between load and capacity. If demand rises above available capacity, lead times will increase unless resource is also increased, for example through overtime or subcontracting work. Therefore, in order to maintain or reduce lead time it is necessary to balance this equation effectively by optimising throughput. Similarly, if a process is out of control, and we are never sure whether a conforming product will be produced, the focus will be on improving the capability of that process.

### Simplify

Simplification is concerned with cutting out sources of process complexity and of product complexity. Process complexity is often caused by many different products *sharing the same process*. This process becomes a bottleneck, and process flows become tangled because they all have to go through this single, central process. In manufacturing, the solutions are based on cellular manufacturing: in distribution, the solutions are based on different distribution channels. Product complexity is often related to the *number of parts*. The more parts there are in a product the more difficult it is to plan, to make and to sell. One way to reduce product complexity is to reduce the number of parts, by integrating several components into one. The other is to reduce the number of parts by standardising them between products.

### Compress

Compressing P-time is concerned with squeezing out waste in each process step. There are two main ways to achieve this. First, straighten the process flow by making a linear flow for each product. Second, reduce the batch size so that flow is improved and queuing time is minimised.

### Integrate

Integrating different value-adding activities so that they work more closely together helps to reduce P-time. Integration is in turn helped by improving the speed and accuracy of information to the process owner. Important issues are demand information (what to do next?), product information (what is it?) and process information (how is it done?). Ways of speeding up information range from simple, paperless systems such as *kanban*, through simple IT systems such as email, to more complex systems such as making EPOS data available in real time through the internet. Integration is also helped by forging relationships between departments or organisations that need to communicate. Teams and partnerships help to integrate activities that are otherwise disconnected.

### Coordinate

Other approaches to reducing P-time aim to reorganise value-adding activities so that they are done in parallel and/or in the best order. Thus running activities at the same time (in parallel) instead of one after another (in series) will reduce lead times. Sometimes it is possible to reduce lead times by doing the same activities in a different order. This may make it possible to combine activities or allow them to be done in parallel. It may also make better use of resources by fitting an extra job into a shift, or by running long tasks that need no supervision overnight.

### Automate

This approach should be used last, once all the others have delivered their improvements (do not automate waste!). Chiefly it is concerned with reducing lead time through the use of robots and IT systems to speed up processes. Such approaches are best focused on bottleneck steps in the overall process. The aim is to improve process capability and reliability as well as speed.

## 5.5 A method for implementing time-based practices

*Key issue:* How can time-based practices be implemented?

Becoming a time-based company means that a systematic approach is essential to improve all three measures of cost, quality and time. This approach means identifying and removing the sources and causes of waste in the supply network, rather than merely treating the symptoms. The method shown here will give you a starting point for implementing a time-based strategy.

First, you need to understand the ways in which customers value responsiveness. Then the method (shown in Figure 5.10) takes you through a series of steps that help you to change your processes to be able to deliver what the customer wants.

### 5.5.1 Step 1: Understand your need to change

The first step in implementing a time-based strategy is to understand whether you *need* to change. This need to change depends on how important responsiveness is to your customers. Here are five key questions that will help to identify the strategic importance of time:

- Is supply responsiveness important to your customers?
- How important is it to them?
- What is the supply D-time target that customers have officially or unofficially set?
- What happens if you do not meet this target?
- What is the total P-time, i.e. the lead time taken from an order arriving in the company until it is fulfilled and finally leaves the company?

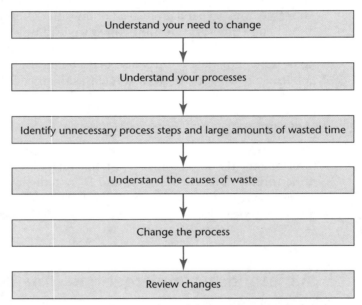

**Figure 5.10   A methodology for time-based process improvement**

## 5.5.2   Step 2: Understand your processes

While you may think you already know your current processes, the only way to make sure is to walk the process in the way described in section 5.3. Mapping a process involves creating a very simple flow chart. This is best done with a pad of paper, a pencil – and a smile. Start at the point where a customer order comes into the company. This could be with a salesman in the field, over a phone, through the fax or via a computer. Write down the name of this step and draw a box around it. Ask whoever picks this order up what happens next. Very probably it gets reviewed, logged in or put on someone's desk. Any of these options is a step. Write this down on your pad of paper below the first step. Draw a box around it too, then join the boxes with an arrow. Keep going, throughout the company, following that order until a product is finally delivered to the customer. Write down every step you encounter.

During your expedition following the process through the company ask the people who undertake each step how long it takes to work on a single, typical order. You need to find out the *activity time* – the time they spend physically working on it, not the time it spends on their desk or next to their machine.

When you have mapped the whole process, compare the total lead time (the P-time) with the time in which your customers are demanding you respond to them (their D-time). How well did you do? If the P-time is greater than the D-time you have a challenge.

Now add up the activity times for all of the steps in the process. How does this compare with the overall lead time (the P-time)? It is likely to be considerably smaller? How does it compare with the D-time? Possibly it is also smaller. If so, you have a real opportunity to improve your responsiveness and get your lead time within that demanded by the customer through applying the ideas listed above, and without the need for extensive investment in technological solutions.

### 5.5.3   Step 3: Identify unnecessary process steps and large amounts of wasted time

Using your process flow chart you should work with the other members of the company involved in the process to identify those steps that do not add value to the customers. Also, identify where large amounts of wasted time are added to the overall lead time.

### 5.5.4   Step 4: Understand the causes of waste

Once again, work with your colleagues and identify the causes of the unnecessary process steps and wasted time. Why do they exist?

### 5.5.5   Step 5: Change the process

Having understood the process, and the causes of waste in it, choose from the generic solutions, described above, those approaches that will make the process more responsive. Apply these solutions with vigour, going for easy ones that deliver early results first to give everyone confidence that you are doing the right thing.

### 5.5.6   Step 6: Review changes

Having altered the way you go about your operations, measure the performance of the process again and find out whether there have been any changes to your performance. Have you become more responsive? If not, why not? Find out and try again. If you have, tell as many people as you can, and have another go at building on your success.

### 5.5.7 Results

The likely result of the above change programme is a situation such as that graphically displayed in the basic four-step supply chain shown in Figure 5.11. Through the implementation of time-based practices or initiatives, cycle times are compressed throughout the supply chain. As a result, delivery can take place in a timely manner more reliably and faster, while more operations can be performed to order within the service window. As a result, lower asset intensity is coupled with enhanced delivery service as possible input to both lean thinking and agility efforts (see Chapters 6 and 7 respectively).

Note that this approach assumes a supply chain point of view, not just a focus on manufacturing or any other segment of the supply chain. A well-known illustration of the importance of this point is that lean approaches have resulted in automotive manufacturing cycle times being compressed to a matter of hours. After manufacture, however, cars are stored in the distribution pipeline or in dealer outlets for weeks, if not months. Lack of supply network thinking results in all of the cycle time investments in manufacturing being wasted.

This does not mean to say that all operations in the supply chain need to be subject to time compression. In the example shown in Figure 5.11, the new delivery cycle times (shown with a broken rule) actually increase in the new structure. But this suboptimisation is allowable, as traditional distribution from local warehouses here is replaced with direct delivery from the factory, where products are made to order. The transition to make to order replaces the need for inventory-holding points, where goods typically are stored for extensive periods of time. Of course this basic example also indicates how time-based initiatives can require structural supply chain redesign, such as the reconfiguration of distribution channels and the adjustment of manufacturing systems and policies.

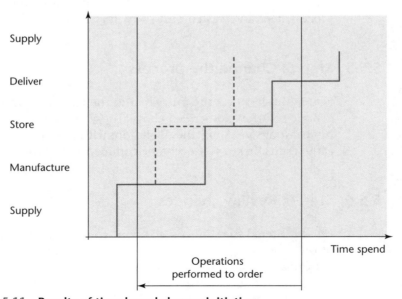

Figure 5.11   **Results of time-based change initiatives**

## 5.6  When, where and how?

There are several tactical considerations to be made when planning a time-based strategy. We have grouped these in the form of three questions to be asked:

- *When?* Time-based competition is only as relevant as the customer perceives it to be. Speed for the sake of speed can create unnecessary costs, and can cut corners, leading to poor quality.

- *Where?* D-times are a measure of the importance of speed as a competitive factor, while P-times measure the ability to deliver. The integration of the two measures the point at which the customer order penetrates the supply chain. In Chapter 5 and Chapter 6, we develop this issue in terms of the customer order decoupling point.

- *How?* The more predictable and lower-priority products and components can be delivered from inventory with less priority given to speed. Shipments of customised products can be assembled from stocks of standard components and modules within the D-time demanded.

## Summary

*What is the lead-time frontier?*

- Competing on time demands a fast response to customer needs. Time-based approaches to strategy focus on the competitive advantage of speed, which helps a network to cope with variety and product innovation, while also improving returns on new products. Speed also means less reliance on long-term forecasts.

- Speed of response helps to lower costs by reducing the need for working capital, and plant and equipment. It also helps to reduce development costs and the cost of quality.

- The lead-time frontier is concerned with reducing P-time (time needed to produce a product or service) to less than D-time (time for which the customer is prepared to wait).

- Differences between P-times and D-times are referred to as the lead-time gap. The gap has strategic implications for marketing, product development and process development. P-time can be reduced by a six-stage process: control, simplify, compress, integrate, coordinate and automate.

*How do we measure and implement time-based strategies?*

- Time-based mapping aims to generate visibility of time in the supply network. A six-step approach to mapping involves creating a task force, selecting the process, collecting data, distinguishing between value-adding and non-value-adding activities, constructing the time-based process map and generating a solution.

- Implementing time-based practices can be accomplished using another six-step process involving understanding the need to change, understanding the processes, identifying non-value-adding processes, understanding the causes of waste, and reviewing what has been done.

## Discussion questions

1 Why is time important to competitive advantage? Identify and explain six key contributions that speed can make to logistics strategy.

2 'Variety yes, complexity no'. Discuss the implications of this statement to logistics strategy.

3 Explain the significance of P:D ratios. How can the production lead time be reduced?

4 Sections 5.3, 5.4 and 5.5 all contain step-by-step models for reducing waste and implementing improved logistics processes. Explain why such models are useful in implementing logistics strategy.

## References

Bicheno, J. and Holweg, M. (2008) *The Lean Toolbox – the essential guide to lean transformation*, 4th edn. Buckingham: Picsie Books.

Cooper, J. and Griffiths, J. (1994) 'Managing variety in automotive logistics with the rule of three', *The International Journal of Logistics Management*, Vol. 5, No. 2, pp. 29–40.

Crosby, P.B. (1979) *Quality is Free: The Art of Making Quality Certain*. New York: McGraw-Hill.

Deming, W.E. (1986) *Out of the Crisis*. Cambridge, MA: MIT.

Edmunds, B. (1999) 'What is complexity?', in *The Evolution of Complexity*, F. Heyhighter, J. Boller and D. Riegle (eds). Dordrecht: Kluwer Academic Publishers.

Galbraith, J. R. (1977) *Organisation Design*. Reading, MA: Addison Wesley.

Garvin, D.A. (1988) 'The multiple dimensions of quality', in *Managing Quality*, Ch. 4. New York: Free Press.

Holweg, M. and Pil, F. (2004) *The Second Century-reconnecting the customer and value chain through build-to-order*. Cambridge, MA: MIT.

Mahler, D. and Bahulkar, A. (2009) 'Smart complexity', *Strategy and Leadership*, Vol. 37, No. 5, pp. 5–11.

Pil, F. and Holweg, M. (2004) 'Linking product variety to order-fulfillment strategies', *Interfaces*, Vol. 43, No. 5, Sept–Oct, pp. 394–403.

Stalk, G. and Hout, T. (1990) *Competing Against Time*. New York: Free Press.

### Suggested further reading

Galloway, D. (1994) *Mapping Work Processes*. Milwaukee, WI: ASQC Quality Press.

Hammer, M. (2007) 'The process audit', *Harvard Business Review,* April, pp. 111–23.

Rother, M. and Shook, J. (1999) *Learning to See,* Version 1.3. Brookline, MA: The Lean Enterprise Institute Inc.

# CHAPTER 6

# Supply chain planning and control

**Objectives**

*The intended objectives of this chapter are to:*

- explain the processes by which material flow is planned and executed within a focal firm and between partners in a supply chain;
- explain the initiatives that have been developed to overcome poor coordination in retail supply chains.

*By the end of this chapter you should be able to:*

- appreciate the sophistication that lies behind an integrated model of material flow in a supply chain, and why this model is so easily corrupted;
- understand how corruption of flow causes loss of focus on ability to meet end-customer demand;
- develop sensitivity for the initiatives that have been developed to restore flow.

## Introduction

In Chapter 3, we introduced the simple framework for coordinated processes across the supply chain that has become known as the 'SCOR model' (Figure 3.15). This model creates a vision of integration of supply chain processes both upstream and downstream. A shared planning process – that coordinates movements seamlessly from one process to the next – orchestrates material flow.

The reality of supply chain management today – summarised in our paper on theory, practice and future challenges (Storey *et al.*, 2006) – shows a very different picture. We conducted a three-year detailed study of six supply chains, which encompassed 72 companies in Europe. The focal firms in each instance were sophisticated, blue-chip corporations operating on an international scale. Managers across at least four echelons of the supply chain were interviewed and the supply chains were traced and observed. We showed that 'supply management is, at best, still emergent in terms of both theory and practice. Few practitioners were able – or even seriously aspired – to extend their reach across the supply chain in the manner prescribed in much modern theory.'

The factors behind the gap between vision and reality are many, reflecting the sophisticated web of processes and coordination that lie behind the vision and the almost endless ways of corrupting it. UK retailer Marks & Spencer (M&S)

introduced vendor managed inventory (VMI – described in Section 6.2.3) to its clothing range, and achieved high levels of coordination with its tier 1 suppliers, low costs and high on-shelf availability. However, events unravelled after a few years due to a number of factors (Storey *et al.*, 2005). Two of the major factors were:

- A change in management structure as M&S created a new category team, many of whom did not like the idea of sharing sales data with suppliers. The method used to generate sales data was changed, and resulted in loss of access to the flow of sales data on which the VMI system depended.

- Suppliers began to outsource their production to new factories in South-East Asia and Morocco to reduce costs, but this resulted in six-week replenishment cycles and loss of responsiveness. Complementary sets of clothes were sourced to different countries, and it proved hard to coordinate deliveries.

Decisions based on advantages internal to a focal firm, and on the search for cheaper prices, are but two common factors in corrupting the flow of materials and information and the focus on the end-customer. Corruption is displayed by poor customer service, stock write-offs or mark-downs, and a lot of resource devoted to 'fire fighting'.

This chapter aims to summarise the detail of an integrated planning and control system. The most comprehensive models originate from manufacturing, and link key activities such as resource planning, demand management and capacity planning into a holistic framework. Individual firms have been quite successful not only in developing effective manufacturing planning and control (MPC) systems, but also in integrating them with other business functions such as finance and human resources through enterprise resource planning (ERP). However, linkages *between* the MPC systems of supply chain partners are relatively weak (Vollman *et al.*, 2005: 578). And linkages between MPC systems at manufacturers and 'service' processes such as distribution and back of store are even weaker. Skim the detail at your peril! Far too many logistics 'decisions' are made on the basis of lack of understanding of the sheer scale and scope of the intricacies of balancing load and capacity, of coordinating marketing wants and supply chain realities.

In section 6.1, we begin by showing how the linkages between manufacturing firms should develop. We then turn to the management of inventory in the supply chain. Finally, we examine the planning and control processes in retail, and explain the implications for integrating material flow across the supply chain. Retail supply chains are of particular interest because end-customer demand is tracked continuously through POS data. There should accordingly be every opportunity to develop a seamless coordination between demand and supply, as envisaged in Figure 1.7. There are challenges enough to cope with, notably the integration of manufacturing, distribution and service processes. However – historically at least – retailers have given priority to the market and have expected manufacturers to keep pace without investing much in terms of coordinating demand and supply. This has resulted in such problems as amplification of demand upstream – the so-called 'bullwhip effect' – high inventories and lengthy P-times. The second part of this chapter therefore continues by reviewing some of the key initiatives that have been developed in recent years to improve planning and control of materials in retail supply chains.

**Key issues** This chapter addresses two key issues as follows:

1 **The supply chain 'game plan':** planning and control in manufacturing. Managing independent demand items. Retail supply chains – driven by the market rather than by the supply chain. Implications for supply chain planning and control.

2 **Overcoming poor coordination in retail supply chains:** initiatives to improve coordination in retail supply chains. Efficient consumer response (ECR). Collaborative planning, forecasting and replenishment (CPFR). Vendor managed inventory (VMI). Quick response (QR).

## 6.1 The supply chain 'game plan'

*Key issues:* **What are the key steps in planning and executing material flow and information flow within the focal firm? What are the key steps in planning and executing material flow and information flow between partners in a supply network? What are the implications for planning and controlling the supply chain as a whole?**

In this section, we consider planning and control processes across a simple supply chain such as that shown in Figure 1.1. We start with planning and control processes at the manufacturer, and the demands this generates on the supplier (well documented in such publications as Vollman *et al.*, 2005). Once it has been made, a fresh batch of product turns into *finished product inventory* – initially stored in the manufacturer's national distribution centre (NDC). So next we turn to the management of inventory in the supply chain, showing that *different* models are likely to be used by manufacturers and retailers to determine how much and when to order. We then explain planning and control from the retailer's perspective, and conclude with the implications for planning and controlling the supply chain as a whole.

### 6.1.1 Planning and control within manufacturing

The purpose of a manufacturing planning and control (MPC) system is to meet customer requirements by enabling managers to make the right decisions. The system coordinates information on key 'source–make–deliver' processes to enable material to flow efficiently and effectively. Three time horizons are involved for all of these processes:

● *Long term*: to support decisions about capacity provision. These decisions are essentially strategic, and answer the questions how much capacity is needed, when and of what type? Thus Mercedes-Benz may plan new model ranges for 20 years ahead – including outline volumes, internal and supplier capacities and distribution strategies.

● *Medium term*: to match supply and demand. Here, Mercedes may plan in more detail over the next 12 months to ensure that forecast demand can be met by correct material provision, together with capacity and resource (such as manpower) availability. The plan would be refreshed monthly.

- *Short term*: to meet day-to-day demand as it unfolds. Here, Mercedes makes weekly production plans to meet specific customer orders. There may be numerous changes that affect achievement of the medium-term plan. These include changes in customer demand, facility problems and supplier shortages. The short-term plan helps managers to decide what corrective actions are needed to resolve such problems, and would be refreshed daily or weekly.

Figure 6.1 shows the main modules in an MPC system. The top section is called the 'front end', and provides an overall match of demand and resource. We here summarise the main front-end modules, followed by a summary of engine and back end:

- *Demand management*: collates demand from all sources – external (forecasts and orders), internal (other firms within the organisation) and spares. Such demand is called *independent* – that is, it is independent of the actions of the focal firm. Referring to Figure 5.3, demand is independent up to the customer order decoupling point (CODP). At this point, demand changes from independent to *dependent*. Upstream from the CODP, in the area referred to as 'P-time–D-time', the focal firm assumes responsibility for sourcing and making speculatively – on the assumption that orders will eventually transpire. Thus *make to order* (MTO, section 5.4) incurs less speculation than *assemble to order* (ATO) and much less than *make to stock* (MTS). Speculation implies that it is necessary to *forecast* demand for the relevant module. Thus, forecasting for sales and operations planning is carried out monthly or quarterly and is at the level of the overall product line. Forecasts for master production scheduling purposes are refreshed frequently for the next few days or weeks, and are made at the level of the individual sku (stock keeping unit).

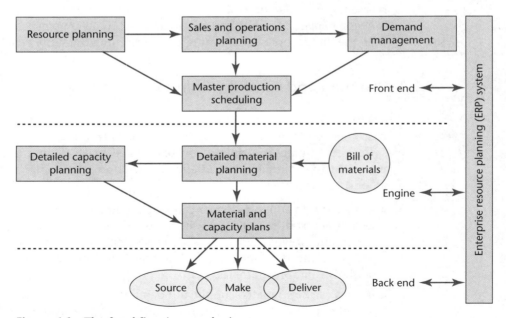

**Figure 6.1  The focal firm 'game plan'**

(Source: From *Manufacturing Planning and Control for Supply Chain Management*, 5th Ed., McGraw-Hill (Vollman, T.E., Berry, W.L., Whybark, D.C. and Jacobs, F.R. 2005), reproduced with permission of the McGraw-Hill Companies.)

Short-term projective forecasting (section 2.3) is carried out using techniques such as *moving averages* and *exponential smoothing*, which are described in Vollman *et al.* (2005: 32). Forecast accuracy (comparing forecast and actual values) is measured by such techniques as mean average deviation (MAD, section 2.3). It is only necessary to forecast for independent demand items: demand for dependent items can be calculated using material requirements planning – described below.

- *Resource planning*: pooling demand and passing it on to manufacturing *must* be moderated by capacity to deliver. Otherwise, a focal firm is at risk of being unable to fulfil marketing plans that do not take into account the realities of what can be done. Again, this would mean that marketing plans are not actionable (section 2.2). Resource planning is concerned with manufacturing capacity in the longer term (output measure), and with machine and man-power loading (input measure) in the shorter term.

- *Sales and operations planning (SOP)*: is the module concerned with matching of demand management and resource planning. Therefore, it is crucial that compatible measures of demand and capacity are used – for example, tonnes/week or '000 units produced/week. Sales and marketing must check with manufacturing that new enquiries can be made and delivered within requested lead times. This may well require coordination across several manufacturing units in different countries. The aim of SOP is to maintain *balance* between demand and supply. Too much demand in terms of capacity, and manufacturing will be under pressure to work overtime and to rush work through. Too little demand, and margins will be under pressure from under-utilised resources, layoffs and price cuts.

- *Master production scheduling (MPS)*: is the disaggregated form of the SOP. This means that the SOP is broken down from high level measures like product families into the detail of skus by major production facility. The MPS is the link between front end and engine of the MPC system. On the one hand, it receives SOP data about sales and forecasts. On the other hand, it feeds data back to SOP on orders and stock replenishment status so that customers and distribution can be kept up to date. The MPS handles the detail of what is planned and what is happening. For MTS environments, the priority is inventory management: for MTO environments, the priority is timely execution of all of the processes from design through to delivery.

- *Material and capacity planning (engine room)*: from overall demand by sku it is next necessary to develop detailed plans by part number. For each part and subassembly, detailed plans show how many and when each must be made. Like the 'big picture' front end logic, not only must a detailed material plan be devised, but it must also be moderated by capacity availability (resources) in each production centre. The logic behind this is called material requirements planning (MRP). This takes MPS data, and explodes it into detailed plans by component and subassembly. Each of these plans must be checked and optimised against available capacity by means of the detailed capacity planning module. An impression of what is involved is given in Victoria SA, Case study 6.1. Engine room logic is described in the form of a novel by Goldratt and Cox (1984); further details are in Vollman *et al.* (2005).

# Victoria SA

Victoria SA makes 'fantastically good cakes' from basic ingredients such as flour, eggs and butter. Demand for Victoria sponge cakes comes from two sources. Some big retailers place their order with the firm two days in advance, while other customers arrive at Victoria's own shops without prior warning and select from cakes that are on display. This means that some cakes are made in line with orders, whilst a forecast is also required to predict day-by-day demand.

Whilst there are many varieties of cake, the bill of material for the famous Victoria sponge cake is shown in Figure 6.2.

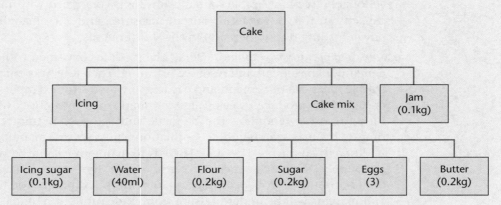

Figure 6.2    **Structured bill of materials for sponge cake**

When overall demand across the range has been collated, Victoria SA is able to determine how much of each ingredient will be needed to make the right number of cakes. Too many and cakes will have to be thrown away, because the shelf life is five to eight days (Victoria does not use stabilisers such as potassium sorbate). Too few and sales will be lost. Accurate planning is thus crucial to the efficiency of the whole operation. The ideal situation is that cakes are made and delivered *just-in-time* to meet customer demand because inventories will be low and freshness at its best.

In an effort to increase sales, Victoria SA decided to increase the product range. Strawberry jam is the traditional filling, but marketing considers that customers would also like other types of filling and decides to try blackberry jam, apricot jam, lemon curd and chocolate. Over the course of the next few months, the experiment appears to be working. Overall sales are up by 10 per cent, with each of the new varieties contributing well. The problem however is that no stable pattern exists in the mix of sales. For example, some days the chocolate-filled cakes sell out, while on other days hardly a single chocolate-filled cake is sold. Major retail customers are complaining about wastage and lost sales opportunities.

The issue appears to be that offering increased variety has led to less stability in the demand pattern as illustrated by the Master Production Schedule (MPS) in Table 6.1. While total daily cake demand is reasonably stable, at around 200 cakes, the demand for each variant is highly erratic. This leads to high inventory levels, due to inaccurate sales forecasts, and increased complexity in the production operation, as shown by the MRP calculation for gross and net requirements in Table 6.2.

Table 6.1   Master production schedule (MPS) for sponge cakes
(before postponement)

| Cake varient | Sales | | | | | | | |
|---|---|---|---|---|---|---|---|---|
| | Orders & forecast | | Forecast only | | | | | |
| | Mon. | Tue. | Wed. | Thur. | Fri. | Sat. | Sun. | TOTAL |
| Strawberry | 34 | 52 | 56 | 13 | 64 | 62 | 57 | 338 |
| Apricot | 58 | 39 | 33 | 43 | 7 | 57 | 28 | 265 |
| Blackberry | 36 | 43 | 9 | 49 | 39 | 37 | 17 | 230 |
| Lemon curd | 40 | 47 | 51 | 67 | 59 | 18 | 61 | 343 |
| Chocolate | 23 | 6 | 46 | 34 | 49 | 49 | 23 | 230 |
| TOTAL | 191 | 187 | 195 | 206 | 218 | 223 | 186 | 1,406 |

Table 6.2   Gross and net requirement calculations for one week demand for sponge cake
(before postponement). 'Exploding' is indicated by arrows

| Component | BOM quantity | units | Inventory | Scheduled receipts | Gross requirement | Net requirement |
|---|---|---|---|---|---|---|
| **Total finished cake** | n/a | cakes | 723 | | 1406 | 683 |
| Strawberry cake | n/a | cakes | 188 | | 338 | 150 |
| Apricot cake | n/a | cakes | 103 | | 265 | 162 |
| Blackberry cake | n/a | cakes | 145 | | 230 | 85 |
| Lemon curd cake | n/a | cakes | 212 | | 343 | 131 |
| Chocolate cake | n/a | cakes | 75 | | 230 | 155 |
| **Flour** | 0.2 | kg | 40 | 40 | 137 | 57 |
| **Sugar** | 0.2 | kg | 40 | 40 | 137 | 57 |
| **Eggs** | 3 | eggs | 600 | 600 | 2049 | 849 |
| **Butter** | 0.2 | kg | 40 | 40 | 137 | 57 |
| **Icing sugar** | 0.1 | kg | 20 | 20 | 68 | 28 |
| Strawberry jam | 0.1 | kg | 21 | 10 | 15 | 0 |
| Apricot jam | 0.1 | kg | 18 | | 16 | 0 |
| Blackberry jam | 0.1 | kg | 14 | | 9 | 0 |
| Lemon curd | 0.1 | kg | 14 | 10 | 13 | 0 |
| Chocolate | 0.1 | kg | 16 | 10 | 16 | 0 |

▶

The MRP calculations, which are shown for the same 1 week period as the MPS, can be explained as follows:

1 'Gross requirement' for 'total finished cakes', and each cake variant, is taken from the MPS.
2 'Net requirement' of cakes is calculated by subtracting the existing inventory from the gross requirement.
3 Inventory of finished cakes is high (equivalent to almost four days' demand) because demand for each variant is highly variable and therefore sales forecasts are inaccurate.
4 The *net requirement* for total finished cakes is exploded (by multiplying it by the BOM quantity for each cake mix ingredient plus icing) to give the gross requirement for each of the cake mix ingredients and the icing.
5 The net requirement for each of the cake ingredients is calculated by subtracting the existing inventory and any 'scheduled receipts'.
6 The inventory of 'cake mix' ingredients is low (equivalent to about one day's demand with another day's demand scheduled for receipt). This is a result of the relatively stable demand for the total number of cakes leading to accurate sales forecasts.
7 The net requirement for each of the 'finished cake variants' is exploded (by multiplying it by the BOM quantity for jam) to give the *gross requirement* for each jam flavour. The net requirement of jam is calculated in the same way as for cake mix ingredients (point 5 above).
8 Inventories of the various jams are high (they cover requirements for the coming weeks without need for scheduled receipts), and therefore the net requirement is zero. This is due to inaccurate sales forecasts caused by the erratic demand for each cake variant.

To fix the unexpected problems, Victoria SA decided on a new way of working. It is recognised that demand is not going to stabilise given the increased product range. The firm decided to adopt a *postponement* strategy by making standard cakes and then postponing final assembly until known demand is available. The basic cake is a *standard component*, while the filling is non-standard and represents the source of complexity and variable customer demand. Cakes are therefore kept in the standard form and only turned into the final form by adding the filling once customer orders have been received. Victoria SA applied postponement to the supply chain and introduced a *decoupling point* (section 5.2.3) at the end of the cake making process. Upstream of the decoupling point, overall demand is forecasted to inform sourcing decisions. Standard components are baked each morning. Downstream of the decoupling point, cakes are assembled to order (section 5.4) in line with customer orders. The time this activity takes has been minimised by setting up a workstation with cakes, filling and spreading tools arranged in a mini flow-line. This brings the production time (P-time: see section 5.2) within the time the customer is prepared to wait (D-time). Carrying out the operation in view of the customer also helps engage them and extends their D-time to a minute or so, long enough to complete the final assembly task.

The flexibility of the new operation means that customers no longer need to place an order two days in advance. Victoria SA can now supply from the new process if orders are received by major customers the day before. An unexpected benefit of the new approach is the ease with which innovations can be test marketed and adopted.

(Source: Dr Heather Skipworth, after an original by Dr Paul Chapman)

*Question*

1  How do you think the MPS, the MRP gross/net requirements calculations and the inventories (finished cake and ingredients) might be different after the implementation of postponement?

- *MPC execution systems (back end)*: the outputs from material and capacity plans in the engine are sets of instructions to suppliers, manufacturing and distribution. These schedules are in the form of purchase orders, works orders (or schedules for MTS) and shipping orders – hence the familiar 'source–make–deliver' processes at the bottom of Figure 6.1. The basic format is 'how many' and 'when' for each part number for each planning process for the relevant planning period (for example the next two weeks, or the next four weeks). Achievement against schedule has to be monitored by minute, by hour or by day. Failures to meet schedule – as a result of for example breakdowns or quality problems – require that remedial action is taken, such as overtime working or outsourcing. An example here is the Nokia supply problem described in Case study 1.4.

Front end, engine and back end MPC modules are all connected to the *enterprise requirements planning* (ERP) database. This enables MPC modules to be seamlessly connected to human resource management, finance and sales and marketing modules. SAP includes MPC systems as part of its supply chain software – supply chain planning, execution, collaboration and coordination.

## 6.1.2  Managing inventory in the supply chain

Planning and controlling factory output is but part of the challenge of managing material flow in the supply chain. A focal firm positioned in a network such as that shown in Figure 1.2 is at the centre of many possible connections with other supplier and customer companies. Upstream processes such as distribution and retail for both finished products and spare parts are subject to independent, random demand. Such demand is independent in that it is not affected by the actions of the focal firm (although demand may of course be stimulated through promotions). Dependent demand, on the other hand, is fixed by the actions of the firm – such as order acceptance and determining forecasts. This section is concerned with the management of inventories of independent demand items using *order point* methods. These are aimed at optimising the trade-off between inventory holding costs and the preparation costs of changeover (manufacturing) or of placing an order (retailing and manufacturing). While the concept of 'economic' batch sizes and order sizes has been widely superseded by other considerations, as we shall see, its principles help us to grasp the nature of some of the hidden costs of inventory decisions.

### 'Economic' batch sizes and order sizes

The question of how many parts to make at a time has traditionally been answered by reference to a longstanding concept called the 'economic' batch quantity (EBQ) formula. Similar principles are used to determine how many parts at a time to order from suppliers in 'economic' order quantities (EOQs). Both EBQ and EOQ assume that parts are used at a uniform rate (i.e. that demand is stable), and that another batch of parts should be made or ordered when stock falls below the *re-order point*. The principle behind reorder point, which sets out to answer the question when to order, is shown in Figure 6.3:

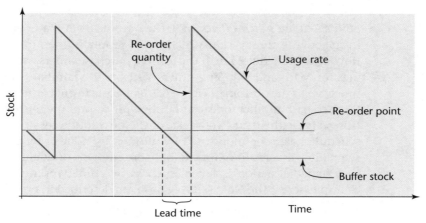

Notes:
1 Re-order point = Demand during lead time + safety stock
2 Re-order quantity = Economic order quantity
3 Buffer stock = *f*(service level.lead time variability.demand variability)

**Figure 6.3   When: the re-order point**

A buffer (or safety) stock line is shown below the re-order level. Buffer stock acts as a 'safety net' in order to cushion the effects of variability in demand and lead times. Buffer stock is a function of the service level (risk of stock outs), lead time variability and demand variability. The re-order point is therefore the sum of the forecast demand during the lead time plus the buffer stock requirement. There are various ways of calculating buffer stock (for a detailed coverage, and for details of EBQ and EOQ calculations, see Vollman *et al.* 2005; Waters, 2003).

In the case of manufacturing batch sizes, the EBQ is determined by optimising the trade-off between changeover cost between one batch and the next (for example, cleaning out the process plant between one type of cheese and the next, or re-setting the packing line from 250g to 500g carton sizes) and inventory carrying cost:

- *Changeover cost per unit, $C_s$.* The cost associated with changing over a given machine from the last good part from a batch to the first good part from the succeeding batch.

- *Inventory carrying cost, C.* The cost of holding stock, calculated from the total inventory cost and the annual rate charged for holding inventory.

To these assumptions we need to add that the usage rate $z$ is known and constant and that the manufactured cost of the sku $c$ is also known and constant. A little algebra applied to these assumptions leads to the so-called Wilson formula:

$$\text{EBQ} = \sqrt{2zC_s/cC}$$

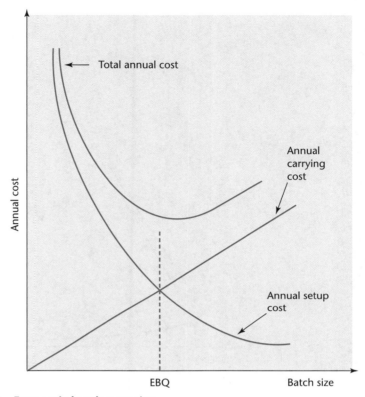

Figure 6.4   **Economic batch quantity**

Thus EBQ increases with usage rate and changeover cost, and reduces with manufactured cost per unit and inventory carrying cost. Figure 6.4 shows how changeover costs reduce as the batch size increases: the bigger the batch size, the lower the changeover costs per unit. On the other hand, inventory carrying costs increase linearly with batch size: the bigger the batch size, the bigger the carrying costs. A total cost line can be added, which is at a minimum when the two lines cross.

All too often overlooked when calculating the EBQ is that the higher the changeover cost, the higher the EBQ. The key point here is that the EBQ can therefore be reduced when the changeover cost is reduced. In the ideal case, the changeover activity should be simplified so that it can be carried out in seconds rather than in hours. Where this is achieved, the changeover cost becomes negligible and the EBQ becomes one (Figure 6.5).

Given zero changeover costs, the EBQ formula obeys the JIT ideal of pull scheduling – only make in response to *actual* demand (section 6.2). Actual demand, of course, is likely to vary from one day to the next, unlike the assumption for demand rate shown in Figures 6.3 and 6.4. Pull scheduling is more sensitive to demand changes, because only what is needed is made. Note that *annual* costs and demand have been quoted in Figures 6.4 and 6.5, but under current market turbulence, this is unrealistic and much shorter history periods (perhaps two or three months) should be used. A further major problem with use of EBQs in manufacturing is that it leads to different stockholdings for different part numbers. Synchronisation of parts movements becomes impossible.

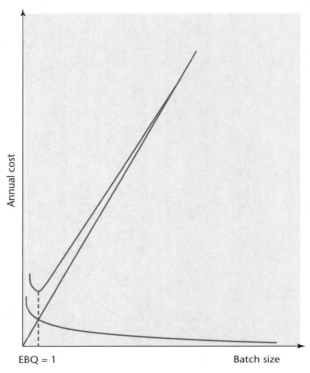

Figure 6.5 **As EBQ → 1**

The concept of the economic order quantity (EOQ) is based on similar assumptions to the EBQ. Here, the calculation addresses the question 'how many parts will we order?' The trade-off this time is between the cost of placing an order and inventory carrying cost, where:

- *Cost of placing an order*: All order related costs, including purchase department costs, transportation costs from the supplier, and goods-in inspection and receiving.

EOQ again increases in line with the cost of placing an order, and reduces in line with the inventory carrying cost. Again the trade-off can be changed. If the cost of placing an order can be simplified to a routine basis whereby parts are ordered by paperless systems such as cards, and collected on regular pickup routes called 'milk rounds', the EOQ can again be reduced towards the JIT ideal. In retailing, similar economies can be made by using POS systems and centralised (as opposed to stores-based) ordering. EOQ principles are still widely used for ordering 'independent demand' items that are not directly used to manufacture products, such as automotive spare parts, class 'C' parts in retail and office supplies.

### Periodic order quantity and target stock levels

Various methods have been adopted to overcome some of the deficiencies of EOQ models, which mean that a set order size is placed on a supplier whenever the inventory level falls below the re-order level. The effect upon suppliers is that – although a regular amount is ordered – the time the order is placed can vary enormously. An EOQ system finds it very difficult to cope if demand goes up or down rapidly. If demand goes up rapidly, then an EOQ system would tend to make replenishments that lag the demand trend.

To illustrate, let us assume a sequence of ten weeks where demand fluctuates between 100 and 1,000 units. The economic order quantity (EOQ) has been established as 1,000 units, and the safety stock at 100 units. Inventories at the start and end of each week can then be calculated as shown in Table 6.3.

Table 6.3   Economic order quantity example

| Week no. | Demand | Ord. quantity | Inv. end | Inv. start | Inv. holding |
|----------|--------|---------------|----------|------------|--------------|
| 1 | 100 | 1,000 | 900 | 1,000 | 950 |
| 2 | 100 | 0 | 800 | 900 | 850 |
| 3 | 200 | 0 | 600 | 800 | 700 |
| 4 | 400 | 0 | 200 | 600 | 400 |
| 5 | 800 | 1,000 | 400 | 200 | 300 |
| 6 | 1,000 | 1,000 | 400 | 400 | 400 |
| 7 | 800 | 1,000 | 600 | 400 | 500 |
| 8 | 400 | 0 | 200 | 600 | 400 |
| 9 | 100 | 0 | 100 | 200 | 150 |
| 10 | 200 | 1,000 | 900 | 100 | 500 |
| Sum | 4,100 | 5,000 | 5,100 | 5,200 | 5,150 |
| Average | 410 | 500 | 510 | 520 | 515 |

An alternative way to deal with variable demand is to use the periodic order quantity. Here, the re-order quantities are revised more frequently. The method uses mean time between orders (TBO), which is calculated by dividing the EOQ by the average demand rate. In the above example, the EOQ is 1,000 and the average demand 410. The economic time interval is therefore approximately 2. An example shown in Table 6.4 illustrates the same situation as in Table 6.3 in terms of demand changes and safety stock level. However, the re-order quantity is based on total demand for the immediate two weeks of history. This re-order method is called *periodic order quantity* (POQ).

POQ normally gives a lower mean inventory level than EOQ in variable demand situations. In this example, the average inventory holding has fallen from 5,150 to 4,150. The same number of orders (Chase *et al.*, 2005) have been used, but the order quantity varies from 200 to 1,800.

Table 6.4  **Periodic order quantity example**

| Week no. | Demand | Ord. quantity | Inv. end | Inv. start | Inv. holding |
|----------|--------|---------------|----------|------------|--------------|
| 1 | 100 | 200 | 100 | 200 | 150 |
| 2 | 100 | 0 | 0 | 100 | 50 |
| 3 | 200 | 600 | 400 | 600 | 500 |
| 4 | 400 | 0 | 0 | 400 | 200 |
| 5 | 800 | 1,800 | 1,000 | 1,800 | 1,400 |
| 6 | 1,000 | 0 | 0 | 1,000 | 500 |
| 7 | 800 | 1,200 | 400 | 1,200 | 800 |
| 8 | 400 | 0 | 0 | 400 | 200 |
| 9 | 100 | 300 | 200 | 300 | 250 |
| 10 | 200 | 0 | 0 | 200 | 100 |
| Sum | 4,100 | 4,100 | 2,100 | 6,200 | 4,150 |
| Average | 410 | 410 | 210 | 620 | 415 |

*Periodic review*

A widely used model for inventory control in retailing is *periodic review*. This works by placing orders of variable size at regular intervals – the *review period*. The quantity ordered is enough to raise stock on hand plus stock on order to a target level called the target stock level (TSL):

**Order quantity  =  Target stock level  −  Stock on hand  −  Stock on order**

The TSL is the sum of cycle stock (average daily demand over the review period and replenishment lead time) and the safety stock. An example of the way the TSL is calculated is:

$$\text{TSL} = \text{cycle stock} + \text{safety stock}$$
$$= D*(T + LT) + Z*\sigma*\sqrt{(T + LT)}$$

where D = average daily demand per sku, T = review period in weeks and LT = lead time in weeks. Z = number of standard deviations from the mean corresponding to the selected service level, and $\sigma$ = standard deviation of demand over T + LT. D may be raised to weekly intervals for slow moving items, and lowered to hours for fast movers.

## 6.1.3  Planning and control in retailing

Retailing is faced with planning and control challenges which are quite distinct from manufacturing:

● A retailer cannot generate sales without stock, and stock that is bought for sales that do not happen 'constitutes a retailer's nightmare' (Varley, 2006).

Retailers are constantly walking the tightrope between too much stock and not enough.

- The product range that has to be supported on the shelf is comparatively wide – 20,000 different products in the Tesco example in Case study 1.1, and perhaps four times that number of individual skus. *On-shelf availability* (OSA) is a key performance indicator. The aim is that OSA targets are maintained across all skus at all times of the day and night so that every product is available at any time that a customer visits a store. In practice, categories such as fresh fish and bread are withdrawn from sale by 18:00 hours to avoid excessive stock write-offs when demand is comparatively low.

- Several stages of the internal supply chain must be coordinated – depots, back of store and front of store. Again, it matters less if a product is in stock at the depot – it *does* matter that it is on the shelf, without which sales cannot be generated.

- Retail profit margins in grocery are tighter (2–4 per cent) than for large, branded manufacturers (8–10 per cent). Retail margins are prone to erosion by *shrinkage*, which is caused by losses resulting from internal and external theft and process failures such as damage and stocktaking errors. Average shrinkage in grocery is 1.52 per cent (Chapman, 2010), and is much higher for categories such as health and beauty, pharmaceutical and floral.

- Demand can be affected by changes that are difficult to forecast, such as seasonality (section 2.3), fashion (Case study 4.4), endorsements (such as the impact of a famous TV chef on the sale of brown eggs) and promotions (Case studies 2.1 and 2.3).

- 'Best before' and 'use by' dates for fresh produce increase obsolescence pressures and inventory turns.

- Reverse logistics (section 4.5) is more complicated because product is being reversed from one point (the store) to a multitude of supply chains (suppliers).

As we have seen in Chapter 2, customers' choices 'drive everything'. Retailers become more connected to the market than to the supply chain. The core capability in retailing is *trading* – buying and selling goods at a profit. To a degree, manufacturing suppliers become the means to an end, and the constraints of manufacturing are poorly understood by retailers.

Consider the demand series shown in Figure 6.6. This is for a high volume ambient product – in this case a washing powder for which demand is comparatively stable.

Examination of this very typical retail demand series shows that the overall demand pattern for each week is similar, but is by no means identical. Peak demand is usually (but not always) on a Saturday, while lowest demand is on Sundays when trading hours are restricted. There is a degree of *uncertainty* (section 2.3) about the actual demand for each day. Retailers expect suppliers to cope with this demand uncertainty – and other uncertainties in the supply chain caused by problems such as shrinkage and variable transport times – by holding *buffer stocks*. Case study 8.3 shows that these buffer stocks – often duplicated in the retailer's depots – can be equivalent to several days of demand.

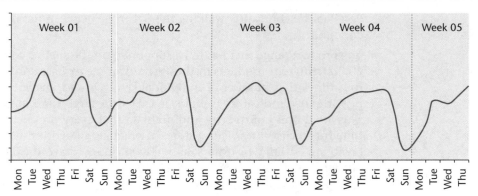

**Figure 6.6   EPOS data for last five weeks**

How does the manufacturer cope with such retailer expectations? Washing powders are manufactured in Europe at Procter & Gamble's (P&G's) factory near London. The process involves mixing the ingredients of individual products (such as Ariel and Bold) in *batches* and then drying and granulating each batch into powder in a 'blowing tower'. While the tower is blowing Bold, it cannot blow Ariel. Each brand has several different formulations, such as Bold Automatic and Bold Low Temperature. This further constrains manufacturing capability (although some products can be finally formulated by clever use of additives at the filling and packing stage). Blowing towers are expensive pieces of capital investment, so the site only has two. It is therefore *impossible* for P&G to produce each product formulation in line with demand. Therefore, P&G has to manufacture its products in advance of retail orders, using the principles of the re-order point shown on Figure 6.3, and must use forecasts to calculate the batch sizes. Further allowance must be made for the time it takes to ship the product from the National Distribution Centre (NDC, which is positioned close to P&G's packing lines on the London factory site), the retailer's depots and its stores. Fortunately, in the case of demand as shown in Figure 6.6, forecast accuracy should be high and it is then possible to plan production batch sizes and buffer stocks accurately as well. But promotions can distort even this high forecast accuracy demand.

In practice, retailers use projective forecasting for planning replenishment quantities of stable demand items such as that shown in Figure 6.6 from suppliers such as P&G. Using sales based ordering (SBO), retailers attempt to match supply with POS demand as closely as possible. POS data from each of the stores that it serves are sent to the depot, which collates sales data and so provides a smoothing effect on demand forecasting. Even when a close logistics relationship has been established with suppliers, coordination comes under strain because of pressures brought by the trading function of the retailer to squeeze suppliers' prices.

Let us next consider the challenges that are created by different processes between one stage of the supply chain and the next, whether caused by manufacturing and retail or by different process requirements between one process and another.

## 6.1.4  Inter-firm planning and control

Both section 6.1.1 on manufacturing MPC systems and 6.1.2 on managing independent demand show that relatively sophisticated modelling data are needed to enable accurate and timely planning and control of logistics in a focal firm. Attention to detail – both in planning and in execution – is key. The greater the product variety, the more component parts and the greater the number of levels in the BOM, the more challenging the task. When it comes to coordinating logistics between supply partners, the challenges multiply because the number of processes at stake is so much greater. There are many other factors that make life even more challenging, resulting from differences between the partners:

- *Differences in process technology*: a supplier of aluminium cans to a soft drinks manufacturer is positioned between producers of aluminium rolled sheet, and high speed canning lines. At the can supplier, the sheet has to be deep drawn and printed with increasingly sophisticated designs. High speed filling machines (1,500 cans/minute) at the soft drinks manufacturer means that the lengthy changeovers are carried out as infrequently as possible. During the peak summer sales period – when sales can double during a hot spell of weather – the whole logistics pipeline is under pressure. The can supplier – situated next to the factory of the drinks manufacturer – supplies cans through a 'hole in the wall' conveyor which enables just-in-time delivery. Coordinating these three quite different manufacturing processes is a major challenge. The default solution is to hold huge stocks at the can supplier – but, even then, you have to hope that the forecasts were correct! If we move to the NDC for the drinks manufacturer, the even tougher challenge is to interface manufacturing with service processes – distribution and retail. Retail demand is not based on manufacturing batch sizes, but on end-customer demand through the till – moderated by weather forecasts and promotions.

- *Differences in working routines*: shift patterns, conditions of employment, holidays and shut-downs are but a few of the possible differences in working routines between partners in a supply chain. Retailers complain that they work 24/7, while manufacturers may only work five days/week. In turn, this means that replenishments for weekend sales (the highest of the week) have to be made up by extra quantities delivered on Monday and Tuesday.

- *Priority planning*: while an order for a major customer may be priority number 1 for the focal firm in Figure 1.3, the existence of the order may not be visible to upstream partners. Each has different priorities to manage – and each has a different perspective about what order should be processed next.

- *Inadequacies in MPC systems design*: we document the case of a manufacturer of electrical cables ('ElectriCo') to specific customer orders against very short lead times (Skipworth and Harrison, 2004). Orders from the customer – a distributor of power leads – were placed daily against generic stocks held at ElectriCo (MTS). Attempts to cut out these stocks at ElectriCo by changing to MTO were frustrated by weekly MRP planning intervals, and by the fact that each planning run took 36 hours to complete. We have surveyed a number of firms to identify best practice in demand planning and forecasting (Harrison *et al.*, 2004).

This survey provided dozens of examples of good practice and bad practice in these areas. Partners in a network who have weak MPC systems potentially create problems for everyone else.

### Implications of poor coordination

One consequence of poor coordination within a supply network is amplification of changes in demand upstream. Amplification of demand changes has been called the *bullwhip effect*. For example, a retailer may order only in full truck loads from its suppliers. Instead of understanding the actual end-customer demand, the suppliers see huge swings in orders that are essentially due to the retailer's desire to minimise transport costs. This has the unfortunate impact of increasing manufacturing costs at the suppliers, because they are asked to make large quantities at irregular time intervals. What may originally have been stable demand through the till becomes heavily distorted.

Figure 6.7 shows an example of the bullwhip effect. Demand through the till is relatively stable, but orders on the supplier are anything but stable! The original range of variation has been amplified into something much worse. The only way in which the manufacturer can respond is to hold stocks – and even those vary enormously from one week to the next. Uncertainty about customer demand leads to large up-and-down swings in the need for capacity and in inventory levels. This effect ripples through the supply chain. Batching rules at the manufacturer make things even worse for its own suppliers upstream. Lee *et al.* (1997) identify four major causes of the bullwhip effect:

- *updating of demand forecasts*: resulting in changes to safety stock and stock in the pipeline;

- *order batching*: while retail customers may buy mostly on Saturdays, MPC systems may batch orders according to different timing rules;

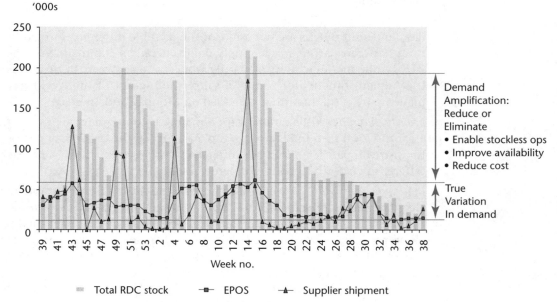

Figure 6.7  **The 'bullwhip effect' at work**

- *price fluctuations*: promotions most often result in lumping of demand into peaks and troughs, when the ongoing pattern is stable;
- *rationing and shortage gaming*: when the latest games console is in short supply, retailers are rationed by manufacturers. Customers place multiple orders on different retailers and apparent demand amplification.

To make matters even worse, it is quite possible for material movements in supply chains to descend into *chaos* (Wilding, 1998). Chaos is characterised by:

- the same state is never repeated ('aperiodic');
- on successive iterations, the state stays within a finite range and does not approach infinity ('bounded');
- there is a definite rule with no random terms governing the dynamics ('deterministic');
- two points that are initially close will drift apart over time.

Wilding lists several implications for management, three of which are:

- *supply chains do not reach stable equilibrium*: small perturbations will always prevent equilibrium being achieved;
- *treat the supply chain as a complete system*. Small changes made to optimise one echelon of the supply chain can result in massive changes in other parts of the chain. Driving down inventory and lead times may not always improve performance. It could result in the system slipping into chaos;
- *remove chaos by focusing on the end-customer*: communicate demand information as far upstream as possible.

### Implications for planning and controlling the supply chain

Based on evidence from MPC systems in manufacturing, the intricacies of managing independent demand and the conclusions of the bullwhip effect and chaos theory, we can conclude that coordinating material flow across the supply network requires attention to detail in both planning and execution on a grand scale. So often, firms have 'orchestrated' (or did we mean 'optimised'?) the supply chain around their own interests – own up auto manufacturers, 'big pharma' and retailers! And simplistic solutions to collaboration and partnership remain at the partial level – especially if limited to dyadic (supplier–customer) relationships. Making MPC systems work together requires hard work, not just a commitment to 'partnership'. We return to these issues in Chapters 9 and 10.

## 6.2 Overcoming poor coordination in retail supply chains

*Key issue:* How can collaboration be extended across the supply chain to focus on meeting consumer demand?

As a result of the challenges listed in section 6.1.4 above, a number of initiatives have been launched to promote better coordination between supply chain processes in retailing (Barratt and Oliveira, 2002). The principle being aimed for is that stock in a retailer's stores is replenished in response to POS data. While retailers initially wanted manufacturers to do this by imposition, more recent initiatives recognise that collaboration is needed – at least between logistics processes at each stage of the supply chain. There are potential benefits all round – more accurate replenishment quantities mean lower inventories, faster response to demand fluctuations and improved on-shelf availability (OSA). They also mean improved sales. We start with efficient consumer response (ECR) which has been targeted primarily in food and fast-moving categories, and end with quick response (QR) which has been targeted primarily at non-food categories.

## 6.2.1 Efficient consumer response (ECR)

Established as a grocery industry initiative, *efficient consumer response* (ECR) is designed to integrate and rationalise product assortment, promotion, new product development and replenishment across the supply chain. It aims to fulfil the changing demands and requirements of the end-customer through effective collaboration across all supply chain members, in order to enhance the effectiveness of merchandising efforts, inventory flow and supply chain administration (PE International, 1997).

The origins of ECR can be traced back to work carried out by Kurt Salmon Associates (in the US) for the apparel sector (Salmon, 1993), and subsequently in the grocery sector (Fernie, 1998). Since then, ECR has increased industrial awareness of the growing problem of non-value-added supply chain costs (section 5.3.5).

Originating within the consumer products industry, ECR emerged partly because of the increased competition from new retail formats entering the traditional grocery industry in the early 1990s, as well as through joint initiatives between Wal-Mart and Procter & Gamble. In Europe, ECR programmes commenced in 1993 with the commissioning of a series of projects, for example the Coopers & Lybrand survey of the grocery supply chain (Coopers & Lybrand, 1996).

The focus of ECR is to integrate supply chain management with demand management. This requires supplier–retailer collaboration – but in spite of the apparent emphasis on the end-consumer, a lot of the early ECR studies focused on the supply side. Subsequent increased focus on demand and category management, however, has led to the adoption of a more holistic view of the supply chain when discussing ECR initiatives. In addition, ECR has stimulated collaborative efforts that have increased the emphasis on key areas such as EDI, cross-docking and continuous replenishment.

Other examples of studies sponsored by ECR-Europe initiatives include an *Optimal Shelf Availability* report (Roland Berger Strategy Consultants, 2003) and the *Shrinkage in Europe* report (Beck, 2004). Generally, ECR initiatives aim to promote greater collaboration between manufacturers and retailers. Effective logistics strategies as well as administrative and information technology are essential for its successful implementation. These techniques are available within most firms, but the most frequent issue is to ensure that existing tools are customised in order to achieve their maximum potential.

The main areas addressed under ECR initiatives are category management, product replenishment and enabling technologies. These can be broken down into 14 areas where individual as well as well-integrated improvements can be made in order to enhance efficiency (see Figure 6.8).

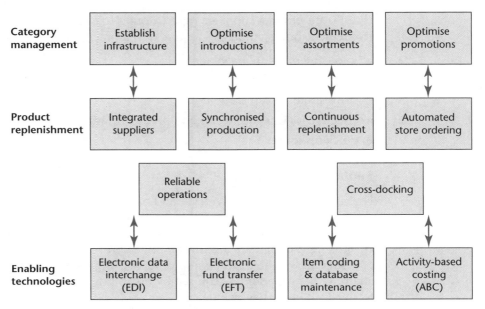

**Figure 6.8   ECR improvement categories**
(Source: Fernie, 1998: 30)

## Category management

As demand management principles have become more important to supply chain initiatives, the category management process has increased in popularity. With an objective of preventing stockout situations and improving supplier–retailer relations, category management aims to balance retailers' product volume and variety objectives. Among activities included in the category management process are the capture and utilisation of knowledge of the drivers behind consumer attitudes and choices.

By focusing on category management and measuring promotional efficiency, ECR enables organisations to utilise their joint resources to reduce supply chain inventory levels, streamline product flows, and use cross-dock options where appropriate. Thus category management represents a focus on the development of at least some of the following capabilities:

- account management;
- demand management;
- multifunctional selling teams;
- price list restructuring;
- effective and customised promotions.

### Continuous replenishment

Continuous replenishment offers both retailers and their suppliers the opportunity to manage their inventory in a more efficient manner (Mitchell, 1997; PE International, 1997). Each of the six stages that make up the product replenishment process (illustrated in Figure 6.8) represents a link that integrates the supply chain from product suppliers right through to end-consumers. In addition, effective replenishment strategies require development of the following capabilities:

- joint inventory management;
- cross-dock operations;
- continuous replenishment;
- effective logistics strategies and product flows;
- quick response.

### Enabling technologies

Enabling technologies drive ECR and make it work. They include scanning data, data warehousing and data mining, which have facilitated our understanding of customer requirements. Examples include EDI, which is increasingly about synchronising trading data among supply chain partners in advance of doing business as it allows the transmission of forecasting data back up through the supply chain. Other capabilities required by organisations in order to implement an effective ECR initiative include:

- effective information sharing;
- automated order generation;
- bar-coding and the use of other scanning technology.

In addition, the data to be shared and communicated at various stages in the supply chain depend on what will provide the most overall benefit. These data should include:

- demand/consumption/sales information;
- cash flow;
- stocks of finished goods/work in progress;
- delivery and output status.

However, many of the problems in sharing and using these data and implementing EDI networks are related to difficulties in achieving a critical mass of companies sufficient to generate substantial benefits.

### Radio frequency identification devices (RFIDs)

Radio frequency identification (RFID) is a product tracking technology that is becoming applied widely in supply chains today (Angeles, 2005). An RFID device, often called a *tag*, can be attached to a piece of merchandise and informs a reader about the nature and location of what it is attached to. Figure 6.9 shows how the reader can relay this information to a management system that can create a

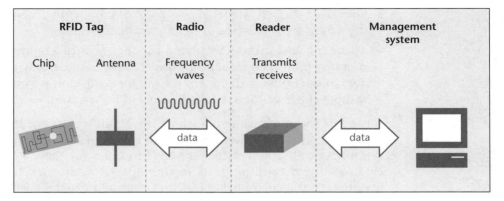

**Figure 6.9   An RFID system**
(Source: Beck, 2004)

picture of what merchandise is where at a level of detail that has not previously been possible.

An active tag has a power source; a passive tag does not. Active tags use a battery, have a limited life and cost far more. The *antenna* is a device that uses radio waves to read and/or write data to the tags. The *reader* manages the interface between antenna and management system. A big advantage of RFID technology over bar-codes is that the tag does not have to be directly in the line of sight of the reader. Tags can be detected by readers remotely because the radio waves can pass through many materials (see, for example, http://www.ems-rfid.com). Trials have been conducted across a range of frequencies – 125 Khz to 2.45 Ghz for chip-based tags – but standards are still being debated in many sectors. The *management system* enables data from tags to be collected and sorted for the purposes of management information and action.

The key piece of information held on a tag is the *electronic product code* (EPC, standards for which were developed by the Auto-ID Center). This 'number plate' is unique to each tag. The unique number can then be linked to information about the product to which it is attached, for example about when and where the product was made, where its components came from and shelf-life details. Some tags may hold this additional information on board however the intention is that most tags will only hold the EPC and additional information will be stored remotely, on a database linked to the management system.

Readers tell us *what* the product is and *where* it is located in the supply chain. The management system compiles this information and allows us to know *how many* products are present at that location for each time bucket. This translates into dynamic data that allows us to know rates of consumption, and stock data at a given point in time – together with what needs to be done. One can already envision that such data will enable supply chain planning and control to be transformed.

Product tagging allows for several interesting applications including:

- tracking products throughout the distribution pipeline ('asset tracking') to provide continuous quantities and position by sku in the supply chain;
- tracking products through back of store to the shelf;

- intelligent shelves, whereby 'sweeping' of product by thieves from shelves in store shows up automatically and raises alarm signals;
- registering sales without involving a cashier: a fancied future state is one where shoppers push their trolley past readers that automatically read EPCs for each item in the trolley, and present the bill for credit card payment to the shopper without the need for retailer personnel to be involved.

Benefits for manufacturers include the ability to understand when products are in the store but not on the shelf (a source of lost sales that manufacturers cannot control) and reducing the opportunities for theft. Retailer benefits include ability to track products in the pipeline against delivery schedules, automation of the checkout process and ability to expand customer information on buying patterns.

Technically, products can be tracked all the way to the customer's home and into it. However, when Benetton planned to track products after the sale, with an eye on returns, it was met with customer resistance on grounds of privacy. This caused Benetton to delay plans for rolling out this idea. The other major hurdle to implementation is the price of the tags. Price/margin levels in most consumer packaged goods tags need to be low enough to be affordable at the individual product level. While Wal-Mart has mandated tag application from its major suppliers, technical issues with readers have so far kept RFID development at pallet level. Beyond product-level tagging in retail channels, many other applications are already in place at case-level, and in higher-value goods such as automotive parts.

---

## CASE STUDY 6.2

## ECR in the UK

Dutchman Paul Polman, now CEO of Unilever, did a stint as General Manager of Procter & Gamble UK and Eire from 1995 to 1999. While admiring the UK's advanced retailing systems, he saw opportunities for all four of the 'pillars of ECR' – range, new items, promotions and replenishment. The following is extracted from the text of a speech he made to the Institute of Grocery Distribution.

### Range

The average store now holds 35 per cent more than five years ago, yet a typical consumer buys just 18 items on a trip. A quarter of these skus sell less than six units a week! The number of skus offered by manufacturers and stores has become too large and complex. My company is equally guilty in this area. No question, we make too many skus. I can assure you we are working on it. Actually, our overall sku count in laundry is already down 20 per cent compared to this time last year. What's more, business is up. Clearly, we have an opportunity to rationalise our ranges. As long as we do this in an ECR way – focusing on what consumers want – we will all win. The consumer will see a clearer range. Retailers and manufacturers will carry less inventory and less complexity. The result will be cost savings across the whole supply chain and stronger margins.

## New items

There were 16,000 new skus last year. Yet 80 per cent lasted less than a year. You don't need to be an accountant to imagine the costs associated with this kind of activity. And look how this has changed. Since 1975, the number of new sku introductions has increased eightfold. Yet their life expectancy has shrunk from around five years in 1975 to about nine months now. We can hardly call this progress.

## Promotions

In promotions it's the same story. Take laundry detergents. This is a fairly stable market. Yet we're spending 50 per cent more on promotions than two years ago, with consumers buying nearly 30 per cent more of their volume on promotions. This not only creates an inefficient supply chain, or in some cases poor in-store availability, but, more importantly, has reduced the value of the category and likely the retailers' profit. We're all aware of the inefficiencies promotions cause in the system, such as problems in production, inventory and in-store availability. They all create extra costs, which ultimately have to be recouped in price. But there's a higher cost. As promotions are increasing, they are decreasing customer loyalty to both stores and brands by 16 per cent during the period of the promotion. We commissioned a report by Professor Barwise of the London Business School. He called it 'Taming the Multi-buy Dragon'. The report shows us that over 70 per cent of laundry promotional investment goes on multi-buys. The level of investment on multi-buys has increased by 60 per cent over the last three years. There's been a 50 per cent increase behind brands and a doubling of investment behind own labels. Contrary to what we thought, most of this volume is not going to a broad base of households. It is going to a small minority. Seventy-one per cent of all multi-buy volume is bought by just 14 per cent of households. Just 2 per cent of multi-buy volume goes to 55 per cent of households. We really are focusing our spending on influencing and rewarding a very small minority of people indeed.

## Replenishment

Based on the escalating activity I've just [referred to], costs are unnecessarily high. There are huge cost savings also here, up to 6 per cent, by removing the non-value-added skus and inefficient new brand and promotional activity.

## Questions

1  Cutting down on range, new items and promotions is presumably going to lead to 'everyday low prices'. Discuss the implications to the trade-off between choice and price.

2  Procter & Gamble's major laundry brand in the US is Tide. This is marketed in some 60 pack presentations, some of which have less than 0.1 per cent share. The proliferation of these pack presentations is considered to have been instrumental in increasing Tide's market share from 20 to 40 per cent of the US market in recent years. Clearly, this is a major issue within P&G. What are the logistics pros and cons of sku proliferation?

## 6.2.2   Collaborative planning, forecasting and replenishment (CPFR)

Collaborative planning, forecasting and replenishment (CPFR) is aimed at improving collaboration between buyer and supplier so that customer service is improved while inventory management is made more efficient. The trade-off between customer service and inventory is thereby altered (Oliveira and Barratt, 2001).

The CPFR movement originated in 1995. It was the initiative of five companies: Wal-Mart, Warner-Lambert, Benchmarking Partners, and two software companies, SAP and Manugistics. The goal was to develop a business model to forecast and replenish inventory collaboratively. An initial pilot was tested between Wal-Mart and Warner-Lambert using the Listerine mouthwash product and focusing on stocks kept in the retail outlets. The concept and process was tested initially by exchanging pieces of paper. This generated clear visibility of the process required and the requirements for the IT specification. The two companies later demonstrated in a computer laboratory that the internet could be used as a channel for this information exchange.

In 1998 the Voluntary Inter-industry Commerce Standards Committee (VICS) became involved in the movement, which enabled it to make major strides forward. VICS was formed in 1986 to develop bar-code and electronic data interchange standards for the retail industry. The involvement of VICS meant that other organisations could participate in the validation and testing of the CPFR concept. With VICS support, organisations including Procter & Gamble, Kmart and Kimberly Clark undertook pilots to test the idea of sharing information to improve inventory handling. One of the pilots in the UK grocery sector is described in Case study 6.3.

---

**CASE STUDY 6.3**

## CPFR trials in the UK grocery sector

CPFR pilots have been a popular diversion in the UK grocery sector. Often, they show – as in this case – that considerable opportunities for improvement exist, but that the problems of scaling up the pilot are too great. The scenario for this pilot, researched by one of our Master's students, Alexander Oliveira, was a manufacturer that supplied a major grocery retailer in the UK. Figure 6.6 shows the typical demand series for one of the ten products in the study, all of which were in the high-volume ambient category. Total sales through the till (EPOS) for a given week were really quite stable. While there is apparent high demand variation, most of this is due to predictable behaviour such as that due to different store opening hours. The day-by-day demand for this product was actually relatively stable over the course of a year. Figure 6.10 places the pilot in context. The manufacturer's national distribution centre (NDC) supplied one of the retailer's regional distribution centres (RDCs), which in turn served ten stores in the pilot (it served a lot more stores in total – about 80).

The starting situation that Alexander found was that forecasting methods were based on a history of the last two–three months. While this gave the correct day-by-day pattern, it was insensitive to actual demand during a given week. As can be seen in Figure 6.6, the actual demand pattern varies from day to day across the series due to a proportion of

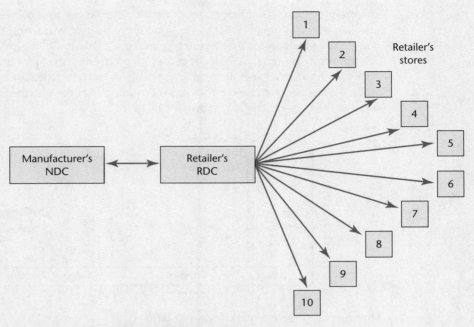

**Figure 6.10    A collaborative planning pilot**

randomness in the pattern. The replenishment cycle was unresponsive because daily deliveries were based on forecasts. This resulted in high safety stocks and poor on-shelf availability. Figure 6.11 provides an inventory profile across the supply chain. The sum of the vertical (average days of stock) and horizontal (average lead time in days) gives the total time for a new batch of product to progress from manufacturing site to shelf. This totals a massive four–five weeks!

Alexander coordinated the provision of forecast data from both manufacturer and supplier. Both forecasts were posted on a website, and he was asked to provide instructions as to how much product the manufacurer should supply each day. Stock for the ten stores was 'ring fenced' at the retailer's RDC – that is, it could not be supplied to any other than the ten stores in the pilot.

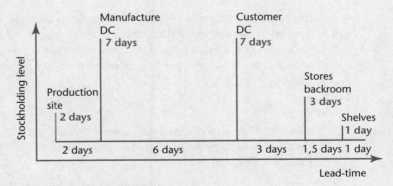

**Figure 6.11    Pipeline map at start**

Alexander soon found that current forecast data did not take daily fluctuations into account, and was based on far too long a history period. By tracking daily demand, it was possible to allow for the randomness without anything like the current quantity of safety stock in the system. He devleoped a new replenishment algorithm that was based on the daily error between forecast and actual, and which added an extra day's buffer stock. It soon became obvious that it was possible to run the system on far lower stock levels at the retailer's NDC, as shown in Figure 6.12.

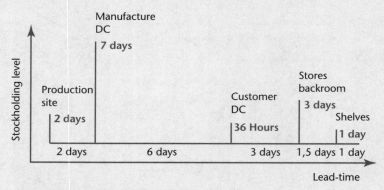

**Figure 6.12   Pipeline map: at end of pilot**

Alexander's work had succeeded in reducing the stock level at the NDC from seven days to 36 hours. In spite of the huge potential savings, the retailer did not go ahead with scaling up the pilot. This can be attributed to several factors. First, many other improvement initiatives were under way. The CPFR initiative would have needed further scarce resources. Second, scaling up would have required a different operating routine at all NDCs and the supporting IT infrastructure would need to have been changed. Third, what worked with one relatively efficient manufacturer may not have worked with others. Nevertheless, Alexander came up with the following five enablers for CPFR implementation (Barratt and Oliveira, 2002):

1 *Define single point of contact for each trading partner:* to ensure that information is neither lost nor deteriorates during the exchange.
2 *Define agenda for collaboration* (short–medium–long term): to stabilise the collaborative goals over time.
3 *Expand collaborative projects* (scope and complexity): to gain critical mass.
4 *Ensure continuous sharing of information:* a key enabler of collaborative planning.
5 *Development of trust:* this takes time. Smaller problems are gradually removed from the CPFR process to help partners develop confidence that the long-term goal is achievable.

## Questions

1 Suppose that the retailer's total sales were €20 billion, and that the ten skus together accounted for 0.4 per cent of these sales. Calculate the approximate savings in inventory to the retailer.

2 Do you consider that the reasons given for not scaling up the pilot are valid?

3 Would there be any benefits to the manufacturer?

In autumn 1999 VICS published a tutorial for CPFR implementation. This is available in hard copy, or can be accessed on its website at http://www.cpfr.org. This 'road map' offers organisations a structured approach to CPFR implementation based on the experiences of the companies involved in the CPFR pilots.

Having shown that the CPFR concept can have bottom-line impact on their businesses, companies are looking to expand the programmes from the handful of items involved in the pilots to the hundreds or thousands of items covered in most trading relationships. This has been a challenge for all organisations, including the software providers, for whom a major focus has been to ensure that software is scaleable; that is, that there are no barriers to the number of organisations and products involved in the CPFR network.

When implementing CPFR, a significant amount of time and effort is required up-front to negotiate specific items such as goals and objectives, frequency of updates to plan, exception criteria and key performance measures. The result is a published document defining the relevant issues for each organisation that has been jointly developed and agreed.

A nine-step business model has been developed that provides an insight into the effort required by both supplier and customer. The model is as follows:

1  Develop front-end agreement.

2  Create joint business plans.

3  Create individual sales forecasts.

4  Identify exceptions to sales forecasts.

5  Resolve/collaborate on exception items.

6  Create order forecast.

7  Identify exceptions to order forecast.

8  Resolve/collaborate on exception items.

9  Generate orders.

In summary, CPFR focuses on the process of forecasting supply and demand by bringing various plans and projections from both the supplier and the customer into synchronisation. CPFR requires extensive support in the form of internet-based products, which can result in major changes to the key business processes. An academic survey of the success of CPFR (Oliveira and Barratt, 2001) found a significant correlation between companies with high information systems capabilities and the success of CPFR projects. The firms with high levels of CPFR implementation use information systems capable of providing timely, accurate, user-friendly and interfunctional information in real time. Skjoett-Larsen *et al.* (2003) propose that CPFR should be seen as a general approach to integrating supply chain processes, and not as a rigid, step-by-step model as proposed by VICS. The electronic integration aspects of collaborative planning are further reviewed in section 8.1.3.

### Benefits of electronic collaboration

Nestlé UK states that the advantages of collaborative systems are significant, and lists the following benefits:

● There is improved availability of product to the consumer, and hence more sales.

- Total service is improved, total costs are reduced (including inventory, waste and resources), and capacities can be reduced owing to the reductions in uncertainty.

- Processes that span two or more companies become far more integrated and hence simple, standard, speedy and certain.

- Information is communicated quickly, in a more structured way, and is transparent across the supply chain to all authorised users. All users know where to find up-to-date information.

- An audit trail can be provided to say when information was amended.

- Email prompts can update users of variance and progress, and can confirm authorisations.

- The data that are in the system can be used for monitoring and evaluation purposes.

- The process can be completed in a quick timescale, at a lower total cost.

- All trading partners become more committed to the shared plans and objectives. Changes are made with more care, and are immediately visible to all.

Many of these benefits are being experienced by those implementing the CPFR philosophy. Wal-Mart and Sara Lee experienced sales increases of 45 per cent and a decline in weeks-on-hand inventory of 23 per cent. The benefits experienced by Procter & Gamble and its retail partners include a reduction in replenishment cycle time of 20 per cent. The increased visibility of the supply chain resulted in a reduction of in-store availability from 99 to 88 per cent being detected with sufficient lead time to respond. This saved three to four days of stockouts for the retailer. Forecast accuracy improvements of 20 per cent have also been experienced.

### 6.2.3  Vendor-managed inventory (VMI)

Vendor-managed inventory (VMI), is an approach to inventory and order fulfilment whereby the supplier, not the customer, is responsible for managing and replenishing inventory. This appears at first sight to counter the principle of pull scheduling, because the preceding process (the manufacturer) is deciding how many and when to send to the next process (the retailer). In practice, the basis on which decisions will be made is agreed with the retailer beforehand, and is based on the retailer's sales information. Under VMI, the supplier assumes responsibility for monitoring sales and inventory, and uses this information to trigger replenishment orders. In effect, suppliers take over the task of stock replenishment.

*Automated VMI* originated in the late 1980s with department stores in the US as a solution to manage the difficulties in predicting demand for seasonal clothing. Prior to this *manual VMI* had been around for many years – particularly in the food industry. Under manual VMI, the manufacturer's salesman took a record of inventory levels and reordered products for delivery to the customer's store, where the manufacturer's representative would restock the shelves. As product variety has increased and lifecycles have shortened, manual VMI has been replaced by automated VMI.

## How VMI works

The supplier tracks their customers' product sales and inventory levels, sending goods only when stocks run low. The decision to supply is taken by the supplier, not the customer as is the case traditionally. The supplier takes this decision based on the ability of the current level of inventory to satisfy prevailing market demand, while factoring in the lead time to resupply. The smooth running of VMI depends on a sound business system. It also requires effective teamwork between the retailer and the manufacturer. In order for both parties to gain full benefit from the system, appropriate performance measures need to be used. The top priority measure is that of product availability at the retailer. It is in both parties' interests to maximise product availability, avoiding lost sales in the short term and building customer buying habits in the long term. By emphasising the supplier's responsibility for maximising product availability, VMI aims to achieve this with minimum inventories. In order to combine both of these apparently conflicting goals, it is necessary to have access to real-time demand at the customer.

The most widely used technology for broadcasting demand data from the retailer customer is *electronic data interchange* (EDI). This provides the means for exchanging data from customer to suppliers in a standard format. Internet-based applications using EDI protocols are increasingly popular, providing the same facility at lower cost. Customer demand and inventory data are often processed through software packages to automate the application of decision rules and identify stock lines that need replenishment.

## Potential benefits

The immediate benefit to a supplier engaged in VMI is access to data on:

- customer sales;
- inventory levels at the customer.

The assumption is that the supplier can use these data to provide better control of the supply chain and so deliver benefits for both the customer and themselves.

Having the supplier take the decision on replenishment aims to minimise the impact of *demand amplification*. This critical problem erodes customer service, loses sales, and increases costs. The ability to dampen demand amplification caused by infrequent, large orders from customers is key to the success of VMI. The surplus capacity and excess finished goods held by suppliers to counteract such variation can then be reduced.

In the longer term, suppliers should integrate demand information into their organisation and develop the capability to drive production with it. This helps to replace the traditional push scheduling, based on forecasts and buffer stocks, with pull scheduling, based on meeting known demand instantaneously out of manufacturing.

### Activity 6.1

There are a number of different ways in which the use of VMI can benefit the supplier and the customer. Make a list of those benefits you think exist under the headings of 'supplier benefits' and 'customer benefits'.

### Potential problems in setting up a VMI system

Other than the practical difficulties of setting up a VMI system, a number of problems can prevent the attainment of the above benefits. Five of them are listed below.

#### Unwillingness to share data

Retailers may be unwilling to share their marketing plans and product range strategies with manufacturers. This is particularly true in the UK, where supermarkets have strong own brands that compete with those of the manufacturers.

Retailers continue to be the owners of information on actual demand passing through their tills. An inability to forward this information, whether due to reluctance or to procedural and technical problems, will prevent suppliers from responding effectively, leading to the need for buffer stocks and increasing the risk of stockouts.

#### Seasonal products

The benefits of VMI are quickly eroded in fashion and seasonal products, especially apparel. VMI in these cases can involve suppliers making to stock based on a pre-season forecast with little scope for manufacturing in season. Small quantities are delivered from this stock to the retailers over the season. Naturally the forecast is regularly at odds with actual demand, so products will be frequently understocked or overstocked. In effect all that has happened is that the burden of owning inventory and disposing of excesses has been moved onto the supplier.

#### Investment and restructuring costs

Adopting a VMI approach incurs a high investment by the customer and supplier. Setting up the processes and procedures for undertaking this new way of working takes time and effort. The customer will need to close their materials management function if they are to make cost savings, while the supplier will need to develop the capability to take over this task.

#### Retailer vulnerability

The process of outsourcing materials management to suppliers makes the retailer more dependent on them.

#### Lack of standard procedures

The practicalities of the processes and procedures that underpin VMI may not be transferable from one customer to another. Customers may ask for different tagging methods or bespoke labelling. With many industrial products there is no bar-code standard.

#### System maintenance

Errors creep into inventory records due to incorrect part counts, mislabelling, damage, loss and theft. These records need to be maintained through manual methods such as stock counts.

## 6.2.4  Quick response (QR)

Quick response (QR) is an approach to meeting customer demand by supplying the right quantity, variety and quality at the right time to the right place at the right price. This concept originated in the US textile and apparel industry in response to the threat posed by overseas competitors. The concepts behind QR are based on taking a total supply chain view of an industry. From this perspective it is possible to understand overall performance and the causes of poor performance, and to identify opportunities for improvement.

Understanding overall performance involves mapping the processes needed to convert raw material into the final product (see Chapter 5). The performance of the process is also assessed to determine its effectiveness. In the case of the apparel industry, mapping followed the process of converting raw material into fibre, then into fabric, then into apparel and finally delivery to the retailer. Key measures of the process were lead times, inventory levels and work in progress.

This investigation found that the total process of converting raw material into clothing took 66 weeks. A basic analysis of the process identified that 55 weeks were taken up with products sitting in various stores as inventory. The principal cause of the need for this inventory was identified as being lack of communication between the organisations in the supply network.

Such analysis is similar to that described in Chapter 5, with the process considered in this case being the whole supply chain from end to end. There are two main differences between QR and a time-based approach to improvement. First, there is an emphasis on using actual customer demand to pull products through the distribution and manufacturing system. Second, there is extensive use of information technology as the preferred way to achieve pull. These two issues are explored in more detail below.

### Role of enabling technologies

High variety in clothing markets – due to different sizes, styles and colours – and in grocery markets has led these industries to use information technologies as a means of enabling QR. These technologies are based around the use of uniform product codes and electronic data interchange (EDI). The process involves collecting merchandise information at the point of sale from the product bar-code. Data are sent to the supplier via EDI, where they are compared with an inventory model for the store concerned. When appropriate, production is ordered for the specific items needed to restock the store to the requirements of the model. Once these items have been made, the cycle is completed when they are packed, shipped to the store and delivered to the shelf.

This process has enormous implications for links across the supply chain. With each retailer having a range of suppliers and each supplier servicing a number of retailers there is the need for common bar-code standards across the industry. The retailer needs to have a scanning and data capture system to identify the item being sold. It will need to have a reordering system that links the item to its manufacturer, and which places an order. Information needs to be exchanged between the parties in a common data format, which can be read by different IT systems. The high volume of transactions means that the systems handling the data exchange need to be robust and reliable. Having been informed of the sale, the supplier inputs this information to its manufacturing planning system in order to schedule production and the ordering of supplies.

It is hardly surprising that it is extremely difficult to achieve this integration across the whole of a supply network. There are significant implications for small businesses, which have difficulty justifying the cost of the IT system and the associated training. These set-up costs can deter new companies with innovative products from being able to supply. Recent developments in internet-based applications are helping to resolve this situation because the implementation and data transfer costs are much lower.

## Summary

*How is material flow planned and controlled in the supply chain?*

- Material planning and control in manufacturing is based on three time periods – long term, medium term and short term.

- The focal firm 'game plan' comprises a set of inter-linked modules ranging from 'front end' (demand management, resource planning, sales and operations planning and master production scheduling) to 'engine' (materials and capacity planning) to 'back end' (detailed planning and control of source–make–deliver processes). All are linked to the enterprise resource planning (ERP) database.

- After manufacture, replenishment of independent demand items in the supply chain is usually managed by order point methods like EOQ and POQ. Periodic review places orders of variable size at fixed intervals.

- Retail processes have other, distinct challenges when it comes to material planning and control. Stock must be available to generate sales, so OSA is a key performance measure. Sales must be supported across a much wider range of skus. The top priority of retailers has been to serve the market, and manufacturers have traditionally been expected to serve retail processes. Shrinkage (stock losses) and the impact of promotions are further challenges.

- Coordinating material planning and control between firms greatly increases the need for management of detail. There are many more ways to inhibit the accurate exchange of data than within a focal firm. This results in undesirable symptoms like the bullwhip effect and even chaotic behaviour of material movements.

*How is it possible to improve coordination between retail and manufacturing processes?*

- Efficient consumer response (ECR) is aimed at integrating SCM with demand management by means of category management, product replenishment and enabling technologies.

- Collaborative planning, forecasting and replenishment (CPFR) aims to improve customer service while inventory management is made more efficient.

- Vendor managed inventory (VMI) refers to the control of inventory management and replenishment by the supplier. The key performance indicator is on-shelf availability (OSA) at the retailer.
- Quick response (QR) is based on taking a total supply chain view, starting with supply chain mapping.

## Discussion questions

1 Apply the MPC framework in Figure 6.1 to a restaurant. Pay special attention to identifying the front end, engine and back end components.

2 Evaluate the impact of international supply chains on the challenges to MPC systems in practice. Does increasing the physical distance between processes mean that they are more difficult to plan and control?

3 Demand changes from independent to dependent at the customer order decoupling point (CODP). What actually happens to end-customer demand, and why is this change so important in managing material flow?

4 What actions are needed to address the problems of inter-firm planning and control listed in section 6.1.3? How would you go about orchestrating material movements (for example the cheese supply chain, shown in Figure 1.1) across a grocery supply chain?

5 Paul Polman, Chief Executive of Unilever, said 'I do not work for the shareholder, to be honest, I work for the customer. I don't drive this business by driving shareholder value.' What matters more: value to the customer or value to the shareholder? Refer to section 3.4 of Chapter 3 in formulating your response. How would you expect this question to impact on Unilever's long-term MPC strategy?

## References

Angeles, R. (2005) 'RFID technologies: supply chain applications and implementation issues', *Information Systems Management*, Vol. 22, No. 1, pp. 51–65.

Barratt, M. and Oliveira, A. (2002) 'Supply chain collaboration: exploring the early initiatives', *Supply Chain Planning*, Vol. 4, No. 1, pp. 16–28.

Beck, A. (2004) *Shrinkage in Europe 2004: A Survey of Stock Loss in the FMCG Sector.* Brussels: ECR-Europe at http://www.ecrnet.org

Chapman, P. (2010) 'Reducing product losses in the food supply chain', in C. Mena and G. Stevens (eds), *Delivering Performance in Food Supply Chains.* New York: McGraw Hill.

Chase, R. Jacobs, R. and Aquilano, N. (2005) *Operations Management for Competitive Advantage*, 10th edn. New York: McGraw Hill.

Coopers & Lybrand (1996) *European Value Chain Analysis: Final Study.* Utrecht: ECR Europe.

Fernie, J. (1998) 'Relationships in the supply chain', in J. Fernie and L. Sparks (eds), *Logistics and Retail Management: Insights into Current Practice and Trends from Leading Experts*, pp. 23–46, London: Kogan Page.

Goldratt, E. and Cox, J. (1984) *The Goal.* New York: North River Press.

Harrison, A., Chapman, P., Rutherford, C. and Stimson, J. (2004) *Demand Planning and Forecasting: Survey of Best Practice.* Cranfield: Cranfield University.

Lee, H.L., Padmanbhan, V. and Whang, S. (1997) 'The Bullwhip Effect in Supply Chains', *Sloan Management Review*, Vol. 38, No. 3, pp. 93–102.

Mitchell, A. (1997) *Efficient Consumer Response: A new paradigm for the European FMCG sector.* London: F/T Pearson Professional.

Oliveira, A. and Barratt, M. (2001) 'Exploring the experience of collaborative planning initiatives', *International Journal of Physical Distribution and Logistics Management,* Vol. 31, No. 4, pp. 266–89.

PE International (1997) *Efficient Consumer Response – Supply Chain Management of the New Millennium.* Corby: Institute of Logistics.

Roland Berger Strategy Consultants (2003) *Optimal Shelf Availability.* Brussels: ECR-Europe, see http://www.ecrnet.org.

Salmon, K. (1993) *Efficient Consumer Response: Enhancing Consumer Value in the Supply Chain.* Washington, DC: Kurt Salmon.

Skipworth, H. and Harrison, A. (2004) 'Implications of form postponement to manufacturing: a case study', *International Journal of Production Research,* Vol. 42, No. 10, pp. 2063–81.

Skjoett-Larsen, T., Therne, C. and Andersen, C. (2003) 'Supply chain collaboration: theoretical perspective and empirical evidence, *International Journal of Physical Distribution and Logistics Management,* Vol. 33, No. 6, pp. 53–49.

Storey, J., Emberson, C. and Reade, D. (2005) 'The barriers to customer responsive supply chain management', *International Journal of Operations and Production Management,* Vol. 25, No. 3/4, pp. 242–61.

Storey, J., Emberson, C., Godsell, J. and Harrison, A. (2006) 'Supply chain management: theory, practice & future challenges', *International Journal of Operations and Production Management,* Vol. 26, No. 7, pp. 754–74.

Varley, R. (2006) *Retail Product Management,* 2nd edn. Abingdon: Routledge.

Vollman, T.E., Berry, W.L., Whybark, D.C. and Jacobs, F.R. (2005) *Manufacturing Planning and Control for Supply Chain Management,* 5th edn, New York: McGraw Hill Higher Education.

Waters, D. (2003) *Inventory Planning and Control,* John Wiley and Sons Ltd.

Wilding, R. (1998) 'The supply chain complexity triangle: uncertainty generation in the supply chain', *International Journal of Physical Distribution and Logistics Management,* Vol. 28, No. 8, pp. 599–616.

## Suggested further reading

Crum, C. and Palmatier, G. (2003) *Demand Management Best Practices: Process, Principles and Collaboration,* Fort Lauderdale, FL: J. Ross Publishing.

Fernie, J. and Sparks, L. (eds) (2004) *Logistics and Retail Management* (2nd edn). London: Kogan Page.

Randall, G. and Seth, A. (2005) *Supermarket Wars: Global Strategies for Food Retailers.* Basingstoke: Palgrave Macmillan.

Wild, A. (2002) *Best Practice in Inventory Management.* Oxford: Elsevier Butterworth Heinemann.

# CHAPTER 7

# Just-in-time and the agile supply chain

**Objectives**

*The intended objectives of this chapter are to:*

- explain how just-in-time can be used to avoid the build-up of waste within and between supply chain processes;
- introduce the concept of the agile supply chain as a broad-based approach to developing responsiveness advantages;
- explore the challenges of coping with volatile demand situations;
- explain how capabilities can be developed and specifically targeted at thriving in conditions of market turbulence.

*By the end of this chapter you should be able to:*

- understand how lean thinking can be used to improve performance of the supply chain in meeting end-customer demand by cutting out waste;
- recognise enemies of flow in the supply chain;
- understand the distinctions between lean and agile strategies, and how the two can work together;
- identify the type of market conditions under which agile strategies are appropriate, and how they can be operationalised.

*In Chapter 9 we consider another key aspect of the agile supply chain – the virtual organisation.*

## Introduction

In Chapter 5, we reviewed the importance of time in supply chain thinking. Time is one of the 'hard objectives' (section 1.3.1), and some supply chains compete on time by delivering products to the end-customer faster than competition. Here, the focus is on reducing the time taken for each process. But time can also be used to alter the trade-offs between competitive priorities – for example, costs do not have to rise proportionately as lead times are reduced (section 5.1.1). This can be achieved by squeezing non-value-adding activities (delays, transport, storage and inspection) from the supply chain by time-based process mapping (section 5.3). Such activities are referred to generically as *waste*, the Japanese word for which is *muda* (the concept of waste was introduced in Chapter 5 and is explored further in section 7.1.2). Such thinking has been developed into a philosophy and accompanying tools and techniques under the banner of 'just-in-time' (JIT). The aim of JIT (Harrison, 1992) is:

**To meet demand instantaneously with perfect quality and no waste.**

All three targets (demand – quality – waste) are ideals which can never be fully achieved. But we can get closer to them over time through continuous improvement. The elimination of waste has been promoted under the banner of 'lean thinking' (Womack and Jones, 2003), who advise:

**To hell with your competitors; compete against *perfection* by identifying all activities that are *muda* and eliminating them. This is an absolute rather than a relative standard which can provide the essential North Star for any organization.**

JIT and lean thinking share the same roots, and originate from competitive strategies developed by the Japanese. Toyota Motor Company is held up as the role model and, although the Toyota brand has been severely damaged in recent years by widespread quality problems (section 1.3.1), this focal firm's operational excellence has had a major influence on logistics thinking today.

A common view is that lean thinking works best where demand is relatively stable – and hence predictable – and where variety is low. But in situations where demand is volatile and customer requirement for variety is high, the elimination of waste in itself becomes a lower priority than the need to respond rapidly to a turbulent marketplace. So the second part of this chapter reviews developments under the banner of the 'agile supply chain'.

In Chapter 6, we reviewed quick response and other time-based approaches to developing the capabilities needed to support the speed advantage. While such logistics capabilities are important enablers to lean and responsive supply chains, the 'agile supply chain' takes the argument a significant step further. Marketplaces of the 21st century are often characterised by proliferation of products and services, shorter product lifecycles and increased rates of product innovation. Simply responding quickly and at the right time are not enough to meet the needs of such marketplaces.

The mission of modern logistics is to ensure that it is the right product – to meet exact end customer needs – that gets delivered in the right place at the right time. Such a mission means that the *end-customer comes first*. Section 7.2 proposes the agile supply chain as an approach that elevates speed capabilities in a given supply chain to much higher levels than would be possible using the tools and techniques discussed in Section 7.1

**Key issues**    This chapter addresses two key issues:

1 **Just-in-time and lean thinking:** the impact of just-in-time on supply chain thinking. Cutting out waste in business processes. Simple, paperless systems v central control. Use and misuse in planning and control.

2 **The agile supply chain:** the dimensions of the agile supply chain, and the environments that favour agility. Agile practices: addressing the challenges of market turbulence, rapid response logistics and managing low volume products.

## 7.1 Just-in-time and lean thinking

*Key issue:* What are the implications of just-in-time and lean thinking for logistics? How can just-in-time principles be applied to other forms of material control such as material requirements planning?

Just-in-time is actually a broad philosophy of management that seeks to eliminate waste and improve quality in all business processes. JIT is put into practice by means of a set of tools and techniques that provide the cutting edge in the 'war on waste'. In this chapter, we focus on the application of JIT to logistics. This partial view of JIT has been called *little JIT* (Chase *et al.*, 2005): there is far more to this wide-ranging approach to management than we present here (see, for example, Harrison, 1992). Nevertheless, little JIT has enormous implications for logistics, and has spawned several logistics versions of JIT concepts.

The partial view of JIT is an approach to material control based on the view that a process should operate only when a customer signals a need for more parts from that process. When a process is operated in the JIT way, goods are produced and delivered just-in-time to be sold. This principle cascades upstream through the supply network, with subassemblies produced and delivered just-in-time to be assembled, parts fabricated and delivered just-in-time to be built into subassemblies, and materials bought and delivered just-in-time to be made into fabricated parts. Throughout the supply network, the trigger to start work is governed by demand from the customer – the next process (Schonberger, 1991). A supply network can be conceived of as a *chain of customers*, with each link coordinated with its neighbours by JIT signals. The whole network is triggered by demand from the end-customer. Only the end-customer is free to place demand whenever he or she wants; after that the system takes over.

The above description of the flow of goods in a supply chain is characteristic of a *pull* system. Parts are pulled through the chain in response to demand from the end-customer. This contrasts with a *push* system, in which products are made whenever resources (people, material and machines) become available in response to a central plan or schedule. The two systems of controlling materials can be distinguished as follows:

- *Pull scheduling*: a system of controlling materials whereby the user signals to the maker or provider that more material is needed. Material is sent only in response to such a signal.

- *Push scheduling*: a system of controlling materials whereby makers and providers make or send material in response to a pre-set schedule, regardless of whether the next process needs them at the time.

The push approach is a common way for processes to be managed, and often seems a sensible option. If some of the people in a factory or an office are idle, it seems a good idea to give them work to do. The assumption is that those products can be sold at some point in the future. A similar assumption is that building up a stock of finished goods will quickly help to satisfy the customer. This argument seems particularly attractive where manufacturing lead times are long, if quality is a problem or if machines often break down. It is better and safer to make product, just in case there's a problem in the future. Unfortunately, this argument has severe limitations. Push scheduling and its associated inventories do *not* always help companies to be more responsive. All too often, the very products the organisation wants to sell are unavailable, while there is too much stock of products that are not selling. And building up stock certainly does not help to make more productive use of spare capacity. Instead it can easily lead to excess costs, and hide opportunities to improve processes.

### 7.1.1  The just-in-time system

Companies achieve the ability to produce and deliver just-in-time to satisfy actual demand because they develop a production system that is capable of working in this way. Such a system can be envisaged as a number of 'factors' that interact with each other, as shown in Figure 7.1. This shows JIT capability as founded on layers of factors that interact together to form a system that is designed for flow. Excellence in each of the six factors determines the effectiveness with which JIT capability can be achieved: that is, how easy it is to get to the top of the pyramid.

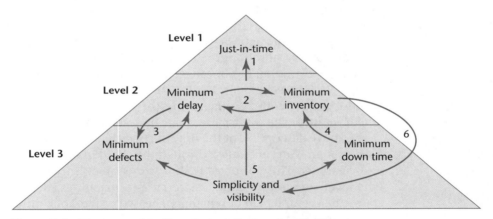

**Figure 7.1   The pyramid of key factors that underpin JIT**

*Factor 1*

The top of the pyramid is full capability for just-in-time supply. This is the level at which a focal firm can produce and deliver according to the demand that is placed on it. The relationships operating within and between levels 2 and 3 form the system that ultimately underpins the achievement of JIT. They are complex, and in some cases there is a long time delay between taking actions and seeing the effects.

*Factor 2*

The two factors *delay* and *inventory* interact with each other in a system of positive amplification; that is, they go up together and they go down together. This interrelationship results in either a virtuous cycle, where things keep getting better, or a vicious cycle, where they keep getting worse. For example, extra delay in a process will result in extra inventory being held to compensate for the delay. Adding more inventory causes further delays as products take longer to flow through the process, which leads to the need for more inventory. Conversely if delays are reduced then less inventory is needed, which results in fewer delays, meaning that inventory can be further reduced. Making sure this relationship operates as a virtuous cycle of reducing delay and inventory instead of a vicious one where they increase depends on the underpinning factors in level 3.

### Factor 3

Defects lead to delays, either through requiring rework or necessitating increased production to compensate for scrap. The likelihood of defects leads to safety stocks being held as a buffer against potential problems. This thinking amplifies quality problems by increasing the time between a defect occurring and its discovery. Not only is the cause harder to identify, but more production will be affected. The attitude that holding inventory can mitigate the effect of quality problems is fundamentally flawed. It stands in opposition to the only successful approach to defect minimisation, where problems are quickly identified, their causes are traced, and permanent solutions are devised and applied.

### Factor 4

Machine downtime relates to a number of issues:

- unplanned downtime – that is, breakdowns;
- planned maintenance;
- changeover times.

Downtime, and particularly the risk of unplanned downtime, is a key cause of the need for safety stocks in a process. Other JIT tools and techniques can help to minimise the problems here. For example, *total productive maintenance* (TPM; Nakajima, 1989) seeks to answer the question 'What can everyone do to help prevent breakdowns?' Regular planned preventive maintenance, closer cooperation between production and maintenance personnel, and equipment sourcing for ease of maintenance are some of the actions that can be taken in response. In other words, increasing planned maintenance costs often results in reduced overall costs of machine downtime. Minimising changeover time is a JIT tool that can be used not only to reduce lost production time but also improve production flexibility. Inflexible facilities delay the rapid production of customer orders.

### Factor 5

Where the flow through a process is easily seen, people in the process will have a better understanding of their colleagues' work and how they themselves affect others. A simple process results from having first *focused* operations around a family of compatible products. Layout is then organised to bring together all the people and equipment needed to undertake the process. These are arranged so that there is a logical flow between the process steps. Arranging the process so that the stations for undertaking the steps are close together not only helps to reduce inventory but also will itself be made easier when inventory is low. A simple process will be more *visible*, allowing it to be better maintained. Not only should there be fewer things to go wrong, they will be more obvious when they do, and will be easier to fix. This attribute helps to minimise both machine downtime and product defects.

Maintenance of the process is underpinned by housekeeping and cleanliness. This starts with designing processes and facilities to create order. There is a place for everything, and everything has its place. Orderliness depends on a thinking workforce that has accepted ownership and responsibility for organising the work place. Attention to detail in terms of 'respect for human' issues is an essential part of JIT philosophy (Harrison and Storey, 2000).

### Factor 6

The levels of work in progress and other types of inventory have a significant impact upon the visibility of a process. It becomes increasingly difficult to see the flow of a process as inventory increases. This may be literally true on a shop floor or in a warehouse, where piles and stacks of goods can isolate workers. The same is true in offices when the process flow becomes lost in assorted piles of work on people's desks.

In order to highlight the limitations of push production we next consider the case of how a focal firm took a rather traditional approach to responding to new demands being placed on the production process.

---

**CASE STUDY 7.1**

## Smog Co.

### The Smog Co. production system

This is the case of Smog Co., a small supplier of well-engineered components. Smog produces a range of products grouped into families. Production of one of the higher-volume product families has been organised into a flow process made up of four steps, which follow one after the other in sequence. Changeover from one product to another is relatively simple, but takes around ten minutes per machine. To minimise delays caused by changeovers, products tend to be made in batches. These batches move from one step to the next, where they queue on a first in, first out basis to be worked on, after which they move to the next step. This process is shown in Figure 7.2.

Step 1        Step 2        Step 3        Step 4

**Figure 7.2   The Smog production process**

Key measures of the performance of this process are the utilisation of people and of machines. The objective is to keep utilisation of both as high as possible. In this situation, if people or machines are idle – and material is available – they are used to make something. Naturally it wouldn't make sense to make anything. Instead the production manager has a feel for what is needed, and uses a forecast from the sales department to make an early start on products that it is considered will be required in the near future.

Fred Hollis, the Smog production manager, felt pleased with performance as he looked out across the factory. He was pleased because his machines and people were busy, there were plenty of finished goods on hand, which the sales team could use to supply customers, and there was stock to call upon if product demand increased. Everything seemed to be under control.

## Changes to customer requirements

The motivation to change from the current system has been low in the past, as the process at Smog Co. is a reliable one, which has worked well for the company. The 'big three' customers, who take three-quarters of sales, tend to order the same things in similar quantities one week in advance of delivery. With a production lead time of three weeks, Smog Co. uses a forecast to schedule production and make sure that finished goods stocks will be available to meet predicted demand. Consistent demand means that forecasts are often close to real demand, so stockouts are rare. In fact the only time this occurred was an incident a couple of years ago, when a key machine went down and a spare part took a long time to source. Current inventory levels now include safety stock to provide cover against a similar problem in the future.

When the company found that certain finished goods were selling slowly, the sales team was particularly good at finding a way to move them. Sometimes prices were cut; at other times sales used special promotions. If production was too high, or the forecast was a bit optimistic, then there were ways of selling surplus stock, and the sales team seemed to enjoy the challenge.

Recently, however, this well-understood position has begun to change. The main customers have started to use a number of new strategies to compete with each other. First one and now a second of them has announced that it will be reducing the call-off time for its products from one week to two working days. At the same time they are all looking for a 5 per cent cost reduction, and are demanding quality improvements.

## A 'traditional' reaction to customer demands for better service

The combination of demands for better services caused Smog management some concern. The obvious response to the changes in ordering patterns was to increase stock levels to cater for unexpected variations in demand. This approach had worked before, when it was used to justify the safety stocks that covered production problems. It seemed worth trying again, so stocks were increased.

Things went well over the first few months, during which time delivery performance remained good, while the customers went ahead with their plan to reduce the order lead time. Keeping up with these orders provided the production manager with a few headaches. Preventing stockouts led to an increase in the number of batches being expedited through the factory. This disrupted the production plan, increased the number of machine changeovers and lowered productivity. As a result, overtime increased in order to maintain output.

▶

The higher level of inventory meant that quality problems were harder to detect. In one case a new operator missed a drilling operation. By the time the first customer discovered the error, nearly two weeks' worth of production had to be recalled and reworked.

The higher inventory levels were also taking up more space. Fred Hollis had submitted a requisition to the finance director to pay for more storage racking. The extra racks were necessary because existing ones were full, and parts stored on the floor were suffering occasional damage in an increasingly cramped factory. Some parts were recently returned by a customer, who felt that damaged packaging indicated damaged products. Naturally, Fred was concerned when his request for more storage space was turned down owing to spending reductions imposed in response to price cuts imposed by customers.

Reflecting on what had happened at Smog, the increase in stock levels had badly affected competitiveness. Smog Co. was experiencing the consequences of trying to forecast demand and using the forecast to determine what to make. Their 'make to stock' approach was responsible for:

- removing the company's ability to be responsive to changes in either quantities or product mix;
- increasing costs and making quality problems worse;
- burying underlying production problems under inventory, and thereby preventing efforts to uncover and resolve them.

In conclusion, while the company had been motivated to change by its customers, the direction it took seemed to have caused many problems.

(Source: After an original by Paul Chapman)

### Questions

1 List the actions that Smog Co. took to respond to the new demands being placed on it by customers. Group your responses under the headings of stock levels, level of expediting and storage space. Briefly describe the effects that these actions had on production performance.

2 Use the 'pyramid of key factors that underpin JIT' to describe the factors that caused these actions to affect the company's ability to respond to the demands being placed on it by customers.

## 7.1.2 The seven wastes

In Chapter 5 we saw how any activity that does not add value is a form of waste. By mapping processes through the supply chain, it is possible to sort value-adding and non-value-adding activities (transport, store, inspect and delay). JIT goes further by adding three more types of 'waste' to make seven in all. They are as follows:

- *The waste of overproduction*: making or delivering too much, too early or 'just in case'. Instead, the aim should be to make 'just-in-time' – neither too early nor too late. Overproduction creates unevenness or lumpiness of material flow, which is bad for quality and productivity. It is often the biggest source of waste.

- *The waste of waiting*: takes place whenever time is not being used effectively. It shows up as waiting by operators, by parts or by customers.

- *The waste of transporting*: moving parts around from one process to the next adds no value. Double handling, conveyors and movements by fork-lift truck are all examples of this waste. Placing processes as close as possible to each other not only minimises the waste of transport but also improves communications between them.

- *The waste of inappropriate processing*: using a large, central process that is shared between several lines (e.g. a heat treatment plant) is an example of this type of waste. Another example is a process that is incapable of meeting quality standards demanded by the customer – so it cannot help making defects.

- *The waste of unnecessary inventory*: inventory is a sign that flow has been disrupted, and that there are inherent problems in the process. Inventory not only hides problems, it also increases lead times and increases space requirements.

- *The waste of unnecessary motions*: if operators have to bend, stretch or extend themselves unduly, then these are unnecessary motions. Other examples are walking between processes, taking a stores requisition for signature, and decanting parts from one container into another.

- *The waste of defects*: producing defects costs time and money. The longer a defect remains undetected (e.g. if it gets into the hands of the end-customer), the more cost is added. Defects are counteracted by the concepts of 'quality at source' and 'prevention, not detection'.

JIT invites us to analyse business processes systematically to establish the baseline of value-adding processes and identify the incidence of these seven wastes. The aim is to get parts and data to flow through business processes evenly and synchronously. The more detailed analysis prompted by the concept of seven wastes encourages a greater analysis and understanding of processes and their relationships than is made by supply chain mapping. This analysis should first start with key business processes such as the supply pipeline.

## 7.1.3   JIT and material requirements planning

As we saw in section 6.1, material requirements planning (MRP) was conceived in order to answer the questions *how many?* and *when?* in ordering parts that are directly used to manufacture end products. MRP is a logical and systematic way of planning materials. It links downstream demand with manufacture and with upstream supply. It can handle detailed parts requirements, even for products that are made infrequently and in low volumes.

On the other hand, MRP is based on a centrally controlled, bureaucratic approach to material planning. Although it is based on a pull scheduling logic, it instructs processes to make more parts whether or not the customer (the next process) is capable of accepting them. Typically, MRP adopts push scheduling characteristics. It remains insensitive to day-to-day issues at shop floor level, and continues to assume that its plans are being carried out to the letter. In other words, MRP is good at planning but weak at control.

Meanwhile, JIT pull scheduling is good at handling relatively stable demand for parts that are made regularly. It is sensitive to problems at shop floor level, and is designed not to flood the next process with parts that it cannot work on. On the other hand, JIT pull scheduling is not good at predicting requirements for the future, especially for parts and products that are in irregular or sporadic demand. JIT is good at control but weak at planning. There are clear opportunities for putting together the strengths of both systems, so that the weaknesses of one are covered by the strengths of the other. For example, even in systems with great variety, many of the parts are common. So JIT can be used to control those parts, while a much downsized MRP plans what is left.

JIT has become associated with the Japanese way of cutting out waste, doing the simple things well and getting better every day. The foundations of Toyota Production System (TPS) are JIT and *jidoka*. *Jidoka* means humanising the man-machine interface so that it is the man who runs the machine, not vice versa. MRP has become associated with the Western way of automating our way out of trouble, and by investing in bigger and better systems that competitors cannot afford to match. Let us next review how these two different approaches apply in motor manufacture by comparing Ford (which has developed its own version of TPS called Ford Production System, FPS) and Toyota.

---

**CASE STUDY 7.2**

## Ford and Toyota

A car assembly plant is built around a simple sequence of tasks that starts in the press shop and ends as a car rolls off the final assembly line. Figure 7.3 shows these basic tasks in summary form:

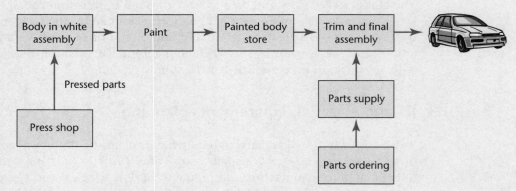

**Figure 7.3 Basic tasks in a car assembly plant**

While these basic tasks are the same for both Ford and Toyota, the way they are managed by the two firms is quite different. We compare policies and practices in relation to small cars such as the Ford Fiesta and the Toyota Yaris:

● Ford is driven by a long-term strategy in Europe. It has invested heavily in fixed assets, and does not seek an early return on them. Currently, it is struggling with a capacity that was designed for a 15 per cent market share when current loading is only 9 per cent. It seeks to make a step change in the production process through high capital investment. Its investment policy has therefore been technically oriented, seeking the 'best' technical solution for each task. For example, Ford's body shop is almost fully automated with robots that are flexible across different parts. When production is changed between one part and another, the robots must be re-programmed. This places high emphasis on technical support for the software, and makes Ford dependent on given equipment suppliers. The layout is designed around the robots and for fixed volumes.

- Toyota has expanded cautiously in Europe. Its investment policy has been step-by-step, and it has sought to make early returns. Key to the Toyota Production System (TPS) are process and quality disciplines through JIT and *jidoka*. Toyota's philosophy is more people-oriented: shop floor people are heavily involved in improvement activities as well as in production work. Toyota's body shop has maybe one third the number of press shop robots as Ford, and tends to use simple multi-welders at low initial cost. It is relatively easy to swap suppliers. Tooling must be changed when production is changed between one batch and another, but people are trained to go for fast set-ups and to improve the process. The layout is designed around people and volume flexibility.

Having learned much from its stake in Mazda, Ford launched its own version of just-in-time called Ford Production System (FPS) a few years ago. Ford has done much to reduce product complexity. This is basically measured by the number of different body styles that are possible. Both Ford and Toyota have three basic body styles, but Ford limits variation to left-hand/right-hand drive and sunroof/no sunroof options. Since these are multiplicative, 12 body shells are possible. Toyota in addition has variations to allow for different engine types and air conditioner types, together with spoiler/no spoiler versions. In total, this means that Toyota has over 70 body shell variations. When multiplied again by the number of painted body colours (say ten for both firms), Toyota ends up with hundreds more painted body options than Ford. This contributes to a surprising difference when it comes to building the car:

- Ford treats the painted body as a commodity. Once they have been painted, bodies are kept in the painted body store, which is a buffer between the body shop and final assembly. The Ford system calculates the number of each painted body type that should be in the store to meet forecast final assembly requirements. Trouble is that the store can be full of the wrong bodies, which means that it is impossible to build the current orders. Up to this point in the sequence, the emphasis is on numbers, not on the end-customer. Bodies are not given a vehicle identification number (VIN) – which allocates the body to a particular customer order – until the painted body is removed from the store and dropped onto the trim and final assembly line.
- Toyota treats the body shell as a customer's car from the start. The VIN is added as the first process at body in white assembly, when panels are welded together to make the shell. In turn, this drives discipline and focus in the paint shop, and helps to improve first time through (FTT) in the paint process. The sequence of bodies through trim and final processes is thereby more predictable, allowing more precise material control downstream.

The parts ordering process for auto assembly is particularly challenging, because some 2,000 individual parts are needed for each vehicle. Most of these parts are added at the trim and final assembly stage. TPS already has a number of advantages when it comes to this task. First, the more predictable sequence of painted bodies into trim and final means that there are few last-minute schedule changes. Second, TPS sets stable lead times that are fixed at certain times for each part.

Third, supplier lead times are allowed for. Ford on the other hand leaves schedules uncommitted until parts are collected. The Ford call-off quantities are set on the day of collection, and don't allow for supplier lead times. Figures 1.8 and 1.9 compare what happens from a supplier point of view – there are huge differences between scheduled and actual demand.

### Question

1  What changes would you propose to both TPS and to FPS in order to cope with customer demands for increasing product variety and more rapid model changes?

## 7.1.4  Lean thinking

Lean thinking (Krafcik and MacDuffie, 1989) developed as a term used to contrast the just-in-time production methods used by Japanese automotive manufacturers with the mass production methods used by most Western manufacturers. Suffering shortages and lack of resources, Japanese car manufacturers responded by developing production processes that operated with minimum waste. Gradually the principle of minimising waste spread from the shopfloor to all manufacturing areas, and from manufacturing to new product development and supply chain management. The term *lean thinking* refers to the elimination of waste in all aspects of a business.

Lean thinking is a cyclical route to seeking perfection by eliminating waste (the Japanese word is *muda*) and thereby enriching value from the customer perspective. The end-customer should not pay for the cost, time and quality penalties of wasteful processes in the supply network. Four principles are involved in achieving the fifth, seeking perfection (see Figure 7.4):

- specifying value;
- identifying the value stream;
- making value flow;
- pull scheduling.

### Specify value

Value is specified from the customer perspective. In Chapter 3 we discussed value from the shareholder perspective. From the end-customer perspective, value is added along the supply network as raw materials from primary manufacture are progressively converted into finished product bought by the end-customer, such as the aluminium ore being converted into one of the constituents of a can of coke (see Chapter 1, section 1.1). From a marketing and sales perspective

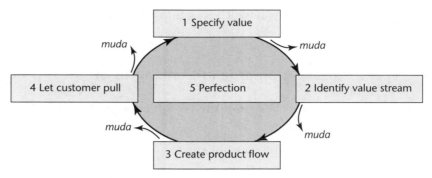

**Figure 7.4  Lean thinking principles**
(Source: After Womack and Jones, 2003)

the can of coke should be 'always within reach of your thirst'. That is an attempt to define value from the end-customer perspective. Another is Porter's concept of the *value chain* (Porter, 1985), which sees two types of activity that are of value to the customer. The first is the primary value activities of transforming raw materials into finished products, then distributing, marketing and servicing them. The second is support activities, such as designing the products, and the manufacturing and distribution processes needed to underpin primary activities.

## Identify the value stream

Following on from the concept of value, the next principle is to identify the whole sequence of processes along the supply network. The principles of time-based mapping are discussed in sections 5.4 and 5.5 of Chapter 5.

## Make value flow

In essence, this means applying the pyramid of key factors that we outlined in section 7.1. Minimising delays, inventories, defects and downtime supports the flow of value in the supply network. Simplicity and visibility are the foundations to achieving these key factors.

## Pull scheduling

Enforce the rules in section 6.1: make only in response to a signal from the customer (the next process) that more is needed. This implies that demand information is made available across the supply chain. Where possible, supply from manufacturing, not from stock. Where possible, use customer orders not forecasts.

While some of these concepts may be distant from current practice, lean thinking shares the philosophy of 'big JIT': seek perfection. This is the fifth principle, and is achieved by gradually getting better at everything we do, squeezing waste out at every step. We continue this section by considering the sources of waste, and the way in which lean thinking can be applied to enriching value in business processes.

### 7.1.5  Application of lean thinking to business processes

Working back from the customer, a focal firm should consider the following processes:

- order to replenishment;
- order to production;
- product development.

In each of these processes, the application of lean thinking involves examining the process, quantifying waste within it, identifying root causes of the waste, and developing and implementing of solutions. Examining the process involves mapping it using a variety of techniques such as flow charting, depending on the nature of the process. Performance is quantified by taking measures of the different kinds of waste. For a first attempt, using the time-based measures of lead time and value-adding time often reveal the main incidences of waste. Having identified waste, lean thinking applies the problem solving tools associated with total quality control (TQC) to identify root causes and develop solutions.

The application of lean thinking is the means by which many companies bring their processes under control. Following a systematic approach to tackling waste, they seek to minimise defects, to minimise downtime and to maximise simplicity and visibility.

#### Order to replenishment

The order replenishment cycle concerns the time taken to replenish what has been sold. Lean thinking seeks to manage the order replenishment cycle by replacing only what has been sold within rapid replenishment lead times. These points are taken up in the next two sections of this chapter, on vendor-managed inventory and on quick response.

#### Order to production

The order to production cycle is the series of steps that are followed to respond to an order, organise and undertake production, and deliver the product to the customer. This 'make to order' process may be contained within a company or can extend down the supply chain.

#### Product development

Product development delivers new products or services that can be sold. This process is essential if an organisation is to have future success. Lean thinking can be applied to this process to make it more effective by supporting the development of products with desirable attributes and features, and achieving this on time. It can also make the process more efficient and ensure that products are developed to cost.

## 7.1.6  Role of lean practices

Lean thinking is associated with a number of operational practices that help to deliver the aim of waste minimisation. Two of the most significant are:

- small-batch production;
- rapid changeover.

These two practices are closely associated with each other, but are considered separately here to aid clarity.

The target in small-batch production is a batch size of 1. The traditional logic behind large batches is to take advantage of reduced costs through economies of scale. This approach is often flawed, as batch size decisions generally consider only production costs, and overlook the costs of inventory and lack of flexibility that is caused by large batches. Lack of flexibility is a major contributor to poor quality of service to the end customer. The rationale behind small batches is that they can reduce total cost across a supply chain, such as removing the waste of overproduction. They help to deliver products that the end customer wants within the expected lead time (D-time – Chapter 5, section 5.2).

The contribution of rapid changeover was graphically shown by the changeover of press tools used to make car body panels. These cumbersome pieces of equipment can weigh up to 10 tonnes, and historically took up to eight hours to change within the large presses. The consequence of these long changeover times was that component production runs were long, often going on for days before the press tools were changed so that another component could be made. Extensive work, again pioneered by Toyota, was undertaken on press design, tooling design and component design over a number of years to help reduce changeover times. The effect has been to reduce changeover times for tools for large pressed parts to around five minutes. Consequently, practices that reduce changeover times are often known as *single minute exchange of dies* (SMED; Shingo, 1988). The ability to undertake rapid changeovers allows a batch of each different body panel to be produced each day in line with current demand instead of having to produce to forecast.

The lesson from the automotive industry is that even very large pieces of equipment can be developed to allow rapid changeovers. This effort may take a number of years, and is reliant upon developments in machinery and product design. The effect is to provide the flexibility to make possible small-batch production that responds to customer needs.

Small-batch production associated with rapid changeover allows productivity to be maintained by taking advantage of economies of scope. Instead of economies of scale, where quantities of the same thing are made, economies of scope lower costs when quantities of similar things that use the same production resources are made.

## 7.2 The concept of agility

The 'agile supply chain' is an essentially practical approach to organising logistics capabilities around end-customer demand. It is about moving from supply chains that are structured around a focal company and its operating guidelines (for example, 'Ford Production System') towards supply chains that are focused on end-customers. Enabling the agile supply chain requires many significant changes: as an example, consider the position of Li and Fung, the largest export trader in Hong Kong. The organisation coordinates manufacturers in the Far East to supply major customers such as *the Limited*, mostly in the US. Chairman Victor Fung says that one of the key features of his approach is to organise for the customer, not on country units that end up competing against each other.

> **So customer-focused divisions are the building blocks of our organisation, and we keep them small and entrepreneurial. They do anywhere from $20 million to $50 million of business. Each is run by a lead entrepreneur.**
>
> (Magretta, 1998)

And capabilities of the supply networks are 'all about flexibility, response time, small production runs, small minimum order quantities, and the ability to shift direction as the trends move'. While some of these ideas reflect JIT approaches, the key is to organise logistics from the customer order back – or 'outside in' – as opposed to pushing product-service offerings into the market – or 'inside out'. Important requirements for that change in mindset include:

- A relentless focus on drivers of customer value in all logistics processes.
- Developing capabilities for responsiveness and flexibility in advance.
- Using those capabilities to align supply chains operations in a dynamic manner.

Mason-Jones *et al.* (1999) developed a helpful comparison between agile and lean supply, shown in Table 7.1. We have extended this table into our comparison of further characteristics of lean and agile supply, shown in Table 7.2.

There is no reason why there should be an 'either-or' approach to logistics strategy. Thus, many supply chains can adopt a 'lean' capability up to a given downstream process, and then adopt an 'agile' capability thereafter. This enables high productivity, low cost processes to start with, followed by responsive processes to allow high levels of customisation thereafter. Such a strategic choice has been referred to as 'leagility' because it combines the benefits of both supply capabilities. The concept of leagility is close to that of postponement, which we discuss later in this chapter.

The comparisons in Tables 7.1 and 7.2 help us to place 'agile' in relation to 'lean', and thus to complement our earlier concept of logistics performance objectives. In Table 1.1 (page 27 in Chapter 1), we considered the issue of competing through logistics. The relative importance of the four ways of competing through logistics (quality, time, cost and dependability) can be assessed with the help of order winners and order qualifiers (see section 1.3.4). *Order qualifiers* comprise the factors that are needed to gain entry into a given market. To actually win orders

Table 7.1   **Comparison of lean supply with agile supply: the distinguishing attributes**

| Distinguishing attributes | Lean supply | Agile supply |
|---|---|---|
| Typical products | Commodities | Fashion goods |
| Marketplace demand | Predictable | Volatile |
| Product variety | Low | High |
| Product lifecycle | Long | Short |
| Customer drivers | Cost | Availability |
| Profit margin | Low | High |
| Dominant costs | Physical costs | Marketability costs |
| Stockout penalties | Long-term contractual | Immediate and volatile |
| Purchasing policy | Buy materials | Assign capacity |
| Information enrichment | Highly desirable | Obligatory |
| Forecasting mechanism | Algorithmic | Consultative |

Table 7.2   **Further characteristics of lean and agile supply**

| Characteristic | Lean | Agile |
|---|---|---|
| Logistics focus | Eliminate waste | Customers and markets |
| Partnerships | Long term, stable | Fluid clusters |
| Key measures | Output measures like productivity and cost | Measure capabilities, and focus on customer satisfaction |
| Process focus | Work standardisation, conformance to standards | Focus on operator self-management to maximise autonomy |
| Logistics planning | Stable, fixed periods | Instantaneous response |

demands that performance of the focal firm on one or more factors must be superior, so that products win orders in the marketplace because the performance of competitors on these factors is not as good. These are called *order winners*. The specification of order qualifiers and order winners helps in the development of logistics strategy. Order winners and qualifiers can *change over time* (Johansson *et al.*, 1993), for example as a result of changes in the product lifecycle. Thus it is essential to re-visit the specification of order winners and qualifiers regularly to ensure that they reflect current market characteristics (Aitken *et al.*, 2005).

The agile mindset aims to align supply capabilities with end-customer demand, so we can view demand characteristics as placing the challenges that supply capabilities must meet. We explored demand characteristics in section 2.3: next we consider how these can be matched by supply capabilities.

### Supply capabilities

Allocation of finished goods to given customer orders is a familiar way of responding quickly to demand – for example, selling cars from a dealer forecourt. But this approach to supply means that inventories of finished goods must first be built up. The problem is that they must be built up in anticipation of *unknown* demand. If stocks pushed by a manufacturer onto its dealer network are too high, they will have to be discounted. If they are too low, sales are lost to competitors. Delaying the exact specification of the car until the customer order is known, and then delivering it within an acceptable D-time, is called *form postponement*. The concept of 'postponement' is now increasingly widely employed by organisations in a range of industries (van Hoek, 2001). Postponement is widely used to improve responsiveness, and is defined (Skipworth and Harrison, 2004) as:

> **The delay, until end-customer orders are received, of the final part of the transformation processes, through which the number of skus proliferates, and for which only a short time period is available. The postponed transformation processes may be manufacturing processes, assembly processes, configuration processes, packaging or labeling processes.**

For example, the aim of the 'three-day car' project is to complete paint, trim, final assembly and delivery of a car to dealer within three days (Holweg and Miemczyck, 2003). Many less ambitious form postponement applications delay packaging, labelling, adding documentation or product peripherals until an order is received. If the decision is limited to peripherals such as type of power supply to a printer, or to whether the number of cans in a pack is 6 or 12, we call this *logistical postponement*.

The appearance of wide customer choice can be created while keeping source, make and deliver processes as simple as possible. This is the thinking behind the principle of *design for logistics*. Creating an agile supply chain requires more than revising logistics and distribution management: it goes all the way to product design. A favourite trick of computer manufacturers such as Dell is to make common electronic boards, and to package them in many ways to create different options. While parts of a board are redundant on many of the finished products, this is more than offset by savings in inbound and manufacturing logistics.

Individual companies in an agile supply chain need to align their operations by redesigning the flow of goods, information and management practices. The aim is the *virtual organisation*, where groups of supply chain partners agree common terms for working together. There are several possible stages in the evolution of a virtual organisation. Traditional sourcing and contract logistics imply an interface between trading partners that is limited to buy–sell transactions. JIT sourcing is an example of a broader interface with sharing of demand data and alignment of logistics processes. Integrated contract manufacturing – in which a third party controls most of the make processes – attempts the integration of demand with supply in the way suggested by Figure 1.6. 'Fourth party logistics' is close to this model in that a third party takes over organisation and coordination of the entire flow of goods, information and management of the entire logistics operation including material planning and control. These supply capabilities which can be deployed to support the agile supply chain are summarised in Figure 7.5.

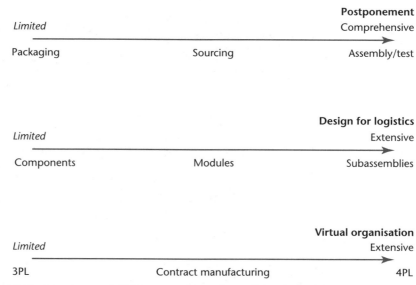

Figure 7.5   **Supply capabilities supporting the agile supply chain**

We explore these approaches further in section 7.2. Meanwhile, Case study 7.3 shows how Xerox developed a 'next generation' logistics strategy by injecting fresh thinking into the position outlined in Case study 1.2.

| CASE STUDY 7.3 | **Segmenting the supply chain at Xerox (Graham Sweet)** |
|---|---|

By the middle of the 1990s Xerox had integrated its European manufacturing and logistics processes and organisations, developing an end-to-end approach to its supply chain. This had delivered massive financials benefits to the company both in terms of inventory reduction and operating cost. At the time it was to launch a new range of products and to extend its market coverage, and it was recognised that the predominantly 'one size fits all' approach to customer fulfillment was not competitive. The company embarked on a programme of asking customers about their requirements for overall fulfillment and understanding supply chain competitive performance.

Based on market/customer expectations the company segmented its supply chain into four different streams across the total source–plan–make–deliver process. The segmentation of the market/customer expectations is shown in Figure 7.6 and the supply chain response in Figure 7.7. *Volume* represents the number of orders/shipments; *variety* reflects the combination of product variation and day-to-day demand variability.

The organisation and the processes of the supply chain needed to operate differently since the priorities of the market and customers were different. Different performance measures and targets were established for each segment and cultures and incentives put in place to drive the change. In all cases the company operated with outsourced partners as part of the supply chain operations but the balance between outsourced and in-house varied depending on the skills and flexibility required. As 'adding

▶

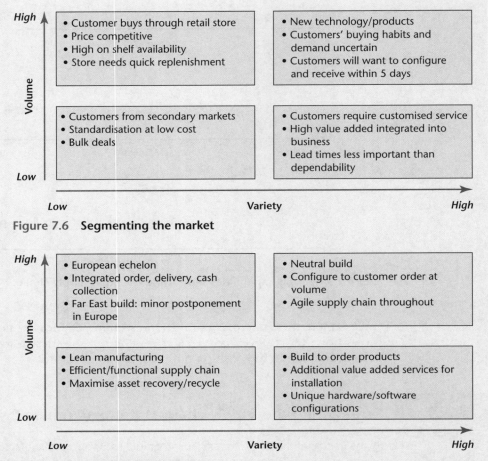

Figure 7.6    **Segmenting the market**

Figure 7.7    **Supply chain response**

customer uniqueness as late as possible' was a key element in the process design, collaboration with the product design teams and suppliers became essential to engineer supply chain-friendly products.

In particular in the high volume/high variety segment the customer order is directed to the integration centre at the end of the line, which has less than five days to finalise the product and deliver to the end-consumer. This could only be achieved by engineering the product to a modular design with final configuration from stock of 'neutral' modules and adding customer-unique options. This capability required flexibility and agility in all areas of the supply chain and investment in the people and skills of demand and supply planning developing key competencies to ensure capacity and inventory to meet the different variations in demand.

At the time the segmentation approach allowed the company to fulfil the majority of its European customer orders from a European supply, with the exception of the high volume/low variety segment which supplied customers through distributors and retailers.

This approach not only improved measures of customer responsiveness but also improved inventory turns, reducing the need for stocks below the European level and overall supply chain costs. Inherent in the design was not only the flexibility in operation but the ability to create and restructure the segments depending on changes to market and customer needs. This configuration of the Xerox supply chain segmentation had a life of approximately four years.

### Question

1  Map the Xerox segments and market response (Figures 7.6 and 7.7) onto demand characteristics in Figure 2.11 and supply capabilities in Figure 7.5 as far as you can, making assumptions where necessary. How closely does the 'actual' match 'theoretical'?

## 7.2.1  Classifying operating environments

Figure 7.8 offers a classification of operating environments based on demand characteristics shown in Figure 2.9 and supply capabilities shown in Figure 7.5. This classification places agility in the context of alternative logistics strategies. First, A, B and C products are positioned. This is based on a Pareto analysis of an organisation's product range (for an example, see Figure 2.1). Typically, class 'A' products comprise 80 per cent of sales value taken on just 20 per cent of orders. They tend to be the more standardised, have lower forecast errors and lower volume variation. Lean logistics methods are therefore often appropriate. Class 'B' products on the other hand are often subject to higher forecast errors, and have higher volume variations. They are often better served by agile approaches.

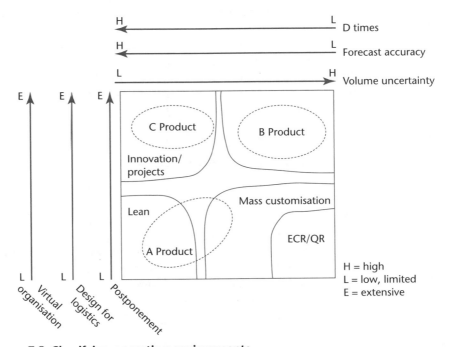

**Figure 7.8 Classifying operating environments**

## 7.2.2 Preconditions for successful agile practice

In addition to the above supply capabilities within the supply chain, there is another set of factors that need to be in place for the agile principles and practices described in section 7.2.4 to pay off or work at all. These are cross-functional alignment and enterprise level focus on the contribution of logistics management and strategy. If revenue-generating functions in particular do not adopt at least a base-level understanding of agile principles, all efforts within logistics may be wasted. And if there is not an enterprise-wide focus on the value potential of logistics, agile efforts are not going to be recognised for what they are worth – and might not provide a compelling enough case for possible investment in them to be made. We propose an *enterprise-level reality check* and a *cost of complexity sanity check* before investing in agile capabilities. We also argue that complexity should be controlled, and that agility will not take away the need for forecasting accuracy.

### Enterprise-level reality check

Starting with the enterprise-wide context, most senior managers know that turning to logistics and the supply chain is a 'good call' when times get tough. Logistics probably gets most mentioned in earnings reports when cost cutting is a response offered to poor performance. In spite of its potential to contribute to cost saving programmes, the value of logistics should not be seen as a first port of call when the bottom line needs to be improved. Agility is centred around the notion of winning in the marketplace based upon service and responsiveness. While such a strategy can be aimed at doing more for less, it may actually – and more importantly – be doing less to earn more. Top line improvement can flow from outperforming competitors through responsiveness to customer needs. Delivery speed and reliability can be such important sources of productivity to customers that we can earn more of their business. An enterprise-level recognition of the contribution of logistics is a precondition for any business case on agile practices.

### Cost of complexity sanity check

The value potential of logistics can only be capitalised on if other functions comply with another key precondition: lowering the cost of complexity where differentiation has no competitive value. As much as agility principles are based on the notion that differentiation is good and 'doable', it does not mean that revenue groups should be given a 'carte blanche' to create proliferating service, product assortments and promotions. There are limits to how much value that variety creates, and the extent to which these demands can be met without the cost of complexity spiralling out of control, even for the most agile supply chain. The key point is not to exceed the capability of the supply chain to deliver the marketing promise.

While differentiation of logistics service can generate short-term gain, the question that revenue-enhancing proposals need to answer is 'will it do so profitably?' Adding a product feature, offering special delivery service and timetables, and engaging in a special promotion might help close a deal in the market in the short term. But such deals can also create added logistics and supply chain costs that are not compensated for by the added revenue. One executive from a manufacturing company put it well:

> **When we showed the financial impact of certain deals our sales teams had closed, it made them realise there were certain deals we should have walked away from.**

Even though it may be hard to assess economic gain or pain from product/service differentiation, reality can be checked by asking questions such as:

- Do customers *really* want fast delivery, or is reliable delivery more important even when slower?
- Do customers *really* want delivery whenever they ask for it, or could a shared forecasting effort resolve fire-drill situations?
- Do we need product proliferation for short-term gain, or because we add sustainable revenue to the business?
- Is there a limit to the number of product variations that the market can recognise and absorb?
- Did we offset added warehousing and distribution costs – even when just directionally right – against added revenue potential?

Heineken, the brewer, offers a powerful example of the last point. During a recent Christmas season it introduced a special product for promotion in the market – the magnum bottle. This seasonal promotion and product won several marketing prizes, and created a lot of buzz (or fizz, even!) in the marketplace. It was also a product that suffered from substantial added shipment, packaging and production costs because different production line setups, bottles, labels and boxes were needed for a very limited demand window. Was it worth the effort and focus of the responsive capabilities that were needed?

Another powerful illustration of the issue is a tactic that one executive calls the 'warehouse dust test':

> **We take our sales people through our warehouse when they come to us asking for new products and promotions and show them the dust levels on other promotional products and product variations that we stock. We ask them 'which products can be discontinued when we introduce a new product?' *or* 'do we need the new product to begin with?'**

### Lowering the cost of complexity: avoiding overly expensive agility

The purpose of responding to customer demand is fundamental to the role of logistics. In this sense, agility is a natural goal. A key qualification is:

> **not at any cost, nor to compensate for mismanagement elsewhere in the organisation.**

Many organisations face challenges related to the risk of driving responsiveness over the top in the wrong areas of focus. Three examples illustrate the cost of complexity (see section 5.1.2):

- Product, packaging and stock keeping unit proliferation leading to extremes of 80 per cent or more of products not even generating 1 per cent of revenue
- Delivery speed is too high, resulting in increased costs for the customer because products arrive too early. This increases handling, storage and related costs.
- Promotions and special events that cause upswings in demand based on sales efforts, not on true customer demand. This leads in turn to downswings shortly thereafter.

In general, complexity in the supply chain is made worse at an organisational level because of aggressive global and international sourcing of materials and products. This reduces the cost of goods sold. However, complexity adds substantial distance, time and dependence on the international logistics pipeline. These increase the as risk of supply chain failures.

There are two key issues at stake here. First, agile capabilities are not the excuse for other functions (such as sales) to ignore supply capabilities in running the business. Second, agility should not be driven by the need for supply chains to compensate for mismanagement in other parts of the business. Cost of complexity is the term that captures the negative consequences of agility in poor organisational contexts. It refers to the costs resulting from unnecessary complexity in the supply chain that agility can reduce. But the key questions are:

- Where is the *value* in this complexity to begin with?
- What customer need does it address to have warehouses with products and materials from old promotions collecting dust?
- Does every shipment really need to be a rush shipment or can some shipments be allowed a bit more time and consolidation with other shipments in cheaper modes of transportation?
- Are promotions and resulting short-term peaks in demand a way to boost short-term revenue, or a way to raise long-term sustainable revenue growth?

The following are some examples of actions to help reduce non-value-added costs of complexity:

- Has the organisation conducted an analysis of revenue contribution by sku?
  - *Consider using a revenue threshold for maintaining a given sku.*
- Does the organisation have a process for reviewing the product portfolio at least annually?
  - *One-off sku reductions do not address the ongoing tendency to proliferate skus over time.*
- Are there hard revenue forecasts related to promotion request that can be evaluated?
  - *Revenue upside potential is most often used to justify adding events and skus reviewing real impact after some time or after the event helps force discipline.*

- Are people ordering shipments aware of the cost of rush orders and are they asked to organise shipment around real and explicit customer request?
  - *Ticking the 'ASAP' ('as soon as possible') box on a shipment form may become standard behaviour, irrespective of customer need.*

In addition to such actions, driving forecast accuracy will assist in avoiding inventories of unsaleable product and panic shipments.

### Forecasting; reducing the need for last-minute crises

As important as fast response may be, organisations cannot make all of their operational decisions in real time and in response to events already taking place. Some advanced preparation and planning is required. Hence, even in the most agile supply chains, forecasting is needed and can be used to avoid expensive panic shipments against orders that could have been anticipated.

Based upon assessment of market potential of new and existing products, promotions and services a demand forecast can be developed. This can be used to prepare and offer input to several internal forecasts. The financial forecast (communicated to financial markets) is impacted by the operational demand forecast and the plan for capacity and asset utilisation. The capacity plan is used in both the mid (example: which warehouse will hold which products from the assortment?) and short term (example: how many products can we make tomorrow?). Asset footprint/forecast is the mid- to long-term plan for capacity needed in the supply chain to cope with volume of demand and nature of demand for services (example: how many warehouse spaces do we need in Europe?).

The more accurate the demand forecast, the better a company can prepare in advance of demand occurring, avoiding the need for last minute response to unexpected demand as well as the cost of preparing for demand that might never occur. However, it is probably impossible to fully and correctly anticipate demand at all time horizons and in all markets, for all products and services, even if revenue groups fully tried and technology (forecasting tools, enterprise resource planning software etc.) were perfect. There are several management approaches to forecasting that will enhance its accuracy and relevance. These include:

- *A 'one forecast' approach*: aggregating product/market specific forecasts to a single global forecast allows the 'big picture' to be developed. It also forces differences in local forecasts to be discussed and resolved. Further, it ensures that the firm executes against a single number, not against several.

- *Ensure forecast accountability*: most often, revenue groups will be asked to develop or crucially impact the demand forecast. These groups have limited incentives to drive forecast accuracy. They don't have to live with the consequences, so under-forecasting makes it easier to hit sales targets. So a focal firm should consider adding a review of quality and accuracy of forecasting input to performance evaluation as one mechanism to drive accountability.

- *Make forecasting business relevant*: in addition to the above, linking demand and operational forecasts to financial forecasts and effort to drive business improvement (such as long-term cost savings) adds relevance to the forecasting process.

- *Use one process*: establishing a single forecasting process for the global supply chain (allowing for minor local variations if need be) allows for consistency in approach, interpretation and measurement.

So far, we have considered 'when' and 'where' agile capabilities should be considered. Some supply chains will be better positioned to support the markets they serve by focusing more on lean approaches – for example, in many low variety, high volume situations. An increasing number of markets will be better served by agile strategies that require responsiveness – for example, because variety is increasing and volumes are decreasing. So next, we consider what capabilities are needed to support the responsiveness objective in more detail.

### 7.2.3   Developing measures that put the end-customer first to improve market sensitivity

All companies include customer service in some form in their performance measurement system. However, almost all operationalise this measurement internally, leading to responsiveness that is misguided and focused wrongly, i.e. not directly and fully on customers, thereby limiting network integration across the supply chain. In particular, most companies measure delivery service in one or multiple ways based upon their internal definition of success. Typically the measures focus on how reliably and fast the company delivered against the timetable it put forward. This misses the point as this timetable might not be aligned with end-customers needs at all. So companies are not tracking responsiveness to these needs. It is much better to ask customers for their desired delivery window and measure execution against that customer-defined measure of success. General Electric realised this when it presented high delivery reliability scores from its own measurement to customers and received a negative reaction. Customers said performance was not as high at all by their measurement, against when they needed deliveries to take place.

GE changed its measurement set towards what it calls Span measurement. Span stands for the range of delivery around customer requested due dates. Essentially, the company now measures, across all deliveries globally, how close it was to the delivery date the customer requested when ordering. In its plastics business the company brought Span down from 30 days to just a few days within a matter of months. This means that every customer can depend upon GE delivering any product, anywhere in the globe, when they ask for it with a maximum variation of just a few days.

The experience of GE suggests the value of several actions to improve measurement for agility:

- Share measurement dashboards with customers.
- Do not measure against your own measures of success, ask the customer what defines success for them.
- Hold all parts of the supply chain accountable against the customer-defined measure of success so that there is no escape from market sensitivity.

### 7.2.4  Shared goals to improve virtual integration

Agility requires the ability to be able to respond to local market requirements and opportunities. However companies should still aim to leverage skills and capabilities across the regions in which they operate. This means they need to establish and strive for shared goals across their business units as a form of virtual integration, with local operations remaining in place and the focus remaining on local customer service (van Hoek *et al.*, 2001).

Most often however, companies trend either towards local responsiveness or strong global standardisation and organisation. Hewlett Packard used to be in the former camp. At one point for example they found that there were dozens of similar B2B exchange efforts underway across the company with informal coordination between teams at best. Rightfully, HP did not respond with, what would have been intuitive to many, a centralisation of efforts and control. Instead, they developed a distributed governance approach that allows for local responsiveness but leverages lessons learned for the company and avoids duplication of efforts.

In order to find a way to balance proliferation of businesses and divisions with high divisional autonomy and complexity in organisation, HP launched a supply chain governance council. The charter that its executive committee set was to implement pan-company efficiency initiatives and uncover supply chain-based revenue opportunities. Specific goals include establishing and driving a coordinated approach to investments pertaining to opportunities that have a pan-enterprise scope and impact and supporting executive awareness of key initiatives to avoid reinventing the wheel.

This means that the HP governance council explicitly does not get involved with initiatives that are specific to an individual business or region; it does not centrally control supply chain governance but it does support larger initiatives from which many parts of the organisation can and should benefit. It also provides senior management with a method for supporting and steering direction on most important opportunities and directions.

Four key operating rules at the council are:

1  mandated senior participation;
2  focus on enterprise-wide initiatives;
3  driving initiative development through divisional sponsorship;
4  fund initiatives from divisional budgets.

The last two are particularly interesting as they help avoid creating a corporate centre approach that can dictate without the businesses caring or paying for it.

Keys to success in a governance approach like this include the need to avoid layering a governance council on top of existing structures. If it generates more governance this can only conflict with existing structures and might enhance bureaucracy rather than agility. Further to that it is important to keep the structure simple and crisp; the governance council serves the purpose of being more agile as a company as opposed to just being agile locally. In order to accomplish that there should be minimal procedure and rules. And finally, what is purely local should remain local; if there is no benefit to leveraging a particular initiative to the global/corporate level then keep it local.

### 7.2.5 Boundary spanning S&OP process to improve process integration

The purpose of the sales and operations planning (SOP, section 6.1.1) module is to set sales forecasts and to translate them into operations plans for sourcing, making, storing and delivering to demand. It requires internal integration, at least between sales and operations, to make the process work. Additionally, forecasting is not just a numbers game, it is a key business process that supports supply chain readiness for market demand.

Alcoa has made some great strides across very diverse business that are very autonomous in their markets to develop a boundary spanning S&OP process to support process and internal integration. Three aspects are particularly noteworthy:

- *Forecast by market, not by business unit.* Alcoa realised that a lot of its businesses were supplying the same markets with all of them developing their own forecast, often hugely varying, based upon a view limited to one business. So what they did was form so-called market sector lead teams that operate across businesses, by market, to come up with one forecast for where that market is going based upon a much more comprehensive view of the market.

- *Coordinate between source-make-deliver.* Alcoa not only translates the forecast into production runs for the factory; in a true process integration fashion they also translate the forecast to what needs to be sourced and what can be expected of the customer's business, hence driving integration along the process, not just at points.

- *Link forecasts to improvement goals.* Forecasting is never going to be fun but it can become more relevant; in that spirit Alcoa links the forecast to 18 months' business improvement goals and have the forecast roll towards that goal. The forecast does disaggregate to six months, four weeks and one week plans but it also maps to the longer-term improvement goal. At Alcoa people are very excited for the new rolling forecast to come out because it tells them whether they are on track to hitting targets. That is much better than the common approach where the sales team just does a forecast for the sake of colleagues in manufacturing while trying not to spend too much time at it because it distracts from selling.

Additionally, the sales and operations planning process is seen as a great way to begin to drive cross-functional integration. One company just setting out on its journey to develop supply chain management started with S&OP because it found it an easy start (calling a meeting) that links to a key activity for many functions (ensuring we forecast what needs to be made so we can serve customers). Hence buy-in is easily gained and joint ownership is quickly established. The company also found that the S&OP table is an effective way to get people across functional silos to start talking and working together. A few ground rules for effective S&OP tables include:

- all key functions need to attend mandatory (sales, finance, production, logistics, procurement) and additional function can be invited if needed (R&D, engineering);

- all attendees need to come with real decision-making authority and mandate for the table to become effective;

- the discussion needs to focus not just on generating a forecast but also on diagnosing forecast errors from the past to learn from them and discuss trade-offs;
- there needs to be a structured (standing) agenda and set of measures used (most typically including forecast error, forecasted volumes and sales amounts, capacity utilisation, new products and upcoming events, sku review).

The vision of creating an agile supply chain is a valuable starting point but until recently it was mostly just vision. The experiences and cases presented in this section show how the vision can be supplemented and how the implementation of agility can be approached practically.

## Summary

*What is JIT, and how does it apply to logistics?*

- JIT is a broad-based philosophy of doing the simple things right and gradually doing them better. As applied to logistics, JIT can be conceived of as a pyramid of key factors that centre on minimum delay and minimum inventory.
- 'How many' and 'when' to order replenishment quantities are key questions that impact on throughput times and inventories. JIT addresses these questions by attacking the sources and causes of waste. Examples are reduction of changeover times and simple, paperless systems of material control based on the principle of pull scheduling.
- Longstanding approaches to material control, such as reorder point stock control, economic order and batch quantities (EOQ, EBQ) and material requirements planning (MRP) can be made to be far more responsive by application of JIT techniques. Examples include reduction of batch sizes, reorder quantities and lead times. All of these help to reduce logistics P-times. Synergies can be delivered too: JIT pull scheduling works best for control, MRP for planning.

*What is lean thinking, and how does it apply to logistics?*

- Lean thinking is a philosophy that has been derived from JIT principles. It seeks perfection by gradually reducing waste from each of four areas: specifying value from the end-customer perspective; identifying the value stream through time-based mapping; making the product flow through the supply network by applying JIT principles; and letting the customer pull through application of pull scheduling.

*What is agility, and how does it contribute to competitiveness of the supply network?*

- Agility is a supply-chain-wide capability that aligns organisational structures, information systems, logistics processes and, in particular, mindsets. It means using market knowledge and a responsive supply chain to exploit profitable opportunities in a volatile marketplace. Agile supply is concerned with developing capabilities proactively to position a supply chain to benefit from marketplaces in which product lifecycles are shrinking, product variety is increasing, and the ability to forecast demand is reducing.

- Lean thinking is concerned primarily with the elimination of waste. The order winners that are supported by this mindset are cost and quality. Agility is concerned primarily with supporting order winners of speed and flexible response. Time compression is a fundamental requirement for leanness, but only one of the enablers of agility.

- A key difference in supply strategy is that lean thinking is concerned with placing orders upstream for products that move in a regular flow. Agile strategy is concerned with assigning capacity so that products can be made rapidly to meet demand that is difficult to forecast.

*What are the agile practices that help to underpin the agile supply chain?*

- Start by understanding the sources and causes of uncertainty in demand, and take steps to position the supply chain to benefit from this uncertainty. The easy option is high-volume, low variety, low demand uncertainty. The tough option is the opposite of all three of these material flow characteristics. Agility seeks to increase responsiveness to volatility and to end-customer demand uncertainty.

- Then, develop capabilities for dealing with shrinking time windows for customer demand fulfillment. Speed of replenishment is usually much better downstream than upstream. Developing upstream time sensitivity is therefore a major enabler. And information dissemination and alignment bring capabilities of dealing with rapid and accurate response using supply-chain-wide dissemination and exchange.

- Third, facilitate servicing the 'market segment of one' by investing in flexible processes, modularity of both product and process, and capabilities to support the information and knowledge content of products and services. Specific practices outlined in this chapter include aligning metrics with true end-customer needs, establishing supply chain governance that allows for decentralised action with central support and coordination, and developing boundary spanning SOP systems.

## Discussion questions

1 Suggest order winning and order qualifying criteria for the following product environments:
   a  reprocessing nuclear fuel
   b  upstream petroleum refining
   c  downstream manufacture of petroleum products
   d  high-value automotive products such as Range Rover or BMW 5 series.

To what extent would lean and agile mindsets contribute to the support of such products in the marketplace?

**2** Dealers have criticised the way auto assemblers use JIT as an excuse for buying parts from the inbound supply network 'so that their costs are kept down'. They then dump finished vehicles onto the dealer by matching '*their* perceptions of a marketplace demand with *their* constraints as a manufacturer, i.e. what they've produced' (adapted from Delbridge and Oliver, 1991). Referring to the Ford/Toyota case study in section 7.1.3, comment on the trade-offs implied in these comments from disgruntled dealers.

**3** What matters more: value to the customer or value to the shareholder? Refer to section 3.4 of Chapter 3 in formulating your response. How does this question impact on the philosophy of lean thinking?

**4** What is meant by the term *overproduction*? Why do you think this has been described as the biggest waste of all?

**5** Explain the difference between pull scheduling and push scheduling. In what circumstances might push scheduling be appropriate?

**6** Explain the difference between surge and base demands. Multi Electronique SA (ME) produces a range of electrical connectors for the automotive industry. Currently, the six production lines at its factory in Toulouse are fully loaded, operating a three-shift system for 5 days per week. One of ME's major customers wants to place an order that would add loading equivalent to a seventh production line, but only for the summer months (May to September). Sales are keen to accept the new order, but it would need to be taken at prices that are no higher than for current business. Suggest options for how ME might manage this order if they accepted it.

**7** Refer back to Figure 2.1 in Chapter 2: it shows a Pareto curve for the sales per sku of a book stockist. A small number of 'hot sellers' constitute most of the sales, while there is a lengthy tail of slow-selling lines and new introductions. The operations people are pressing for the 'tail' to be chopped in half, arguing that it adds cost, not value, to the business. They argue that each order is taken at fixed cost, regardless of size. Sales order processing and pick and dispatch from the warehouse are examples of such fixed costs. 'Instead, we should focus on the core of the business: 90 per cent of our business comes from just 10 per cent of the titles,' the operations director argues. 'We could chop our costs in half and only lose 5–7 per cent of the business. Think of the effect on margin!' Sales, on the other hand, are reluctant to give up any of the titles, arguing that it is customer choice that drives the business. 'We have built up this business on the strength of our product range', the sales director argues. 'Retailers come to us because we are a one-stop shop. If we haven't got it in stock, we get it.' Explain the above in terms of a lean versus agile debate, using the concepts of market winners and qualifiers and benefiting from small volumes.

# References

Aitken, J., Childerhouse, P., Christopher, M. and Towill, D. (2005) 'Designing and Managing Multiple Pipelines', Journal of Business Logistics, Vol. 26, No. 2, pp. 73–96.

Chase, R.B., Jacobs, R. and Aquilano, N.J. (2005) *Operations Management for competitive advantage*, 10th edn. London: McGraw-Hill.

Delbridge, R. and Oliver, N. (1991) 'Just-in-time or just the same? Developments in the auto industry: the retailer's views', *International Journal of Retail and Distribution Management*, Vol. 19, No. 2, pp. 20–60.

Harrison, A. (1992) *Just-in-Time Manufacturing in Perspective*. Hemel Hempstead: Prentice Hall.

Harrison, A. and Storey, J. (2000) 'Coping with world class manufacturing', *New Technology, Work and Employment*, Vol. 13, No. 3, pp. 643–64.

Holweg, M. and Miemczyk, J. (2003) 'Delivering the "3-day car" – the strategic implications for automotive logistics operations', *Journal of Purchasing and Supply Management*, Vol. 9, No. 2, pp. 63–7.

Johansson, H.J., McHugh, P., Pendlebury, A.J. and Wheeler, W.A. (1993) *Business Process Reengineering: Breakpoint Strategies for Market Dominance*, Chichester: John Wiley & Sons.

Krafcik, J.F. and MacDuffie, J.P. (1989) *Explaining High Performance Manufacturing: The International Automotive Assembly Plant Study*. MIT: International Motor Vehicle Program.

Magretta, J. (1998) 'Fast, global and entrepreneurial: supply chain management Hong Kong style', *Harvard Business Review*, Issue Sept/Oct, pp. 102–14.

Mason-Jones, R., Naylor, R. and Towill, D.R. (1999) 'Lean, agile or leagile: matching your supply chain to the market place', *International Journal of Production Research*, Vol. 38, No. 17, pp. 4061–70.

Nakajima, S. (ed.) (1989) *TPM Development Program: Implementing total productive maintenance*. Cambridge, MA: Productivity Press.

Porter, M.E. (1985) *Competitive Advantage: Creating and sustaining superior performance*. New York: Free Press.

Schonberger, R.J. (1991) *Building a Chain of Customers: Linking business functions to build the world class company*. New York: Free Press.

Shingo, S. (1988) *Non-Stock Production*. Cambridge: Productivity Press.

Skipworth, H. and Harrison, A. (2004) 'Implications of form postponement to manufacturing: a case study', *International Journal of Production Research*, Vol. 42, No. 1, pp. 2063–81.

van Hoek, R. (2001) 'The rediscovery of postponement: a literature review and directions for research', *Journal of Operations Management*, Vol. 19, No. 2, pp. 161–84.

Womack, J. and Jones, D. (2003) *Lean Thinking*. 2nd edn. New York: Simon and Schuster.

## Suggested further reading

Goldman, S., Nagel, R. and Preiss, K. (1995) *Agile Competitors and Virtual Organizations*, New York: Van Nostrand Reinhard.

Harrison, A.S. (1992) *Just in Time Manufacturing in Perspective*. Hemel Hempstead: Prentice Hall.

Lee, H.L. (2004) 'The Triple A supply chain', *Harvard Business Review*, Issue No. 10, Oct., pp. 1–11.

Womack, J. and Jones, D. (2003) *Lean Thinking*, 2nd edn. New York: Simon and Schuster.

# Part Three

# WORKING TOGETHER

In a supply network, no firm is an island that stands on its own. Nor does it compete on its own. A focal firm depends on its network partners for components to assemble, for products to sell, for the movement of goods and so on. While Part Two focused on the central logistics task of achieving responsiveness to customer demand, most firms cannot achieve this without the support of their network partners. Complete vertical integration of an industry is unusual today – although 'vertical retailers' have developed a similar strategy, as we saw in Case study 4.4. Functional specialisation of suppliers on those parts of the value proposition in which they excel, coupled with integration into the supply network, is more common.

This is becoming especially relevant today. Some manufacturing firms, for example in the electronics and automotive industries, add only 10–20 per cent of total added value internally. The rest is created in the supply base – by commodity suppliers, by co-designers and co-manufacturers, by main suppliers and by their supply partners. Chapter 8 offers approaches to integration and collaboration in the supply chain, and Chapter 9 offers insights into sourcing and supply management.

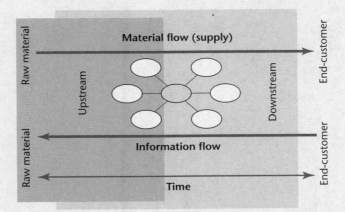

# Integrating the supply chain

**Objectives**

*The intended objectives of this chapter are to:*

- explain the need to coordinate processes, and the opportunities for collaboration between partners within supply chains;
- introduce a range of options for buyer–supplier relationships;
- describe the spectrum of supply relationships;
- describe the implications for suppliers of entering into partnerships.

*By the end of this chapter, you should be able to understand:*

- the benefits of collaboration within supply chains;
- the range of alternative inter-company relationships;
- the benefits and challenges of operating supply chain partnerships;
- ways of approaching implementation issues;
- key aspects of managing the supply chain.

## Introduction

A number of alternative supply chain structures have emerged, based upon networks and the degree of inter-firm collaboration. A well-known view is that of Sako (1992), who distinguishes a 'spectrum' of possible supply relationships, ranging from:

- *arm's length*: a detailed contract specifies the responsibilities of both parties including terms and conditions. Undue familiarity is avoided, and neither party is controlled by the other. Divorce is a readily available option when the contract finishes;
- *obligational*: individual contracts are still in evidence but embedded within a broader relationship of mutual trust. Outline specifications are more common, but there is 'an incentive to do more than is expected'.

Optimising the supply chain process inevitably leads to a growing interdependence among supply chain partners, and obligational behaviour becomes more in evidence. With this interdependence, a realisation develops that increasing levels of *adaptation* are necessary to achieve long-term mutual benefit.

Adaptation means making changes to a firm's internal processes in order to accommodate the needs of supply partners. Supply partners may have to develop a common set of control mechanisms. Hunter *et al.* (1996) comment:

> The two organisations will still be subject to independent governance, but will have in common a similar set of governance procedures and mechanisms specific to their joint working relationship, thus replicating in some measure the conditions within an integrated organisation.

Such common governance is more in keeping with the obligational view. The implications for competitive strategy of this growth of collaborative supply chains are considerable – in particular the need to develop those skills that enable a company to re-engineer established buyer–supplier relationships and successfully to manage them on a day-to-day basis.

But a one-sided view of the relationship may be the norm elsewhere, and have quite different implications for the firms involved. For example, Rubery *et al.* (2004) studied the way that a customer firm may 'extend its tentacles inside the [supplier firm] to re-shape the internal human resource practices'. The customer firm may exert pressure on a supplier's HR practices in areas such as hours worked (to fit with their own), performance assessment and associated bonus payments.

Centralised purchasing decisions may also greatly impact supplier relationships. While operations and logistics are developing supplier relationship management, purchasing may replace existing suppliers with new ones with whom there is no current relationship. And while centralisation lowered purchasing costs overall, manufacturing and logistics costs were increased (Pagell, 2004). Purchasing may be measured on the visible reductions in piece part prices, but the invisible costs of longer transport times, extra inventories and poor delivery reliability go unchallenged.

The overall aim of this chapter is to explore the need for integrating supply chain processes, and then to review different types of supply relationship, the impact on the firms involved, and the situations where a given type of relationship is most relevant to a supply chain's competitive position.

**Key issues**  This chapter addresses eight key issues:

1 **Integration in the supply chain:** the benefits of internal and external co-ordination.

2 **Choosing the right relationship:** which relationship is appropriate in different circumstances – bottleneck items, strategic items, non-critical items and leverage items.

3 **Partnerships in the supply chain:** cooperative, coordinated and collaborative relationships; their advantages and disadvantages.

4 **Supply base rationalisation:** dealing with a smaller number of suppliers to enable high-intensity relationships to develop.

5 **Supplier networks:** the development of supplier associations and the Japanese equivalent, *keiretsu*.

6 **Supplier development:** managing upstream suppliers through integrated processes and synchronous production.

7 **Implementing partnerships:** the potential pitfalls in moving from open market negotiations to collaborative relationships.

8 **Managing supply chain relationships:** the objective of deeper, closer relationships in the supply chain and factors for achieving them.

## 8.1 Integration in the supply chain

*Key issue:* **How can we integrate internally, externally and electronically?**

What drives integration in the supply chain? Procter & Gamble's desire is to design the supply chain to meet the needs of end-customers, starting from point of sale and working backwards to deliver the right product, in the right place, at the right time, of the right quality. The following are four principles of Procter & Gamble's supply chain strategy:

- Produce every product that needs to be produced every day through short cycle production.
- Communicate with suppliers in real time – suppliers with whom we have built long-term relationships and with whom we have integrated systems.
- Draw demand data from the point nearest to the end-customer – in this case, the retail cash register.
- Collaboration between all supply chain partners using a multifunctional approach (commercial and supply chain working together) and aligned metrics focusing on delivering to the end-customer.

All of these principles involve integration – both internal and external. 'Integration' in the context of the supply chain is concerned with *coordination*: establishing the 'rules of the road' whereby material and information flows work in practice.

Evidence that improved integration (both upstream and downstream) leads to improved performance for the supply chain as a whole has been found by survey research for firms in fabricated metal products, machinery and equipment manufacturing (Frohlich and Westbrook, 2001). Integration was measured across eight variables, as follows:

1 Access to planning systems.

2 Sharing production plans.

3 Joint EDI access/networks.

4 Knowledge of inventory mix/levels.

5 Packaging customisation.

6 Delivery frequencies.

7 Common logistical equipment/containers.

8 Common use of third party logistics.

The authors found that the broadest integration strategies led to the highest rates of significant performance improvements. They pictured this in terms of 'arcs of integration', our version of which is shown in Figure 8.1. We can propose that broader integration reduces uncertainty of material flow through the supply network. In turn, this improves efficiency and reduces the P-time (Chapter 5).

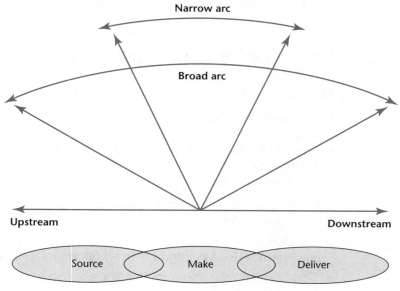

**Figure 8.1    Arcs of integration**
(Source: After Frohlich and Westbrook, 2001)

## 8.1.1  Internal integration: function to function

Another survey – this time of over 300 organisations in the US – probed integration between marketing and logistics functions within a focal firm (Stank *et al.*, 1999). More frequent integrative behaviour between marketing and logistics resulted in better performance and better interdepartmental effectiveness. This may seem obvious, but the improvements in performance included cycle time reduction, better in-stock performance, increased product availability levels and improvements in order-to-delivery lead times.

Firms with higher internal integration demonstrated higher relative logistics performance compared with less integrated firms. There was no difference between 'high' and 'low' integration firms on basic service; that is, consistent delivery on request data and advance notification of delays and shortages. However, on the 'higher value' service elements, such as delivery reliability, there was a significant difference. High-integration firms had higher performance in terms of meeting customer needs, accommodating special customer requests and new product introductions. This resulted in an enhanced customer perception of the organisations. Similar conclusions are arrived at by Windahl and Lakemond (2006), especially where the firm is developing integrated products and services such as 'power for life' (see Case study 2.5). And a study of Spanish food manufacturers by Gimenez (2006) shows that the highest levels of external integration are achieved by firms that have already achieved the highest levels of internal integration between logistics, production and marketing.

The implications of this research are that firms should continue to work at improving internal integration. For example, functional barriers between purchasing, manufacturing and distribution may lead to the following scenarios:

- Purchasing buys castings on the basis of low price, but the supplier has a poor record for delivery reliability and quality. Manufacturing is faced with uncertain deliveries and high reject rates.
- Manufacturing aims to keep machine and labour productivity high, so batch sizes are kept high. Distribution is faced with poor availability, especially of class B and C parts.
- Distribution wants to maintain a fast throughput warehousing operation, so resists carrying out any post-manufacturing operations. Manufacturing is faced with the additional complexity of customising products.

Internal integration is the key starting point for broader integration across the supply chain. As Robert Lynch said (cited in Kirby, 2003: 69), 'For some reason alliance professionals find it easier to create alliances with their major competitors than with other divisions in their own companies. We don't deal with our own internal integration. How can we integrate externally if we can't do it internally?'

## Activity 8.1

Taking your business (or one well known to you) as an example, how well do the internal functions integrate? Consider the purchasing–manufacturing–distribution example above and develop a scenario for the company, using the company's names for the functions concerned. What impact does your scenario have on material flow?

### 8.1.2  Inter-company integration: a manual approach

If significant improvements can be achieved by internal integration, potential for the benefits of external integration could be even higher. This was demonstrated by the Bose Corporation (a US-based manufacturer of hi-fi equipment) in the early 1990s when they developed the *JIT2* concept. Bose recognised that, if the traditional buyer–supplier relationships were to be made more effective, more people would be required in their organisation. However, budget constraints meant that no additional people could be employed in this role. This acted as a driver to develop the JIT2 concept.

A logical extension of the just-in-time concept described in Chapter 6 is to place customer and supplier processes closer together. The JIT2 approach goes a stage further by eliminating the buyer and the salesman from the customer–supplier relationship, thus fostering increased communication between the parties. The principle is simple: a supplier employee who resides full time in the customer's purchasing office replaces the buyer and supplier. This *supplier-in-plant* is empowered to use the customer's scheduling system to place orders with their own company. In addition, the supplier-in-plant does the material planning for the materials supplied by his company.

The 'supplier in-plant' is also part of the production planning process, so production is planned concurrently with the supplier organisation. This form of integration streamlines the supply process by removing the multi-level planner–buyer–salesman–supplier plant process by making this the responsibility of one individual. This dramatically reduces the demand uncertainty experienced by the supplier organisations. The benefits of this streamlining have also resulted in major business improvements for Bose. These include:

- 50 per cent improvement in terms of on-time deliveries, damage and shortages;
- 6 per cent reduction in material costs;
- 26 per cent improvement in equipment utilisation;
- major reductions in inventory holdings.

The Bose supplier-in-plant concept demonstrates how collaboration and integration can benefit the supply chain. The supplier-in-plant can, to a large degree, be superseded by today's electronic integration techniques.

### Activity 8.2

What are the opportunities for the JIT2 supplier-in-plant principle in your chosen company? Could the principle help to improve integration, either by a company representative working in the customer's organisation, or by representatives from major suppliers working in your chosen company?

### 8.1.3  Electronic integration

Much of the pioneering work for electronic integration has been in the fast-moving consumer goods (FMCG) sector between retailers and manufacturers. The traditional way to exchange orders and delivery information has been by means of electronic data interchange (EDI). But EDI systems are generally incompatible with each other, and have high development and installation costs. Technologies based on the internet offer worldwide connectivity and relative ease of access.

Achieving visibility throughout the supply chain is of paramount importance in the search for competitive advantage. The exponential development of internet technology together with the increased power of the personal computer offers organisations a relatively cheap means of integrating information systems across the supply chain.

The internet provides a platform-independent communications highway that can be used as a cross-company interface to enable electronic commerce. Thereby, it fosters operationally efficient, connected and cooperative relationships among manufacturers, suppliers and distributors. Using the internet can provide an easy and cost-effective answer that is available to all partners in a network.

E-business is a term used to cover trading with a firm's suppliers and business customers – that is, business-to-business – by electronic means. A feature of B2B is the formation of online trading communities (see, for example, Ariba, http://www.ariba.net) and electronic marketplaces. Such structures have been enabled by the explosion of internet technology and seek to offer cost reductions in procurement of both direct and indirect goods, and also in the processing of such transactions. The relationship of these terms in the context of the 'e-supply chain' is shown in Figure 8.2.

Trading partners can integrate electronically in three ways: transactional, information sharing and collaborative planning.

### Transactional: the electronic execution of transactions

This is usually found in business to business (B2B) e-commerce, with the trading partners focusing on the automation of business transactions such as purchase orders, invoices, order and advanced shipment notices, load tendering and acknowledgements, and freight invoices and payments. These transactions involve the electronic transmission of a fixed-format document with predefined data and information fields.

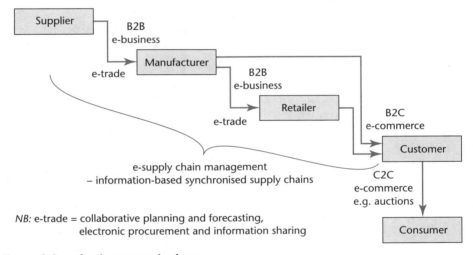

**Figure 8.2   e-business terminology**

### Information sharing: the electronic sharing or exchange of information

Trading partners are given access to a system with shared information. Often, however, one partner transmits shared information to another. The information is sent on a 'for your information' basis; the recipient uses the data as it stands, and no feedback is given. Shared information may include product descriptions and pricing, promotional calendars, inventory levels, shipment tracking and tracing. This type of arrangement only supports independent planning by each partner. Uncertainty is reduced by each partner becoming aware of other partners' activities. However, trading partners do not have the opportunity to comment on or change the plan in any way.

We develop the concept of information sharing by means of a case study in *continuous replenishment* (CR). Continuous replenishment logistics is a pioneering approach to using developments in IT to supply demand quickly from the manufacturer. Using electronic point of sale (EPOS) data to track customer demand through the till, CR shares data from retailer to supplier. The aim is for the supplier to replace quickly what has been sold today, so that stock availability on the shelf is maintained at the retailer. Case study 8.1 gives a view of where fashion logistics is heading.

<table>
<tr><td>CASE STUDY<br>8.1</td><td></td></tr>
</table>

## Continuous replenishment in the apparel industry

Case study 4.4 describes some of the competitive pressures in the apparel industry and trade-offs in developing global 'vertical' supply strategies. (Vertical strategies aim to emulate retailers such as Zara, which source everything from set manufacturing plants that are situated close to their retail outlets.) Setting up a similar operation in the US would be problematic – for a start, there is not much left of the apparel manufacturing base because it went overseas long ago for cost reasons. Competitive pressures are constantly increasing – a significant percentage of the industry is fashion-driven – and fashion changes continuously. Thus, time-to-market is increasingly important. Kumar and Arbi (2008) note:

> turnaround time is important for US fashion retailers intending to compete with Europe's low-cost fashion providers, including H&M and Zara. Both European stores have created production models that deliver inexpensive fashion apparel in weeks, rather than months. Zara designs, produces and delivers a garment in 15 days to US stores according to a 2005 profile by Harvard Business School's Working Knowledge. For American apparel chains, Central America is a potential outsourcing destination, with lower production costs than the USA, falling tariffs and approximately 21 days to get designs made and delivered, 43 days if American material is used.

Retailers drive the industry, and – in a fragmented and very competitive marketplace – they are moving quickly to address its longstanding logistics problems. Increasingly, they are turning to suppliers to respond faster to better quality information, including the use of systems such as Product Lifecycle Management (PLM). Kurt Salmon Associates (Rubman and del Corrado, 2009), consultants to the industry, have highlighted that many retailers have embraced the concept of integrating retailer PLM and supplier sourcing systems, including JC Penney and Guess Inc. Real-time collaboration is essential to driving product development in the industry. Also a shorter product development lead time enables the delay of design and colour decisions to maximise the on-trend opportunity.

Kuhel (2002) proposes an apparel supply chain of the future that is based on continuous replenishment, which we have adapted. Let us assume a designer and retailer of fashion apparel is situated in the north-eastern US. A new range has been designed, and early sales are encouraging. These early sales figures are used to refine forecasts quickly, and to prime the logistics pipeline with a flow of product that matches expected demand. After this, it is essential to regulate the flow of finished goods to match actual demand. This is how it is done.

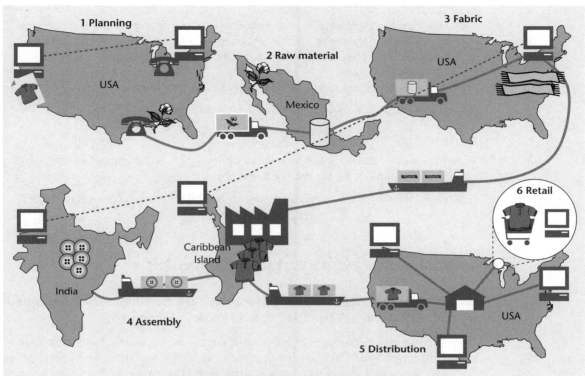

**Figure 8.3    Continuous replenishment in the apparel industry**
(Source: After Kuhel, 2002)

As soon as an item is purchased, the retailer collates the electronic point of sale (EPOS) data from its stores, and sends the data upstream. The 'pull' signal (Chapter 6) goes back all the way to the yarn manufacturer. Figure 8.3 represents the path that a garment might take from concept to delivery. Six stages are involved.

1 **Planning:** apparel retailer determines design for a product, evaluates costing with the supplier and then sends demand data and forecast upstream. These signals set the supply chain in motion. Later, once the product has gone to market, a web-based link from the retailer's EPOS system to the manufacturer triggers replenishment responses.

2 **Raw material:** suppliers respond to demand signals via phone, fax, email or integrated system. Raw cotton is compressed into bales, and fitted with radio frequency identification device (RFID) tags (see section 6.2.1) to specify source and type.

3 **Fabric:** manufacturers weave and ship product in response to demand from the retailer. Inventory/shipment tracking starts here. In-transit data are passed downstream via the internet or integrated system workflow.

4 **Assembly:** fabrics and trims come together at the final assembly plant, which in this example is situated in the Caribbean. (Manufacturers situated within short shipping times of the US are favoured over Far East suppliers.) The plant has an ERP system that processes orders received electronically. Finished goods are assembled and bar-coded by store prior to despatch. All suppliers to the apparel retailer use compatible or integrated systems.

▶

**5 Distribution:** the product is shipped by container to the retailer's national distribution centre (NDC). Here, store orders are cross-docked using the bar-code to identify the destination store. They are then forwarded to regional distribution centres (RDCs) that serve 50–100 stores.

**6 Retail:** as items are purchased, EPOS triggers replenishment responses.

Sources: Kuhel (2002); updated by Harrison (2005); updated by Baker (2010)

*Questions*

1  Summarise the 'current state' problems that are typical of the apparel industry, and their implications for supply chain integration.

2  Identify potential barriers to executing the proposed apparel 'supply chain of the future'.

## 8.2  Choosing the right supply relationships

*Key issues:* **What types of supply relationships can be adopted? How can each type of relationship be tailored to different types of product?**

There are many possible types of relationship in the supply chain. A development of Sako's view mentioned in the introduction to this chapter is that the different options can be viewed in the form of a continuum. This can range from *arm's length*, where the relationship is conducted through the marketplace with price as its foundation, to *vertical integration*, where the relationship is cemented through ownership. Vertical integration can *extend* for one or more tiers and its *direction* may be upstream, downstream or both. A continuum of relationship options is shown in Figure 8.4. Each of these relationship styles has motivating factors that drive development, and which govern the operating environment. The duration, breadth, strength and closeness of the relationship vary from case to case and over time.

| Arm's length | Partnership | Strategic alliance | Joint venture | Vertical integration |

**Figure 8.4    Relationship styles continuum**
Source: After Cooper and Gardiner, 1993

A focal firm may not have the same type of relationship with all of its customers and suppliers. The firm may adopt a range of styles: choosing which type of relationship to adopt in a given supply chain situation is an important strategic issue. For example, grocery retailers often adopt an arm's length style for 'own brand' goods such as kitchen paper, and use on-line auctions (Smart and Harrison, 2003) to obtain lowest price solutions. Elsewhere, they may use a strategic alliance to develop petrol forecourts, such as the alliance between Tesco Express (Case study 1.1) and forecourts of Esso fuel stations.

Companies tend to deal with a large number of suppliers, even after the supply base has been rationalised. Treating them all in the same way fails to recognise that some have different needs from others. Differentiating the role of suppliers and applying appropriate practices towards them allows a focal firm to target purchasing and supply chain management resources to better effect.

A popular view is that Japanese companies consider all of their tier 1 suppliers as partners. This is not really true: for example, Japanese automotive manufacturers do not regard all of their suppliers as equal. In fact among the typical 100–200 tier 1 suppliers to an OEM only about a dozen will enjoy partnership status. Typically, these elite few tend to be large organisations. Inspired by the Japanese version of supply relationships with partners, outlined in the introduction to this chapter under Sako's 'obligational' description, Western auto manufacturers have been developing their own versions. The model for these has been the *keiretsu* structure shown in Figure 8.8, which is similar to the structure we showed in Figure 1.2. A number of lead suppliers such as Robert Bosch and Delphi supply to their customers worldwide and have developed sophisticated marketing, development and logistics capabilities.

This leads to the development of another type of supplier in addition to the 'lead' product/service suppliers. This is the group of firms that has been 'demoted' to the second tier. Here, they will have to compete against global players on price, delivery and flexibility. Case study 8.2 explains some of the dynamics in automotive inbound supply chains, and the changing roles and responsibilities of suppliers.

| CASE STUDY 8.2 | ## Automotive supply chains: a range of inbound logistics solutions |
|---|---|

Automotive assemblers and their inbound supply chains have developed many solutions to orchestrate the manufacturing and delivery of the thousands of parts that go to make up a vehicle. The many potential inbound logistics solutions are summarised in Figure 8.5.

Changes are of increasing value to the vehicle assemblers, where the complexity of the logistics operation has been greatly downsized by reducing the number of tier 1 suppliers and broadening their responsibilities. Yet the ability of the assemblers to customise their finished products has increased. Quality consistency is expected at 50 ppm, while demanding price reduction targets are the norm.

### Supplier delivers CIF (carriage, insurance and freight)

The supplier delivers the ordered parts to the assembler's factory, and includes the distribution costs in the piece part price.

### Assembler collects *ex-works*

The assembler subcontracts the process of parts collection from a number of suppliers visited on a daily frequency. Parts are taken to a consolidation centre, where they are

▶

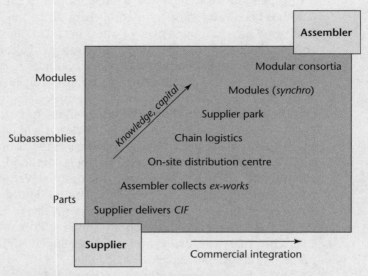

**Figure 8.5   Evolving inbound supply relationships**

decanted into trailers destined for different assembly plants. An example is the Ford operation run by Exel at Birmingham in the UK. Parts collections are made from the Midlands region of the UK, and dispatched to 22 Ford plants around Europe.

## Automotive supplier community

This is a dedicated co-location of suppliers in the region of dedicated vehicle manufacturers. The big difference from all the other integration types is that deliveries are made to more than one vehicle assembly plant. An example for more than one OEM plant is the BMW Innovation Estate in Wackersdorf where several suppliers provide parts for four BMW sites.

## On-site distribution centre

Instead of delivering parts directly into the assembler's plant, the logistics partner may deliver into a distribution centre positioned close to the assembler's plant. The advantages are much more controlled inbound parts movements into the plant. The assembler is able to call up parts that are needed for a relatively short time period, thus improving material flow into the plant and reducing vehicle congestion. Additional value-adding activities may also be carried out in the DC. Thus, for example, suppliers carry out some final assembly and sequencing tasks in the new Integrated Logistics Centre at BMW, Cowley.

## Supply centres

These are co-located supplier clusters on site and could be part invested by the VM and service provider (3PL). Supplier proximity enables late module configuration with smooth material flow. BMW Leipzig uses an electrical conveyor system to connect external and internal suppliers to the assembly line.

## Chain logistics

Here the objective is to increase the *speed* of the inbound supply chain. If not planned and managed, drivers' hours regulations across Europe can lead to waste as the supply chain stops to allow for rests. The higher the speed of inbound supply, the lower the stock that needs to be held at the assembly plant. A useful further advantage is that the higher the speed, the less packaging and containers are needed in the supply chain. An example of chain logistics is the ALUK operation that supports the Toyota plant at Burnaston in the UK. Parts movements from a supplier in southern Spain are planned in four-hour stages, where the full trailer is swapped for an empty one in a similar fashion to the Pony Express in the days of the Wild West!

## Supplier park

A supplier park is a cluster of suppliers located outside but close to a final assembly plant; popular with JIS suppliers and associated with new assembly plants linked to supplier by conveyor belts, tunnels or bridges. (JIS = just in sequence: the capability to supply a module in accordance with the drumbeat requirements of an assembler.) Major tier 1 subassembly manufacturers are positioned on a supplier park close to the assembly hall. Major sub-assemblies are then sequenced into the assembly hall in response to a 'drumbeat' (based on the master schedule – see Chapter 6), which identifies the precise specification of the next body to be dropped onto the trim and final assembly track. Suppliers then have a finite amount of time to complete assembly and deliver to the point of use on the track. An example here is the Exel operation at the VW–Seat plant at Martorell near Barcelona, where material movements on the supplier park are specified and orchestrated by means of Exel's IT systems.

## Modules

The VW–Seat plant at Martorell demonstrates a further advance in logistics thinking. Instead of delivering a large number of subassemblies, why not get the tier 1 suppliers to coordinate all the parts needed to produce a complete module that can then be simply bolted onto the car? Product variety can be increased by customisation of the modules. The advantages are illustrated in Figure 8.6.

Modular designs offer less WIP and a considerably downsized process for the assembler, and greater variety for the customer. Downsizing of the assembly process means that it is shorter, and can be positioned closer to customer demand. Complexity can then be added later in the pipeline between customer order and delivery of the specified car into the customer's hands – a concept called postponed variety. The term *synchronous supply* has been used to describe the delivery of modules not just at the correct quality and correct time, but on a real-time basis with the assembler and with the added challenge of zero safety stock. The condominium approach goes a step further in integration. In this case the suppliers reside and operate under the same roof as the vehicle manufacturers. Due to outsourcing and the lean management, VMs often do not need adjacent space at the final assembly track and can thus offer their factory space to suppliers. Suppliers then assemble their own modules inside the assembly area. An example for the condominium is the Ford Industrial Complex at Camacari in Brazil.

▶

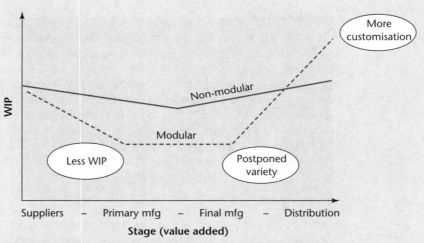

**Figure 8.6    Modularisation: doing more with less**
(Source: van Hoek and Weken, 1998)

## Modular consortia

This is the highest possible integration step for suppliers in the automotive industry. The whole assembly operation is divided into separate modules, with a supplier responsible for each. Therefore the suppliers not only assemble the modules, but they also perform part of the final vehicle assembly.

The VW bus and truck plant in Brazil is an experiment in the further development of the modular concept. The truck assembly operation has been divided into seven modules, with a supplier responsible for each. All the direct workers are on the supplier's payroll, and the supplier not only assembles the module, but also performs final assembly of the vehicle. The assembler's task has been downsized to engineering, design, supervision and administration. The Mercedes plant at Hambach in France, which produces the micro compact Smart car, divides the vehicle into five main modules. Seven suppliers are fully integrated into the final assembly plant, while 16 non-integrated suppliers deliver submodules and parts. The whole information system – which supports manufacturing, logistics and distribution – is outsourced to Accenture.

## Implications for suppliers

The demands on tier 1 suppliers increase in proportion to the various logistics solutions described earlier. A clear trend towards supplier parks and modularisation can be seen in the logistics strategies of automotive assemblers. Increasingly, tier 1 suppliers are being expected to control subsequent tiers in the supply chain, while ensuring delivery and quality to the assembler. At the same time, challenging cost reduction targets are being set, while the whole process is facilitated by tier 1 outbound defect levels that are less than 50 ppm. Many suppliers question whether the draconian demands for 'cost down' targets are compatible with such defect levels.

*Four* distinct stages can be seen in the development of capabilities by tier 1 suppliers:

- *Tier 1 basic*: suppliers with in-house design capability and project management capability who can ensure timely delivery and reasonable quality reliability (50 ppm).

An example would be a tyre manufacturer who holds four–five days' stock and who delivers to set time windows: that is, limited logistics capability.

- *Tier 1 synchro*: suppliers who provide all of the basic capabilities, but with virtually no safety stock. Additional capabilities for the supplier are synchro logistics and IT expertise which is closely integrated with the assembler, greater flexibility and more secure emergency procedures. They operate through 'clone' plants that are situated on supplier parks no more than ten minutes' travel time from the assembler's production line.
- *Tier 0.5*: full service providers, who integrate component manufacturing through supply chain management to achieve the optimum design of a given module. They carry out pre-emptive market research and develop innovative designs through shelf engineering (designs that are prepared proactively in advance of need and placed 'on the shelf', thus saving time in the event that the need does arise). They are partners in major cost reduction projects at each model change, and in continuous improvement projects in between.
- *Tier 0*: the highest possible integration. In addition to tier 0.5 responsibilities, the tier 0 supplier is responsible for a vehicle manufacturer's main assembly operations divided into separate modules, with a tier 0 supplier responsible for each. Therefore the supplier performs final VM module assembly operations. Final VM assembly line work retention is a matter of the VM's strategic choice but it could be performed by the tier 0 as exhibited on line by supplier Magna for BMW.

There is a substantial passing of risk from the assembler to the tier 1 supplier at each stage. Increasingly, the supplier takes responsibility for designing and developing new products of increasing complexity in advance of new model programmes. And there is no guarantee that the supplier will get the work, because competitive tenders are issued for each new model. This forces suppliers to keep primary manufacturing and core business at a 'home' location, and to construct low cost, late-configuration 'postponement' plants near the OEM's assembly hall to enable synchro deliveries. The decision by BMW to switch R50 (Mini) assembly from Longbridge to Cowley left a number of suppliers with £2 million synchro assembly units in the wrong place.

The strategic dilemma for tier 1 suppliers who currently supply the assemblers directly is whether to expand into system integrators (tier 0.5), or to become indirect suppliers to such organisations. Siegfried Wolf of Magna International described the tier 0.5 transition as follows:

> To become part of this new tier, companies will require a worldwide presence, global sourcing, programme management, technology, JIT and JIS know-how and specialist production knowledge. They will also require a high level of R&D spend.

So, after tier 0.5, where do the competitive challenges lie? Tier 2 suppliers will still be largely low-overhead, product-based companies that have limited service capability. Price pressure will continue to be severe, and return on sales often little above break-even. Tier 2 suppliers often cannot afford expensive inspection and test resources, so defect levels will continue to be relatively high, often in the range 1,000–2,000 ppm (i.e. 1–2 per cent). This will present major challenges for tier 0.5 suppliers, who must also guarantee delivery reliability to the assembly track, and a module that fits perfectly at all times.

▶

As an example of tier 0.5 evolution, the joint venture between Canada's Magna International and Japan's Calsonic Kansei ('Magna Kansei') produces the complete fascia ('cockpit module') for the Nissan Micra at a new facility close to Nissan's Washington plant in north-east England. Sales of the joint venture have almost trebled as it assumes responsibility for all of the components and subassemblies that make up the module. Calsonic Kansei designed, developed and tested the Micra fascia from a Nissan-engineered concept design. Co-location of supplier engineers at the Nissan development HQ in Atsugi City meant that Nissan product development teams supervised the design and development process. Magna Kansei assumes responsibility for parts it makes itself, for sourcing externally made parts, and for final module assembly and shipment JIS to the Nissan plant. There are 32 tier 2 suppliers: 18 are *imposed*, where Nissan sets the price and commercial details. The rest are *nominated* by Magna Kansei. This effectively limits the amount of integration that can take place at the design stage. Imposed suppliers that have been selected mainly on price act as barriers for improvement of quality capability.

(Sources: Harrison, 2000, 2004; Bennett and Klug 2010).

### Questions

1 Summarise the advantages and risks to suppliers who want to achieve tier 0.5 status.

2 Consider the differences that can be seen between the logistics conditions of the supplier integration models discussed above. Comment on the geograghic proximity, shared investment, asset specificity, IT-system integration and transport costs connected with the above models in a drive towards a 'tier zero' status for progressive suppliers and their vehicle manufacturers.

## 8.3 Partnerships in the supply chain

*Key issues:* **What are partnerships, and what are their advantages and disadvantages?**

So far, we have used the term 'partners' in a supply chain to apply to all firms that are involved in a given network. In section 8.7, we develop the term 'strategic partners'. Here, we review the added value that partnerships may bring. Generally, cooperative relationships or 'partnerships' have been characterised as being based upon:

● the sharing of information;

● trust and openness;

● coordination and planning;

● mutual benefits and sharing of risks;

● a recognition of mutual interdependence;

● shared goals;

● compatibility of corporate philosophies.

Among these, perhaps the key characteristic is that concerning the sharing of information. This should include demand and supply information. Chapter 6 showed how collaborative planning is being used to share information between retailers and manufacturers.

### 8.3.1 Economic justification for partnerships

Entering into a partnership with a company, to whatever extent, implies a transition away from the rules of the open marketplace and towards alternatives. These different structures must demonstrate benefits otherwise they will not deliver competitive advantage.

Open market relationships are typified by short-term contracts, arm's length relations, little joint development and many suppliers per part. Observing that Japanese practice – and consequently the 'lean' model of supply differs significantly from this – indicates that other, non-market mechanisms must be operating.

The Japanese tend to infuse their transactions with the non-economic qualities of commitment and trust. These characteristics are important in successful partnerships. While this may increase transaction costs and risks, it appears that the 'non-economic qualities' help to secure other economic and strategic advantages that are difficult to achieve through the open market system.

### 8.3.2 Advantages of partnerships

Within partnerships, savings come in the form of reduced negotiations and drawing up of separate contracts, reduced monitoring of supplier soundness, including supply quality and increased productivity. These are accompanied by strategic advantages of shortened lead times and product cycles, and conditions amenable to longer-term investment.

These advantages, however, need to be set against the problems that can be associated with the introduction of commitment and trust.

### 8.3.3 Disadvantages of partnerships

Some of the examples of potential disadvantages of partnerships include the following:

- the inability to price accurately qualitative matters such as design work;
- the need for organisations to gather substantial information about potential partners on which to base decisions;
- the risk of divulging sensitive information to competitors;
- potential opportunism by suppliers.

In the long term, additional factors occur when companies enter into partnerships. With the outsourcing of the R&D of components and subsystems, buyers benefit from the decreased investment they have to make. Working with suppliers who fund their own R&D leads to their earlier involvement in new product development where buyers benefit from suppliers' ability to cut costs and develop better-performing products. This scenario leads to greater buyer risk owing to dependence on a smaller number of suppliers for designs, and also the potential for opportunism through the smaller number of other companies able to compete with the incumbent suppliers for their work.

Consider the reasons why a company would wish to enter into a partnership with a customer or supplier. List the advantages and disadvantages you can think of.

## 8.4 Supply base rationalisation

*Key issue:* **What are the drivers for reducing the numbers of direct suppliers?**

Integrating a supply chain means that a focal firm's processes align with those of its upstream and downstream partners. It becomes impractical to integrate processes of the focal firm with the processes of a substantial inbound network of suppliers. Instead, high-intensity relationships can be managed with a limited supplier base. Such considerations argue for the appointment of a limited number of lead suppliers, each responsible for managing their portion of the inbound supply chain. Clearly one of the key concerns for logistics management is the criteria by which lead suppliers are chosen (see Section 9.2).

### 8.4.1 Supplier management

Supplier management is the aspect of supply chain management that seeks to organise the sourcing of materials and components from a suitable set of suppliers. The emphasis in this area is on the 'suitable set of suppliers'. The automotive case study above explains some of the considerations in this process.

Generally, companies are seeking to reduce the numbers of suppliers they deal with by focusing on those with the 'right' set of capabilities. The extent to which companies have undertaken this and have tiered their supply chains is exceptional. Even in the early 1990s, two-thirds of companies were reported to be reducing their supplier base. Anecdotal accounts of the reductions abound. For example, Sun Microsystems was reported to have consolidated the top 85 per cent of its purchasing spend from across 100 suppliers in 1990 to just 20 a few years later.

Consider an organisation of your choice: have its major customers consolidated their supply base over the past five years? If so, by how much? What criteria did these customers use to decide which companies to keep and which to 'demote' to a lower tier?

### 8.4.2 Lead suppliers

While true single-sourcing strategies are the exception rather than the rule, the concept of the *lead supplier* is now widely accepted. Over the past ten years many large companies have consolidated their supplier base. In some cases this has seen the number of suppliers reduce from around 2,000 to 1,000 or so. However, many of the original suppliers still contribute to the OEM's products, but they now do so from lower tiers. The responsibility for managing them now lies with the suppliers left at the first tier. In some cases this responsibility is new and has had to be learnt.

Has the position of your selected organisation changed in the supply chain? If it has risen up the supply chain, or remained at the same tier whilst others were 'demoted', what new capabilities had to be developed? If it was demoted, why did this happen? Was it a good thing or a bad thing to happen?

## 8.5 Supplier networks

*Key issues:* What are supplier associations and the Japanese *keiretsu*?

Supplier networks can be formal or informal groups of companies whose common interest is that they all supply a particular customer, or support an entire industry. Four such networks are considered here:

- supplier associations;
- Japanese *keiretsu*;
- Italian districts;
- Chinese industrial areas.

### 8.5.1 Supplier associations

Aitken (1998) defines a supplier association as:

> the network of a company's important suppliers brought together for the purpose of coordination and development. Through the supplier association forum this company provides training and resource for production and logistics process improvements. The association also provides the opportunity for its members to improve the quality and frequency of communications, a critical factor for improving operational performance.

Supplier associations may be traced back to the late 1930s with the oldest known group being one linked to Japanese automotive manufacturer Toyota. This early group consisted of 18 suppliers producing basic commodity items such as screws, nuts and bolts. These suppliers formed the group for the benefit of themselves. The Toyota organisation itself did not perform an active role in the beginning of the association. However, the distant role of Toyota was to change, as raw materials became scarce during the Second World War. As part of wartime – control by the Japanese government, small and medium-sized firms were directed to supply larger firms, which were being utilised as distributors of raw material by the government. Prescribing the flow of materials forced the movement of scarce raw materials to key manufacturers. Through this direct interventionist approach the government tried to force assemblers and the subcontractors to work together to increase the efficiency of the supply chain.

The policy employed by the government therefore encouraged assemblers to establish links with suppliers to ensure component supplies. The carrot and stick approach of the government assisted the foundation of several associations. The institutionalist approach by government succeeded in determining the future structure of the supply chain for Japanese automotive companies. Japanese car assemblers changed their *modus operandi* to align with the prevailing governmental coercive isomorphic forces, thereby obtaining social legitimacy. However, it was not until the early 1940s that assemblers began to recognise the potential benefits of becoming active members of the associations. In 1943 Toyota became interested in the management of the association. Through the provision of management support Toyota started to develop and improve confidence and trust between members and itself.

There can be many improvement objectives of a supplier association, and these will vary between associations and industry sectors. Research has identified ten primary objectives for establishing and developing an association, as shown in Table 8.1.

**Table 8.1   Primary objectives for establishing and developing supplier associations**

| Objective | Rationale |
|---|---|
| The provision of manufacturing tools and techniques such as JIT, Kanban and TQM | *Improve knowledge and application of best practice tools and techniques within the supply base* |
| Produce a uniform supply system | *Remove muda (waste) from the system then standardise process management in all parts of the supply chain* |
| Facilitate flow of information and strategy formulation | *The assembler assists the suppliers in formulating an improvement strategy by providing best practice information* |
| Increase trust between buyer and supplier | *The result of gaining improvements in the first three objectives is an improvement in trust* |
| Keep suppliers & customers in touch with market need | *Assemblers aid their suppliers in understanding the needs of the customer through sharing market intelligence, sales plans and development opportunities* |
| Enhance reputation of assembler within supply base | *Assemblers attempt to prove to their suppliers that they are worth dealing with* |
| Aid smaller suppliers | *Some supplier associations are established to aid smaller associations who could not support the development or improvement programmes necessary to achieve world class manufacturing standards from their own internal resources* |
| Increase length of trading relationship | *Through supporting suppliers in the development of their operations the assembler needs to invest resource. Through committing resource the assembler increases the asset specificity of the supplier and it is therefore important that the relationship is maintained* |
| Sharing development benefits | *The association forum supports not only supplier–assembler improvements but also supplier–supplier knowledge sharing* |
| Providing examples to suppliers of how to develop their own supply base | *The performance of the entire supply chain is improved by cascading supply chain management technique into it* |

# Supplier association

A major supplier of digital telecommunications systems, which we shall call 'Cymru', had established a successful manufacturing plant in Wales. The European region had been restructured into five customer-facing divisions, which would provide major customers with a single point of contact for integrated solutions. This would in turn focus operations by key account, and boost Cymru's commitment to quality and customer satisfaction. Cymru's major customer was TELE, a national telecomms service provider. Following deregulation of markets in Europe, TELE started to buy telephone handsets in the global market at prices that were well below those of Cymru. A two-year contract was replaced by a four-month contract, and call-off quantities became much more uncertain for Cymru and its suppliers.

In order to compete, Cymru decided that it would have to improve customer service in terms of availability, speed of new product introduction and cost. A new logistics programme was conceived whereby Cymru bypassed TELE's internal distribution structure and delivered direct to TELE's customers. This meant that TELE carried no inventories and that Cymru took over the distribution task with superior service levels. TELE signed a five-year deal with Cymru, and both parties enjoyed better margins.

In order to support the better service levels, it was essential that Cymru's supply base was integrated into the new logistics programme. This meant that the relationship style (Figure 8.4) would need to be moved from arm's length to strategic. As the procurement manager commented:

> **I quickly realised that the old way of communicating on a one-to-one basis would no longer work. I'd never get round the suppliers quickly enough to get them all in a mindset of what had to change and when.**

Suppliers had previously been informed of future plans on a 'need to know' basis through their organisational 'gatekeepers' in the purchasing department at Cymru. New work was put out to tender, and the lowest-price bid secured the business.

Setting up a supplier association was viewed as the best way to address the needs and timescales for changing the supply chain. Suppliers could be involved simultaneously in reducing lead times from two weeks to two days (receipt of order from TELE to delivery at end-user's site). This would be achieved through improved responsiveness, both inbound and outbound. Far Eastern competitors would be unable to match such service levels and total logistics costs.

In setting up the supplier association, priority was given to suppliers who supplied parts for final assembly of the telephone, especially those that supplied colour-related and mechanical parts which would have maximum impact on lead-time reduction. Seven tier 1 suppliers and one tier 2 supplier agreed to take part, and the network is shown in Figure 8.7.

The Cymru supplier association was therefore formed from a wide variety of companies, in terms of both size and industry sector. In a marked break with the past, Cymru kicked off the association with an inaugural meeting that presented confidential product development and market information. The aim of the association was 'to promote best practice, improve overall supply chain performance and support product development'. This was to be achieved by self-help teams committed to sharing knowledge and experience in an open and cooperative manner. Many suppliers were concerned that

▶

the association was being formed 'as a disguise for margin reduction', and were reassured when Cymru insisted that the main task was cost reduction. More open communications and an emphasis on mutual cost reduction were seen by suppliers as essential foundations for the new association.

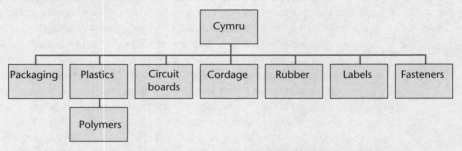

**Figure 8.7    Cymru supplier association inbound supply relationships**

The initial activity was to benchmark all members to 'gain an understanding of the strengths and weaknesses of current processes and practices relative to a best practice model'. Areas for benchmarking were those that Cymru had itself established already as competitive priorities. They were:

- quality: ppm of components received, goods produced and goods shipped;
- productivity: value added per employee, throughput and operation times;
- delivery: percentage of deliveries on time to customer and from suppliers;
- stock turns: stock turn ratio;
- continuous improvement: improvement plans, team activities and employee development programmes.

The results of the benchmarking process stimulated much interest among the suppliers. The account manager of one of them commented:

> **Benchmarking is very important. We need to know from the customer what he thinks of us. How do we rate against other suppliers in the association? I want to know because it could be I've got something to learn from another supplier.**

Following the benchmarking phase, suppliers met every quarter to formulate strategy, share market and product development information, and share plans for implementing best practice. The new plans were then deployed within individual supplier companies by training workshops. In turn, these plans spawned improvement projects aimed at achieving the competitive priorities.

(Source: Aitken, 1998)

### Question

**1** The supplier association described above eventually collapsed. What causes do you think might have led to this collapse?

## 8.5.2 Japanese *keiretsu*

One of the Japanese business structures that have received interest from Western business is the *keiretsu*. *Keiretsu* is a term used to describe Japanese business consortia based on cooperation, coordination, joint ownership and control.

The *keiretsu* possesses the particular characteristic of having ownership and control based on equity exchanges between supply chain members. Despite the complexities of their ownership structure, *keiretsu* represents a supply chain model that helps to explain the organisation of most companies in the automotive and electronics sectors in Japan.

The supply chain *keiretsu* is a network in which activities are organised by a lead firm. The typical supplier networks of large automobile and electronics firms are managed and led by the major assemblers, as shown in Figure 8.8.

The formation of *keiretsus* occurred as a result of the strategy in the 1960s of assemblers outsourcing subassemblies to increase capacity, leading *de facto* to the emergence of a tiered structure. The *keiretsu* became instrumental in developing the pyramidal structure of the supply base with its tiered arrangement to ensure that the assembler only works directly with a reduced number of suppliers. These suppliers in turn take responsibility for managing the next level down and so on. The tiered *keiretsu* style of arrangement has now become the favourite supply structure in the automotive industry worldwide.

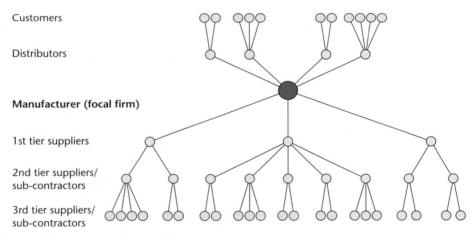

**Figure 8.8   Japanese *keiretsu* structure**
(Source: Aitken, 1998)

---

### Activity 8.6

Brazilian-born Carlos Ghosn was despatched to Nissan after Renault took a 36.8 per cent stake in the Japanese car maker in 1999. What he has done in turning round Nissan's €15 billion of debt and chronic losses has sent shock waves through Japanese business thinking. One of his main targets for change has been the *keiretsu* system, which he described as a 'gross waste of capital'. Ghosn has broken up Nissan's *keiretsu* system, and is reducing the number of suppliers from 1,200 to 600. Masaaki Kanno, head of economic research at JP Morgan's Asian office, is quoted as saying: 'While many people in Japan realised this system should be changed, it has taken a foreigner to change it. I am not exaggerating when I say Ghosn is a hero in Japan now. People believe that he has saved Nissan from death.'

The system that has acted as a model for Western auto inbound logistics is being dismantled by Nissan. Is this anomalous? Discuss.

### 8.5.3 Italian districts

A third way of organising supply partnerships has been popularised and led by industrial districts in Italy (Becattini, 2002). Porter (1990) commented on the strengths of the Italian ceramic tile 'cluster' in the Sassuolo district in his *Competitive Advantage of Nations*. Producers benefited from 'a highly developed set of suppliers, support industries, services and infrastructure', and the geographic concentration of firms in the district 'supercharged the whole process'. Districts are characterised by hundreds or even thousands of small, family owned firms with a handful of employees working single shifts. The great majority of firms are led by entrepreneurs who are craftsmen, often relying on the most basic planning and control tools. Concern currently focuses on the ability of districts to adapt to changes in global competition, as Case study 8.4 explores.

---

**CASE STUDY 8.4**

## Supply chain internationalisation in the Marche shoe district

The National Association of Italian Footwear Manufacturers (ANCI – http://www.anci-calzature.com) explains 'The success of the footwear sector in Italy is linked to an enterprising spirit and to the structure of the sector. The structure is a "web" of raw material suppliers, tanneries, components, accessories, machinery manufacturers, model makers and designers. This has resulted in a territorial concentration of firms and the formation of shoe manufacturing districts such as Marche, Tuscany, Venetia and Lombardy. The leading position of the Italian shoe industry is due to superior product quality and high levels of innovation.'

The Marche shoe district is the largest concentration of producers of shoes and accessories in Europe. There are more than 3,000 shoes firms, almost 500 shoe components firms and more than 100 leather firms employing almost 50,000 workers, with combined sales of over €3 billion. The district is export-oriented, with more than 75 per cent of production going abroad – mainly to Germany, the USA, Russia and increasingly to Asia, including China.

District firms are mostly small family businesses with fewer than 20 employees, but there are also a few larger firms with internationally recognised brands. The district leader, Della Valle Group, produces high quality shoes and bags, matching a classic style design with comfort and a sporty look. Traded on the Milan Stock Exchange, it has sales of €570 million, and has developed strong international brands – such as Tod's, Hogan and Fay, plus a growing network of directly owned stores. Leading positions in specific market niches are occupied by Fornari (focused on trendy female teenager shoes with its brand Fornarina), by Falc (specialising in children's top-quality shoes under Falcotto and Naturino brand names) and by Santoni (focused on top quality handmade shoes with prices up to €1,500). Top fashion firms such as Prada, Dolce & Gabbana and Hugo Boss have signed licensing agreements with Macerata district firms for the production of their shoe collections. Figure 8.9 shows two products from the Santoni website.

The shoe district has developed as an integrated supply network, offering the vast and competitive range of components and equipment required for making shoes – from leather processing to soles, from cutting machinery to packaging. Logistics is simplified by the geographical concentration of firms in the district and the personal

**Figure 8.9    Italian style from the Santoni Collection**

knowledge and trust that characterises relationships among district entrepreneurs. Flexibility by the small firms supply network enables the ups or downs of fashions to be met.

Since the 90s, however, the district network has had to come to terms with an outsourcing trend to low labour cost countries that is always a threat to mature and labour intensive industries in developed economies. As a result, production of low cost shoes has been almost fully outsourced, first to Eastern Europe and then to the Far East. In low price product ranges, district companies retain only high value activities of design, marketing and distribution in the Macerata district.

Outsourcing has also affected the core district products in medium to high quality footwear. Here, however, foreign partners are involved only in less complex tasks to preserve Italian style and quality. The result is an increasingly widespread network. Processed leather is brought into the district after initial processing in Asia (mainly India and China). The leather is then checked, cut and prepared to be sent to Eastern Europe for further processing (mainly to Romania and Albania for sewing and hemming). Prepared leather is returned to the district for finishing and assembly. Such partial outsourcing – called outward processing traffic – preserves the high quality standards of district shoes while cutting down on costs.

This makes logistics a critical activity. Transportation costs per unit have increased, and responsiveness has been put at risk. This is of particular concern to a business that is linked to fashion, where season collections and sales campaign deadlines cannot be missed. While offshore sourcing has led to significantly longer lead-times, increasing inventories and lot sizes are not an effective answer. Most district firms offer differentiated products based on fashion trends, and would therefore face a high risk of mark-downs at the end of season. Therefore, firms normally order only 25–30 per cent of forecast requirements for a seasonal collection from their suppliers. Orders for the rest of the collection are made in line with incoming orders from distributors and boutiques.

The new international network (including a sales network that is progressively extending towards Asia) has become so complex that even large companies find it difficult to manage. Leading district firms are tackling logistics issues through increased information processing capabilities and through advanced services from logistics service providers. In order to manage a production network spanning from nearby district suppliers to Eastern Europe (mainly for shoes) and China (for clothing), Fornari has installed SAP–AFS (Apparel and Footwear Solution). This new ERP system has allowed the company to improve visibility over production planning and tighten control over suppliers. Fornari has outsourced outbound logistics, and is considering a logistics platform to handle information exchange for district subcontractors and foreign suppliers to reduce

▶

costs, an RFID system to improve responsiveness to European customers and a logistics network to support its strong selling presence in China.

However, most district companies are not large enough to become attractive propositions for IT or logistics service providers. While they can't afford to lose outsourcing opportunities, these small firms risk being unable to manage the more complex networks that result. Moreover, most district entrepreneurs do not fully support the potential advantages of sharing outsourced services. Since they lack the accounting tools for getting a complete picture of logistic costs, they do not perceive logistics as a competitive weapon. They only care about emergencies when a rush order is required or when a planned delivery is late, but dealing with such emergencies becomes more difficult when distant foreign partners are involved. Therefore the District Committee is supporting development of a new logistics approach through its service company and through regional incentives. Such a radical change in international supply chain management cannot be limited to setting up new infrastructures and new services alone, but will also require cultural changes that – led by larger firms – alter the mindsets of district entrepreneurs.

Source: Professor Corrado Cerruti, University of Rome Tor Vergata

## Question

1 Analyse strengths and weaknesses of the Italian shoe district logistics model.

### 8.5.4 Chinese industrial areas

Manufacturing of goods has been extensively transferred to low cost countries such as China, and trade between China and Europe has increased dramatically in the past 20 years. Europe's imports from China have grown by around 21 per cent per year for the last five years. In 2008, the EU imported €247.6 billion worth of goods from China (European Commission, 2009). This comprises mainly industrial goods: machinery and transport equipment and miscellaneous manufactured articles. China imported €78.4 billion from Europe, again mainly manufactured goods (for example, Liu, 2005). China is the EU's second-largest trade partner, while the EU is China's top trade partner. Europe invested some €4.5 billion in China in 2009.

In order to keep pace with these burgeoning trade flows, China has developed massive industrial areas. But 'one of the unique characteristics of industrial policy in China is that it involves government intervention at all levels, from the political elite all the way down to village leaders' (Liu, 2005). Government intervention has created another way of organising supply partnerships by means of industrial areas. First was Shenzhen in Guangdong province (1980s), then Pudong of Shanghai (1990s). The latest has been Tianjin included in China's 11th Five-Year Programme (2006–10) as part of the country's effort to boost regional development of the Bohai Gulf Region in particular and the north-east and north-west China in general.

CASE STUDY
8.5

## Binhai New Area – North China's latest international logistics centre

Located on the coast of east Tianjin, Binhai New Area (BNA) is at the intersection of the Bohai Economic Belt and Jing-Jin-Ji Metropolitan Circle and Bohai Economic Sphere. This is also the starting point of the Eurasian Continental Bridge and an important outlet for countries adjacent to China, as shown in Figure 8.10:

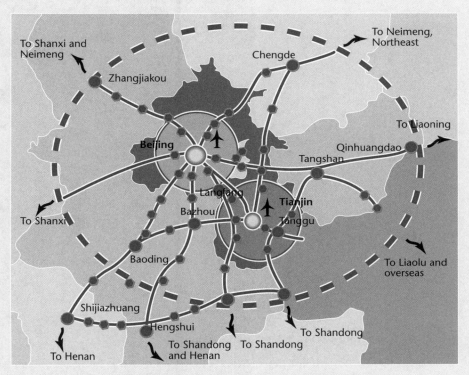

**Figure 8.10    Bohai Economic Sphere: BNA is on the coast, near to Tianj**

BNA has been under construction for ten years, and is composed of three functional areas:

- Technological and Economic Development Area (TEDA);
- Tianjin Port Free Trade Zone and Tianjin Port;
- an integrated administrative area – Binhai New Area Government.

With an area of 2,270km², a coastline of 153km and a population of some 2 million, the function of BNA is to service the northern regions of China. It is a base for modern manufacturing and research applications, and a centre for international shipping and logistics. A clear development plan was formed after continual amendment and optimisation, and the nine functional areas have been defined – such as the advanced manufacturing zone, airport industry zone and the Binhai high-tech industry development zone, shown in Figure 8.11.

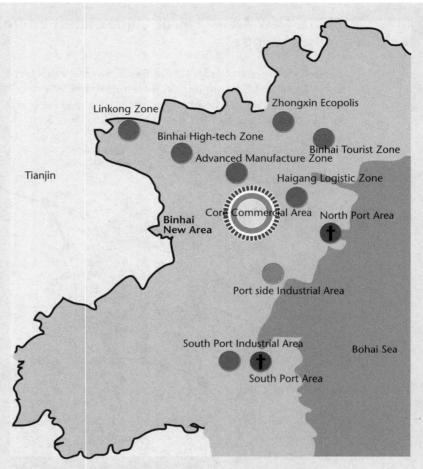

**Figure 8.11 Nine functional areas**

The vision is for BNA to become a focus for the development of new technology industries and so support the overall development of the whole region. A major advance has been the location of Airbus A320 production facilities in BNA. The Area's success has been built around:

- *Location*: the Eurasian Continental Bridge to Japan and South Korea, and the closest port to central and west Asia, Tianjin serves as the link connecting domestic and foreign markets. Modern logistics development in the new area will support the constant enlargement of international trade and foreign direct investment.
- *Excellent facilities*: BNA has become China's largest deep-sea port, and its sea routes connect to more than 400 ports in over 180 countries. The port has a modern EDI network, and benefits from development of an International Trade and Shipment Service Centre and the Tianjin Electric Port. As one of the four biggest cargo airports in China, the Area has four channels connected to Europe. Tianjin will be the first international airport that can transfer goods from one aircraft to another aircraft or from aircraft to land. It has an effective highway system and is well connected to the national train network.

- *Growth*: the Area has attracted many part-owned or fully foreign-owned firms. More than half of the Fortune 500 list of companies have constructed factories in BNA, which has transformed the Area into a major manufacturing base. Addressing economic needs of the 21st century, BNA is focusing on aerospace, oil and chemical engineering, equipment manufacturing, electronic goods, biomedical, new energy and materials, light industries and textiles, and defence-related science and technology.

- *Logistics*: The last government plan called for a target for logistics added value of RMB65 billion (€8 billion), taking 58 per cent of the service industry as a whole. To achieve this goal, BNA is constructing six new logistics bases to form a large-scale, multi-level logistics network, supplemented by sub-centres such as assembly, transit, storage, processing and distribution. In order to develop a systematic operation of shipment, harbour and port, Dongjiang Bonded port area was constructed. It implements a comprehensive international transfer, distribution, storage and related service systems.

In spite of these success factors, a number of challenges to building an international logistics centre remains:

- *Third party logistics providers*: there are more than 20,000 logistics-related firms in Tianjin, 500 of which are located in the free trade zone – including more than 50 international logistics operators. BNA aims to be a logistics centre of excellence, so it is important that the best international operators are there in strength. However, only a few third party logistics operators are there which can provide integral services, and few large international logistic firms have their headquarters in Tianjin. It is of great concern to the government that firms can be persuaded to establish their headquarters in the new Area.

- *Construction work*: the shipment centre is fundamental to the success of the logistics centre, but construction work is behind schedule. The two centres – international shipment and logistics – are seen by the State Council as having consistent goals due to their overlapping roles. There is a need to develop a more unified plan for development, with a coordinated policy and infrastructure construction logistics. The coordination of policy and the relationship between different industries and adjacent provinces is needed to achieve joint development and integral operation of the shipment and logistics centres.

- *Supporting services*: a comprehensive set of supporting services – especially for the financial industry – has developed relatively slowly. The environment for the development of banking, security, insurance, finance, asset management, and consultancy and information services, needs to be improved. Trade services, market operation, exhibition and spot sale, information collecting and broadcasting, social supervision and talent exchange are currently weak. Supporting services such as these are need to create a more favourable business environment, and to support development of shipment, warehouse and logistics activities.

(*Source*: Professor Huo Yanfang, Tianjin University School of Management)

## Questions

1 What measures would you recommend to BNA management to enhance the development of its logistics capabilities?

▶

**2** There are further concerns which government intervention finds hard to resolve. 'Lack of coordination from within Tianjin and between Tianjin and other regions has resulted in duplicated developments and cut-throat competition in the Bohai Gulf Region in general and in Tianjin in particular. The dependence on water diverted from the Yangtze River Basin or from desalination is also challenging the sustainable development of Tianjin' (*the Tianjin Binhai New Area as China's next growth pole*, http://www.eai.nus.edu.sg/BB331.pdf) Check out this website and find others to explore the sustainability concerns of the Chinese logistics centre model.

## 8.6  Supplier development

*Key issue:* **How can upstream supply processes be integrated to improve material flow?**

One of the keys to increased responsiveness in the supply chain is a high level of integration with upstream suppliers. Analysis of the supply chain often shows that product lead time is usually measured in weeks rather than days. This is caused by excessive inventories of raw materials, packaging materials and intermediate products being held upstream of the final point of manufacture. Not only does this represent a cost burden, it also increases the P-time of the supply chain as a whole.

Where suppliers appear unable to make improvements, or fail to do so sufficiently quickly, customers who feel their own performance is being hampered – yet remain committed to the relationship with the supplier – often seek ways to remedy the situation. Many buying firms actively facilitate supplier performance and capability through supplier development. This typically results in activities aimed at developing and improving overall capabilities and performance of the supplier towards the goal of meeting and serving the needs of the customer.

Supplier development consists of any effort of a buying firm with a supplier to increase its performance or capabilities and meet the buying firm's short-term or long-term supply needs. Unfortunately the temptation for buyers to gain short-term advantage still exists in supplier development to the detriment of long-term partnerships. Also, meeting the needs of buying firms is not necessarily linked to development that would enhance overall supply chain competitiveness. Therefore care must be taken not to lose sight of end-customer needs in the transactions between specific pairs of companies.

Various trends are observable as leading-edge companies seek to improve their management of the upstream supply chain, including:

● integrated processes;
● synchronous production.

### 8.6.1  Integrated processes

A key focus of supplier development should be the alignment of critical processes: that is, new product development, material replenishment and payment. This alignment needs to consider collaborative planning and strategy development.

It is perhaps the concept of joint strategy development that distinguishes integrated supply chains from mere 'marriages of convenience'. While the customer will always be pre-eminent in the determination of joint strategic goals, involvement of key suppliers in this process benefits all parties.

Process integration can be enhanced through the creation of *supplier development teams*. The purpose of these teams is to work with suppliers to explore ways in which process alignment can be achieved; for example, seeking to establish a common 'information highway' between the vendor and the customer, or working to establish common product identification codes. Nissan in the UK reports that supplier development teams have been a significant element in its success in creating a more responsive supply chain.

### 8.6.2 Synchronous production

Linking upstream production schedules with downstream demand helps to improve material flow. The creation of a 'seamless' network of processes aims to dramatically reduce inventories while greatly enhancing responsiveness. The Japanese concept of *heijunka* seeks coordination of material movements between different processes in the supply network. *Heijunka* is often referred to as 'levelled scheduling', which involves distributing volume and mix evenly over a given time period. Output of each major process in the supply chain therefore matches end-customer demand as closely as possible throughout that time period (Harrison, 2005).

Transparency of information upstream and downstream is essential for synchronisation to work. For example, the supplier must be able to access the customer's forward production schedules, and the customer must be able to see into the supplier's 'stockroom'. The *virtual supply chain* envisages partners in the chain being linked together by a common information system, so that information replaces the need for inventories.

Another approach that seeks to improve synchronous supply chain processes is that of *vendor-managed inventory* (VMI). Here, the supplier takes responsibility for planning and controlling inventory at the customer (see section 8.4). The advantage is that a large element of uncertainty in the supply chain is removed through shared information. The need for safety stock can thereby be dramatically reduced.

## 8.7 Implementing strategic partnerships

*Key issue:* What are the barriers to achieving strategic partnerships in the supply chain?

In earlier chapters, we referred to 'partners' as other firms who happen to share the supply network with a focal firm. And in section 8.3, we started to develop the term 'partnership' to address the evolution of additional features from a basic, arm's length relationship. Here, we use the term 'strategic partner' to refer to a supply partner with whom a focal firm has decided to develop a long-term, collaborative relationship. 'Collaboration' may be the ultimate objective of a number of phases through which a supply relationship may evolve. A transition route from open market negotiation to collaboration is shown in Figure 8.12:

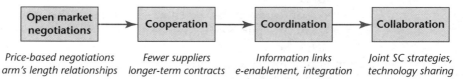

| Open market negotiations | Cooperation | Coordination | Collaboration |
| :---: | :---: | :---: | :---: |
| Price-based negotiations arm's length relationships | Fewer suppliers longer-term contracts | Information links e-enablement, integration | Joint SC strategies, technology sharing |

**Figure 8.12   The transition from open market negotiations to collaboration**
(Source: After Speckman *et al.*, 1998)

Obligational aspects of the relationship increase from cooperation to collaboration. Coordination can be defined in terms of establishing 'rules of the road' whereby partners can work together. This is the key step to integrating the supply chain. Collaboration goes beyond integration by including long-term commitments to technology sharing and to closely integrated planning and control systems. The two firms become interdependent, that is, they adapt to each other and develop common logistics governance processes. Case study 8.6 describes what happened in one such relationship.

---

**CASE STUDY 8.6**

## A strategic partnership at WheatCo–ChemCo

WheatCo and ChemCo are two US chemical corporations, both leaders in their fields and with similar sales (around $2 billion per year). Eight years prior to our study, the two companies formed a 20-year strategic partnership with the objective of gaining competitive advantage through mutual access to low cost raw materials. One outcome was the establishment in the UK of a small ChemCo facility (70 employees) on a large WheatCo site (700 employees). The ChemCo facility was located next to the WheatCo 'Basics' unit, and linked by a bridge. While a fence divided the two plants, selected employees were able to pass between the two by means of swipe card access. A ChemCo manager commented:

> **We are symbiotically linked. If you take away the ChemCo and WheatCo signs, we're really one site . . . we have a relationship and it's an umbilical cord.**

ChemCo was dedicated to production of a chemical additive used in the production of rubbers, paints and other compositions. The feedstock used in the ChemCo process was supplied by the WheatCo 'Basics' unit. The manufacturing process of the additive generated a gaseous by-product, which was recycled back into the WheatCo feedstock. Half of the additive made on the ChemCo site was sold to WheatCo's 'Rubber' unit, and the rest to other customers in Europe and the US (see Figure 8.13). The two firms thereby formed a 'closed loop' supply chain – whereby they were both customer of, and supplier to, each other. The production processes operated on a round-the-clock basis and there was very little buffer stock within the supply loop: 'if we have a problem, then ChemCo has a problem ten seconds later'. This close interdependency of logistics processes meant that operating teams were in contact on a 24-hour basis. There was a

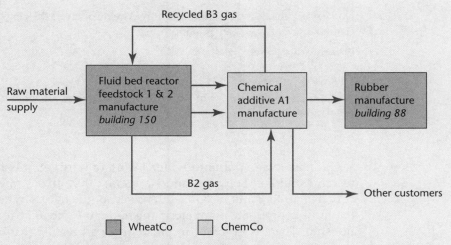

**Figure 8.13    The WheatCo–ChemCo relationship**

direct telephone link between WheatCo and ChemCo operators to allow easy communication and instant warning of changes in either of the processes, or to inform of production stoppages.

The supply relationship was multifaceted, with interactions taking place at many levels. Locally it included plant management, engineers and operators. In the US, an executive contact was appointed by each firm to manage the relationship at a strategic level. This applied in particular to the global contract agreement, which provided the commercial terms for the relationship. A joint Steering Committee determined the local operational strategy for the relationship and provided guidelines to two other joint teams: 'quality improvement' and 'technical'.

Eight years after the supply relationship began, the upstream WheatCo process had become unreliable. There were also quality issues with the chemical additive supplied by ChemCo, which impacted rubber production at the downstream WheatCo unit. In the early days of the relationship, operators had been encouraged to socialise through company events and plant visits. This allowed a common language to be developed, through interaction:

> 'we may spend a day there, they spend a day here' and thus 'we didn't need to communicate where if something did go wrong they would automatically take care of it'.

More recently, the relationship had developed some disturbing 'arm's length' characteristics. Both partners were implementing internal programmes which drew attention away from the supply relationship. At shop floor level, less interaction and fewer visits were allowed. This was made worse by employee turnover. As a consequence, operators felt that they could no longer 'put a face to a name'. Lack of interaction, together with the recurring technical issues, put a strain on the overall relationship. Recognising that a blame culture had developed, site management from WheatCo and ChemCo decided to organise a 'Team Day' to ensure that operators, shift managers and engineers from the three manufacturing units could meet, socialise and be trained on the specifics of the supply loop. However, the 'Team Day' was cancelled due to a company-wide

▶

workforce reduction plan announced by WheatCo: given the circumstances, such a socialisation event was seen as inappropriate.

(Source: Koulikoff-Souviron and Harrison, 2007)

### Question

1  Use the template shown in Figure 8.14 to help describe what had happened to the relationship between ChemCo and WheatCo.

And here it is important to offer a word of warning. It is apparent from our research (Koulikoff-Souviron and Harrison, 2007) that strategic partnerships are very demanding and resource intensive. So it is necessary to determine where is the most appropriate point along the route in Figure 8.12 for a given supply relationship. There is no point in pursuing a partnership just because it is 'more to the right' in Figure 8.12. In some cases, as stated earlier, open market negotiations will be most appropriate.

The transition from multiple sourcing and arm's length negotiation of short-term, purchase-price-allocated contracts to one based on cooperation, collaboration, trust and commitment requires a supply chain process to be put in place which needs designing, developing, optimising and managing. A key step in achieving this is to ensure that supplier development and purchasing teams are fully involved in the changes.

Failure to do this often leads to purchasing executives undertaking behaviour incompatible with fostering successful strategic partnerships. While many are familiar with – and voice support for – partnerships, in practice their approach and practices are not supportive. Barriers that have been identified include the following:

● There is an inappropriate use of *power* over the supply chain partner.

● Buyers focus on their own company's *self-interest*, often because they are incentivised to do so.

● There is a focus on the *negative implications* of entering into partnership.

● While buyers value trust, commitment and reliability, they continue to be *opportunistic* and seek gains at their partner's expense.

● *Price* is viewed as the key attribute in supplier selection.

These barriers, which are explained below, show that the decision criteria used by buyers retain a legacy of the traditional approach where the choice of lowest price remains the most defining characteristic. Unless such behaviour is changed, it prevents supply chain relationships from developing beyond a crude application of commercial power, where the free market is used to instil discipline and promote a supply base in which it is assumed that the fit survive. An explanation of the above barriers is as follows.

### Power

The ability of one member in the supply chain to control another member at a different level can be detrimental to the overall supply network, and can provide a source of conflict. Conflict is clearly associated with power, arising when one organisation impedes the achievement of the goals of another. For example, in retailing, shelf space is a key resource that has potentially conflicting implications for the retailer and for its suppliers. The retailer looks for maximum return on space and contribution to its image, while the supplier seeks maximum shelf space, trial for new products and preference over competitors.

### Focus on negative implications of partnership

Buyers consider the benefits gained through heightened dependence on a smaller number of suppliers less favourably, and tend to highlight the risks. Buyers also consistently view the cost-saving aspects of supply chain management as more important than the revenue-enhancing benefits.

### Opportunism

A key issue that prevents partnerships from enduring appears to be the gap between the strategic requirements of long-term partnerships and tactical-level manoeuvring – in particular, opportunism. It is a problem to resolve this, given that the dimensions that characterise close working relationships also provide both opportunity and increased incentive for opportunistic behaviour. This is caused when partners cannot easily obtain similar benefits outside the relationship and when specialised investments have been made. Buyers often assume that suppliers will take advantage if they become too important, and as such act to prevent this. The consequences for the partnership relationship come second in their considerations.

### Self-interest

Companies face difficulties in establishing and maintaining supply chain partnerships. Even in the automotive industry, often considered the supply chain exemplar, companies keen to implement single sourcing continue to multi-source, particularly for non-critical items and commodity items. They rarely enter into collaboration even when the customer is dependent on the supplier – that is, when the product is strategically important and alternatives are limited – and instead set their self-interest higher than the need to act according to common best interest.

### Focus on price

The focus on price may be due in some part to buyers having trouble valuing matters such as know-how, technological capability, a particular style of production or a spirit of innovation and therefore being unable to price them accurately. Their concern that suppliers may act opportunistically tends to lead them to avoid entering into areas where these factors prevail. Significantly, one of the key areas that feature these traits is that of design and development. It seems that, in this area, buyers find it extremely difficult to measure designer performance or the amount of productive time spent during design, and therefore feel the need to guard against high bids from suppliers.

## 8.8    Managing supply chain relationships

*Key issue:* **How can broader-based relationships be formed between trading partners in the supply chain?**

### 8.8.1    Creating closer relationships

The traditional supplier–customer relationship has been limited to contact primarily between the customer's buyer and the supplier's salesperson. Other functions, such as information systems, are kept very much at arm's length. Indeed,. the customer's buyer argues that dealings with the supplier should only go through him or her: in that way, they ensure that sensitive communications, such as those affecting price, are limited to a single channel.

This traditional style of relationship ('bow-tie') is contrasted with a multiple-contact model ('diamond') alternative in Figure 2.6. In the 'diamond' version, contacts between different functions are positively encouraged, and the arm's length relationship of the 'bow-tie' is replaced by active relationship management and supplier development processes. This is exemplified by the remarkable changes in the supplier portfolio at the UK high street retailer BhS. In the early 1990s BhS had over 1,000 suppliers. Now it has just 50. But the nature of the relationship with the 50 is quite different. There are now multi-level connections between the supply chain players, and a high level of electronic collaboration. There is also a much greater involvement by the remaining 50 suppliers in high-level strategy development at BhS.

We found that even the closest and most interdependent supply relationships in practice exhibit a tension between *togetherness* (a tendency to see the requirements for working together in the supply relationship) and *separateness* (the frustration of joint work or the positive aspects of working separately. Koulikoff-Souviron and Harrison, 2007). Figure 8.14 shows this tension as an arrow that connects two contrasting behaviours.

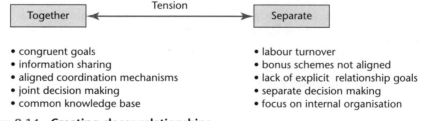

**Figure 8.14    Creating closer relationships**
(Source: After Koulikoff-Souviron and Harrison, 2007)

We concluded that logistics disciplines provide a focus for coordination around which other aspects of a supply relationship revolve. If failures such as product quality and process breakdowns did not happen, then adjustments would not be necessary. It is the *failures* inherent in the management of physical product flows that make these adjustments necessary, and which encourage the partners to work together. Management of physical flows demands heavy-duty coordination mechanisms between supply partners. This can be overlooked by senior managers – who tend to focus on contractual aspects of a relationship, and to overlook its procedural implications and the necessary resource commitment.

Coordination manifests itself as a tension between mechanisms that bring the partners together – hence stressing the benefits of achieving shared success – as well as mechanisms that drive the partners apart. Separateness can be derived either from a failure to coordinate (because of various technical or organisational reasons) or from the need to focus on the requirements of the internal organisation.

However attractive such processes of bonding may appear, in practice the organisational boundaries and vested interests inhibit the rate at which relationships deepen. These have been described as a series of factors as a result of research in the auto industry.

## 8.8.2  Factors in forming supply chain relationships

Lamming (1993) proposed nine factors for analysing customer–supplier relationships, which have been modified and extended below:

- *What the order winners are*: for example, price, product range, technology advantage, superior product quality.
- *How sourcing decisions are made*: is it, for example, competitive tender, auctions, supplier accreditation and sole source?
- *The nature of electronic collaboration*: is it transactional, information sharing or collaborative?
- *The attitude to capacity planning*: is this seen as the supplier's problem, as a problem for the buyer (tactical make/buy/additional sources) or as a shared strategic issue?
- *Call-off requirements*: does the customer (for example) alter schedules with no notice, require JIT delivery against specified time windows, or require synchronised deliveries of major subassemblies to the point of use?
- *Price negotiations*: are price reductions imposed by the buyer subject to game playing by both parties, the result of joint continuous improvement projects, etc.?
- *Managing product quality*: does the customer help the supplier to improve process capability? Are aggressive targets (e.g. 50 ppm defects) set by the customer? Is the supplier responsible for quality of incoming goods and warranty of the parts in service?
- *Managing research and development*: does the customer impose new designs and have the supplier follow instructions? Does the supplier become involved in new product development? Is the supplier expected to design and develop the complete product for the next model?
- *The level of pressure*: how far does the customer place pressure for improvement on the supplier to avoid complacency (e.g. 30 per cent price reduction in the next two years)?

Within the European auto industry at present, the most significant factor seems to be the last. Overcapacity among the assemblers has created massive pressures for cost reduction. The supply chain accounts for 70–80 per cent of an assembler's costs, so this is the primary target. Figure 8.15 shows the inventory profile for volume assemblers in Europe (Holweg and Miemczyk, 2002).

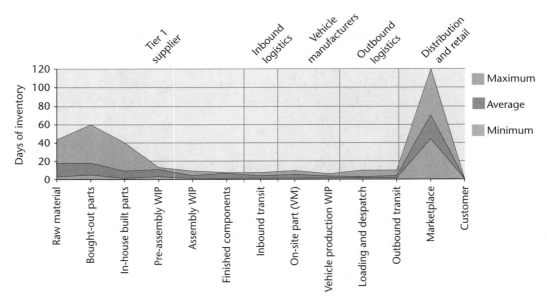

**Figure 8.15   Automotive supply chain: inventory profile**
(Source: After Holweg and Miemczyk, 2002)

It is apparent that assemblers have been using their power in the supply chain to optimise inventories around their own processes. Meanwhile, component manufacturers upstream and dealers downstream are carrying huge inventories. Dealer networks were holding some €18 billion of stock in disused airfields around Europe! While long-term mutually beneficial relationships are often talked about, the reality can be very different.

## Activity 8.7

Select an industry of your choice and, within this, review the nine factors listed in section 8.8.2. How would you classify the state of supply chain relationships in this industry?

## Summary

*What are the benefits of integration in the supply chain?*

● Integration in the supply chain is developed through improved coordination upstream and downstream. Coordination is concerned with establishing the 'rules of the road', whereby material and information flows work in practice.

- Research has shown that improved coordination between marketing and logistics results in better performance in areas such as cycle times, inventories, product availability and order-to-delivery lead times. Internal integration is the essential precursor to external integration.

- Benefits of electronic collaboration listed by Nestlé UK include improved availability of product to the consumer and hence more sales. The total service is improved, total costs are reduced (including inventory, waste and resources), and capacities can be reduced owing to the reductions in uncertainty achieved. In addition, processes that span two or more companies become far more integrated and hence simple, standard, speedy and certain. Trading partners become more committed to the shared plans and objectives.

- The closest supply relationships exhibit both 'together' and 'separate' tensions. Separation, especially during periods when the relationship is under pressure as a result of logistics failures, demands continuous remedial work. Research in the auto industry indicates that heavy downward cost pressures on suppliers limit the progress at which relationships deepen.

- JIT2 aims to achieve inter-company collaboration manually by placing customer and supplier together as supplier-in-plant.

- Electronic collaboration can be undertaken in three ways: transactional (the transmission of fixed-format documents with predefined data and information fields); information sharing (a one-way process of providing access to information such as product description and pricing, sales information, inventory and promotional calendars); and collaborative planning (electronic collaboration at strategic, operational and tactical levels).

### What are the different types of relationship in the supply chain?

- Supply chain relationships can vary from arm's length (characterised by a focus on price, and by few points of contact between the organisations concerned), to vertical integration at the other (characterised by integration of processes and by contacts at all levels).

- The choice of the appropriate relationship is helped by recognising that some suppliers are more strategic than others. One way to segment the supplier base is to use the purchase portfolio index, and to divide suppliers according to strategic, bottleneck, non-critical and leverage characteristics.

- Partnerships may bring added value to supply relationships, and have been described using seven factors: the sharing of information, trust and openness, coordination and planning, mutual benefits and sharing of risks, a recognition of mutual interdependence, shared goals, and compatibility of corporate philosophies.

- Three stages of the development of partnerships have been defined: cooperation, coordination and collaboration. The move towards collaborative partnerships is characterised by increases in the time horizon and the scope of activities involved.

### How can closer supply chain relationships be implemented?

- Supply base rationalisation seeks to reduce the suppliers with whom an organisation deals directly to a smaller number of strategic suppliers. Rationalisation involves re-tiering the supply chain so that other suppliers are placed under a lead supplier, or 'tier 1' supplier.

- Supplier associations bring suppliers to an OEM or tier 1 supplier together for the purpose of coordination and development. They also aim to improve the quality and frequency of communications between members. In practice, association companies benchmark each other, and formulate improvement projects aimed at increasing the competitiveness of the overall network.

- *Keiretsu* is the term used to describe the supplier association in Japan. Here, the additional characteristics are that ownership and control of the network are based on equity exchanges between members. *Keiretsu* structures have attracted recent criticism because of their relative inflexibility and high capital cost.

- Districts are a distinctly Italian solution to competitive advantage which involve the clustering of numerous SMEs in a focused network with close geographic distances between partners. Again, flexibility to respond to globalisation issues is proving to be a challenge.

- Industrial areas have supported China's extraordinary economic growth over the last 20–30 years. They have been developed by long-term, detailed government planning and financing. Binhai New Area exhibits many textbook features – such as clustering of firms around the state-of-the art port and airport. There are challenges too, including better third party logistics, development of the shipment centre and supporting services.

- Improved responsiveness from supply chains is facilitated by integrated processes (including joint strategy determination) and synchronisation (coordinated flow facilitated by transparency of information upstream and downstream).

- Barriers to implementation include the inappropriate use of power, self-interest, a focus on negative implications, opportunism, and a pre-occupation with price.

## Discussion questions

1  Consider the use of partnerships with customers to improve competitiveness. Discuss this within a group scenario using the following guidelines:

   a  Make a list of companies in your chosen company's industry known to undertake supplier development. This should include all its customers and other companies that are potential customers.

   b  Make a list of all the types of development and improvement that your chosen company would like help with.

   c  Assemble these lists along the two sides of a grid, following the example shown in Figure 8.16. Mark on the grid where each of the companies is able to provide the necessary help.

   d  Examine the grid you have constructed and identify the following:
      - issues that require help that current customers provide;
      - issues that require help that only potential customers provide;

- issues that require help that no one provides;
- customers (current or potential) that provide a great deal of help;
- customers (current or potential) that provide little or no help.

e  Use these five criteria as the basis for identifying companies that should be valuable in ensuring your company's long-term success. These companies are the ones that should be considered as likely partners.

f  Having identified the likely partners, identify the difficulties in establishing partnerships and the problems in maintaining them.

g  Conclude with the actions that you would undertake to overcome the problems associated with partnerships in order to achieve their advantages.

|  | | Companies that help suppliers | | | |
| --- | --- | --- | --- | --- | --- |
|  | | Company A | Company B | Company C | Company D |
| Improvement help required | ISO 9000 | ● | | | |
| | Process improvement | | ● | ○ | |
| | Communication systems | | ● | ● | |
| | Environmental legislation | | ○ | ○ | ● |

Key

● Strong positive link

○ Weak positive link

Figure 8.16   **A supplier development grid**

**2**  'Supply chain relationships don't mean anything. At the end of the day, it depends entirely on who has the most power. It's the big boys in the supply chain who decide just how much of a relationship there's going to be.'

Discuss the implications of this statement.

## References

Aitken, J. (1998) *Integration of the Supply Chain: The Effect of Inter-organisational Interactions between Purchasing-Sales-Logistics*. PhD thesis, Cranfield School of Management.

Becattini, G. (2002) 'Industrial sectors and industrial districts: tools for industrial analysis', *European Planning Studies*, Vol. 10, No. 4, pp. 483–93.

Bennett, D. and Klug, F. (2009) *Automotive Supplier Integration from Automotive Supplier Community to Modular Consortium*, proceedings of the 14th Annual Logistics Research Network Conference, 9–11 September 2009, Cardiff.

Cooper, M. and Gardner, J. (1993) 'Building good business relationships – more than just partnering or strategic alliances', *International Journal of Physical Distribution and Logistics Management*, Vol. 23, No. 2, pp. 14–26.

European Commission (2009) at http://europa.eu/rapid/pressReleasesAction.do? reference=MEMO/08/580&type=HTML&aged=0&language=EN&guiLanguage=en

Frohlich, M. and Westbrook, R. (2001) 'Arcs of integration: an international study of supply chain strategies', *Journal of Operations Management*, Vol. 19, No. 2, pp. 185–200.

Gimenez, C. (2006) 'Logistics integration processes in the food industry', *International Journal of Physical Distribution and Logistics Management*, Vol. 36, No. 3, pp. 231–49.

Harrison, A.S. (2000) 'Perestroika in automotive inbound', *Supply Chain Practice,* Vol. 2, No. 3, pp. 28–39.

Harrison, A.S. (2004) 'Outsourcing in the automotive industry: the elusive goal of tier 0.5', *Manufacturing Engineer,* February/March, pp. 42–45.

Harrison, A. (2005) 'Leveled scheduling', in Slack, N. (ed.), *Blackwell Encyclopedic Dictionary of Operations Management*, pp. 151–2, 2nd edn, Oxford: Blackwell.

Holweg, M. and Miemczyk, J. (2002) 'Logistics in the "three day car" age: assessing the responsiveness of vehicle distribution logistics in the UK', *International Journal of Physical Distribution and Logistics Management*, Vol. 32, No. 10, pp. 829–50.

Hunter, L., Beaumont, P. and Sinclair, D. (1996) 'A "partnership" route to human resource management?', *Journal of Management Studies,* Vol. 33, No. 2, pp. 235–57.

Kirby, J. (2003) 'Supply chain challenges: building relationships', *Harvard Business Review*, July, pp. 65–73.

Koulikoff-Souviron, M. and Harrison, A. (2007) 'The pervasive human resource picture in interdependent supply relationships', *International Journal of Operations and Production Management*, Vol. 27, No. 1, pp. 8–27.

Kuhel, J. (2002) 'Clothes call', *Supply Chain Technology News*, Vol. 4, No. 2, pp. 18–21.

Kumar, S. and Arbi, A.S. (2008) 'Outsourcing strategies for apparel manufacture: a case study', *Journal of Manufacturing Technology Management*, Vol. 19, No. 1, pp. 73–91.

Lamming, R. (1993) *Beyond Partnership*. Hemel Hempstead: Prentice Hall.

Liu, L. (2005) *China's Industrial Policies and the Global Business Revolution – the Case of the Domestic Appliance Industry*. Abingdon: Routledge.

Pagell, M. (2004) 'Understanding the factors that enable and inhibit the integration of operations, purchasing and logistics', *Journal of Operations Management*, Vol. 22, No. 5, pp. 459–87.

Porter, M. (1990) *The Competitive Advantage of Nations*. London and Basingstoke: Macmillan.

Rubery, J., Carroll, M., Cooke F., Grugulis, I. and Earnshaw, J. (2004) 'Human resource management and the permeable organization: the case of the multi-client call center', *Journal of Management Studies,* Vol. 41, No. 7, pp. 1199–222.

Rubman, J. and del Corrado (2009) Creating Competitive Advantage through Integrated PLM and Sourcing System, Kurt Salmon Associates, at http://www.kurtsalmon.com

Sako, M. (1992) *Prices, Quality and Trust – Interfirm Relations in Britain and Japan*. Cambridge: Cambridge University Press.

Smart, A. and Harrison, A. (2003) 'On-line reverse auctions and their role in buyer–supplier relationships', *Journal of Purchasing and Supply Management*, Vol. 9, pp. 257–68.

Speckman, R.E., Kamauff, J.W. and Myhr, N. (1998) 'An empirical investigation into supply chain management', *International Journal of Physical Distribution and Logistics Management*, Vol. 28, No. 8, pp. 630–50.

Stank, T.P., Daughtery, P.J. and Ellinger, A.E. (1999) 'Marketing/logistics integration and firm performance', *The International Journal of Logistics Management*, Vol. 10, No. 1, pp. 11–24.

Van Hoek, R. and Weken, H.A.M. 'The impact of modular production on the dynamics of supply chains', *International Journal of Logistics Management*, Vol. 9, No. 2, pp. 25–50.

Windahl, C. and Lakemond, M. (2006) 'Developing integrated solutions: the importance of relationships within the network', *Industrial Marketing Management*, Vol. 35, No. 7, pp. 816–18.

## Suggested further reading

Brown, S. and Cousins, P. (2004) 'Supply and operations: parallel paths and integrated strategies', *British Journal of Management*, Vol. 15, No. 4, pp. 302–20.

Cousins, P., Handfield, R., Lawson, B. and Petersen, K. (2006) 'Creating supply chain relational capital: the impact of formal and informal socialisation processes', *Journal of Operations Management*, Vol. 24, No. 6, pp. 851–63.

Das, T.K. and Teng, B.S. (1998) 'Between trust and control: developing confidence in partner co-operation in alliances', *Academy of Management Review*, Vol. 23, No. 3, pp. 491–513.

Fawcett, S. and Magnan, G. (2002) 'The rhetoric and reality of supply chain integration', *International Journal of Physical Distribution and Logistics Management*, Vol. 32, No. 5, pp. 339–62.

Fernie, J. and Sparks, L. (eds) (2004) *Logistics and Retail Management* (2nd edn). London: Kogan Page.

Li, S., Ragu-Nathan, B., Ragu-Nathan, T. and Subba Rao, S. (2006) 'The impact of supply chain management practices on competitive advantage and organisational performance', *Omega*, Vol. 43, No. 2, pp. 107–24.

Ploetner, O. and Ehret, M. (2006) 'From relationships to partnerships – new forms of cooperation between buyer and seller', *Industrial Marketing Management*, Vol. 335, No. 1, pp. 4–9.

Randall, G. and Seth, A. (2005) *Supermarket Wars: Global strategies for food retailers*. Basingstoke: Palgrave Mcmillan.

Scarborough, H. (2000) 'The HR implications of supply chain relationships', *Human Resource Management Journal*, Vol. 10, No. 1, pp. 5–17.

# CHAPTER 9

# Sourcing and supply management

**Objectives**

*The planned objectives of this chapter are to explain:*

- value contributions that procurement can make to the supply chain;
- what procurement does or the basic procurement process, strategically, tactically and operationally;
- four operating principles for good procurement practice aimed at leveraging supply market value;
  - a align internally before turning attention externally
  - b involve procurement early and completely to develop category strategies
  - c focus on total cost of ownership, not just price
  - d after the order has been placed, the harder work of supplier relationship management begins;
- the new talent profile for procurement professionals.

*By the end of this chapter, you should be able to understand the principles of:*

- the drivers of procurement value;
- rationalising the supply base;
- how to segment the supply base.

## Introduction

Supply management, enshrined in Kraljic's (1983) formative article 'Purchasing must become supply management', is concerned with inbound logistics (Figure 1.2), and addresses the broad task of coordinating the inbound flow of materials – including supplier selection, risk management, and material planning and control. 'Procurement', or 'purchasing', focuses on the upstream part of the supply chain, and on interfaces with suppliers in particular. One of Kraljic's forward-looking comments was:

> Few focal firms today can allow procurement to be managed in isolation from the other elements of their business systems. Greater integration, stronger cross-functional relations and more top management involvement are all necessary. Every facet of the purchasing organisation, from system support to top management style, will ultimately need to adapt to these requirements.

Sourcing is concerned with the strategic decision of whether to obtain parts or services internally (within the focal firm) or externally. If externally, then the next decision is, which supplier to source from? Reflecting the literature, we use the terms 'supply management', 'procurement' and 'sourcing' interchangeably. Procurement is essentially a functional domain of the supply chain, just like manufacturing or distribution. The operational focus of procurement is to ensure that supplies of goods and services are in place so that a focal firm can produce its product and/or service and ship it to the end-customer. Tactically, procurement also contributes to basic value drivers – such as price competitiveness and service levels. Strategically, procurement holds the potential to accelerate innovation, and drive step changes in costs and performance levels. In recent years there has been an increasing focus on procurement, which is being regarded as more important and strategically relevant. Figure 9.1 shows how more than half of the respondents to a recent survey indicate that modern-day economic dynamics and circumstances raise procurement's importance and strategic visibility. Procurement provides an important perspective on the supply chain.

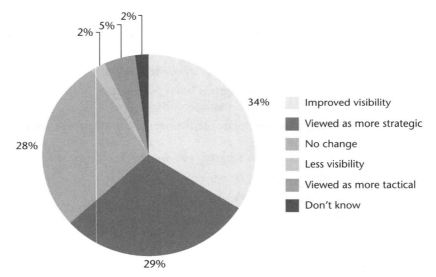

**Figure 9.1   Changing perspectives of procurement**

This change in perception can be explained by the parts and services that are procured by a focal firm as a portion of total value add created. With outsourcing and Far East sourcing dominant in many supply chains, firms have become increasingly dependent on suppliers for the customer value they generate. Procurement professionals have become more of a critical group of supply chain agents whose role is to create supplier value and align it with customer value creation. That is a significant migration towards an increasingly strategic role for these professionals, away from their traditional roots as order processors and/or price negotiators.

**Key issues**   This chapter addresses three key issues:

1 **What does procurement do?:** the strategic, tactical and operational roles of the procurement function. Drivers of procurement value.

2 **Rationalising the supply base:** supplier rationalisation programmes and why they are needed.

3 **Segmenting the supply base:** strategic, bottleneck, non-critical and leverage items. The impact of sustainable supply chain management (SSCM). Preferred suppliers, policies per segment, vendor rating – leading to 'customer of choice' status. Procurement talent.

## 9.1　What does procurement do?

If the purpose of the procurement process is to help ensure 'supply' in the 'supply chain', how is that achieved? Essentially there are two key subprocesses to consider, as shown in Figure 9.2. After specifying needs for supplies, there is a supply market search for the supplies that are needed. This is followed by the selection of supplies and the firms who make them. After this process, the suppliers have been contracted, but they have *not yet delivered* the physical goods. For this, we have the operational process in which supplies are ordered and received, and suppliers are paid for their services.

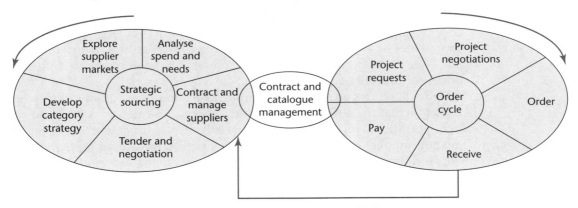

**Figure 9.2　Procurement strategic sourcing, tactical contract management and operational ordering cycle**

In Figure 9.2 strategic, tactical and operational procurement are shown as interlinked circular processes. On the right are the operational procurement activities that focus on placing orders, receiving goods and paying invoices. In order for these processes to run smoothly, automation through ERP (section 6.1) or e-procurement tools is often valuable. But aligning procurement processes with suppliers can be even more valuable, linking ordering systems on the 'buy' side with shipment systems on the 'supply' side. Thus EDI helps to reduce errors, accelerate shipments and reduce transaction costs. Managerial integration can create even greater benefits. This type of integration takes time, effort and investment, and, as a result, it cannot be achieved with all suppliers. So focal firms contract with selected suppliers and agree upon product and service catalogues (middle circle of Figure 9.2) so that – in the operational process – not every purchase needs to be treated as a new one. Buyers can order from selected and pre-qualified suppliers so that they do not have to find fresh sources and negotiate new commercial terms for every order.

Aligning contract and catalogue management effectively means that the left circle in Figure 9.2 is needed – strategic sourcing. Suppliers are selected and contracted for longer-term relationships in a particular area of spend. But prior to that, the company's need for procured products and services is assessed in depth, its current spend with suppliers in each area of spend is assessed, the supplier market is studied, and a strategy to meet business needs by means of a procurement strategy is developed. Typically, this strategy is developed by a team of buyers, but includes business users and stakeholders such as manufacturing. Often senior management is asked to sponsor and sign off on strategies. In short, there is a lot that happens before procurement actions such as tendering for framework agreements even begins. Development of a strategy for a given category of spend might lead to the conclusion that the category would be better made in-house, and so should not be tendered at all. The result of the strategic sourcing process typically is the appointment of suppliers whose contracts are used in tactical procurement (production planning, project sourcing, etc.) and operational procurement. Based upon tactical and operational experiences with contracted suppliers, performance is often evaluated and rated. Vendor ratings can then be used as the basis for supplier development and relationship management (section 9.2).

Figure 9.2 can be used to assess the maturity of a procurement function. If procurement is mostly focused on 'procure and pay' and 'operational' activities, then its buyers are more tactical in nature. If a focal firm allocates staff and time to activities more to the left, it can be expected to see greater returns on its efforts and have the opportunity to align procurement more deeply with strategies and drivers of customer value.

Figure 9.3 offers an indication of time allocation based upon industry benchmarks for staff in different parts of the process. Staff mostly focused on the far right operational procurement activities will allocate little time to strategic sourcing and supplier relationship activities, whereas staff focused on the left should not be allocating too much time on ordering, pricing orders and tracing shipments and payments. If that is the case, it is likely that operational processes are not running smoothly enough, leading to the escalation of many operational issues and/or staff is not strategic enough in capability or positioning all together to deliver procurement value.

## 9.1.1 Drivers of procurement value

Depending upon the drivers of customer value and industry, structure procurement has different contributions to a supply chain's competitiveness to make. The most well known is to ensure cost efficient supply of goods and services. This driver is particularly valuable in:

- narrow margin industries;
- price-sensitive markets;
- focal firms that have a high procured value ratio, meaning that the value of procured goods and services is high in comparison to revenue generated. In such environments a high share of total costs is managed in the procurement process.

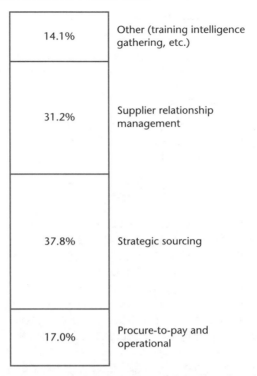

**Figure 9.3    Indication of time allocation for procurement value generation**

Figure 9.4 shows an example of such an operating environment. A company with €1.1 billion in revenues buys in €754 million. So, in this example, procured goods and services amount to almost 70 per cent of revenues. After investments, other costs and salaries, the company makes a narrow 2.5 per cent or €28 million in profit. If procurement is able to lower prices on all the procured goods and services by only 5 per cent it will more than double profits. This explains why, especially in recessionary periods, more attention is paid to the cost reduction potential that procurement holds, as shown in Figure 9.1.

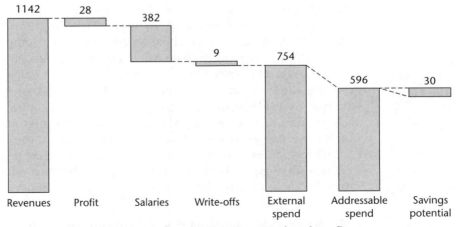

**Figure 9.4    'Waterfall' of revenue, purchasing spend and profit**

But viewing procurement as essentially a function to drive down costs ignores its enormous strategic potential. As Cousins and Speckman (2003) say:

> **To view procurement as a cost savings activity only is to sentence one's company to competitive failure. Many firms are only now recognizing that by leveraging the expertise of their supply base gains can be made that lead to a sustainable competitive advantage.**

Research of the Procurement Intelligence Unit, as shown in Figure 9.5, shows that cost savings are the still the most commonly used measures of procurement performance today.

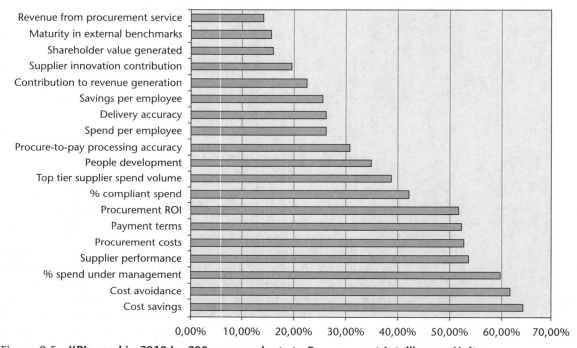

**Figure 9.5** **KPIs used in 2010 by 200+ respondents to Procurement Intelligence Unit survey**

However, cost savings are not the only contribution that procurement can make towards competitiveness of a supply chain. Ensuring reliable delivery of supply helps ensure that production schedules are met and customer deliveries are not at risk. Also JIT delivery needs to be negotiated and implemented with suppliers. In lean operating environments this reliability is of high value for seamless process execution. In more agile environments (section 7.2) responsiveness of the supply base is of particular value and, again, capable suppliers need to be selected. Also, avoiding risks of discontinued supply and supplier bankruptcies or supply interruptions are among the contributions that procurement can make to supply chain performance. Innovations and contributions to step changes in services and service levels are more easily achieved through close supplier relations.

It is for these reasons that it is commonly recommended that four operating principles should be followed:

- Align procurement internally towards its broader strategic role within the focal firm before turning to supplier relations.

- Involve procurement early and fully in supply chain design and development, not just when a contract needs to be drawn up about prices for a supplier already selected.
- Focus on total costs of ownership (see below) or customer value sought, not solely on price.
- Do not consider the procurement job done when a supplier contract is signed; this moment marks the start of the supplier relationship management work (principle IV below) that is arguably harder than the initial sourcing and contracting work, and more time and resource intensive.

If these four principles are met, procurement staff will be provided with the incentive to allocate substantially more time to strategic and supplier relationship management tasks. Such changes are not without their detractors. A common view is that it is hard to show the savings for such broad-based and long-term developments, whereas it is easy to show how much procurement has saved by squeezing prices. And it is risky to become dependent on suppliers who may then take advantage of the buyer's perceived weakness. But 'strategic supply implies that supply chain wide skills, expertise and capabilities are brought to bear by the full set of supply chain partners. They are united in the belief that by working collaboratively they will accomplish goals that they could not otherwise have achieved' (Cousins and Speckman, 2003).

## Activity 9.1

Consider procurement contributions to managing the supply chain in three different sectors: construction, consumer electronics and grocery retailing. Include in your consideration margins, price v service as drivers of customer value, and the ratio of procured value against revenues.

### Operating principle I: Business alignment

The first operating principle touches upon the work that an organisation needs to do internally, before it turns to the supply base. Given procurements focus on and dominant role in supplying these upfront steps are often ignored or not focused on sufficiently. The downside of that is that procurement might be sourcing supplies that are not fully right for business needs, running the risk of focusing on the wrong supplies, wasting supplier time and credibility internally, as well as company credibility in the supply market.

So if procurement's role is to assure the inbound flow of materials, it is important for procurement professionals to be closely aligned with their peers in the supply chain. Without that it will be hard to know exactly what to buy and what opportunities in the supply market are most valid to consider. Achieving this alignment takes consistent effort, much of it on the part of procurement professionals themselves.

Often, however, procurement is governed as a staff department, implying a degree of remoteness from supply chain operations. Even though in principle any governance system can work, it does require talent to achieve that. Figure 9.6

Figure 9.6    **Weight of factors associated with 1-point increase in purchasing performance score**

shows how, according to McKinsey, talent-related factors help explain the majority of improvement in procurement performance (Reinecke *et al.*, 2007). Organisational structure is found at the very bottom of Figure 9.6. So when procurement professionals ask for better organisational position or a more central role in the supply chain (and this happens frequently) this is a reflection of weakness. Alignment needs to be achieved – while position is earned by means of talent.

How is alignment achieved in procurement? It is achieved at a number of stages, times and levels. Business plan alignment is achieved around the annual business planning and review cycle at a senior level between business unit management and procurement leadership. Alignment around specific business objectives that need to be addressed can be achieved through cross-functional operation of a project team. Coordination around specific contracts can be regulated by ordering policies and authorisations which specify that orders over a certain value need to be co-signed by procurement.

## CASE STUDY 9.1    Refreshing strategic sourcing at Heineken

Heineken, the world's third largest brewer, based in the Netherlands, with worldwide annual sales of over €14 billion and purchased value of over €7.5 billion annually has taken procurement very seriously for years. And it does so not only within the supply chain discipline but across the business. There is senior executive ownership for the function and presidents of operating companies will host 'president meetings' where purchasing best practices are exchanged. For strategic sourcing there are cross-functional project teams that run projects. Peers from the business collaborate with procurement professionals in the team to ensure proper specification of needs and processes. And regional buyers collaborate in regional purchasing platforms to align priorities, strategies and tactics. Strategic questions that tend to be discussed in the meetings with the regional presidents include:

● development of multiyear alliances;
● backward integration through the acquisition of a glass, can, PET or malting plant;

- approval of new sources;
- substitution of packaging or ingredients;
- roles and responsibilities in promoting innovation through accessing suppliers' innovation capability.

In short, through careful alignment of purchasing within the function and externally with top management and other functions within the business, purchasing is involved in some important strategic discussions.

## Question

*Supply Management* (27 August 2009, web reference below) commented: 'The world's third-largest brewing company, which brews and sells more than 170 beers and ciders globally including Heineken, Amstel, Foster's, and Strongbow, announced the savings in its half-year financial report. The company said they were achieved through Heineken's 'Total Cost Management programme', a three-year cost reduction initiative for 2009–2011 targeting areas of supply chain, commerce and wholesale. In total, the programme delivered savings of €50 million up to the end of June. Of this, 28 per cent was achieved through using the company's buying power to drive down costs and secure more competitive contracts with suppliers.

Does the centralisation of procurement of major variable spend items (such as agricultural inputs, production materials, packaging and labels) count as 'alignment'?

(http://www.supplymanagement.com/news/2009/beer-money-for-heineken-as-supply-chain-makes-savings/)

Alignment requires of professionals:

- The ability to identify potential levers for alignment and for spotting business needs.
- Willingness to see functional expertise as a price of entry, not a differentiator, as peers expect you to be knowledgeable about procurement, that is not a likely subject of conversation: business needs are.
- Service focus to centre the effort around peer needs, not procurement desire to drive value.
- Flexibility in articulating the agenda differently depending upon business needs and creativity to find a way to stick to the agenda, despite different business needs.
- The ability to 'sell' ideas through participation rather than through the use of authority or position (again, asking for that is a sign of reluctance to engage).
- Standing strong on business values, such as 'customers first, positions last'; 'improvement forever, complacency never'; 'value centricity, position focus eccentricity,' to help keep the discussion focused.

Ways to achieve alignment include:

- Embedding/stationing key procurement staff in the businesses to make the part of the business 'fabric'.
- Using metrics of the business to evaluate performance.
- Study business plans and business training material.

- Interview executives, get invited to business meetings to understand the agenda of priorities and issues.

  Markers of aligned procurement organisations include:

- Strong business partner focus among staff.

- Incentives and performance indicators are not solely financial – such as cost savings based on PPV (purchase price variance – the 'standard cost' that has been budgeted and then used as a measure of procurement's performance. This ignores other performance measures such as those based on quality and delivery reliability).

- Results are not claimed by procurement but procurement contributions are reference in business results (annual reports, for example).

- Procedures and authorisations exist but are hardly referenced due to seamless working relationships in which peers acknowledge each other's role and have clarity about roles and responsibilities.

---

**CASE STUDY 9.2**

## Business alignment at Cofely

Cofely, in the Netherlands, is an installation and technical services company with annual revenues of €1.3 billion and with some 7,000 staff. The firm is organised into 14 distinct businesses with their own profit and loss accounts. These businesses either serve particular regions of the country or particular market segments. Specialised market segments include the infrastructure business that focuses specifically on infrastructural works, including traffic management and control systems, and the oil and gas business that serves the oil industry at oil rigs and drilling locations.

Alignment at the highest level is achieved by the CEO's inclusion of procurement in his so-called 'high five': the top five strategic priorities for the company. It is not strange that, as a result, procurement is featured in the company's annual report management letter and featured articles. The inclusion of procurement in the strategy is explained by the strategy's focus on improving margins in a narrow margin industry and the company's high procurement ratio.

The strategic mandate is used by the procurement leadership team to engage in business alignment efforts with the heads of the company's 14 business units. Account plans are developed for each business unit based upon consultation of management teams during the annual planning process. The account plan, similar to what sales management would develop for external clients, contains (among other things):

- Business objectives that procurement can help meet.
- Projects and operational priorities that can help achieve these objectives and that become joint priorities.
- Performance indicators to evaluate progress and results.
- A review and evaluation setup (frequency of review, participants, etc.) to ensure that the account plan becomes a living document for collaboration during the business plan execution.

Project teams tend to be cross-functional, involving business peers that have a key interest in the project and getting the specs right.

These three levels of business alignment are hardwired into ordering policies and authorisations that specify that large orders need to be co-signed by procurement.

## Principle II: Developing strategies for procurement categories

Principle II calls for involvement of procurement early and fully, right across the product lifecycle, from design through to disposal. This broad-based involvement allows procurement to adopt a long-term, strategic role and to seek innovative opportunities to leverage supplier market value. The focal firm can encourage innovation by reducing or eliminating three kinds of problems (Henke and Chun, 2010):

- conflicting objectives among the customer's functional areas through alignment – principle I;
- excessive and often late engineering or specification changes;
- price-reduction pressures on suppliers that consider only the focal firm's financial needs.

When approaching the procurement of goods and services in a particular category or area of the supplier market strategically, the focal firm can be much smarter about how to approach the supplier market. Procurement will already be knowledgeable about supply market opportunities against business needs, and have benchmarked its approaches against competition. Developing strategic sourcing requires the following to be in place (Kocabasoglu and Suresh, 2006):

- elevation of the procurement function from a traditional, transaction-processing mode to a more strategic role;
- effective cross-functional coordination of procurement with other functions of the firm (principle I again);
- information sharing with and development of key suppliers.

Strategic sourcing can be defined as a systematic process that 'begins with thorough analysis of spend across a focal firm, and then organises that spend by focusing on selected suppliers for best results on cost, new product development, quality and service' (Smock, 2004). A procurement strategy is typically focused on a category of products or services (category management is described in section 6.2.1), and so is often referred to as a *category strategy* (for example, Monckza *et al.*, 2009). Categories could range from health and beauty in grocery, to surfacing products in the construction sector. Chapter headings of a strategy document for a procurement category typically include:

- Specification of supply chain stakeholders engaged in the development of the strategy for the purpose of properly specifying business needs and aligning business stakeholders.
- Overview of current procured value and existing supply base.
- Analysis of the supply market and supply market trends (what are the major suppliers, what are their strategies, how interesting are we as a customer?).
- Competitor approaches and benchmark performance in the category.
- Consideration of the need to buy versus the opportunity to in-source; should we procure at all, and if we do, how will suppliers connect into our supply chain processes?

- Total cost of ownership considerations (see following section).

- Supply facing strategic options and relevant performance indicators for this category; taking in all of the above how should we approach the supply base, including relationship considerations; do we want to negotiate or form a partnership, for example?

- Implementation and communication plans that focus on engaging the user base in the business and along the supply chain during and after the procurement project.

The availability of strategies for procurement categories rather than the more limited procurement role in buying is a key indicator of a focal firm's supply chain maturity.

### Principle III: Total cost of ownership, not just price

Because savings are such a predominant traditional focus of procurement, it is understandable that negotiating lower prices is a captive domain for procurement professionals. While price is an important aspect of the value exchange with the supplier, it might be a limited focus (see logistics strategy drivers in section 2.5). Price is typically the order winner in commoditised markets, where products and services are easily exchangeable. But delivery speed and reliability, product quality and innovation are more often the order winners in other markets. So, when squeezing prices relentlessly, service levels may drop in order to compensate for the price discounts. In section 1.4, we reviewed the *trade-off* between cost and time: more of one means less of the other. It is for this reason that it is wiser to analyse total cost of ownership before negotiating price.

The total cost of ownership (TCO) concept acknowledges that price might only be the tip of the iceberg of cost drivers. Figure 9.7 displays this graphically. For example, price matters when buying a car. But so do maintenance costs, warranty, durability of the car, how quickly you can take delivery, what are the running

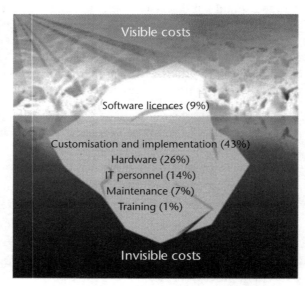

**Figure 9.7  Total cost of ownership – initial purchase price might only be a fraction**

Table 9.1  **TCO summary report**

| CPC#: PO678496 Volume 100 | | | Description: NT9X7601PCB151X105 Component Family: 21 |
|---|---|---|---|
| **Suppliers:** | **Supplier A** | **Supplier B** | **Supplier C** |
| • Price per unit: | 98.62 | 106.48 | 104.7 |
| • Lifecycle costs/unit | | | |
| Divisional purchasing | 1.498 | 0.899 | 0.449 |
| Materials engineering | 0.288 | 0.288 | 0.288 |
| Transportation | 19.955 | 4.455 | 0.179 |
| Receiving | 0.413 | 0.158 | 0.073 |
| Inspect/screen | 2.281 | 0.872 | 0.403 |
| Work in progress quality | 1.422 | | 6.692 |
| Accounts payable | | 0.033 | 0.015 |
| Store/select | 0.003 | 0.003 | 0.003 |
| Deliver to workstation | 0.006 | 0.006 | 0.006 |
| Waste disposal | 0.055 | 0.055 | 0.055 |
| After-sale quality | | | |
| • Total (Price + LCC) | $124.54 | $113.25 | $112.86 |

(Source: After Ellram and Siferd, 1998)

costs (fuel, oil) and related costs (insurance, taxes). Beyond the initial purchase price there are costs that occur over time, during the lifecycle of the product, such as warranty. TCO is the equivalent to inbound logistics that cost to serve (CTS, section 3.3.3) is to outbound logistics.

The objective of TCO is to get below the price of a purchase, and to identify how much it costs a focal firm over the product lifecycle. This includes pre-purchase costs such as supplier evaluation and QA. Table 9.1 shows a TCO model for three suppliers of a component to a focal firm in the telecoms sector (Ellram and Siferd, 1998). While supplier A appeared to be the low-price supplier, it was highest TCO once transportation and QA costs had been added to the basic piece part price.

The TCO situation can change over time. Figure 9.8 compares costs of products A and B: product A has a lower purchase price but higher maintenance costs. As a result, over time product A is more expensive than product B. If the purchase had been made with the intention to use the product for >5 years, it would be advisable to purchase product B over product A.

Figure 9.9 compares costs of product C and D over time. Product C again has a lower initial purchase price, but that price does not include shipping and packaging. The price of product D *does* include shipping and packaging – making it a cheaper product once at the factory (total delivered costs).

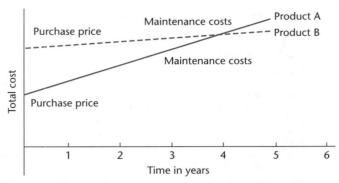

**Figure 9.8   Cost of ownership over time for product A and product B**

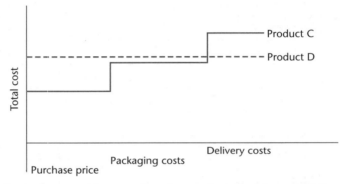

**Figure 9.9   Cost of ownership over time for product C and product D**

While it may be difficult fully to quantify total costs, simply *considering* total costs before buying provides an advantage in procurement. For example, service terms could be more important than price for a particular supply, and the category strategy would show this. Alternatively, it could be that technological edge is more of a differentiator between competitors, so this should be reflected in the search criteria for suppliers. Table 9.2 lists cost items for different costs areas over the product lifecycle, and activity 9.2 invites you to apply these.

### Activity 9.2

Using the TCO checklist in Table 9.2, consider the purchase of: 1) a computer; and 2) a newspaper. List which cost factors might be relevant in the respective purchases, and compare your views for the two.

## Principle IV: Supplier relationship management (SRM)

After the contract with suppliers has been signed for a particular category, the work of procurement is not done – even though traditionally that is what might

Table 9.2   **Drivers of total cost of ownership**

| Cost area | Cost item | Applicable? Yes/No, how? |
|---|---|---|
| Purchase price | Price | |
| Delivery service | Shipping | |
| | Packaging | |
| | Extra charge for express shipping | |
| | Taxes and duties | |
| Warranty | Repairs | |
| | Service | |
| Operating costs | Insurance | |
| | Training | |
| Implementation costs | Phasing out existing product | |
| | Disposing of existing product | |

have been thought. When a contract has been signed, it still needs to be implemented. A lot of contracts that have been closed have never been fully implemented due to lack of business support, lack of leadership with the new supplier(s), or lack of alignment with business needs. So, again, without business alignment and category strategies, contracting could be a wasted effort. But a contract supplier that is not managed might be equally ineffective. Without implementation and supplier relationship management, many of the contracted benefits evaporate before realising them during the contract's duration. So, if not managed past contract agreement, the procurement process will likely generate limited value.

SRM aims for collaboration with suppliers so that a focal firm can 'develop new products competitively and produce goods efficiently' (Park *et al.*, 2010). The basic steps to supplier relationship management are:

1  Reduce the supply-base.
2  Segment the supply-base.
3  Establish policies per supply market segment.
4  Implement vendor rating and improvement planning.
5  Assign executive ownership to most important suppliers to foster relationship potential.
6  Manage towards customer of choice status.

Figure 9.10 proposes an integrative framework for SRM. The process of continuous improvement is facilitated by the alignment of commodity strategies, supplier selection, and long-term supplier collaboration supported by assessment and development (Park *et al.*, 2010).

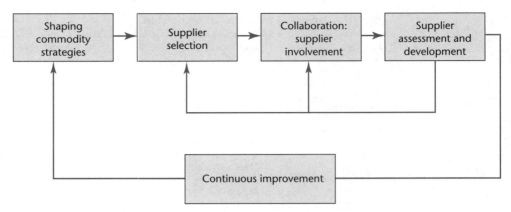

**Figure 9.10   A proposed integrative SRM framework**
(Source: Park *et al*, 2010)

## 9.2  Rationalising the supply base

Paradoxically, the first step to managing the supply base for value through relationships is to get rid of the majority of suppliers. The rationale for this action is the inability of a focal firm to allocate development resource to suppliers when there are simply too many of them.

One of the steps to prepare for reduction of the supply base is to collect the list across business units and operating entities, together with the amount of annual spend and which parts of the organisation are buying from which suppliers. This information also proves valuable in strategic sourcing efforts because it is helpful to have this information available in advance of developing a category strategy. Based on this spend information, the opportunity to rationalise much of the supply base may be revealed. For example, it may reveal that different business units within a focal firm are buying from the same suppliers under different contractual terms, or that a number of different suppliers are used for non-critical items (next section) without anybody ever considering to contract a few with better terms. It also tends to reveal that the majority of spend is concentrated with a few suppliers, and that the remaining suppliers are high in number, low in spend. The few suppliers with whom a lot of business is done are obvious candidates for relationship management, others may not provide returns on the substantial investments involved (section 8.7).

| CASE STUDY 9.3 | Supplier rationalisation at Nuon |

Nuon, a Dutch-based utility company, had about 12,000 suppliers, the total spend with whom was about €1 billion. The procurement team analysed this supply-base, and was helped in this task because there was one single list of suppliers – which is not at all always the case! In more internationally operating companies there are often as many lists of suppliers as there are operating countries or subsidiaries. When studying the list of suppliers, several issues emerged:

- All suppliers were essentially treated in the same way; their invoices were paid in strict sequence of arrival, they all operated under the same generic terms and conditions, and no time was invested in any of these suppliers unless there were problems. Part of the reason for this was that the list was simply too long for procurement professionals to work other than in 'firefighting' mode.
- The list was too long for procurement professionals to be familiar with, let alone manage all suppliers effectively.
- The list contained errors because it was not owned by procurement; there was a supplier called IBM and a supplier called I.B.M. and a supplier called IBM the Netherlands

What the procurement team did was:

1 Assign ownership for the supplier list to the management team, and appoint a 'point person' in the operational procurement team to administer the list. This person periodically sat down with procurement teams (which all had respective categories under their control) during 'drive in' days.
2 During these days the procurement teams met with the supplier list manager consecutively to review their list and correct errors, relocate suppliers when in the wrong category, remove inactive suppliers or suppliers that did not fit within the category strategy.
3 The supplier list manager also created 'speed bumps' (barriers) to introducing new suppliers; new suppliers had to be submitted for inclusion and procurement might be asked to underwrite their inclusion in the list.

It was found that simply assuming ownership over the list – a role not contested by anybody – helped drive progress and awareness. Additionally, supplier rationalisation targets were set, and the supplier count was placed on the management team's 'dashboard' (Case study 10.2) in order to consistently ensure managerial focus and scope being devoted to the supply base.

After clearing a lot of errors and 'clutter' from the supplier list, it was found that less than 10 per cent of the suppliers generated more than 90 per cent of the spend. In other words, there was a long 'tail' of suppliers (activity 2.1) that had very little spend and that were only supplying infrequently.

In order to reduce the supplier list further, the expenses policy was adjusted to eliminate a substantial portion of the list where lunch places, restaurants and bars had been asked to invoice rather than have the employee pre-pay and then claim. Also, a purchasing card was introduced. This is a credit card in an employee's name but linked to the firm's accounts. The introduction of this payment method allowed for a lot of small purchases (for example, books, team outings and flowers) to be made by credit card – without the need to have the supplier on the list. Finally, the ongoing focus of the organisation strategically to source categories of spend helped reduce the supply-base. For example, when contracts were developed for IT consultants, the list of IT consultants was reduced from 200 to a manageable 16.

In just three years, these efforts helped to drive down the supplier list from 12,000 to 4,000 – making for a much more manageable supply-base. Also the structural focus on the list helped track compliance with contracts (for example – are there suppliers on the list that are not contracted? Are there old suppliers returning?) – simply because the list was being actively managed and down to a controllable size.

A fundamental factor in supply base rationalisation is 'which suppliers should be selected for partnership'? Section 8.3 defines the characteristics of partnerships in the supply chain. Selection criteria for partnership should be based on the products involved and 'the supplier's competencies – particularly their capability to contribute to new product development' (Goffin *et al.*, 2006).

## 9.3  Segmenting the supply base

Not all suppliers are created equal. There are large and small suppliers by spend; suppliers that do business with multiple parts of a focal firm; suppliers that have been contracted through a strategic sourcing effort – and those that are not. Therefore it is advisable to *segment* the supply-base, just as we segment markets and customers (section 2.2). In the best case scenario, supplier segmentation should align with market segmentation, based on the notion that supply chains should be organised from the customer back, across the businesses and companies involved ('vertical integration').

Basic segmentation criteria tend to include:

- the amount of spend with the supplier, and
- criticality of supplies for the smooth operation of the supply chain and for delivery to the customer.

### Activity 9.3

Supplier segmentation is the supplier-facing version of customer segmentation in a B2B market. So a salesperson meeting with a procurement person is like two different parts of the business meeting each other, creating a match or a mis-match. Consider the conversation between a salesperson visiting a client considered to be a non-core 'cash cow' (customers who can be depended on for steady, dependable cash flow with little opportunity for growth), while the procurement person is considering the customer in terms of forming a strategic relationship. Also consider the reverse situation.

A number of approaches seek to segment suppliers. The widely used *purchase portfolio matrix* (Kraljic, 1983), one version of which is presented in Figure 9.11, is based on the notion that a focal firm will seek to maximise purchasing power when it can. This approach assumes that the key factors that affect the relationship are the strength of the buying company in the buyer–supplier relationship, and the number of suppliers able and willing to supply a product in the short term.

### Strategic items

Strategic items are those for which the buyer has strength but there are few available suppliers. In this situation, procurement should use its power strategically to draw suppliers into a relationship that ensures supply in the long term.

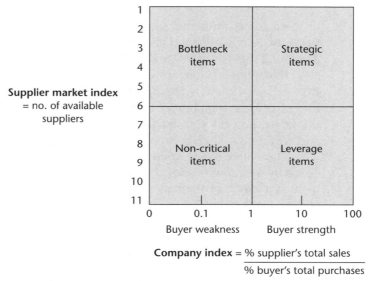

**Figure 9.11   Purchase portfolio matrix**

## Bottleneck items

Where the buyer has little power and there are few alternatives then these items are termed *bottlenecks*. The aim of purchasing in this situation is to reduce dependence on these items through diversification to find additional suppliers, seek substitute products and work with design teams to ensure that bottleneck items are avoided in new products where possible.

## Non-critical items

With a good choice of suppliers, possibly through following a strategy of using standardised parts, the traditional buying mechanism of competitive tendering is most valid for non-critical items. Such items are the ones with the following characteristics:

- not jointly developed;
- unbranded;
- do not affect performance and safety in particular;
- have required low investment in specific tools and equipment.

## Leverage items

Where there are a large number of available suppliers and the buyer has high spending power, then the buyer will be able to exercise this power to reduce prices and push for preferential treatment. Naturally, care should be taken not to antagonise suppliers just in case these favourable market conditions change. A more tactical approach may be appropriate.

This approach to segmentation is heavily weighted towards the buyer's viewpoint. It is also a little unfashionable because it uses the term 'power' in supplier relationships, and assumes that traditional market-based negotiations will be used for some product groups. However, it applies to many firms today, and reflects the tough approach taken by purchasing teams in some of their customers. Accepting that these sorts of conditions are likely to prevail or even intensify, it is clear that suppliers need to work on their relative strategic importance to a focal firm in order to strengthen their position in a supply relationship. Indeed, this may already be happening in the strategic quadrant, where the supplier tends to dominate, according to a Dutch survey of procurement professionals (Marjolein and Gelderman, 2007).

A major value of the Kraljic framework is that it helps procurement professionals 'to move commodities and suppliers around specific segments in the portfolio in such a way that the dependence on specific suppliers is reduced' (Gelderman and van Weele, 2002). Thereby, it is possible for positions to be changed *within* the matrix – either by suppliers or commodities. For example, some bottleneck items (such as, maintenance, repair and overhaul – MRO) might be migrated into the leverage segment by simplifying the specification – or making it more generic and so allowing pooling of demand between different product groups. Figure 9.12 shows such possible migration routes from 'bottleneck' to 'leverage'. Such migrations and more strategic supply relationships help in the implementation of *target pricing*, whereby marketing in a focal firm establishes the price of a product that will support the target market share. Target price less margin leaves the *target cost*, which is then used to establish prices for suppliers (as well as design and manufacturing target costs). Target pricing encourages more collaborative partnerships, and less adversarial relationships (section 8.3). As Newman and McKeller (1995) state, 'cohesiveness is an ingredient of target pricing'.

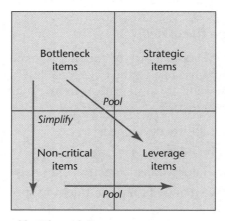

Figure 9.12   **Migration of bottleneck items**

## Activity 9.4

Selecting a focal firm of your choice, use a copy of the purchase portfolio matrix (Figure 9.11) and plot on it the names of its top ten customers and top ten suppliers. Which position would your chosen focal firm prefer to be in?

Suggest actions that would improve the situation.

But, in what may be a departure from the Kraljic framework, the impact of sustainable supply chain management (SSCM) has apparently been to distort the familiar relationships. By replacing the axes by risk to the triple bottom line (TBL, section 1.3.2) and risk to supply, Pagell *et al.* (2010) created modified segments (Figure 9.13). 'Price' becomes subordinated to 'TBL risk', with all three values – environmental, social and economic – at stake. Some segments remained relatively unchanged – bottleneck and non-critical items are in the same positions when TBL risk is low. In the strategic segment, risks have been expanded to encompass all three TBL values. The biggest change was in leverage items. In SSCM, focal firms are dividing leverage items into three sub-segments:

- *True commodities:* retain the characteristics of the 'traditional' leverage items: suppliers would have an impact on only a single value of the TBL.

- *Strategic commodities:* are recognised for their potential ability to be leveraged in terms of their long-term competitive advantage. Instead of using buyer power, small numbers of selected suppliers were being given long-term contracts and premium prices to invest in new product development.

- *Transitional commodities*: these may initially be regarded as strategic commodities. But by working to reduce TBL risk, it may be possible to convert them over time into true commodities.

The emphasis is less on price, more on *supply-base continuity*. Partners in SSCM aim to work together in a manner that 'allows them to thrive, invest, innovate and grow' (Pagell *et al.*, 2010).

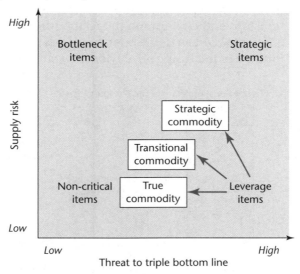

**Figure 9.13    The sustainable purchasing portfolio matrix**

## 9.3.1  Preferred suppliers

Suppliers that win contracts as part of a strategic sourcing project tend to be considered as *preferred suppliers*. These are favoured over non-contracted suppliers, and with the implementation of these contracts the suppliers get support and stewardship from the customer. Often, their success is a target for a procurement professional, and contract usage is measured as a key performance indicator. So these suppliers are kept closer, and the relationship receives attention. But time and resources are not committed by the customer to the extent allocated to strategic relationships.

### 9.3.2 Strategic relationships

A very small number of suppliers can become of strategic importance to the fundamental success of a focal firm, and to performance of the supply chain. The single most important characteristic of such relationships is that there can be very few. Unfortunately partnership-type terminology is one of the most inflated business terms. The term is often used by sales personnel to try to establish an appearance of commitment, whereas the real commitment for these types of relationships is simply unaffordable and uneconomical to spread too thinly.

### 9.3.3 Establishing policies per supplier segment

If suppliers are segmented as a reflection of how they are not all similar, the obvious next step is to agree upon, and implement, policies that reflect the differing nature of relationships with suppliers in different segments. These tend to be centred around the amount of time and resources allocated to the relationship (for example, from few in the commercial segment to many in the strategic segment) and the degree to which the relationships are embedded and stewarded inside the company.

Typical policy considerations are shown in Figure 9.14. After this step, we move from preparing for supplier relationship success by weeding out select relationships and establishing the relationship framework. This helps to implement differentiated levels of resource towards capturing relationship value. These efforts are of increasing selectivity and commitment.

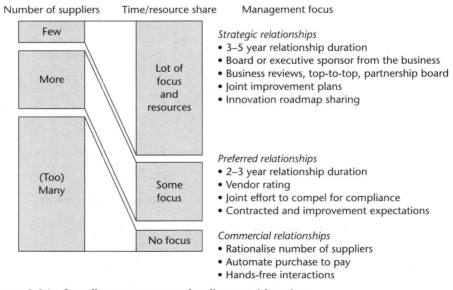

Figure 9.14 **Supplier segments and policy considerations**

## 9.3.4 Vendor rating

Vendor rating is a measurement effort focused on supplier performance. Basic spot checks on delivery reliability (correct quantities and times) are typically used for commercial suppliers. Broader-based measures are needed for strategic and pre-ferred relationships as shown in Figure 9.14. Vendor rating is not 'measuring for the sake of measuring': it is measuring for the sake of *jointly improving* both supplier and customer processes. In the best cases, vendor rating results are used as a basis for a standing discussion of joint improvement opportunities between a supplier and customer team of stakeholders. Joint action plans are developed and progress is evaluated, joint improvement projects and teams may be involved. The supplier is explicitly asked to offer improvement suggestions to the customer and perform-ance challenges are jointly owned. They are not just reported to the supplier with a one-sided assignment to 'fix them'. In short, vendor rating is a mechanism to de-velop and advance the relationship, and to centre relationship management on business-relevant improvement opportunities, structurally and consistently. The vendor rating results are discussed on a regular basis, and use an agreed set of met-rics to provide structure and consistency in focus and commitment.

The steps involved in setting up a vendor rating system are:

1 *Select the team*: vendor rating is best undertaken by a cross-functional team of stakeholders who have various interests in a given commodity from design through to logistics. The process is not exclusive to the procurement function – vendor rating works better when there are business peers of procure-ment professionals involved in the dialogue to represent a broad internal client-base. Often, performance data are partially collected based upon qualitative input from users, and improvement suggestions should not come from procure-ment alone. So, as in strategic sourcing, business engagement and alignment is important preparation for vendor rating effectiveness.

2 *Establish the rating criteria*: the actual set of metrics used is a tool, and there is some sophistication that goes into its design. For example, the metrics cate-gories may be consistent across categories but with different weighting between the categories depending upon the category strategy. Also metrics should be consistent between suppliers in the same category to allow for comparison be-tween suppliers. The metrics categories typically include price, delivery reliabil-ity and quality, with innovation and process improvement as possible extras. Delivery tends to be reliability more than operational in nature: an on time in full (OTIF) measure, for example, that can be extracted from the focal firm's ERP system. Quality and innovation may be more subjective in nature.

3 *Determine the effective weighting*: this establishes the team's view of the relative importance of each criterion. This may be achieved by asking members to un-dertake a paired comparison of the criteria that have been defined in step 2.

4 *Score each supplier's performance*: team members are asked to rate the criteria for each supplier. To minimise the risk of bias, a set of rating guidelines is estab-lished for each criterion, and a scale agreed – for example, from 1 = poor to 10 = excellent.

An example of the output of a vendor rating for a supplier (Yayha and Kingsman, 1999) is shown in Figure 9.15.

| Criteria | Sub-criteria | Effective weight | Criteria score | Sub-total |
|---|---|---|---|---|
| Quality | Customer reject | 0.171 | 8 | 1.368 |
| | Factory audit | 0.075 | 7 | 0.525 |
| Responsive | Urgent delivery | 0.13 | 9 | 0.117 |
| | Quality problem | 0.18 | 9 | 0.162 |
| Discipline | Honesty | 0.024 | 7 | 0.168 |
| | Procedural compliance | 0.012 | 6 | 0.072 |
| Delivery | | 0.336 | 7 | 2.352 |
| Financial | | 0.067 | 9 | 0.603 |
| Management | Attitude | 0.038 | 7 | 0.266 |
| | Business skill | 0.010 | 9 | 0.09 |
| Tech. capability | Tech. prob. solving | 0.068 | 9 | 0.612 |
| | Product ranges | 0.016 | 9 | 0.144 |
| Facility | Machinery | 0.102 | 9 | 0.918 |
| | Infrastructure | 0.02 | | 0.18 |
| | Layout | 0.03 | | 0.27 |
| Total vendor rating | | | | 7.847 |

Figure 9.15   **Vendor rating example**

Sharing performance feedback may occasionally be considered risky or as giving up negotiation leverage when the supplier performance is good. That would be true if negotiation leverage is all that matters, but in preferred supplier relationships that is not at all the case. These are the relationships in which good performance is celebrated and shared as a joint success. Essentially, the customer wants the supplier to do well. Additionally, with a continuous improvement focus, no performance is perfect, so there is always work to be done and the performance bar is always rising. Figure 9.16 shows the output for three areas – price, quality and delivery reliability. While supplier A scores very positively on price, it shows weaker performance on delivery reliability, prompting supplier and customer to work on forecasting processes collaboratively.

Beyond vendor rating, there are advanced levels of business involvement in supplier relationship management when it gets to more exclusive relationships, as we explain next.

## 9.3.5  Executive ownership of supply relationships

The rationale behind executive ownership is that there is so much value to be gained from select supplier relationships that it should not be left to procurement alone to manage them – and that it is worth the involvement of senior executives

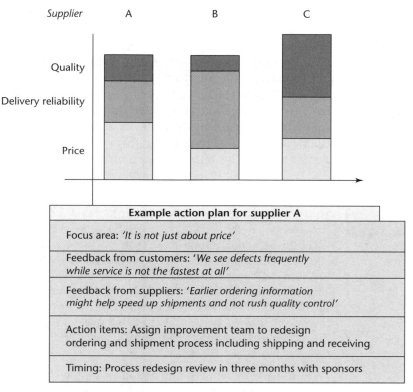

**Figure 9.16    Example vendor rating report and action planning**

from across business units that use supplier services and goods. Typically, companies will short-list their most important suppliers and invite senior executives of business units that are prominent users of the suppliers on the list to assume ownership of between one and three supplier relationships.

The role of an *executive owner* of the relationship includes:

- hosting two–three top-to-top meetings with peers from the supplier to discuss the relationship and business opportunities;
- serving as a steward of the supplier inside the organisation;
- serving as an escalation point for usage and performance issues with the supplier;
- serving as a sponsor of joint improvement projects and ensuring proper resource allocation towards these projects.

Procurement may do most of the detailed work to support the executive owner, but should not seek to take over the relationship. Rather, procurement should seek to enable the relationship. If it is hard in a business to find executives who are willing to take on ownership of a few supplier relationships, the value of suppliers is not being properly recognised within the focal firm. In such cases, procurement has some internal marketing to do. Alternatively, it may be that executives already have suppliers that they regularly interact with, but on a more informal basis. Here, procurement needs to infuse the systematic selection of the shortlist and rigour into the way that relationships are managed. The value that can be derived from this should provide the incentive. Finally, it may be that the supplier will predominantly offer up salesforce resources to the exchange. In that case there is work for procurement to do to ensure appropriate commitment to the relationship on the supplier side. Without it the exchange will eventually unravel and attention will shift away.

In addition to the very close 'one on one' engagement with select suppliers, a lot of companies also use supplier awards and events to acknowledge and award suppliers more publicly. These events can include a broader range of preferred suppliers and be tied to vendor rating continuous improvement efforts. They also serve as an effective channel for communication and supplier engagement.

---

**CASE STUDY 9.4**

## Acknowledgement of suppliers by P&G

P&G host an annual supplier appreciation event where it makes awards to its best suppliers. As a sign of the importance and prominence associated with this event by P&G, the 2009 event was published on the very front page of the company's website. Suppliers of the year, such as Novozymes of Bagsvaerd in Denmark – a strategic enzyme supplier for P&G's laundry and cleaning products – achieved this recognition by 'consistently scoring the highest in broad-based qualitative and quantitative evaluations by P&G employees throughout the supply chain'. The company's global head of procurement said during the event:

> From market changing innovation to supply chain excellence, our supplier partners are foundational for building a stronger future. P&G is at our best when we have fostered relationships with our external business partners that enable collaboration in achieving mutual goals, addressing challenges, and delivering ongoing innovation.

(Rick Hughes, VP Global Purchases, P&G)

But perhaps more importantly – and as a sign of business ownership that could not be more clear – the company CEO participated in the event and said:

> I want to acknowledge the tremendous contributions and commitments that our external business partners make to help us achieve our strategies and goals.

(Bob McDonald, CEO P&G)

(Source: Company website press release 4 November 2009 http://www.pginvestor.com/phoenix.zhtml?c=104574&p=irol-newsArticle&ID=1350941&highlight=)

---

### 9.3.6 Migrating towards *customer of choice* status

A final stage in implementing and rolling out supplier relationship management is more of an aspirational stage that is not achieved by many focal firms. In this stage all the investment in the preparation for focus on a select few suppliers and the resource allocation geared towards selected suppliers, begins to pay off at an advanced level of supplier privileges. Supplier relationship management in many respects is 'reverse marketing' – it is the marketing of a focal firm to its suppliers, seeking to acquire preferred status as a customer. Think back to the segmentation activity 9.3: does this not have a lot to do with 'selling' the supplier? Again, this goes well beyond the traditional approach of procurement as the function that drives prices down through tough negotiations. This has everything to do with unleashing the full power of business-aligned procurement – with business engagement, ownership and involvement at multiple levels, from category strategy development, through strategic sourcing, through account planning and segmentation and strategic relationship ownership. The purpose of seeking customer of choice status is to acquire a level of support from suppliers, not just in price points or shipment conditions but wholly and fully that is preferred to competition. In search of this goal, supplier relationship management might pay off as a competitive differentiator. This obviously requires an organisation's ability to achieve a status with its supplier making it worthy of such investment.

The recent recession seems to have driven US-owned auto manufacturers towards this goal. Planning Perspectives carry out an annual survey of supplier relations in the sector. CEO John Henke said:

> **If there was a silver lining to the recession for US suppliers, it has to be that it caused the domestic automakers to wake up and realise how important their suppliers are to their future fortunes.**

Henke 'believes the US firms' improvement reflects the fact that many of their suppliers went bankrupt or were nearly bankrupt to the extent that it threatened the auto businesses. This led to companies working hard to be fair and manage their suppliers more equitably, while continuing to consolidate their overall number of suppliers' (Allen, 2010).

*Customer of choice* status entails several benefits, including:

- First access to innovations and R&D.
- Customised solutions on a technology, process, service and product level hardwired into company supply chain processes.
- Best account management staff allocated to the account.
- Supplier wanting to do more than needed.
- All senior executive ownership met with equal level engagement, both in seniority, resource allocation, account management support and time commitment.

The box below offers a set of tips and suggestions for supplier relationship management.

---

Tips for effective supplier relationship management

1 Supplier relationship management is a process not a one-off activity.

2 We need to align internally before looking outward, but often look outside first.

3 Again, this is also not just about price: do not set all measures in a one-sided way but have the discussion about which measures to use as a basic level engagement with suppliers, ending up with joint and shared scorecards.

4 Procurement challenges suppliers but should steward them internally.

▶

5 Don't try to do it on your own, the more sponsors and business interactions the better (including for vendor rating).

6 If you do not know how suppliers are graded, the supplier might, as suppliers very often conduct customer satisfaction surveys.

7 Measuring is less important than joint action planning, also share relative positions of a supplier against its competition to drive up performance.

8 Any feedback conversation is an improvement opportunity to drive progress.

## 9.4 Procurement technology

As is the case with many parts of the supply chain there are several types of technology dedicated to procurement (sub-)processes. In the late 1980s during the technology boom there were a lot of portals and e-auction sites and technologies considered part of the big revolution. These technologies are however mostly related to the operational ordering and buying part of the process. Hence, one of the reasons for it going bust was that its value contribution was mostly limited to ease of operational ordering and price reductions but excluding more strategic domains and advanced value drivers of procurement contribution.

Today, there are procurement technologies related to all process, from e-auction technology (including B2B versions of eBay) for ordering in commodity markets to e-sourcing process support software that can facilitate a strategic sourcing process. Catalogues (supplier generated or internally managed) and e-procurement technologies are often used in the operational process. Then there are linkages into supply chain technology that are used in procurement including ordering in the ERP system or the use of EDI linkages to suppliers to accelerate paperless ordering, order confirmation and paying. Self-billing is often used by suppliers that are hooked into the operational software of their customers; these suppliers can just bill for orders generated in the ERP. Technology can help create ease of ordering and in fact this can both be a way to compel the business into using preferred suppliers or a way for procurement to create some basic-level customer satisfaction (making the life of peers in the business easier). It should be noted however that technology in procurement can make processes run smoother and more efficiently but can never replace the value of top procurement talent (see following sections).

## 9.5 Markers of boardroom value

If procurement is such a lever of supply chain performance and competitiveness in more and more operating environments and companies, it is understandable that there are markers of boardroom value that may be found in advanced organisations. These markers include:

- Explicit mention and coverage of procurement in the annual report, investors' updates and CEO/CFO speeches. An increasing number of purchasing executives are finding their way to board-level appointments (Hall, 2010): 'our study found a 41 per cent increase over the past year in the number of European companies with procurement represented on the board. And last year was up 32 per cent from the 2008 study. So, while we've frequently found that US companies gave procurement far more recognition than European counterparts, that simply isn't the case any more.'

- Published targets for procurement return in mergers, savings or supplier innovation targets.

- Procurement targets are explicitly mentioned in the budget letter to the businesses at the start of the budgeting season, preferably with an expectation of paragraphs of the business plan to include procurement references.

- All businesses have stated plans, objectives and key performance indicators on their dashboard (see Case study 10.2) that relate to procurement so that they are managing towards clear business-centric and mission-critical procurement (related) targets.

- Internal service awards are being won by procurement professionals as a sign of recognition within the company of its service and valuable business contributions.

- A 'tour of duty' in procurement becomes a plus for general managers and heads of business units, just like a 'tour of duty' in sales is – once this stage is reached it is clear that, as a function, procurement has arrived and its impact in business is acknowledged. Talent in procurement is not the sole property of the function but becomes a company or supply chain asset. The nature of this talent is not unique to procurement either as the next section will help clarify.

## 9.6  What does top procurement talent look like?

Obviously talent needs vary by supply chain segment, and within the procurement segment it varies by subprocess. If savings are very important then negotiating skills are important, particularly in the operational buying process. For strategic sourcing, seeking to unleash contributions to supply chain competitiveness, a lot more skills are needed. Whereas, traditionally, negotiations skills are emphasised in procurement, the list of skill requirements has grown long and far beyond that. Skill requirements include:

- Strategic thinking in order to approach supply markets smarter and with company strategic priorities in mind.
- Entrepreneurial focus to be able to spot opportunities in the supply market against end-market needs.
- Creativity and solution orientation to be able to find ways around supply market constraints and barriers.
- Communication skills to engage internally and build bridges to suppliers.
- Quality and improvement focus to continue to improve the performance of the supply base over time.

- Relationship skills, not to 'wheel and deal' but to develop joint ongoing improvement focus with suppliers and grow those relationships over time.
- Stewardship skills to represent suppliers internally and ensure they achieve proper alignment with the business.
- Consultative skills to engage with the business and ensure proper articulation of business needs for suppliers to fulfil.
- Service posture towards business partners who specify and order, and towards suppliers who actually do the majority of the work. While it is fine to report results, procurement talent should not seek the spotlight over suppliers and its internal customers.

In short, this profile is ideally suited to Master's graduates in the supply chain domain. Often, procurement roles are much sought after, even if just for a few years, due to the opportunity to make a clear and visible impact on large parts of the business. Procurement results are clear and often targeted in investment updates, merger and acquisition plans, budgets and business plans. So procurement allows for demonstrable impact with senior exposure, which in turn makes it an even more relevant milestone along the career path of future CEOs.

## Summary

*What is the role of procurement in logistics?*

- Procurement is the upstream part of the supply chain that faces suppliers. Given the amount of value procured in by most companies procurement plays a key role not only in helping manage the company bottom line, but also in ensuring critical suppliers and delivery service and product quality.
- Essentially, most companies and supply chains are critically dependent on supplies and suppliers for customer service and performance. It is therefore recommended that procurement is involved early and fully, so that strategies can be developed per product category, strategies that appreciate total cost of ownership, not just purchase price.
- Supplier relationships should be managed proactively with segments, performance measurement and management, policies per segment, and executive ownership for key relationships.
- The talent profile required for effectiveness in procurement is that of (future) top leaders of the company.
- The ability to demonstrate high level, concrete business impact within procurement makes it a function much sought out by aspiring and ambitious talent.

*How can a procurement strategy be crafted and delivered?*

- Procurement strategy begins with internal business alignment of procurement with other business functions. It continues with developing strategies for procurement categories. It is guided by total cost of ownership, rather than purchase price variance (PPV). And it facilitated by supplier relationship management.

- Supplier relationship management starts with rationalising the supply base. The remaining supply base is then segmented. Strategic relationships are formed with a small number of suppliers, and policies established for each supplier segment. Supplier performance is established and monitored collaboratively using vendor rating. The longer-term aim is to migrate towards 'customer of choice' status.

## Discussion questions

1 List 'before' and 'after' descriptions for procurement as a function and the professionals within that function when considering what procurement came from (staff order processor negotiating discounts after supplier selection was made by others) and how it is described in this chapter when it comes to:
   a  business alignment and business involvement;
   b  stage and degree of involvement of procurement in supply chain design and strategy;
   c  amount of time devoted to strategy discussion;
   d  link between category strategy, supplier segmentation, and vendor rating, and company and supply chain strategic priorities;
   e  calibre of staff in the function (defined as: potential to migrate to other parts of the business, potentially make CEO one day and have a visible impact on company and supply chain performance, both on a day-to-day basis as well as in terms of progressing strategy).

Please also offer descriptions/examples of what these differences look like.

2 A recent CAPS report (Monckza and Petersen, 2009) listed ten top issues relating to the implementation of procurement strategy:
   - Vision, Mission and the Strategic Plan
   - Commodity and Supplier Strategy Process
   - Strategic Cost Management
   - Engagement by Corporate Executives and Business Unit Leaders
   - Human Resource Development
   - Procurement & Supply Organisation Structure & Governance
   - Measurement & Evaluation
   - Total Cost of Ownership
   - Functional & Business Processes, Practices & Systems
   - Structuring & Maintaining the Supply Base.

Explain how each of these issues contributes to a well-crafted procurement strategy.

3 Explain what is meant by the term 'triple bottom line' (TBL), and why it is important to procurement strategy. Elaborate the significance of TBL to supplier segmentation strategy, paying particular attention to its impact on strategic and leverage items.

## References

Allen, A. (2010) *US Motor Giants Move up Supplier Relations Ranking, Supply Management,* at http://www.supplymanagement.com/news/2010/us-motor-giants-move-up-supplier-relations-ranking/

Cousins, P. and Speckman, R. (2003) 'Strategic supply and the management of inter- and intra-organisational relationships', *Journal of Purchasing and Supply Management*, Vol. 9, No. 1, pp. 19–29.

Ellram, L. and Siferd, S. (1998) 'Total cost of ownership: a key concept in strategic cost management decisions', *Journal of Business Logistics*, Vol. 19, No. 1, pp. 55–63.

Gelderman, C. and van Weele, A. (2002) 'Strategic direction through purchasing portfolio management: a case study', *International Journal of Supply Chain Management*, Vol. 38, No. 2, pp. 30–8

Goffin, K., Lemke, F. and Szwejczewski, M. (2006) 'An exploratory study of "close" supplier–manufacturer relationships', *Journal of Operations Management*, Vol. 24, pp. 186–209.

Hall, S. (2010) *Procurement Leaders Jump on Board*, Procurement Leaders, http://blog.procurementleaders.com/procurement-blog/2010/4/28/procurement-and-supply-chain-jump-on-board.html

Henke, J.W. Jr and Chun, Z. (2010) 'Increasing supplier-driven innovation', *Sloan Management Review*, Vol. 51, No. 2, pp. 41–6.

Kocabasoglu, C. and Suresh, N. (2006) 'Strategic sourcing: an empirical investigation of the concept and its practices in US manufacturing firms', *Journal of Supply Chain Management: A Global Review of Purchasing and Supply*, Vol. 42, No. 2, pp. 4–16,

Kraljic, P. (1983) 'Purchasing must become supply management', *Harvard Business Review*, Sept/Oct, pp. 109–17.

Marjolein, C. and, Gelderman, C. (2007) 'Power and interdependence in buyer supplier relationships: a purchasing portfolio approach', *Industrial Marketing Management*, Vol. 36, No. 2, p. 219.

Monckza, R., Handfield, R., Guinipero, L. and Patterson, J. (2009) *Purchasing and Supply Management*, 4th edn. Mason, OH: Cengage Learning.

Monckza, R. and Petersen, K. (2009) *Supply Strategy Implementation: Current State and Future Opportunities, CAPS Research*, Arizona State University, at http://www.capsresearch.org/publications/pdfs-public/monczka2009es.pdf

Newman, R. and McKeller, J. (1995) 'Target pricing – a challenge for purchasing', *International Journal of Purchasing and Materials Management*, Vol. 31, No. 3, pp. 13–20.

Pagell, M., Wu, Z. and Wasserman, M. (2010) 'Thinking differently about purchasing portfolios: an assessment of sustainable sourcing', *Journal of Supply Chain Management: A Global Review of Purchasing & Supply*, Vol. 46, No. 1, pp. 57–73.

Park, J., Shin, K., Chang, T.-W. and Park, J. (2010) 'An integrative framework for supplier relationship management', *Industrial Management and Data Systems,* Vol. 110, No. 4, pp. 495–515.

Reinecke, N., Spiller, P. and Ungerman, D. (2007) 'The talent factor in purchasing', *McKinsey Quarterly*, Vol. 1, pp. 6–13.

Smock, D. (2004) 'Strategic sourcing: it's now deeply rooted in US buying', *Purchasing*, 2 September, pp. 15–16.

Yayha, S. and Kingsman, B. (1999) 'Vendor rating for an entrepreneur development programme: a case study using the analytic hierarchy process method', *Journal of the Operations Research Society*, Vol. 50, pp. 916–1030.

## Suggested further reading

Monckza, R.M., Handfield, R.B., Giuipero, L.C., Patterson, J.L. and Waters, D. (2010) *Purchasing and Supply Chain Management*. Andover: South Western Cengage.

Van Weele, A. (2009) *Purchasing and Supply Chain Management – Analysis, Strategy, Planning and Practice*, 5th edn. Andover: Cengage.

# Part Four

# CHANGING THE FUTURE

The final part of this book takes a somewhat different approach. It takes the lessons learned in the previous nine chapters and considers how future changes can be expected. The rationale for these changes is based on earlier lessons combined with current leading-edge thinking on logistics. Chapter 10 assesses current approaches to the supply network, and their impact on logistics in several areas such as internal alignment, spotting opportunities for collaborative developments, managing cost-to-serve for company growth, and the creation of supply chains and supply chain managers of the future. We hope that this will provide input to the process of taking the lessons learned in this book off the page and putting them into practice to create improvements in tomorrow's supply chains.

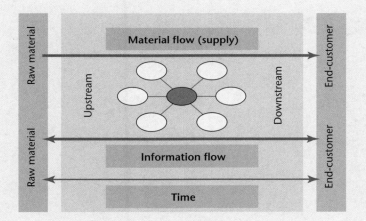

# CHAPTER 10

# Logistics future challenges and opportunities

**Objectives**

*The intended objectives of this chapter are to:*

- collect together four major changes that are impacting on supply chain strategies (the what);
- identify how management of the supply chains of the future will be affected by the advance of new structures and approaches to aligning the organisation, external partners and management development;
- list key issues in managing the transition towards future state supply chains (the how).

*By the end of this chapter, you should be able to understand:*

- key issues in four key areas that will affect the way supply chains of the future will be structured;
- improved ways in which supply chains may compete in the marketplace;
- ways of approaching implementation in four major change areas.

## Introduction

We are looking at an exciting future for logistics in general and logistics managers in particular. Everything you have learned in the book so far offers you crucial basics to travel on the journey towards supply chain management becoming a key enabler of a firm's competitive position. So the question becomes, what is it that we will be working on in the next few years as we strive to deliver on the promise of supply chain management? There is not one single answer to this question. If one thing should be clear from the cases and examples offered in this book so far, it is that there are multiple answers depending upon markets, company maturity and strategy. No two supply chains are alike, and companies often participate in multiple supply chains. Furthermore, there are multiple scenarios and initiative areas on which both practice and research focus. There is accordingly plenty of scope for progress, both in terms of basics and in the more innovative areas. The difference between 'satisfactory' focal firms and managers, and 'excellent' focal firms and managers will be in the degree of executing concepts such as those covered in this book and implementing them for real. In this chapter we both offer key areas where work is to be done even for the best companies as well as levers to develop for successful supply chain managers of the future. So we look both at the 'what' and the 'how' of supply chains of the future in this chapter.

Key issues This chapter addresses five key issues:

1 *Wrapping the chain around the heart of the focal firm,* **or, achieving internal alignment:** improving internal alignment (wrapping around) with key other parts of the internal organisation (the heart) to help the supply chain become front and centre and well positioned internally to be able to further integration externally.

2 Selectively *hooking up the chain,* **or, external improvement priorities:** picking upstream and downstream collaborative opportunities.

3 *Pulling the chain* **the right direction, or, cost-to-serve:** how do we manage full service costs (pull from the customer) for healthy (right direction), profitable growth?

4 The *critical link in the chain,* **or, supply chain managers of the future:** the major influences on creating supply chain managers of the future and the rapidly migrating talent profile needed for success.

5 *Changing chains*: practical lessons on how the massive changes needed to create the supply chain of the future can be managed and achieved.

## 10.1 Changing economics?

*Key issue:* **Supply chain integration assumes integration that does not come naturally to firms and managers.**

Supporting the concept of integrated logistics and supply chain management is the fundamental belief that when functions, regions and companies are closely aligned and work collaboratively, the customer will be served better. The reality of course is that these are big assumptions that are very hard to achieve in practice. Focal firms still have to report their financial results and set their strategies. Different functions in the supply chain have different priorities and internal challenges. Cultural differences between firms and countries still play a big role along the supply chain (Case study 4.5 refers to some of these).

Economically, supply chain integration has many benefits – for example, lower inventories and faster response times. Implementation may be less about changing economics and more about changing mindsets and behaviours. Godsell and van Hoek (2009) list five common practices that companies adopt for the benefit of sales or financial reporting that really hurt supply chain efforts. They are:

1 Pulling forward sales to hit a revenue target causing huge short-term surges in demand and related possible inventory shortages to be followed by a drop in demand and inventory build.

2 Reporting on time in full measures against delivery dates promised by the focal firm – not those requested by the customer. This creates the illusion of 'customer focus', while potentially being too late or too early from the *actual* customer's point of view.

3 Having an inventory policy that is applied generally across the product range to focus on the challenges of seasonal peaks and long lead times – when demand for some products in the range can be more accurately forecast (for example, T-shirts in Table 1.1).

4 Manipulating orders in favour of reporting ambitions – for example, stopping inventory build towards the end of a reporting period to improve the balance sheet, but ordering extra quantities after the period has ended. Quarterly financial reporting requirements in the US can encourage this behaviour.

5 Manipulating sales forecasts so that they will add up to the numbers promised by finance to the investor community and result in poor ordering policies.

In short the point is:

a Can we stop treating the supply chain like a concept or a philosophy and start working towards its operational benefits in meeting end-customer needs?

b Can we stop using the supply chain as a playground for the strategically poor who are seeking short term gains from other functional angles?

The major change is to prioritise internal alignment above making increasingly sophisticated demands on suppliers for JIT and JIS deliveries and modular construction (case study 8.3 illustrates this transition). This has everything to do with day-to-day working practices inside the company and between functions. Before we cover internal alignment, one more point needs to be made about changing economics and it has to do with sustainability, which we addressed in section 4.7.

There is a lot of talk these days about how sustainability means that focal firms have to change their ways of thinking and the economics they use in making decisions. While we agree that sustainability needs to be factored into decision making widely and generally as a consideration of importance (the Akzo Case study 4.8 refers) we do not believe this challenges existing economic frameworks such as the trade-off between lead time and transportation costs (for example, Figure 4.7). This trade-off implies that shorter lead times create higher transportation costs (for example, air freight), while lowering transportation costs (for example, container vessel) increase lead times. Increased fuel prices, or transportation costs due to factoring in more environmental considerations and costs, may lead to some longer lead times But while the curves in the trade-off model may change, the framework still applies.

This scenario became a reality when fuel prices increased rapidly in advance of the 2009 recession. Many firms were reconsidering global sourcing and shifting sourcing back locally to save on transportation costs. Essentially the equilibrium of the trade-off between lead time and transportation costs shifted with changes in fuel prices. But the framework was still valid. Also, when the costs of capital increased with the credit crisis prior to the 2009 recession, inventory holding became more expensive and as a result companies were reconsidering centralised inventories. But the model of centralisation of inventory to reduce inventory costs v longer transportation routes remained valid. In short, sustainability considerations might change the economic equilibrium but the basic economic trade-offs are still the same (van Hoek and Johnson, 2010).

## 10.2  Internal alignment

*Key issue*: **How do we align the internal organisation around supply chain opportunities, priorities and efforts?**

External integration between partners in a supply network is an important destination. But internal integration is the essential precursor to external integration, the case for which we outlined in section 8.1.1. Key functional domains that form parts of the supply chain or impact supply chain performance need to align around priorities, opportunities and approaches. The fact that this is often not the case impedes supply chain efforts and might be what stands between 'great plan' and 'great success'. As quoted in section 8.1.1, 'how can we integrate externally if we can't do it internally?'

Figure 10.1 shows a chart from van Hoek and Mitchell (2006) that demonstrates the challenge of internal alignment. This chart captures findings from an internal survey of a globally operating manufacturing company (and repeated in many other companies with similar results). The survey included existing supply chain priorities and initiatives. In a way it lists supply chain targets and supply chain efforts already underway; that is, the existing plan that the supply chain is

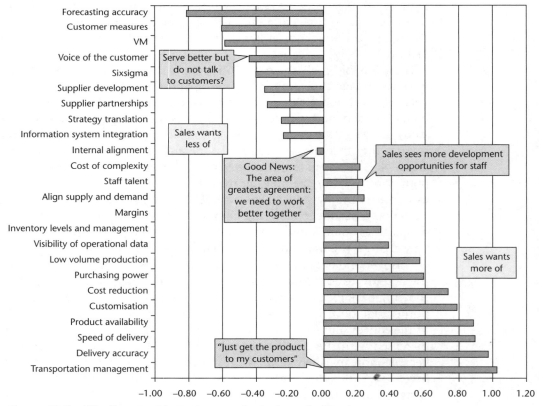

**Figure 10.1  Misalignment between supply chain and sales**

(Source: van Hoek and Mitchell, 2006)

operating against – and that is board-approved. The supply chain team and peers in other functions – in particular sales – were surveyed. They were asked for their opinion about the importance of these priorities and the current performance on them. The difference between importance and performance is considered to be an indication of the opportunity for improvement.

Figure 10.1 shows that, when contrasting opportunity scores of respondents from sales with respondents from the supply chain, important differences in opinion are found. When bars point to the right, sales sees a greater priority; when bars point to the left, the supply chain sees a greater priority. Taken together, the chart tells a shocking story of misalignment. Not least, when looking at the smallest bar in the centre of the graph, it appears that there is one and only one area where supply chain and sales more or less agree – the area of internal alignment. An interpretation of this is that the only thing we agree upon is that we do not agree on anything, and that we need to align better. Another obvious area of misalignment is that sales is asking for improved transportation management and delivery services. But sales is asking for less focus on the enablers of improved delivery service, such as forecasting accuracy. The chart reveals the painful challenge many supply chain managers face on a day-to-day basis: complaints about shipments and little support for its efforts at improvement that are critically dependent on support from other functions.

## CASE STUDY 10.1  Alfa Laval

When the senior supply chain executive team from Alfa Laval conducted an alignment analysis throughout the company, as exemplified in Figure 10.1, it realised there were a lot of basics to be improved. The team identified four areas where alignment improvement efforts could be focused: in interactions with peers from other functions; in interactions with their bosses and the board; in interactions with their teams; and in their own day-to-day behaviour. Some of the mechanisms and actions defined by the team are captured in Figure 10.2, which they termed their 'alignment compass'.

In this effort, two key areas received a lot of attention – improving communication and training in supply chain and operations, and improving the initiative planning process. Starting with the latter, it was surprising for the executive team to see that there was no appreciation from peers in other functions for some of the strategic initiatives under way in the supply chain. The team realised that this was going to make the journey through those efforts harder at least and impossible at worst. It was decided that improvements could be made in the initiative planning process by expanding pilots in cross-functional efforts in the supply chain already underway and that the planning process could be improved to capture the voice of the organisation up-front. Areas earmarked as valuable included initial discussions with key peers to ensure engagement, time and resource commitment, and the effective focusing of initiatives.

In the communication area it was realised that the case for supply chain initiatives was not clearly communicated to begin with, and that peers were not committed to the implementation journey. Specific communication tactics for improving this situation included:

- using training in other functions as a channel for communication;
- moving away from jargon and technical language;

▶

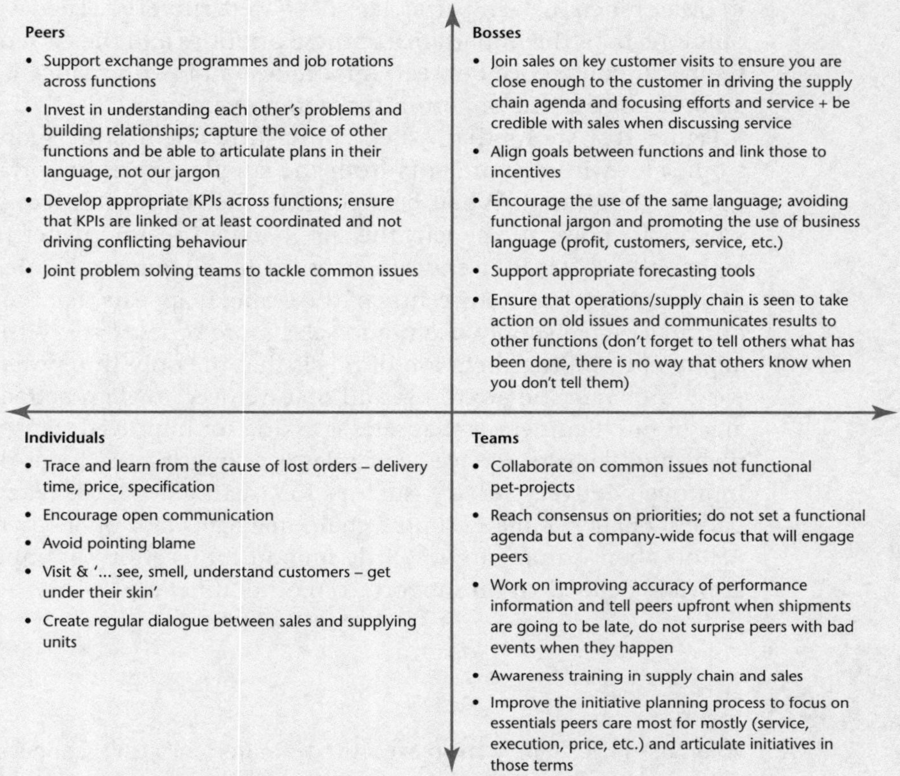

**Peers**

- Support exchange programmes and job rotations across functions
- Invest in understanding each other's problems and building relationships; capture the voice of other functions and be able to articulate plans in their language, not our jargon
- Develop appropriate KPIs across functions; ensure that KPIs are linked or at least coordinated and not driving conflicting behaviour
- Joint problem solving teams to tackle common issues

**Bosses**

- Join sales on key customer visits to ensure you are close enough to the customer in driving the supply chain agenda and focusing efforts and service + be credible with sales when discussing service
- Align goals between functions and link those to incentives
- Encourage the use of the same language; avoiding functional jargon and promoting the use of business language (profit, customers, service, etc.)
- Support appropriate forecasting tools
- Ensure that operations/supply chain is seen to take action on old issues and communicates results to other functions (don't forget to tell others what has been done, there is no way that others know when you don't tell them)

**Individuals**

- Trace and learn from the cause of lost orders – delivery time, price, specification
- Encourage open communication
- Avoid pointing blame
- Visit & '... see, smell, understand customers – get under their skin'
- Create regular dialogue between sales and supplying units

**Teams**

- Collaborate on common issues not functional pet-projects
- Reach consensus on priorities; do not set a functional agenda but a company-wide focus that will engage peers
- Work on improving accuracy of performance information and tell peers upfront when shipments are going to be late, do not surprise peers with bad events when they happen
- Awareness training in supply chain and sales
- Improve the initiative planning process to focus on essentials peers care most for mostly (service, execution, price, etc.) and articulate initiatives in those terms

**Figure 10.2    Alfa Laval's alignment compass**

- moving towards using shared business language that puts initiatives in terms of shared output objectives and in terms of benefits to priorities in other functions;
- communicating the case for initiatives from the start, and frequently updating peers on progress and, more importantly, results against shared output objectives.

It is important to note that these communication improvements are also intended to be personal in nature. These communication issues should not be left to an internal communications department. They need to be incorporated into the personal toolkit of supply chain managers in order to increase the likelihood of initiative success, effective cross-functional management, and, most importantly, their personal effectiveness. It was found that driving success in these areas will require some training, coaching and possible 'tag teaming' with peers – or even job rotation.

(Source: After van Hoek and Mitchell, 2006)

## Questions

1  Can you provide examples of how functional agendas might clash, leading to challenges in supply chain initiatives?

2  Can you suggest additional integrative mechanisms along the axes of the alignment compass?

In addition to improving internal alignment with sales, new product development is a key peer function that deserves internal alignment focus. It is often pointed out that the impact of the supply chain on new product development (NPD) and new product introduction is important in areas such as:

- shipping products to market fast enough (before product launch dates);
- ensuring sufficient inventory at the launch date; and
- ensuring a flow of parts and components for new product manufacturing.

Examples of how this presents itself in practice are provided by Nike and Reckitt Benckiser (van Hoek and Chapman, 2006). At Nike (see Case study 4.3) – as in most fashion companies – it is important to ensure that all key accounts have sufficient stock available at the start of each of the four seasons in a year when a rush for products begins. That means ensuring supply of several thousand skus from multiple suppliers globally, through the distribution channel to all customers on time simultaneously. Missing the launch date disappoints customers and affects overall product revenue. Equally, when a new blockbuster videogame is introduced in the market, one-third or more of the entire sales take place within the first 24 hours of the product becoming available, with people lining up in front of stores before a midnight release. Obviously in this example it is also crucial to ensure sufficient supply to stores in order to avoid lost sales, and disappointed customers and accounts. In conclusion, new product development and the supply chain is another key area where internal alignment must be targeted.

Like many companies, Reckitt Benckiser, a consumer products company, found forecasts for new products to be one area where misalignment between supply chain and NPD was particularly costly and challenging. A major challenge with new products is that there is less historical reference data to use as a base number for forecasting and there are more uncertainties to contend with around such important issues as an exact launch date, and supply volumes. Misalignment was found to be costly because poor forecasts led to limited product availability, disappointed customers and lots of firefighting and last-minute fixes. Several reasons were found for the underperformance of the forecasting process. These included tendencies to average out forecasts when functions do not agree, delayed response due to lack of group consensus, and even forecasts that become available late as a result of forecasting being given a low priority for too long.

In order to address these shortcomings and contribute to supply chain readiness, Reckitt Benckiser created a new role in the supply chain team – a new product introduction forecasting manager. This manager is dedicated to working with functions involved in the NPD process specifically to drive alignment around the forecast. The manager flags forecasting differences between functions, and spots possible challenges in assumptions and works across functions to arrive at a more accurate forecast. Next, the forecasting manager supports the translation of the forecast into a supply chain capacity plan, and forms a natural spotlight in the organisation for avoiding bottlenecks.

With supply chain readiness for NPD improved and with fewer execution issues and firefighting the supply chain team has manoeuvred itself into a better position. It is less likely to be distracted by last-minute crises and more likely to be considered a useful member of the NPD team that can make valuable contributions based upon the capability it has to offer.

---

**Activity 10.1**

Assume for a moment that you are a supply chain manager invited into a new product development team meeting. What questions would you ask of the team to ensure you can prepare your supply chain for effective product launch?

---

## 10.3 Selecting collaborative opportunities upstream and downstream

*Key issue:* **Where and how to place bets on collaborative opportunities upstream and downstream in the supply chain.**

Once a company has its internal organisation more aligned around supply chain opportunities, priorities and initiatives, it is in a better position to select external collaborative opportunities. In some respects, this is like placing bets – but not like playing roulette, if managed carefully! There are new developments pertaining to selecting opportunities downstream (with customers) and upstream (with suppliers and partners). Specifically, the notion of being selective is key. Some argue that the term 'partnership' is one of the most inflated terms in modern business and it is well known that you can only truly partner with a few. So where should we focus upstream and downstream in the supply chain for maximum benefit?

### Selecting upstream collaboration opportunities

Beyond sourcing parts and services needed to make and deliver products and service for customers, firms are increasingly looking at collaboration opportunities in new product development and R&D. Of course companies can only do this really effectively when they are aligned internally first (see section 10.1 above). Procter & Gamble has a stated objective to move towards having 50 per cent or more of its innovation from external partners, and has launched a programme called 'Connect + Develop' to enable this (see Figures 10.3 and 10.4). The company has tackled this diligently:

- The programme has CEO-level support and public endorsement making it crystal clear that this is not just a supply chain initiative or playground but that this is mission critical for the company.
- They have established a dedicated organisation with senior leadership, programme management, deal makers, business developers and engineers.
- They have developed a 'needs list' containing technologies in which the company is interested. This helps to focus the search for innovation, and serves as a screening tool for assessing collaborative opportunities. Note also that this

means the company is publicly and on record sharing areas where it could use help. This is completely counter to old procurement practices of playing divide and rule with information.

- Account managers will steward partner innovations into the organisation and throughout a structured and well-defined process.
- P&G can structure partnerships in multiple forms depending on the type of innovation and application.

Figure 10.3 shows the P&G 'Connect + Develop' philosophy, and Figure 10.4 illustrates examples of 'Connect + Develop' efforts.

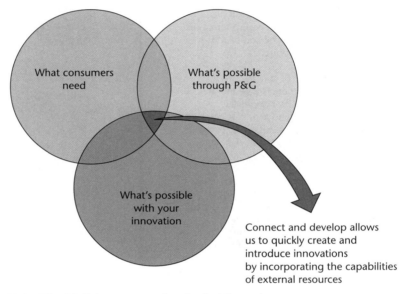

**Figure 10.3    The P&G 'connect + develop' philosophy**
(Source: Procter & Gamble Connect + Develop programme)

## Selecting downstream opportunities: which customers to give the keys to our car

Partnering with customers can be a much scarier notion than partnering upstream. It implies sharing a lot of inside information with customers and talking openly about what a company *cannot* do. Traditionally, this is not how companies (and sales staff) sell. When making the mind-shift, however, there is a lot of potential on the table. Specifically, some companies are initiating customer collaboration efforts that involve working to resolve supply chain problems jointly with customers to serve the end-consumer better. Among the areas where fruitful collaboration opportunities have been found are several process integration areas, including:

- linking supplier delivery to customer warehousing and materials handling processes;
- linking supplier to customer forecasting;
- linking customer ordering to supplier delivery planning systems.

### Connect + Develop successes

Consumers around the world have already realised the benefits of P&G's Connect + Develop strategy. The following products and technologies are examples of the mutually beneficial collaborations we have established through external connections.

### Ready-to-go technologies

P&G introduced Bounce, the world's first dryer-added softener, after acquiring the product technology from the independent inventor who developed the innovative fabric-care solution.

### Ready-to-go products

By acquiring the newly introduced SpinBrush, P&G was able to bring a superior oral care brand to market quickly, without undertaking the time and expense of developing an entirely new product.

### Ready-to-go packaging

Several of our Olay Skin Care products now utilise new consumer-preferred pump dispenser originally developed by a European packaging products company. P&G led a collaborative improvement process to make the original pumps more effective prior to their launch in Olay's North American markets.

### Commercial partnerships

P&G found the perfect complement to the Swiffer brand in a hand-held duster developed by a Japanese competitor. After purchasing the product, P&G leveraged elements of existing manufacturing processes and advertising components to launch Swiffer Duster within 18 months.

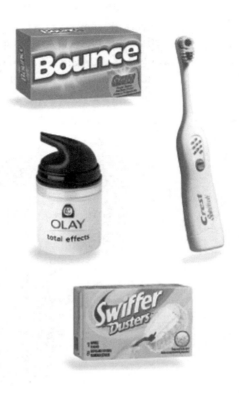

**Figure 10.4   Examples of 'Connect + Develop'**
(Source: Procter & Gamble Connect + Develop programme)

Additionally, a focus on serving the end-consumer better implies collaborative opportunities such as:

- supplier suggestions for campaigns and merchandising;
- joint product and packaging design;
- joint product mix development to improve inventory turns on the retailer's shelf.

An example of the latter would be for a consumer product company to suggest replacing certain of its own products on a retailer's shelf with others, and suggesting improved store and shelf planograms. Essentially, these collaborations centre around a supplier actively (re-)designing part of the customer's operation and adjusting its own systems accordingly. These efforts can come at an investment premium and involve market risks. Hence it is important to select wisely which customer relationships to engage with in these collaborative efforts. One global manufacturer uses a set of screens to evaluate customer relations in terms of collaboration opportunities. Counter to common wisdom, they do not look so much at the size of the customer account but rather at the nature of the customer's business and their relationship. The company may select smaller customers for investment in collaboration for reasons such as: it could be one of the rising stars in the industry worth investing in now, or it might be a particularly innovative customer investment which could have a much broader spin-off. The characteristics the company uses to evaluate customer relationships are not so much financial or sales-oriented, but focus on 'soft' factors (see section 1.3.3) such as openness to innovative suggestions and willingness to experiment. The company found that its efforts to evaluate customer relationships before offering up collaborative options helped in prioritising projects for greater returns and greater opportunities for success.

## Activity 10.2

1 What are the main risks involved in collaborating with customers? Consider industrial as well as consumer sectors by referring to Table 2.2.
2 Why are internal stewardship and process ownership necessary for collaborations?

## 10.4 Managing with cost-to-serve to support growth and profitability

*Key issue:* How do we leverage full service costs management for growth and profit?

Assessing the *cost-to-serve* uses ABC methodology to quantify the actual costs involved in fulfilling customer orders (see section 3.3.3). Despite all the progress in the last few years on moving from functional organisations to process and supply chain organisations, most firms today are still focused on managing efficient supply of products against customer demand. Cost rationalisation efforts centre on using global sourcing and purchasing to reduce material costs. As a result, supply chain cost reduction has been executed in isolation of customer value and revenue generation. The undesirable outcome is to rationalise service to the most valuable customers. This has been brought about by lack of a clear sense of customer relationship investment opportunities, and by the inability to have a constructive discussion with sales and customer service about what services are valuable for which customers, and what services do not contribute. Figure 10.5 shows how costs and revenue have been moving in opposing directions. Customer profitability analysis helps dispose of that shortcoming, as it assesses focal firms' ability to profitably fulfil individual customer orders, and to serve individual customer accounts and distribution channels with current supply chain design and customer service systems. Essentially, this analysis changes the economic starting point from internal costs to working from customer orders upstream.

Figure 3.11 showed how customer profitability analysis can reveal how the profits are generated by 50 per cent of the customer base, and how the other 50 per cent of customers are currently unprofitable. This finding assumes that most traditional accounting systems are very accurate in tracking cost of goods sold (*source* and *make* costs) but underperform in tracking logistics costs to individual customers (*deliver* costs). Once shipment, service and customisation costs are added on a 'per customer' basis, a different profitability curve emerges.

Cost and revenue spinning in opposite directions ...

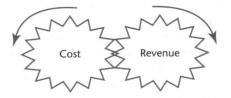

... lead to an unfavourable profit distribution

Figure 10.5   **The dynamics of customer profitability**

This analysis has several implications, including:

- service terms and conditions for unprofitable accounts need to be changed, and converted into profitable alternatives;
- the most important customers need more attention, by focusing more customer service efforts on these customers;
- prices should be increased for unprofitable customers, or they should be gradually removed from the focal firm's sales portfolio altogether.

Most importantly, customer profitability analysis enables focal firms to link supply chain efforts to customer value and market opportunity in a way that improves customer relations and revenues in a profitable manner.

The concept of cost-to-serve shows that outbound logistics contribute significantly to profitability. Cost-to-serve also enables a firm to home in on the best growth opportunities, which would otherwise be difficult to identify. While it also focuses internal and external alignment opportunities, now we are aligning the entire supply chain around customer service opportunities that are not just doable but also have the greatest impact on profitability and competitiveness.

Rationalising a product mix is a good area of application, as shown in Case study 10.2 below.

| CASE STUDY 10.2 | **Clorox supports growth by cutting skus** |

Companies want to grow, and one of their commonest strategies is to create new products. These may increase revenues, but of course they do not guarantee profits. In fact, product proliferation often reduces margins. One company we studied found that the bottom 40 per cent of its products generated less than 3 per cent of revenue, and the bottom 25 per cent of its products were highly unprofitable.

Several years ago, Clorox, a $4 billion consumer products company, realised it needed to address the problem of underperforming products. At the time, 30 per cent of the company's stock keeping units (skus) were falling short of sales volume and profit targets. Clorox responded by developing a formal process for evaluating sku performance and making decisions about which products to cut.

As part of the annual business planning process, annual reduction goals are established for underperforming skus, as well as a 'glidepath' (specific goals by month) and specific action items for reaching the reduction goal. Specific action items may include discontinuance, substitution or increasing distribution. A cross-functional sku management process team, sponsored by the CFO and led by the director of supply chain planning, meets monthly to track progress, spotlight businesses that are off-target, discuss process improvements and resolve policy issues. The team includes director- or VP-level representatives from sales, marketing, finance and product supply.

This team uses a 'dashboard' (selected key measures of performance) to evaluate the performance of skus against annual sales volume and profit goals (or hurdles). The dashboard also rates the performance of each business according to the proportion of skus that meet hurdles. Businesses are graded green if they are exceeding goals; yellow if they are within 5 per cent of target and red if they are more than 5 per cent from target. 'Red' businesses are required to specify tactics to bring their proportion of products meeting hurdle rates in line with goals. The executive teams of 'red' businesses typically must identify underperforming skus that will be eliminated, and specify the strategy for eliminating them.

Like any business tactic, product rationalisation must be used cautiously. Many companies have tried to tackle this issue by ruthlessly cutting the product portfolio. The risk, though, is that a company cuts too deeply into its revenue streams and finds it has discontinued products that key customers care for, damaging important customer relationships. Clorox frequently reviews product lines with customers to optimise the product mix on the shelf.

Today, more than 90 per cent of Clorox's skus meet volume and profit hurdles, up from 70 per cent four years ago. Retail sales per sku have grown by more than 25 per cent, the return on products has increased and retail customer service levels have improved. Clorox now leads its peers in retail sales per sku in the majority of its categories.

(Source: Based on van Hoek and Pegels, 2006)

*Questions*

1  What reasons for and against product proliferations might different functions use?

2  What reasons need to be considered for discontinuing and continuing skus?

## 10.5  The supply chain manager of the future

*Key issue:* **What are the changing needs and requirements that apply to the most effective supply chain managers?**

Ultimately, the purpose of this book is to support the development of effective supply chain managers. This is arguably the most important job to begin with. In that respect it should be noted that today's and tomorrow's supply chain managers look very different from the supply chain staff of the recent past. There are several key capabilities that will make or break supply chain managers of the near future:

- These managers need to be effective at interfacing with customers. This is new because in the past supply chain staff used to be almost completely internally and operationally focused. Sales monopolised the customer, leaving supply chain managers short of 'supply chain relevant' customer insight.

- Functional knowledge is a base requirement (this used to be a differentiator, now it is a qualifier).

- They need to have strong interpersonal skills (van Hoek *et al.*, 2002) Supply chain staff used to be technical and operational in background and training. They were heavily focused internally, without the ability to align peers around efforts and priorities, and unable to engage business people in their efforts.

- They need to have general management and strategic management capabilities and skills. Hence, they should no longer be solely operationally focused and boxed in, which makes them unable to integrate and be seen as contributing to corporate strategic goals.

- They need to be able to develop and foster relationships internally and externally (as opposed to being focused only on running an operation).

- They need to be able to translate supply chain efforts and jargon into business language that their peers can respond to and relate to their own day-to-day efforts.

- They need to have a service ethic that does not include always saying 'yes'. Traditionally, supply chain people have either been very good at saying 'no' to special requests, or saying 'yes' all the time. They therefore need to manage trade-offs in operations, while finding creative ways to serve the customer and becoming an essential part of the business organisation (chain wrapped around the heart) and being considered key business partners.

- They need to be 'business people' that help build and grow the business and use supply chain as a tool not the purpose in doing so, so creativity, innovative approaches to business problems and entrepreneurial approaches to leveraging supply chain capabilities and practices to the benefit of the customer are key.

This will help supply chain managers avoid traditional pitfalls such as:

- being unable to align the organisation around supply chain opportunities;
- lacking crucial *voice of the customer* (VoC) insights to achieve success with final customers (VoC processes aim to go beyond customer satisfaction measurement by crafting a more comprehensive, cross-functional exchange with selected customers – for example, Delgado-Hernandez *et al.*, 2007);
- being only operationally focused, with limited insight into strategic business goals;
- taking initiatives in an effort to help peers, but not succeeding due to the points listed above;
- being great at supply chain concepts, but weak at solving customer problems and becoming a partner that is mission critical for the focal firm.

## Activity 10.3

1 Consider what personal development courses are key for a supply chain student to follow, in addition to supply chain programmes.
2 Find an example of a recent supply chain job advertisement at a management level, critique it for competency requirements and propose how it might be modified to fit the future challenges in the area.

Finally, we have a few pointers for the supply chain managers of the future:

- Traditional logistics people are often seen as being best at saying 'no', often because of initiative overload. Avoid saying 'no' for technical reasons, but ask about the business need that a request serves.

- One way to select what initiatives to support is to avoid being caught out by those without clear business and cross-functional involvement, ownership, sponsorship and goal sharing.

- Do not rely on technology as a 'be all and end all'. Most of the tough supply chain challenges can at best be supported by technology, but they mostly involve people and processes – and management of change skills.

- Traditional supply chain people often spend a lot of time taking calls about problems, fighting fires and being the hero of the day. But this can distract from working on structural solutions that will prevent those problem calls from happening to begin with. So stop fixing things and start solving problems.

- Traditional logistics people were born and raised in areas of functional expertise and have built their careers around those skills. This leads to communication and business alignment issues. Supply chain management is a cross-functional job. So stop being a functional expert and start being a business general manager.

- Think growth, not just cost containment. The supply chain is often called on first to deliver savings and operational synergies – most often in tough times and during mergers. While the supply chain has a key role to play here, an emphasis on cost containment underestimates the contribution of the supply chain to growth, and keeps it in a negative box – insulated from the happy times during periods of growth!

- Put the end-customer first – as ally and ultimately as judge.

## 10.6 Changing chains

*Key issue:* How do we actually make the transition to supply chain effectiveness happen?

Based upon the experiences of having worked with and for many companies and the detailed study of companies in different industries, countries, stages of development and parts of the supply (details in van Hoek *et al.,* 2010) it appears that there are some big lessons about changing supply chains that are being learned today. Most textbooks and research on supply chains pay too much attention to the technical aspects of management, leaving change management largely uncovered and unstudied. We have found that there are some clear pointers in making change happen in a supply chain. While this list is not exhaustive, we intend it to be informative and useful.

Focal firms that make change happen in supply chains over and over again experience the following:

1 *Prepare for the (longer) run*: major supply chain change efforts tend to take longer than initially planned and longer than might be anticipated up-front. And there are typically no short cuts to true implementation of the plan (no matter what consultants and vendors might say).

2 *Plan to re-plan*: most major supply chain change efforts end up being executed differently than initially planned and the change programmes are often revised along the way in order to be able to respond to changed circumstances or additional change issues found along the change journey.

3 *A voyage of discovery*: there is real learning as you go along. As change programmes evolve and progress, managers learn about new changes and behavioural challenges – and how to incorporate them into the change programme.

4 *The boardroom pitch is only the start of the test*: after pitching successfully to senior management and gaining their buy-in, middle management and staff across the organisation need to be engaged in the effort to give the programme a chance for real implementation. Additionally, given the learning that needs to happen along the way and the extended time period, real reconfiguration and implementation changes require (senior) management commitment which needs to be earned repeatedly. So, in short, boardroom support helps launch the change but is not merely sufficient when it comes to making the change actually happen.

5 *Integrative but not integral*: change programmes in supply chains often focus on different parts of the supply chain. While they all require integrative actions to ensure business alignment and cross-functional peer support they often do not address the whole supply chain. Often it might be one part of the supply chain taking the lead; logistics or procurement, for example, and that is fine, the supply chain is big and comprehensive enough for many strides forward, some even simultaneous.

6 *Internal customers are a proxy for end-customers*: customer service first is key in all good supply chain efforts but not all parts of the supply chain have direct access to the customer, let alone the end-customer. For those, often more upstream, segments of the supply chain, internal customers might be focused on as a proxy for end-customers. Just like external integration requires internal alignment as a basis, focusing on internal service is a good foundation for external service capability, good service ethic also runs everywhere in your blood, not just when in front of a customer.

7 *Inside first*: many supply chain reconfigurations start internally to the company before they impact other segments of the supply chain externally, following the lessons on internal alignment.

8 *IT integration*: this was also a hot topic in the early 1990s but it appears to still be hard to achieve and is not easily enabled but rather a source of a lot of work. It is important to keep that in mind, and not to assume that technology makes it easy to change broken processes. Technology cannot change broken process or poor alignment without the hard managerial change work to support it.

9  *Benchmarks and best practices open eyes and help change programmes to stay on track*: external benchmarks are useful to set direction, make the case for change and audit progress on the change journey using externally verifiable standards.

10  *Cross-functionality*: is key to engaging relevant stakeholders in the supply chain, although not all functions and businesses need to engage. Rather than full supply chain integration, the concept of selective integration is key and specific to company and context. This also helps make change management more focused and perhaps doable.

11  *Consistent cross-functionality*: is a key characteristic of supply chain reconfiguration. Together with the complexity of the change process we suggest this is a marker of effective supply chain change management.

12  *Training and communication*: these are well-known levers. Training staff and management are key enablers of change effectiveness and readiness. Communications – to remind and reinforce across the organisation – are useful tactics as long as they are updated with the change journey adjustments and learnings during the change journey.

## Summary

*What does the supply chain of the future look like?*

- The chain is wrapped around the heart, or, the ability to align the organisation internally around supply chain opportunities, priorities and efforts in order to avoid partial, ineffective or failed supply chain improvement efforts.
- Hook on the chain, or, the capability to spot and select the limited number of collaborative opportunities upstream with partners and suppliers, and downstream with customers.
- Pulling the chain, or, the capability to map true and complete cost to fulfil customer orders and to manage services and costs for increased profitable growth.
- Critical link in the chain, or, the development of a 'new breed' of supply chain managers that will help realise all of the above.
- Changing chains, or, the capability to make the change actually happen for real.

We hope the readers of this book will have picked up insights and lessons that they can use on their journey to create supply chains of the future. In our experience of working for many different companies in different industries and countries, and based upon our research from across the past decade we are convinced about one thing: most of the progress in supply chain management is still 'up for grabs'. Both at the basic and more advanced levels, most focal firms still have only started on the journey of opportunity and possibility. Actually making the change happen will be the characteristic that sets leaders apart in our field. We wish readers the best in making change happen, and in working for a better supply chain of the future.

## Discussion questions

1  We started out in Chapter 1 by defining supply chain management as 'Planning and controlling all of the business processes that link together partners in a supply chain in order to serve the needs of the end-customer'. How will leading-edge developments covered in this chapter contribute to this vision?

2  Suggest how the five change areas discussed in this chapter apply to our model of the supply network (Figure 1.2) and to the integration of demand and supply shown in Figure 1.7.

## References

Delgado-Hernandez, D., Benites-Thomas, A. and Aspinwall, E. (2007) 'New product development studies in the UK', *International Journal of Product Development*, Vol. 4, No. 5, pp. 413–29.

Godsell, J. and van Hoek, R. (2009) 'Fudging the supply chain to hit the number: five common practices that sacrifice the supply chain and what financial analysts should ask about them', *Supply Chain Management, An International Journal*, Vol. 14, No. 3, pp. 171–6.

van Hoek, R. and Chapman, P. (2006) 'From tinkering around the edge to enhancing revenue growth: supply chain – new product development alignment', *Supply Chain Management, An International Journal*, Vol. 11, No. 5, pp. 385–9.

van Hoek, R.I., Chatham, R. and Wilding, R.D. (2002), 'People in supply chains: the critical dimension', *Supply Chain Management, An International Journal*, Vol. 7, No. 3, pp. 119–25.

van Hoek, R. and Johnson, M. (2010) 'Sustainability and energy efficiency', *International Journal of Physical Distribution & Logistics Management*, Vol. 40, Nos. 1–2. pp. 148–58.

van Hoek, R., Johnson, M., Godsell, J. and Birtwistle, A. (2010) 'Changing chains. Three case studies of the change management needed to reconfigure European supply chains', *International Journal of Logistics Management*, Vol. 21, No. 2 (to come).

van Hoek, R. and Mitchell, A. (2006) 'Why supply chain efforts fail; the crisis of misalignment', *International Journal of Logistics, Research and Applications*, Vol. 9, No. 3, pp. 269–81.

van Hoek, R. and Pegels, K. (2006) 'Growing by cutting sku's at Clorox', *Harvard Business Review*, April, p. 23.

### Suggested further reading

*2016: The future value chain*, Global Commerce Initiative, Capgemini, Intel.

Harrison, A. and White, A. (2006) *Intelligent distribution and logistics, IEE Proceedings of Intelligent Transportation Systems*, Vol. 153, No. 2, pp. 167–80.

# Index

Accenture 268
accommodate strategy 29
account plans 308
activity times 92
activity-based costing 89–95, 102, 343
   cost-time profile 92–4
   cost-to-serve 94–5
   maintenance costs, allocation of 91
adaptation 255–6
after sales 57
agile supply chain 21–3, 236–49
   boundary spanning sales and operations
      planning process 248–9
   classification of operating environments 241
   complexity costs reduction 243–5
   cost of complexity sanity check 242–3
   customer service and market sensitivity 246
   enterprise-level reality check 242
   forecasting 245–6
   lean and agile supply characteristics 237
   supply capabilities 238–41
   virtual integration improvement 247
   Xerox: segmenting supply chain 239–41
air miles 117
Airbus A380 113–14
Akzo 149, 335
Alcoa 248
Alfa Laval 337–8
alignment 31, 305–8
   internal 335, 336–40
Amazon.com 37
annual costs 195
apparel industry 136–9, 262–4
appraisal cost driver 88
arm's length relationships 255, 264, 288
assemble to order 165, 188
assembler collects *ex-works* 265–6
asset:
   efficiency 100
   footprint 245
Atlanta Agreement 146
attitude (customer loyalty) 51
Australia 23
authority 133
AutoCo 58, 62, 64
automation 178, 179
automotive supply chains 265–70, 292

Bacalao (dried fish) 64–8
back to school surge 39
balanced measurement portfolio 95–100
   balanced measures 96–7

supply chain financial model 99–100
supply chain management and balanced
      scorecard 97–9
batching rules 202
behaviour (customer loyalty) 51
benchmarking 103, 276, 349
Benchmarking Partners 210
Benetton 208
best alternative use 74
best before dates 199
best in class 103
best practices 349
BhS 290
Binhai New Area 281–4
BMW 25–6, 62, 176, 266, 269
boardroom value markers 326–7
BOM 201
Bond SA – marginal costing 84
Boots the Chemist 40
Bose Corporation 259–60
bottleneck items 317, 318
boundary spanning sales and operations
      planning process 248–9
break points, multiple 125–6
break-even point 81–2, 84
break-even time 158, 159
bricks and mortar model 37
Bruntland report 23
buffer capacity 62, 63
buffer stock 194, 199, 212
bullwhip effect 186, 202, 203
business customers 36
business to business (B2B) 37, 38, 50, 247, 316, 326
   electronic 260–1
business to customer (B2C) 37–8, 50
buying behaviour 59

call-off quantity 20
call-off requirements 291
Calsonic Kansei 270
capability, full 224
capacity planning 291
cash:
   and debtors 76
   generation 100
   to cash cycle 78
catalogues 326
category:
   management 205
   strategy 309
cause-and-effect diagram 175
change, understanding necessity for 179–80

changeover cost per unit 194–5
changeover, rapid 235
chaos 203
child labour elimination in Sialkot soccer ball
        industry (Pakistan) 146–7
Chinese industrial areas 280–4
Christmas surge 39–40
Chrysler 144
Cisco Systems value recovery programme 142–3
classical strategy 29
CleanCo 44–5, 58, 59
cleanliness 226
Clorox 344–5
Coca-Cola 111–12
Cofely 308
collaboration 286, 288, 340–3
    electronic 291
collaborative planning, forecasting
        and replenishment 210–14
commercial partnerships 342
commitment 288
commodities 319
communication skills 327, 337–8, 349
competing through logistics 16–27
    hard objectives 17–19
    soft objectives 25–6
    see also supportive capabilities
competitive environment 104
competitive moves 113
competitive profile 60, 62
completeness 57
complexity 155–6
    costs reduction 243–5
    costs sanity check 242–3
compression and lead time 178
compromise strategy 64
concentration of firms at specific sites 117–18
condominium approach 267
confidence 25
'Connect and Develop' examples 342
consolidation:
    global 116–18
    multiple 125–6
consultative skills 328
Continental Tyres 144
continuity 31
continuous replenishment in apparel industry 262–4
contractual terms 94
contribution 81–2, 84
control and lead time 178
control process 7
cooperation 288
coordination 49, 178, 179, 257, 291, 306
    global 130
coordination in retail supply chains 203–18
    collaborative planning, forecasting
        and replenishment 210–14
    efficient consumer response 204–9
    quick response 217–18
    vendor-managed inventory 214–16

core competencies 137
Corporate Social Responsibility 23, 145–9
correctness 57
corruption 186
cost 16, 31, 76
    advantage 18–19
    options, multiple 126
    of placing an order 86, 196
    rationalisation 343–4
    reduction 98, 154–5, 159–61
    -time profile 92–4
    -to-serve 94–5, 343–5
    see also activity-based costing
countermeasures 21
creativity and solution orientation 327
creditors 77
cross-functionality 349
cultural differences 334
currency fluctuations 126–8
customer 37, 96
    of choice status 324–6
    demands for better service 227–8
    expectations 37
    facing teams 58–9
    intimacy 53
    loyalty 51–2
    needs, increased responsiveness to 157
    order decoupling point 166, 176, 188
    profitability curve 95
    relationship management 53–6
    requirements 227
    satisfaction 51–2
    service and market sensitivity 246
    value analysis 60
    value profiles 62
    see also end-customers
customisation 60, 63, 64, 73
cycle stock 198

D-time (demand time) 60, 164–8, 181, 183, 188,
        192, 238
data:
    collection 170
    sharing 216
Dawnfresh 117
debtors 76
decoupling point 192
defect rates, internal 98
defects 225, 229
delay 57, 224–5
delivery:
    accuracy 122
    costs 343
    frequency 57, 94
    process 102
Dell 165, 176, 238
Della Valle Group 278
Delphi 265
demand 11
    actual 20–1, 195

amplification 215
average 197
base 31, 48
chain 15
dependent 188, 193
forecasts 202
independent 188, 193, 196, 201
management 188
peaks and troughs 62
profile 46–9, 60
-pull system 39
schedule 20–1
and supply chains, integration of 15
surge 31
total 48
trend 48
unknown 238
variable 197
dependability advantage 19, 21
design for logistics 238
development costs reduction 160
differential advantage 41
direct costs 80, 85–7
direct product profitability 84–7
disaggregation 49
discounting 59
discretionary costs 80, 87–9, 103
distress purchases 30
distribution 6
    centres, changing role of 132
    channels 94
    of shipment cycles times in days 161
domestic and international logistics pipelines,
        comparison of 126
downstream organisations 236, 257, 272, 285,
        292, 341–3
    end-customers 36, 58
    supply chain 6, 9, 10, 11, 14
drivers of internationalisation 111–19
    Airbus A380 113–14
    dimensions of strategies 113
    fourth generation global shift in Europe 112
    global consolidation 116–18
    handling 115
    inventory 114
    risk 119
    time-to-market 115
    transport 115
drivers, measurement of 60–3
drivers of procurement value 302–14
    business alignment 305–8
    Procurement Intelligence Unit survey 304
    purchasing performance score 306
    strategic sourcing at Heineken 306–7
    strategies for procurement categories 309–10
    supplier relationship management 312–14
    time allocation 303
    total cost of ownership 310–12, 313
    'waterfall' of revenue, purchasing spend
        and profit 303

e-auction technology 326
e-business 260–1
e-information 57
e-procurement 301, 326
e-sourcing process support software 326
'economic' batch sizes 193–6
'economic' order sizes 193–6, 197
economic values 24
EDF (France) 26
efficient consumer response 76, 204–9
Electro-Coatings Ltd 172–6
electronic data interchange 5, 200, 206, 215, 217,
        260, 301, 326
electronic point of sale 5, 40, 210, 262, 263
electronic product code 207
enabling technologies 205, 206, 217–18
end-customers 35–70
    demand profiling 46–9
    marketing perspective 36–8
    quality of service 50–6
    see also priorities setting; quality of service;
        segmentation
endorsements 199
engineered costs 80, 87–9, 103
engineered to order 166, 176
engineering instructions 167
enquiry processing 167
enterprise resource planning 186, 193, 263, 279,
        301, 321, 326
enterprise-level reality check 242
entrepreneurial focus 327
Environmental Protection Agency 23
environmental values 23
Ericsson 22
events management and promotions in retail
        sector 39–40
Everglo Battery 54–6
evolve strategy 28
executive ownership of supply
        relationships 322–4
exponential smoothing 189
external metrics 104

failure driver, internal and external 88
fair trade products 147, 148
Fairtrade Foundation 23
fashion industry 199
    see also apparel industry
fast-moving consumer goods
        sector 38, 43
field sales 44
Filmco 86–7
financial bonds 53
financial flexibility 98
financial incentives 53
financial ratios 77–9
finished product inventory 187
fixed assets 77
fixed costs 77, 80, 81–4
flexibility 22, 57, 98

flow 225–6
  charts 170
  information 6, 11, 15
  material 6, 11, 12–14
  value 233
focal firm 9–10, 60, 102, 123, 155, 334
  supply chain integration 258, 264
  supply chain planning and control 185,
    188, 193
focus 29, 132, 133
focused factories: from geographical to product
    segmentation 120–1
Food and Drug Administration 47
Ford 10, 62, 230–2, 266
forecast/forecasting 46–7, 158–9, 245–6, 248–9
  demand 49, 188–9, 202
  error 31, 60
  projective 47, 200
form postponement 238
fourth party logistics 238
freight modes, multiple 126
funds flow 73
future challenges and opportunities 333–50
  Alfa Laval 337–8
  changing economics 334–5
  Clorox 344–5
  cost-to-serve 343–5
  downstream collaboration opportunities 341–3
  internal alignment 336–40
  supply chain effectiveness 347–9
  supply chain management 345–7
  upstream collaboration opportunities 340–1

Gantt chart technique 171
General Electric 246
General Motors 143
geopolitical threats 119
global consolidation 116–18
global coordination and local operation
    maxim 130
global sourcing arrangements 144
Glup SA 88–9
governance 256
government 96
gross requirement 191–2
growth functions 47

handling 115
hard objectives 17–19, 221
  see also cost; quality; time
harmfulness 57
heijunka (leveled scheduling) 285
Heineken 156, 243, 306–7
Henkel 144–5
heritage in market 133
Hewlett-Packard 130–1, 144, 147, 247
historical analogy 47
housekeeping 226
human rights 148

IBM 36
Ikea 51
impulse shoppers 39
in full 19
in-store availability, improved 88–9
inbound logistics 10, 265–70
inbound strategies 67
indirect costs 80, 85–7
individual plants/factories, evolving role of 131–2
industrial marketing 42
information flow 6, 11, 15
information revolution 37–8
information security 148
information sharing 261–4
information technology 217–18, 348
initiative planning process 337
initiatives, time-based 156
inputs 12
inside out 236
integration 10, 178, 301
  contract manufacturing 238
  external 336
  high 258
  improvement, virtual 247
  internal 336
  and lead time 178–9
  processes 284–5
  vertical 136, 264
  see also supply chain integration
inter-firm planning and control 201–3
internal logistics 10, 13
International Labour Organisation 146
internationalisation 109–51
  Akzo 149
  Asian facilities, location of 128
  child labour elimination in Sialkot soccer ball
    industry (Pakistan) 146–7
  Cisco Systems value recovery programme 142–3
  consolidation and break points, multiple 125–6
  corporate social responsibility in the supply
    chain 145–9
  distribution centres, changing role of 132
  domestic and international logistics pipelines
    118, 126
  focused factories: from geographical to product
    segmentation 120–1
  freight modes and cost options, multiple 126
  individual plants, evolving role of 131–2
  inventories, centralised 121–4
  layering and tiering 130–1
  lead time of supply, extended 125
  location analysis 128–30
  price and currency fluctuations 126–8
  reverse logistics 141–3
  risk readiness 143–5
  trade-off between cost and time for shipping 127
  transit times 125
  Wal-Mart sustainability programme 149
  see also drivers; reconfiguration processes

internet technology 260
    *see also* e-entries
inventory 76, 114, 192, 224–5, 226
    /availability 57
    average turnover 78
    carrying cost 194–5
    centralised 121–4
    -holding costs 115
    management 193–8
    policies to reflect volatility levels 143–4
    profile 13–14, 292
    vendor-managed 185–6, 214–16, 285
    waste, unnecessary 229
investment 74–5, 216
    *see also* return on investment
invoice price 86
ISO 9000 168
ISO 14001 23
Italian districts 278–80

*jidoka* 230–1
JP Morgan Chase Vastera 73–4
judgemental methods 47
just-in-sequence 269–70
just-in-time 13, 14, 161, 166–7, 190, 195–6,
        269, 291
    JIT2 concept 259
just-in-time and lean thinking 221–2, 223–35
    defects 225
    delay and inventory 224–5
    flow 225–6
    Ford and Toyota 230–2
    full capability 224
    inventory 226
    machine downtime 225
    material requirements planning 229–32
    order to production 234
    order to replenishment 234
    product development 234–5
    pull scheduling 233–4
    role of lean practices 235
    Smog Co. production system 226–8
    value flows 233
    value specification 232–3
    value stream identification 233
    waste 228–9

*keiretsu* 265, 276–7
Kimberly-Clark 210
Kmart 210

LaCrosse Footwear 144
layering 130–1
lead suppliers 272–3
lead-time 57, 64, 335
    of supply, extended 125
lead-time frontier 153–84
    implementation of time-based practices 179–82
    P-time greater than D-time 176, 177, 178–9

    *see also* P:D ratios and differences;
        time-based competition;
        time-based process mapping
leagility 236
lean capability 236
lean logistics 241
lean thinking 222
    *see also* just-in-time and lean thinking
leverage items 317–19
Li and Fung Co. 236
lifecycle curves 47
local community 96
location analysis 128–30
loyalty 6
    programme 52

M&S 24–5, 27, 185–6
McDonald's/McColonisation 111
machine downtime 225
Magna International 269, 270
maintenance costs, allocation of 91
make process 102
make to order 176, 188, 189, 201
make to stock 176, 177, 188
management system 207
managerial (short- and medium-term) aspects 8
manufacturing costs 80, 86–7
manufacturing planning and control 186, 187–8,
        201–2, 203
manufacturing supply chain planning
        and control 187–93
Manugistics 210
Marche shoe district 278–80
margin of safety 84
margin-driven behaviour 59
market/marketing 57, 177
    approach 113
    and logistics 67–8
    mix 41–2
    participation 113
    perspective 36–8
    sector lead teams 248
    sensitivity 246
master production scheduling 167, 168, 189,
        190–2, 193
Matalan 27
material and capacity planning (engine room) 189
material flow 6, 11, 12–14
material requirements planning 189, 190, 201,
        229–32
matrix twist 45
maximum variable, minimum fixed policy 77
mean absolute deviation 48
mean average deviation 189
Mercedes 155–6, 268
merchandising requirements 45
milk rounds 196
modelling trend 47–8
modules 267, 268

Monte Carlo experiments 162
motions waste, unnecessary 229
moving averages 189
multiple-contact model (diamond) 290

national accounts 44
national distribution centres 8–9, 17, 40, 80, 94
    supply chain planning and control 187, 200,
        210, 212
NEC 147, 148
Nestlé UK 213–14
net requirement 191–2
networks 10–11
    and capacity planning 6
    logistical 113
    see also supplier networks
new items 209
new pharmaceutical entities 47
new product development 164, 339–40
new product introduction rate 98
new product launches 89
Nike 23, 24, 123–4, 146, 147, 158, 339
Nissan 270, 277, 285
Nokia 22, 25, 193
non-critical items 317
non-standard 192
non-value-adding time 170, 172–3
Nuon 314–15

obligational relationships 255, 256, 286
obsolescence 158
occupational health and safety 148
on quality 19
on shelf availability 176, 199, 204
on site distribution centre 266
on time 19
on time in full 98, 122, 321
one size fits all 73
open market relationships 271
operating environments, classification of 241
operation release tickets 167–8
operational excellence 53
operational ordering cycle 301–2
opportunism 288, 289
opportunity costs 87
order:
    batching 202
    management 57
    point methods 193
    qualifiers 26–7, 59, 236–7
    to delivery lead time 98
    to production 234
    to replenishment 234
    winners 26–7, 41, 59, 61, 237, 291
orderliness 226
organisational structure 306
original equipment manufacturing 131, 265, 266,
    269, 272
outbound logistics 10, 13

outputs 12
outside in 236
outsourcing 77, 136, 271, 279
overheads see indirect costs
overproduction waste 228

P:D ratios and differences 162–8
    consequences when P-time is greater than
        D-time 165–8
    getting ideas to market 165
    supply pipeline performance, using time
        to measure 163–5
    time, use of as a performance measure 162–3
    Wiltshire Distribution Transformers 166–8
    see also D-time; P-time
P-time (production time) 176–7, 181, 183, 186, 188,
    192, 258
pace 133
Pareto analysis 41
partnerships 270–2, 285–9, 342
perceived benefit 74
performance objectives 27
periodic order quantity 196–8
periodic review 198
Philips 22
physical and accounting correspondence 57
physical distribution 10
physical infrastructure set-up with LLP origin
    in Asia 138
physical product 16
pick accuracy 17
pipeline map 211, 212
planning process 7, 102
plant and equipment capital reduction 160
point of sale 47, 186, 196, 200, 204
    see also electronic point of sale
policy establishment per supplier segment 320
postponement 14, 131, 192
    logistical 238
power 288–9
Powerdrive Motors 42–3
PowerGen (UK) 26
presentation (supply condition) 57
pressure 291
prevention cost driver 88
price 42
    fluctuations 126–8, 203
    focus on 289
    negotiations 291
priorities setting 56–68
    Bacalao (dried fish) 64–8
    buying behaviour 59
    current approach to market segmentation 58–9
    customer value analysis 60
    drivers, measurement of 60–3
    market segmentation, future approach to 63–4
    selected service level measurements 57
priority planning 201
Probo Koala ship 145

process:
  improvement 177
  steps, unnecessary 181
  technology 201
processes, understanding of 180–1
processing costs 80
Procter & Gamble 112, 118, 200, 204, 210, 214,
    257, 324
  Connect + Develop 340–1, 342
procurement:
  business-aligned 325
  technology 326
  *see also* sourcing and supply management
product 42
  development 177, 234–5
  innovation, increased 157–8
  leadership 53
  lifecycle management 262
  obsolescence 115
  offering 113
  profile 60, 63
  quality and safety 148, 291
  range 45
  segmentation 120–1
  types 45
profit (margin) 80, 82–3
promotional efficiency 205
promotions 42, 45, 59, 89, 199, 209
pull scheduling 195, 214, 223, 230, 233–4
pull signal 263
punctuality 57
purchase portfolio matrix 316, 317, 319
purchasing 10
  performance score 306
push production 226
push scheduling 223–4, 229

qualifying criteria 41
quality 16, 156, 162
  advantage 17
  assurance audits 55
  costs 88, 160
  improvement 154–5, 327
  standards 168
quality of service 35, 50–6
  customer loyalty 51–2
  Everglo Battery 54–6
  Ikea 51
  measurement 56
  relationship marketing and customer relationship
      management 53–6
  service quality gap model 50
  value disciplines 53
quick response 204, 217–18

radio frequency identification devices 206–8,
    263, 280
randomness *see* uncertainty
range of items 208

rationalisation 314–16
rationing 203
re-order point 194
ready-to-go packaging/products/technologies 342
reality check 242
Reckitt Benckiser 339
reconfiguration processes 132–40
  global structure 133
  localisation structure 133
  postponed manufacturing 134, 135
  Smiths Aerospace 139–40
  trade-off between time and cost in global supply
      chains: apparel industry 136–9
regional distribution centres 8–9, 17, 40, 80, 210–11
regularity (service care) 57
relationships:
  management 290–2
  marketing 53–6
  skills 327
  strategic 320
reliability of delivery 122
remote factory system 18
replenishment of stock 206, 209
representation of logistics costs 79–89
  Bond SA – marginal costing 84
  break-even chart 82, 83
  direct material costs against volume of activity 82
  direct product profitability 86–7
  direct/indirect costs 85–7
  engineered/discretionary costs 87–9
  fixed/variable costs 81–4
  Glup SA 88–9
  rent cost against volume of activity 81
  total cost cube 80
research and development 291
resource planning 189
response time 57
responsibility: sustainability advantage 23–5
restructuring costs 216
retailer vulnerability 216
retailing supply chain planning and control
    198–200
return on capital employed 75
return on investment 75–9, 84, 100, 103
return on new products, improved 158
return process 102
returns 7
reverse logistics 9, 141–3, 199
reverse marketing 324–5
review period 198
risk:
  in international logistics 119
  readiness 143–5
  reduction 158–9
Robert Bosch 265
Royal Mail 19

safety stock 197, 198
Saga Sports 147

sales 76
  based ordering 200
  order processing 189
SAP 210
  -AFS (Apparel and Footwear Solution) 279
Sara Lee 214
scheduled receipts 192
seasonality 39, 47–9, 62, 199, 216
security of information and property 25
segmentation 38–45, 58–9, 63–4, 240–1
  annual sales per customer for book distributor 41
  behavioural 39, 44
  CleanCo 44–5
  consumer and industrial marketing, comparison
    between 42
  demographic 38
  events management and promotions in retail
    sector 39–40
  geographical 38, 120–1
  Powerdrive Motors 42–3
  product 120–1
  technical 39
segmentation of supply base 316–28
  boardroom value markers 326–7
  bottleneck items 317, 318
  customer of choice status 324–6
  executive ownership of supply relationships 322–4
  leverage items 317–19
  non-critical items 317
  policy establishment per supplier segment 320
  preferred suppliers 319–20
  Procter & Gamble 324
  procurement technology 326
  strategic items 316
  strategic relationships 320
  top procurement talent 327–8
  vendor rating 321–2, 323
self-billing 326
self-interest 289
separateness (in supply relationships) 290–1
service 16
  care 57
  level measurements 57
  posture 328
  see also quality of service
settlement period for creditors/debtors, average 78
shareholders 96
shipped quantity 57
shop scheduling 167–8
shortage gaming 203
shrinkage 199
Silicon Fen (Cambridge) 117
Silicon Valley 117
simplicity 156
simplification 178
single business concept 111
single minute exchange of dies 235
small-batch production 235
Smiths Aerospace 139–40

Smog Co. production system 226–8
social bonds 53
social values 23
soft objectives 16, 25–6
solution generation 171–6
source and make costs 343
source process 102
source-make-deliver processes 187, 193
source-plan-make-deliver process 239
sourcing:
  commodity items from low-wage economies 116–17
  decisions 291
  multiple 288
  sole 144
  strategic 301, 302, 306–7
  see also outsourcing
sourcing and supply management 299–329
  supplier rationalisation 314–16
  see also drivers of procurement value; segmentation
    of supply base
Span measurement 246
speed 161
  of delivery 122
  of response 57
standard component 192
standard procedures, lack of 216
starting point 133
steady state replenishment policy 39
stewardship skills 327
stock:
  replenishment 176
  turnover 57
  turns 98
stockout 57
storage costs 87
strategic alliance 264
strategic customers 58
strategic items 316
strategic (long-term planning) aspects 8
strategic partnerships integration 285–9
strategic relationships 320
strategic sourcing 301, 302, 306–7
strategic suppliers 58
strategic thinking 327
strategy 155
  for procurement categories 309–10
strategy drivers 63, 64
strategy of logistics 27–31
  aligning strategies 29–30
  definition 28–9
  differentiating strategies 30–1
  Talleres Auto 30
  trade-offs 31
structural bonds 53
Sun Microsystems 272
supplier 96
  codes of conduct 24
  delivers carriage, insurance and freight 265
  development 284–5

-in-plant 259–60
management 272
networks 9, 10–12, 273–84
    Chinese industrial areas 280–4
    Italian districts 278–80
    Japanese *keiretsu* 276–7
    supplier associations 273–6
park 267
preferred 319–20
rationalisation 314–16
relationship management 312–14
strategic 58
supply 10, 11
supply capabilities 238–41
supply centres 266
supply chain 3–33
    automotive 265–70, 292
    closed loop 286
    of customers 223
    definitions and concepts 6–8
    development 6
    effectiveness 347–9
    financial model 99–100, 101
    governance council 247
    implications 38
    information flow 15
    integration 255–95
        arcs 258
        continuous replenishment in apparel
            industry 262–4
        electronic 260–4
        external 257
        inter-company 259–60
        internal 257, 358–9
        partnerships 270–2
        relationships management 290–2
        strategic partnerships 285–9
        supplier development 284–5
        supply base rationalisation 272–3
        *see also* supplier networks; supply relationships
    logistics 21
    management 6, 7, 100, 319, 345–7
        and balanced scorecard 97–9
        network, global 137
        tools and trade-offs in supply chain 138
    material flow 12–14
    operations reference model 15, 101–4, 185
    performance 103–4
    planning and control 185–219
        inter-firm 201–3
        inventory management 193–8
        retailing 198–200
        Victoria SA 190–3
        within manufacturing 187–93
        *see also* coordination in retail supply chains
    ratio 100
    scope/activities 132, 133
    structure and tiering 8–12
    tailored 31

Tesco 4–5
virtual 285
Xerox 13–14
*see also* agile supply chain; competing through
    logistics; strategy of logistics
supply conditions 57
supply management *see* sourcing and supply
    management
supply pipeline performance, using time to
    measure 163–5
supply relationships 264–70
    automotive supply chains: inbound logistics
        solutions 265–70
supply-base continuity 319
support activities 233
supportive capabilities 19–25
    responsibility: sustainability advantage 23–5
    uncertainty: agility advantage 21–3
    variability control: dependability advantage 19–21
sustainability 16, 19, 23–5, 145, 335
synchronous production 13, 267, 285
system maintenance 216
systemic strategy 29

tactical contract management 301–2
tags 207
Talleres Auto 30, 162
target:
    pricing/cost 318
    stock levels 196–8
task force creation 169
TBL 24
tendency (in reconfiguration process) 132, 133
Tesco 4–5, 6, 8, 21, 23, 39, 199
    corporate store steering wheel 98–9
    Express and Esso 264
    Information Exchange 5
    loyalty programme 52
    regional distribution centre 17
third party logistics providers 77, 131
tier 0 269
tier 0.5 269, 270
tier 1 basic 268–9
tier 1 customers 36
tier 1 suppliers 186, 265, 267, 269
tier 1 synchro 269
tier 2 265
tiers 10, 130–1
time 16, 31
    advantage 17–18
    allocation 302, 303
    between orders (TBO) 197
    break-even 158, 159
    elasticity of price 162
    horizons 187–8
    -to-market 115, 137
    use of as a performance measure 162–3
    wasted 181
    *see also* just-in-time

time-based competition 154–61
   adding value opportunities 157–9
   cost reductions 159–61
   definition and concepts 154–5
   distribution of shipment cycles times in days 161
   initiatives 156
   limitations 161
   variety and complexity 155–6
time-based process mapping 92, 168–76
   cause-and-effect diagram 175
   construction 171
   current 174
   data collection 170
   Electro-Coatings Ltd 172–6
   example document 169
   flow charting process 170
   identification of each step 173
   re-engineered 175
   selection of process to map 169
   solution generation 171–6
   task force creation 169
   time-based analysis data 174
   value-adding and non-value adding time 170
   walking the process 172
   waste, sources of 171
timetable 133
togetherness (supply relationships) 290
tolerance zone 96
top procurement talent 327–8
top-down decisions 100
top-up shoppers 39
total cost of ownership 310–12, 313
total costs 80, 87
   re-balancing 94
total order cycle time 57
total productive maintenance 225
total quality control 234
Toyota 17, 18–19, 22, 143, 161, 222, 230–2, 235, 267
   supplier associations 273–4
   UK 21
trade-offs 31, 78–9, 127, 130, 154–5, 310, 335
   between cost and time in global supply chains:
      apparel industry 136–9
   between cost and time for international
      shipping 127
   between two locations 130
   identification 31
trading 199
tradition 133
traditional style of relationship (bow-tie) 290
training 337–8, 349
transactional electronic integration 261
transit times, extended and unreliable 125
transport/transportation 115
   breakdowns 119
   bulk 118
   costs 80, 87, 89
   network redesign 144
   of wastes 229
triple bottom line 23, 145, 319
trust 288

uncertainty 16, 19, 21–3, 46, 49, 199
Unilever 112
unique value proposition 31
upstream organisations 58, 257, 272, 285, 292, 340–1
   supply chain logistics 6, 9, 10, 11, 14
   supply chain planning and control 193, 201, 202
use by dates 199

value:
   activities 233
   -adding 7, 54–6, 113
   -adding time 157–9, 170, 172–3
   chain 233
   disciplines 53
   flows 233
   and logistics costs 73–106
      financial ratios 77–9
      return on investment 75–9
      supply chain operations reference
         model 101–4
      *see also* activity-based costing; balanced
         measurement portfolio; representation of
         logistics costs
   specification 232–3
   stream identification 233
variability control 16, 19–21
variable costs 80, 81–4
variety 155–6, 157, 239–40
vendor rating 321–2, 323, 324
vendor-managed inventory 185–6, 214–16, 285
vicious cycle 225
Victoria SA 190–3
virtual organisation 238
virtuous cycle 225
Vision Express 18, 19
VM modules 267, 269
voice of the customer 346
volatility levels 143–4
Volkswagen 17–18, 268
volume 239–40
   of activity 81
   -driven behaviour 59
   -driven customers 44
   variation 62
Voluntary Inter-industry Commerce Standards
      Committee 210

Wal-Mart 23, 39, 149, 204, 208, 210, 214
walking the process 170
warehouse dust test 243
Warner-Lambert 210
waste 9, 181, 221–2, 228–9, 232, 233–4
whale curve 94
WheatCo-ChemCo 286–8
Wilson formula 194
Wiltshire Distribution 166–8, 176
working capital 76, 159–60
working routines 201
world wide web 37–8

Xerox 13–14, 15, 239–41